Leveling Crowds

Comparative Studies in Religion and Society
Mark Juergensmeyer, editor

Leveling Crowds

Ethnonationalist Conflicts and Collective Violence in South Asia

STANLEY J. TAMBIAH

University of California Press

BERKELEY   LOS ANGELES   LONDON

University of California Press
Berkeley and Los Angeles, California

University of California Press, Ltd.
London, England

© 1996 by
The Regents of the University of California

Library of Congress Cataloging-in-Publication Data

Tambiah, Stanley Jeyaraja, 1929–
    Leveling crowds : ethnonationalist conflicts and collective violence
in South Asia / Stanley J. Tambiah.
        p.   cm.—(Comparative studies in religion and society ; 10)
    Includes bibliographic references and index
    ISBN 0-520-20002-0 (alk. paper).—ISBN 0-520-20642-8 (pbk. : alk.
paper)
        1. Riots—South Asia.   2. Crowds—South Asia.
3. Communalism—South Asia.   4. Violence—South Asia.   5. South
Asia—Ethnic relations.   I. Title.   II. Series.
    HV6485.S64T35   1997
    303.6′23′0954—dc 20   95-48114

Contents

Figures, Maps, and Tables

Figures

Maps

Tables

Preface

This book has taken a fairly long time to complete. The flow of pertinent contemporary political events made closure difficult, and my own academic and administrative and other professional commitments forced me to put it aside from time to time. With the help and generosity of Karen Colvard of the Harry Frank Guggenheim Foundation, Mark Juergensmeyer was able to assemble Ainslie Embree, Jack Hawley, W. H. McLeod, Bruce Lawrence, and David Rapaport in Hawaii in September 1991 for a two-day discussion of the first draft, completed a month earlier. Their comments, and those of Karen Colvard, were encouraging, thoughtful, and helpful.

By the time of the Hawaii discussions, the Hindutva movement in India and the various processional campaigns of the Hindu nationalists to build a temple to Ram in Ayodhya at the site of the Babri mosque had intensified, while also provoking some violent incidents. Also in 1991, the Bharatiya Janata Party (BJP) had its first notable electoral success and became India's largest opposition party. I therefore determined to add a substantial account of the Ayodhya issue to this book.

In 1992, I began the projected chapter on the Ayodhya debate, but I soon realized that this not only required lengthy treatment but also raised issues that were outside the scope of a book focused on collective violence. In fact, I found myself writing a second book, and having more or less followed the events associated with the Ayodhya issue to the climactic demolition of the mosque in December 1992 and the aftermath of violence and political consequences, I returned in the summer of 1993 to the text of the first manuscript. After delays caused by various academic commitments, and after taking into account advice to include at least a brief chapter on Hindu ethnonationalism and its political impact, I managed in early August 1995 to complete this book, covering events in India and Pakistan up to around 1992–93. It is hoped that a second book dealing with Hindu nationalism, the demolition of the Ayodhya mosque, and the alleged crisis of secular politics in India will be written in due course.

It is difficult to give a coherent account of the motivations that directed the writing of this book. Having already published two short books exclusively focused on the current painful and prolonged ethnonationalist conflict in Sri Lanka, and living at a time of explosions in many places of ethnonationalist violence, all seemingly sharing a family resemblance, I found myself realizing that there were substantive and theoretical issues of a general and comparative nature that invited study. South Asia seemed a manageable arena to visit for selected case studies and comparative study. Especially as regards recent developments in India and Pakistan, I do not claim much expert and "original" knowledge, although I am no stranger to these countries. I stood on the shoulders of many others to put together my narrative. I did not begin this book because I already knew what I wanted to say. I only knew what I wanted to find out. I did most of my learning during the reading and writing process. I also benefited from co-teaching two seminars at Harvard on nationalism, pluralism, ethnicity, and violence with Nur Yalman and Begonia Aretxaga. I naturally expect readers, especially the experts, to evaluate this book according to their standards, but I hope they will not condemn me for my audacity and my willingness to take risks.

I wish to thank the Harry Frank Guggenheim Foundation for giving me a grant to visit India. Friends have kindly provided me with relevant documents, and I thank in particular Diana Eck, Bina Agarwal, H. L. Seneviratne, and Ashkutosh Varshney. I am especially indebted to Rebecca Grow for typing the bulk of the book manuscript, a task efficiently completed by Annemarie Bestor and Nicole Thornton-Burnett, and to Dan Rosenberg for a close reading of the proofs for mistakes and for compiling an informative index. Finally, I must express my appreciation for those associated with University of California Press—particularly Doug Abrams Arava, Erika Bűky, and Peter Dreyer—for overseeing the production of this large and complex book.

PART ONE

SELECTED SITES OF CONFLICT IN SOUTH ASIA

1   The Wider Context

A somber reality and disillusionment of our epoch, which emerged from the ashes of World War II, is that although there have been successes in the push toward development and modernization, eradication of disease, and the spread of literacy, economic and political development programs have generated and stimulated, whether by collusion or in reaction, in good faith and poor anticipation, massive civil war and gruesome interracial and interethnic bloodshed. The same epoch has witnessed the rise in many countries of repressive authoritarianism in both military and democratic guises, equipped with Western weaponry, inflamed by populist slogans and fundamentalist doctrines, and assisted by a flagrant manipulation of the mass media, which have vastly expanded their reach.

The optimism of the sociologists, political scientists, and anthropologists who naively foretold an "integrative revolution" and the inevitable decline of "primordial loyalties" such as kinship, caste, and ethnicity in third world countries, has by now waned and dimmed. The introduction of constitutions and democratic institutions, enshrining human rights, universal franchise, the party system, elected legislatures, majority rule, and so on, has often resulted in strange malformations that are far removed from the goals of liberty, justice, and tolerance that were the ideological supports of Western European and North American liberal-democratic syntheses. Something has gone awry in center-periphery relations throughout the world, and a manifestation of this is the occurrence of widespread ethnic conflict, accompanied in many instances by collective violence among people who are not aliens but enemies intimately known.

THE UBIQUITY OF ETHNIC CONFLICT

At different times, certain ranges of phenomena, grouped under embracing labels such as "social class," "caste," "race," "gender inequality," "modernization," "the colonial encounter," and so on, have become foci of intensified scholarly interest. Then these inquiries fade away, not only because of diminishing marginal returns, but also because the phenomena themselves, as reflected on the screen of history, either lose their salience or are transformed into other events, which are more revealingly grouped under new labels.

One such label subsuming a range of phenomena with a family resemblance is "ethnicity." It is significant that the term *ethnicity* has come into vogue and found its way into standard English dictionaries, especially since the 1960s. Linguistic, national, religious, tribal, and racial divisions and identifications, and competitions and conflicts based on them, are not, of course, new phenomena, yet the recent salience of the term *ethnicity* "reflects a new reality and a new usage reflects a change in that reality" on a global scale in the latter half of the twentieth century, both in the industrialized first world and the "developing" third world.[1]

It seems that the term *ethnicity* gained popularity in the social science literature of the 1960s and early 1970s, not only to describe certain manifestations in the third world, but also in reaction to the emergence of ethnic movements in the industrialized and affluent world, especially in the United States, Canada, and Western Europe.[2] And since the dismantling of the USSR and the other communist regimes of Eastern Europe, the spate of internal conflicts that have exploded there are also viewed as ethnic and ethnonationalist in kind.

Ethnic conflict is a major reality of our time. This is confirmed, not simply by its ubiquity alone, but also by the cumulative increase in the frequency and intensity of its occurrence. According to a recent enumeration, some forty-eight countries (including the republics that have supplanted the USSR) are experiencing ethnonationalist conflicts of one kind or other. Since the 1960s conflicts have occurred or been perpetuated between anglophone and francophone in Canada; Catholics and Protestants in Northern Ireland; Walloons and Flemings in Belgium; Chinese and Malays in Malaysia; Greeks and Turks in Cyprus; Turks and Kurds in eastern Turkey; Basques and Spaniards; Jews and other minorities on the one hand and Great Russians on the other; Ibo, Hausa, and Yoruba in Nigeria; and East Indians and Creoles in Guyana.[3] Add to these upheavals that have become climactic in recent years, among them the Sinhala-Tamil war in Sri Lanka, the Sikh-Hindu and Muslim-Hindu confrontations in Kashmir, and the turmoil engendered by the Ayodhya temple dispute; the Chackma-Muslim turmoil in Bangladesh, the actions of the Fijians against Indians in Fiji, the Pathan-Bihari clashes in Pakistan, and preceding the recent political settlement, the inferno in Lebanon, and the erosion of human rights previously manifest in Israeli actions in Gaza and the West Bank and the assassinations exchanged between Israel and the PLO; and, finally, the century-old difference exploded again between Christian Armenians and Muslim Azerbaijanis in March 1988.[4]

Eastern Europe has been on the boil since the vast Soviet empire was dismantled, and old "nationalities" have been resurfacing and jostling for power and for separate recognition. The death toll has been rising in the republics of the former USSR in tandem with the politics of secession.[5] In Yugoslavia, at first the Slovenes and Croats were ranged against the Serbs and declared their independence, and we have read daily since 1992 about the triangular warfare and carnage in Bosnia-Herzegovina between Serbs, Croats, and Muslim Slavs. Another recent phenomenon is the exodus of refugees from Albania into Greece and Italy. And the list lengthens every month.[6] It is this parade of disasters (on top of two world wars, economic crises, and authoritarianisms of the right and left) that probably prompted Isaiah Berlin to say, "At eighty-two, I have lived . . . the worst century Europe has ever had."

Most of these conflicts have involved violence, homicide, arson, and destruction of property. Civilian riots have evoked action by security forces, sometimes to quell them, sometimes in collusion with civilian aggressors, sometimes both in sequence. Events of this nature have happened in Sri Lanka, Malaysia, India, Zaire, Guyana, and Nigeria. Mass killings of civilians by armed forces have occurred in Uganda and in Guatemala, and large losses of civilian lives have been recorded in Indonesia, Pakistan, India, Sri Lanka, and Rwanda.

Some dissident ethnic groups have declared secessionist aims that threaten to break up extant polities, and these aims in turn have invited invasion of one country by another (for example, the Somali invasion of Ethiopia), or armed intervention, such as by India in Sri Lanka in 1987. Moreover, ethnic conflict has also frequently caused massive displacements of people, many of them being deposited in refugee camps in neighboring countries, as in Africa, the Middle East, India, Sri Lanka and elsewhere. Nor, finally, should we forget large-scale expulsions of people, as happened to Asians in Uganda in the 1970s.[7]

The escalation of ethnic conflicts has been considerably aided by gun-running and free trade in the technology of violence, which not only enable dissident groups to resist the armed forces of the state, but allow civilians to battle one another with lethal weapons.

The classic definition of the state as the authority invested with the monopoly of force has become a sick joke.[8] After so many successful liberations and resistance movements in many parts of the globe, the techniques of guerrilla resistance are now systematized and exportable knowledge. Furthermore, easy access to the technology of warfare by groups in countries that are otherwise deemed low in literacy and in economic development—we have seen what Afghan resistance can do with American guns—is paralleled by another kind of international fraternization among resistance groups—who have little in common save their resistance to the status quo in their own countries, and who exchange knowledge of guerrilla tactics and the art of resistance. Militant groups in Japan, Germany, Lebanon, Libya, Sri Lanka, and India have international networks of collaboration, not unlike—perhaps more solidary than—the diplomatic channels that exist between mutually wary sovereign countries and the great powers. There are, of course, global politico-economic processes at work, which cause disparities between countries, structure metropolitan centers and peripheries into configurations of uneven development, and stimulate neighbors of unequal power and status to confront one another.

Another development, not unknown in the past in the form of mercenaries for hire, but today reaching a sinister significance, is the "privatization of war"—that is, the ability of governments with extraterritorial geopolitical aims to fight their foreign wars, not by committing their own professional armies, but by farming out contracts for subversive military and political action to private professional groups willing to be hired or capable of being mobilized. The employment of ex-SAS (British Special Air Service) veterans by the Sri Lankan government to help in the war against the Tamil militants is one of many such examples. Analogously, the lessons the United States learned in Vietnam were later applied with zest in Nicaragua and Afghanistan, where local dissidents were armed and trained in the use of weaponry and the arts of destabilization. Professionalized killing is no longer the monopoly of state armies and police forces. The internationalization of the technology of destruction, evidenced in terrorism and counterterrorism, has shown a face of free-market capitalism and long-distance trade in action unsuspected by Adam Smith and by Immanuel Wallerstein. The ubiquity, the increased frequency and intensity, of ethnic conflict, serviced by modern technology of destruction and communication, and publicized by the mass media, makes such conflict a special reality of the late twentieth century. Faced with recent disturbances in South Russia, Mikhail Gorbachev was moved to say that [ethnic] nationalism was the "most fundamental vital issue of our society."[9] And on a visit to Yugoslavia, a country that has a long history of tensions between "nationalities," he is reported to have said, "Show me a country without nationalist problems, and I will move there right away."[10] What a shift there has been in historical consciousness from Victorian times to the computer age of instant information! The Victorian perception of the people of the world was, as we well know, that they could be placed on a ladder of evolution and progress, with the Europeans at the summit. Other peoples were not really contemporaneous with the West, and archaeological metaphors such as "survivals" and the "contemporaneity of the noncontemporaneous" (a phrase coined by Karl Mannheim) were used to describe a global population whose development was assumed to be both uneven and discontinuous. Edward Tylor gave a vintage expression to this consciousness when he wrote:

> The educated world of Europe and America practically settles a standard by simply placing its own nations at one end of the social series. The principal criteria of classification are the absence or presence, high or low development, of the industrial arts . . . agricultural, architecture, etc., the extent of scientific knowledge, the definiteness of moral principles, the conditions of religious belief and ceremony, the degree of social and political organization and so forth.[11]

This Victorian perspective in the main persisted perhaps until World War II, but there has been a recent change in paradigms, positing common world historical processes that hold centers and peripheries in one dialectical and interlocked field. There are specific developments that have contributed to a shift in historical consciousness that views our present world as a global village. The revolution in the media, instant transmission of visual images and auditory messages, linking metropolitan centers and distant places, and wide coverage of events, so that news broadcasts (whether by NBC, CBS, ABC, or CNN) present diverse events occurring at diverse places as a single synchronic and simultaneously occurring reality. These communication processes bind us in a synchronicity of fellow witnesses of world events. We come to feel that the worldwide incidents of ethnic conflict are of the same order and are mutually implicated: strife in Northern Ireland; kidnappings in Lebanon; beatings on the West Bank; fire bombings in Germany; killing of civilians in Sri Lanka; riots against the Sikhs in Delhi; massing of Korean youth against a rightist government; attacks on the "bush negroes" by the townsmen of Suriname, sniping by the Contras in Nicaragua, explosive tensions between Armenians and Azerbaijanis, unrelenting Serb attacks on the beleaguered Muslim Slavs of Bosnia, mutual massacres of Tutsi and Hutu—all belong to a contemporary world suffused by violence. The internationalization of violence and the simultaneity of its occurrences viewed on our TV screens make us all spectators and vicarious participants responding with our respective sympathies and our prejudices.

THE POLITICIZATION OF ETHNICITY

A major issue today is the transition from the politics of the nation-state to the politics of ethnic pluralism. It is useful at this juncture to take as our point of reference Benedict Anderson's *Imagined Communities: Reflections on the Origins and Spread of Nationalism* (1983), in order to recognize its contribution and also to go beyond it to take account of newer developments.

Immanuel Wallerstein contends that after its inception in Europe in the sixteenth century, world capitalism spread like a tidal wave from the metropolitan capitals and gradually inundated the peripheries. The versions of the "dependency" theory of world capitalism variously proposed by Wallerstein, André Gunder Frank, Paul Baran, Samir Amin, and Claude Meillassoux all in the end posit a monolithic global historical process. However, they leave out of account the parallel process by which the world was fragmented, differentiated and carved up as "nation-states." Anderson shows how easily the modular concepts of the "nation-state" and "nationalism" were pirated by third world colonial and postcolonial elites. Under colonialism, the "historical consciousness" of nineteenth-century Europe was transmitted to and imbibed by local elites subjected to the textbook learning propagated by colonial schools.

In Anderson's account, historically speaking, it was the creole communities of Latin America, the former colonies of Spain, that developed "the conception of nation-ness well before most of Europe." Simultaneously "a colonial community and an upper class," the creoles mounted the first national liberation movement against the Spanish empire.

Anderson's plotting of the rise in Europe of national consciousness in the late eighteenth and early nineteenth centuries, inspired by linguistic and vernacularizing revolutions, followed from the mid nineteenth century on by the promotion and manipulation of "official nationalism" by the European monarchies, based on a national identification projected onto vernacular languages, led him quite correctly to perceive that the nation-building policies of the new states of the third world consisted of "both a genuine, popular nationalist enthusiasm and a systematic, even Machiavellian, instilling of nationalist ideology through the mass media, the educational system, administrative regulations, and so forth. In turn, this blend of popular and official nationalism has been the product of anomalies created by European imperialism: the well-known arbitrariness of frontiers, and bilingual intelligentsias poised precariously over diverse populations."[12]

A weakness in Anderson's thesis, especially when we contemplate developments in pre- and postindependence India (a country he does not discuss), is his suggestion that nationalism in the colonies and the third world was largely a more or less passive or borrowed response to the European impact. An examination of India's nationalist discourse as articulated by three different personalities—the "early" thinker Bankimchandra Chattopadhyay; Mohandas Gandhi, who consolidated the national, while decrying the modern; and Jawaharlal Nehru, who married the national to the agency of the state—suggests that, although indeed derivative and mostly taking the form of "passive revolutions," the colonial and postcolonial responses were also dialectically engendered and filtered through the experiences and motivations of differently positioned local elites and leaders, whose voices were by no means unitary and homogeneous.

Similarly, in Sri Lanka, in the decades immediately preceding independence, while the dominant voice of the politicians of the Ceylon National Congress and their successors (including D. S. Senanayake and S. W. R. D. Bandaranaike) was collaborative with the British Colonial Office, there were other distinctive oppositional voices, such as that of Anagarika Dharmapala, the father of Sinhala Buddhist nationalism, and the radical communists and Trotskyites, whose rhetoric was revolutionary and anticolonial.

Anderson's Eurocentric sequencing is, in fact, locked into the project of nation-state making, as, indeed, is the more complex "derivative discourse" proposed by Partha Chatterjee,[13] and both have to be taken a stage further, which requires a radical transformation of their master narratives. The politics of the newly independent states, framed initially in terms of "nation-state" ideologies and policies, have by virtue of various internal dialectics and differences led to a new phase of politics dominated by the competitions and conflicts of "ethnic collectivities," who question unitary nationalist and "nation-state" dogmas. The politics of ethnicity is indeed a product of the interweaving and collision of the two global processes we mentioned earlier: world capitalism and its operation through multinational corporations, and widespread nation building by liberated colonies now ruled by elite intelligentsias, who, however, have to react to their divided civilian constituencies. These interacting global processes, while having certain homogenizing effects, have simultaneously spawned differentiation and opposition within the new polities, manifested as ethnic conflict.

We have recently discovered with shocked surprise that the politics of ethnicity is not only a main preoccupation of the newly independent countries of the third world, but has emerged with a vengeance in what used to be called the second world: the recently dismantled Soviet empire and its erstwhile satellites in Eastern Europe. The dismantling and dismembering of the earlier formations have resulted in the creation and the demand for creation of new states on an ethnonationalist basis, and thereby the intensification of ethnonationalist conflicts, of which the Azerbaijani-Armenian conflict over Nagorno-Karabakh, and the triangular struggles between Croats, Serbs and Muslims in what used to be Yugoslavia are the most spectacular.

There appear to be two interrelated developments in this part of the world, which are characterized by both positive and negative features. The collapse of totalitarian political systems has opened space for their replacement by democratic regimes. While one can see the obvious virtues of democracy and representative government compared with totalitarian Communist party rule, yet the fact is that the alleged changeover to electoral democratic methods in Eastern Europe (and the Commonwealth of Independent States) has actually unleashed and/or intensified ethnic conflicts, and ethnic majorities have used their electoral dominance to inferiorize and assault or displace their minorities (while seceding former minorities do the same to their own minorities). This phenomenon of "ethnic cleansing" reached its most virulent climax in the former Yugoslavia with a battery of devices: food blockade, incessant shelling, causing the flight of people from their homes, killing of captured "enemies," systematic raping of women (causing them to become pregnant, so that they will carry the enemy's children—inasmuch as the Serbian, Muslim Slav, and Croat peoples are strongly patrilineal and male-dominated, the father's ethnic identity primarily determines the child's).

The second development concerns the effects—particularly in the short term—of the dismantling of the command economies of the former USSR and Eastern European countries and the change to market economies and free enterprise. Here various economic ills—the hijacking of enterprises by the bureaucracy in place; increasing unemployment, caused by the closing of inefficient firms; black-market operations; and the lack or weak functioning of capital, labor, and commodity markets—have fed into the frag-

mentation and uncertainties of sociopolitical systems increasingly dislo‐
cated by ethnic conflict, fascist racist propaganda, and ethnic cleansing.

Simultaneously, we are also witnessing a shakeup in the confidence and
complacency of Western Europe, which has recently shown disturbing ev‐
idence of chauvinism, racism, discrimination, identity panic, and a thrust
toward national separateness, accompanied by attacks on foreign workers
and migrants, as economies worsen and unemployment rises. The Maas‐
tricht Treaty, with its hope of a unified currency, is falling apart; the con‐
cept of Europe as an entity is being questioned by British, Danish, and
lately French misgivings; the European Community is suffering the strain
of differential national economic interests. Britain has a history of racial
problems vis-à-vis its West Indian, Pakistani, and Indian emigrants; and
the German fire-bombings of Turkish guest workers and French assaults
on Algerians and other North Africans led by Jean-Marie Le Pen and his
Petits Blancs raise the specter of incipient racism, which mercifully is re‐
jected, if not firmly resisted, by millions of citizens.

Our complacent assumptions of civilizational progress have been
shaken. Lessons swept under the carpet and conveniently forgotten are
resurfacing: that democratic politics and free-market capitalism have their
prerequisites, their sociocultural conventions and contexts, and their own
constructed myths; that they are not immune from their own internally
generated contradictions and tensions; that they are not pills that surely
and automatically cure illness.

There is another recipe for progress that is currently being tested: the
idea of the nation-state as the desirable basis for structuring political life, a
previously hegemonic concept that is currently undermined by regional
and subnational resistances.

THE NATION-STATE IN CRISIS AND THE RISE
OF ETHNONATIONALISM

An alternative title to this section might be "A Tale of Two Nationalisms."
Ignoring the many nuances, there are two models of nationalism that are
in interaction, as well as contention, in many parts of the world. Each
model has its benefits and its costs, and our existential task at the close of
the twentieth century is to find a way of reconciling the two and of con‐
structing a new synthesis in the political lives of collectivities of people.

First, there is the nationalism of the *nation-state*, which was historically
conceived and substantially first realized in Europe, particularly Western
Europe. Second, there is what I call *ethnonationalism*, which has arisen

separately in many parts of the globe. Ethnonationalism has had and continues to have its European formulation and presence in (parts of) Germany, and today more vigorously in Eastern Europe. It also manifests itself in distinctive and similar ways in many other parts of the world—in Africa, in the Middle East, in South and Southeast Asia, and in Latin America. Ethnonationalism in its variant forms is most definitely not solely a Western construction. Regional and minority ethnonationalist movements in earlier empires and conquest states historically predate the appearance of the nation-state in Western Europe. Being more general in its stimulus, ethnonationalism has independently emerged at many different sites, although today global processes may drive them to converge.

In their global role as imperial powers, the nation-state's European progenitors sought to transplant the form to their third world dependencies and colonies, a process that accelerated with decolonization after World War II. Its impact on the social forms and practices of these erstwhile colonies in fact brought into prominence an intensified form of ethnonationalism in regional reaction to the excessive or unwelcome centralizing and homogenizing policies of the nation-state. In Eastern Europe, a similar imposition after World War I of the nation-state blueprint on a terrain differentiated by linguistic, religious, and ethnic cleavages, followed by the subsequent imposition on the same terrain after World War II of authoritarian communist regimes, has been succeeded today by an outbreak of ethnonationalist and regional claims that are competitive, divisive, intolerant, and violent, as well as euphoric and full of aggrandizing ambitions and collective promises for the participants.

It is this historic meeting, collision, and dialectic between the project of nation-state making and the counterclaims of ethnonationalism that provides the primary focus for this book. It is suggested that what is happening in the countries of South Asia (and in many other newly independent third world countries) is not very different from what is happening in Eastern Europe and the newly founded Commonwealth of Independent States.

THE NATION-STATE AS A HISTORICAL CONSTRUCTION

In its Western European form, the secular nation-state was predicated on the ideals proclaimed by the French Revolution, on the one hand, and the universalist claims of Enlightenment rationalism, on the other. Essential components of this nation-state were separation of church and state (and the virtual privatization of religion), the conception of citizenship based on the formal equality of all individuals who are its members; the jurisdiction of the nation-state as valid in the territory that it covers and that is defined by its frontiers; and finally, the arguable notion that politics is a secularized domain of activity shaped by its own objectives of power and by its own logic and rules. ④

The secularization of politics carried distinctive entailments, which are worth underscoring. In Western European history, the separation of church and state, and the relegation or confinement of religion to the private domain, was linked to the stimulation given the scientific revolution and experimentation by certain trends in Protestant Reformation thought. In maintaining that God had instituted the laws of nature, and that scientists could legitimately discover these laws, the Protestant Reformation thereby also in the long run had opened the door for God to become otiose or distant with regard to the pursuit of science. The scientists' religious beliefs and attachments, if they had any, were supposedly irrelevant to establishing the laws of science.

Historically, the development of the Western nation-state was linked to the launching of the Industrial Revolution, and the impulsion of capitalism as an expansionary force, creating wide-ranging, interlocking markets for goods, relatively free geographic mobility of labor, and a progressive erasing of parochial boundaries. Capitalism was a dynamic homogenizing agent in the newly industrializing countries. It also generated the expectations and hopes of a continuing economic expansion, despite "temporary" slumps and downturns. The expectation of economic growth and expansion generated aspirations to social mobility, cultural homogenization, and more egalitarian distributions of wealth.

We may also introduce into this heady mix another tendency: the drive to create a national culture, usually around a common dominant language, which gains precedence over other dialects or minority languages. (Switzerland is an exception in this respect.) The growth in literacy rates, linked to expanding educational facilities, and opportunities, and the explosion of cheap printing are other integral components of the Western success story.

In the creation of the Western nation-state, political integration, continuous economic expansion, and, frequently, linguistic homogenization for administrative purposes and for "high" cultural productions went hand in hand. The concepts of nation and state were fused into an entity, the bounded nation-state. And in the end, above all, national identity required from the citizen a loyalty to the state conceived of as a *secular* entity. This was the ideal-typical construction, claiming *normative* authority, whatever the deviations in actual fact.

Now, since the secular nation-state has been advocated by many Western theorists and third world intellectuals and political leaders as the bedrock on which modernization and economic development can be raised, it is extremely relevant to bear in mind two warnings.

First, historically, the Western European nation-state was achieved as the end result of very special developments, including social upheavals, internal strains, revolutions, and divisive wars between states. (We tend to forget this when we are impatient with the problems of governance and economic development in other countries.) Second, there is the possibility of a fundamental fallacy being perpetrated when an attempt is made to impose a historical construction such as the nation-state, achieved on distinctive soil, on a dependent world, as if its realization were a necessary stage in Universal History. This supposition, derived from Enlightenment assumptions, perhaps has near "hegemonic" status in global affairs (although in Europe itself it has been questioned and contested).

What happens—and indeed how do we perceive and represent and interpret what happens—in many parts of the world where the events that led to the realization of the European secular nation-state have not taken place, are slow to take place, take place unevenly, or are actively *resisted* as harmful (as for example in Iran by Shiite fundamentalism or in India by Hindu nationalists)? Is it now time to shift from the language of "obstacles" to "development" to the language of active subaltern "resistance" to it?

In trying to sort out these issues, it is relevant to consider that the other side of the Western model of the secular nation-state is its aggressive nationalism and imperialist expansion and penetration into what became its colonial dependencies. Liberal democracies in Western Europe and the United States frequently imposed authoritarian rule abroad, the exploitation of native labor and resources, and the inferiorization, if not erosion, of the cultures of the colonized. Marxists explain these processes in terms of capitalism gaining a new lease on life through colonial exploitation. This inferiorization and threat of cultural extinction in large part lies behind the rise of Islamic fundamentalism, Buddhist "nationalism," Hindu nationalism, and other such reactions, and their retaliatory attitude to Western economic affluence and domination, political supremacy, alleged consumerist values, celebration of sexual eroticism, erosion of family durability, alleged "privatization" of religion and separation of religion from affairs of state, and so on.

THE THREE PHASES OF INDEPENDENCE

Keeping in mind that their political objective was the establishment of nation-states, we may discern three phases in the political history of third world countries like India, Sri Lanka, Malaysia, Guyana, and Nigeria, which received their independence soon after the end of World War II. The characteristic issues of each phase are stated in terms of the ideological rhetoric and distinctive labels used by politicians and academic commentators alike. (I do not intend these phases to be taken as discontinuous shifts but merely as showing different emphases.)

The first stage was the actual "decolonization" process itself, when Western imperial powers, following World War II, "transferred power" to local elite groups. Decolonization was preceded and accompanied by violence when, as was the case with Algeria, the colonized fought a "war of liberation." In other colonies, such as Sri Lanka and Burma, the transfer of power was more peaceful, although not entirely without the staging of civil disobedience movements and other forms of resistance, such as, for example, those mounted in India by the Indian National Congress and in Malaya by the communist guerrillas. India underwent the horrific trauma of Partition, the political and economic and social consequences of which continue to have grave costs.

The second phase, spanning the late 1950s and gathering momentum in the 1960s, was characterized by optimistic and even strident claims in the newly independent countries about their objectives of "nation making," strengthening "national sovereignty," creating "national culture" and "national identity," and achieving "national integration." The slogans of the time accented "national" dimensions, and in doing so played down and wished away internal diversity and social cleavages in favor of the primacy of nation-states as the accredited units of the United Nations and the modern world system. Frantz Fanon's book *The Wretched of the Earth*, with its programmatic celebration of "national consciousness," "national culture," and "national literature" in African states newly delivered from the chains of colonialism, belongs to this phase. Fanon proclaimed that "to fight for national culture means in the first place the fight for the liberation of the nation, that material keystone which makes the building of a culture possible."[14] For many intellectuals of South Asian origins, it was Jawaharlal Nehru, in his autobiography and his much-read book *The Discovery of India*, who eloquently preached the promise of Indian nationalism and cultural renaissance wedded to the organizing institutions of the state, a marriage that would deliver social justice, economic growth, and scientific progress.[15]

This phase of optimistic nation building was enacted as the work of "national coalition governments," examples of which were Nehru presiding
over the monolithic Congress Party; Cheddi Jagan, an East Asian, and L. F. S.
Burnham, a Creole, heading the People's Progressive Party in Guyana in the
early 1950s; Tengku Abdul Rahman presiding over the Malaysian Alliance,
again in the 1950s; and D. S. Senanayake's leadership of the United National Party in Ceylon in the same period. Political parties seemed willing
to collaborate, rather than emphasizing their separate interests and their
special constituencies. This phase was also marked by confident expectations of expanding economic horizons, instanced by faith in economic
planning and growth and the spawning of "five-year plans" funded by foreign aid, whose smooth flow, it was hoped, would make the world safe for
capitalism and democracy.

In a dislocating and sometimes disconcerting manner this hopeful, ex-
pansive phase of nation building has been put to the test and even reversed
in the third phase, from the 1960s onward, by the eruption of ethnic conflicts. The divisiveness has revolved around issues of language, race, religion, and territory. Accordingly, there has been a shift again in slogans and
concepts. *Ethnic groups* and *ethnic conflict* are the salient labels for talking
about these events. The terms *plural society, devolution of powers, traditional homelands,* and *self-determination*—old words given new force and
urgency—have begun to frame the political debate and academic analyses.
The central political authority, the state, which in the previous phase of nation building and economic growth was designated as the prime actor and
central intelligence in initiating, directing, and controlling the country's
future and historical trajectory, is now, after years of escalating ethnic divisiveness and pluralistic awareness, counseled to be a "referee," adjudicating
differences and enabling regional cultures and societies to attain their "authentic" identities and interests.

In our present phase of ethnonationalism, characterized by the politicization of ethnicity, there are two salient features. The ethnic groups qua
groups demand and bargain for collective entitlements (the concepts of individual rights and individual identity are secondary here), and it is usually
a majority group that demands affirmative action on its behalf to put to
right an alleged historical injustice, thereby once again giving new content
to affirmative action, which is usually undertaken on behalf of depressed
minorities and underclasses.

What I call ethnonationalism relates to the generation of regional or
subnational reactions and resistances to what is seen as an overcentralized
and hegemonic state, and their drive to achieve their own regional and local

sociopolitical formations. Now let me enumerate four issues that have posed problems with regard to nation-state making and "modernization" in newly independent and so-called developing third world countries, and that have increasingly generated the politics of ethnonationalism. They are the four rocks on which the nation-state project has foundered:

1. The question of what the language or languages of education and administration ought to be, and of whether to replace English with *swabasha* (indigenous languages), is a postcolonial problem that has taxed countries with plural languages, such as India, Pakistan, Burma, Sri Lanka, Malaysia, which all have their own written languages and literatures. The ramifications of this language issue are many.

2. Closely related is the "modernization" program that has entailed the launching of ambitious literacy and educational programs. The result has been an explosion of literacy in the context of a population explosion, and the creation of large numbers of educated or semi-educated youths seeking employment in economies slow in growth and unable to accommodate them. It is this category of unemployed youth at urban sites that has everywhere been the most visible and activist participant in ethnonationalist movements and ethnic riots.

3. A major divisive and contentious issue, generated by economic development and modernization in countries of low income and high-population density and rural underemployment, is large-scale population movements and migrations that cause dramatic speedy changes in the demographic ratios of peoples in a region who perceive themselves as different on the basis of ethnic origins, religion, length of residence, and so on. Myron Weiner has proposed two hypotheses concerning "the social and political consequences of internal migration in a multi-ethnic low-income society": (a) "that the process of modernization, by providing incentives and opportunity for mobility, creates the conditions for increasing internal migration"; and (b) "that the modernization process nurtures the growth of ethnic identification and ethnic cohesions."[16]

The second proposition is especially true when migration and the collision of groups produces "competition for control over or access to economic wealth, political power and social status"; and when there is a strong concept of "territorial ethnicity"—the notion that certain ethnic groups are rooted in space as *bhumiputra* (sons of the soil), especially among the indigenous folk of the region into which migrants are coming; and when migration changes the demographic balance and the mix of ethnic groups within a given space. Migrants belonging to a particular ethnic group may move in from the periphery to work in subordinate positions to the ethnic group or nationality predominating in the core region. This situation results in a "dual labor market" and applies to Turkish and Greek guest workers in Germany, Moroccans in France, and Mexican labor migrants to the United States, who frequently become depressed minorities victimized by discrimination.

Quite different outcomes ensue, however, when the population flow is in the opposite direction—that is, when the migrants have skills and capacities superior to those of the locals and come to enjoy affluence and social prestige. This second situation can become particularly acrimonious and contentious, especially in postcolonial and postindependence times, when power shifts to and is exercised by the most numerous, usually the local "sons of the soil," who then wish to displace these successful so-called "aliens" and newcomers. Frequently, this thrust coincides with the "indigenous" or local population producing its own educated youth, who aspire to move into occupations held and enterprises managed by the migrants. Such moves to displace people in favored positions are particularly acute when the avenues of employment in the modern sector are not expanding fast enough to incorporate the number of entrants among the locals into the ranks of the middle class. When such bottlenecks occur, the successful migrants are viewed as obstacles to the social mobility and well-being of the indigenous majority.

I need mention only these well-known examples in illustration: in northeastern India, in Assam and Tripura and elsewhere, the collisions between the local hill tribes and the incoming West Bengali Hindu and Bangladeshi Muslim migrants; in Pakistan, the animus against the Muhajir who migrated to Sind after Partition and became prominent in Karachi; in Uganda, Idi Amin's expulsion of Indian merchants and professionals; in Fiji the tensions between Fijians and Indian immigrants. With the dissolution of the USSR, many Russian professionals and administrators who had been sent or migrated to the various non-Russian republics were faced with similar displacement by "indigenous" populations.

4. The fourth issue pertains to the degree of viability of secularism as specified in Western nation-state philosophy in civilizational contexts of the sort prevailing in many parts of the world—in the Middle East, in South and Southeast Asia, and elsewhere—where many persons reject the relegation of religion to the private domain and are earnestly committed to the idea that religious values and beliefs must necessarily inform politics and economic activities. The vexed issue is how to implement this worldview in a context where multiple religions with distinctive practices, and whose followers differ in their numbers, exist together in the same politi-

new forms of secular. *(brkhls)*

cal arena. It has been asserted that India has been the home of a concept of secularism, different from the Western one, in which the state, rather than excluding religion from politics, is exhorted to be evenhanded in its dealings with multiple coexisting religions that give direction to the lives of their adherents. Mahatma Gandhi, who once said that those who want to separate religion from politics understand neither, is held to be the quintessential proponent of the distilled wisdom of India that religions must and can coexist in a spirit of tolerance and mutual respect within the same polity.

Precedents for this were allegedly set by two celebrated Indian rulers, Aśoka, who ruled over most of India, except the deep south, in the third century B.C., and whose "righteous rule" was influenced by Buddhist values of tolerance and nonviolence, and the sixteenth-century Moghul ruler Bābur, who ecumenically reached out to Hinduism. These are indeed glorious precedents. But recent developments in India in the form of Sikh fundamentalism and the cry for Khalistan, and in the form of Hindu nationalism, propagated and propagandized with great effect by such organizations as the Rashtriya Swayamsevak Sangh (RSS), the Bharatiya Janata Party (BJP), the Vishwa Hindu Parishad (VHP), and that generated the Ayodhya temple dispute (the Babri Masjid–Ram Janmabhumi clash), are putting India's capacity to negotiate a viable relation between a unified polity and sectarian religio-politics severely to the test. There are similar developments in neighboring countries, including Sri Lanka.

The conundrum that faces many of us South Asians is this: while we all should make the effort to comprehend and appreciate the reasons for the rejection of Western secularism by certain religious communities, we also have to face up to the question of what policy to put in its place in an arena where multiple religious communities with divergent political agendas contest one another and make claims that threaten to engender discrimination and inequality among citizens who in principle must enjoy the same civil rights and should peacefully coexist.

2   Orientation and Objectives

By *discourse*, I mean the aggregate of speech acts, utterances, interactions, and practices that together constitute a shared arena of public conduct for a collectivity of people.

Ethnic identity is above all a collective identity: we are self-proclaimed Sinhalese, Malays, Ibos, Thais, and so on. It is a self-conscious and vocalized identity that substantializes and naturalizes one or more attributes—the usual ones being skin color, language, religion, and territorial occupation—and attaches them to collectivities as their innate possession and their mytho-historical legacy. This is a "primordialist" claim. The central components in this description of identity are emotively charged ideas of inheritance, ancestry, and descent, place or territory of origin, and the sharing of kinship, any one or combination of which may be invoked as a claim according to context and calculation of advantages. These ethnic collectivities are believed to be bounded, self-producing, and enduring through time.

Although the actors themselves, invoking these claims, speak as though ethnic boundaries were clear-cut and defined for all time, and think of ethnic collectivities as self-reproducing, bounded groups, it is also clear that from a dynamic and processual perspective, many actors, as well as outside commentators, recognize that there are many precedents for "passing" and change of identity, for incorporations and assimilations of new members, and for changing the scale and criteria of collective identity motivated by dynamic contextual considerations. From this perspective, ethnic labels and membership are "instrumental" in construction and manipulable and porous in application.

There is also a third, "constructionist" perspective, which is allied to the "instrumentalist" view. Borrowing a phrase from Benedict Anderson, we may say that it characterizes ethnic collectivities as "imagined communities,"[1] in the sense that the members of the collectivity, although scarcely sharing interpersonal relations and face-to-face familiarity, are persuaded by disseminated literary manifestoes and media messages transmitted by ideologues that they are a community sharing origins, traditions, and aspirations. There has been an expansion of their mental horizons and subjective imaginings.

Ethnicity embodies and combines two interwoven processes, which constitute its double helix. One is the substantialization and reification of qualities and attributes as enduring collective possessions, made realistic and imaginable by mytho-historical charters and the claims of blood, descent, and race. This results in what has aptly been called "pseudo-speciation"— that is, the collectivities in a certain sociopolitical space think of themselves as being of separate social kinds. Internal unity and homogeneity, and external difference and opposition, are integral to this condition. The other contrapuntal and complementary process is that ethnic boundary-making has always been flexible and volatile, and ethnic groups have assimilated and expanded, or, in the opposite direction, differentiated and segmented, according to ideological causes and persuasions, historical circumstances, and political-economic possibilities. Ethnic identity unites the semantics of primordial and historical claims of distinctiveness with the pragmatics of calculated choice and opportunism in dynamic contexts of political and economic competition between interest groups.

Ethnic groups, especially in contemporary times of widespread ethnic conflict, seem to be intermediate between local kinship groupings (such as lineages, clans, kindreds, and so on) and the nation as a maximal collectivity. Moreover, especially marked in the modern context, and within that context conspicuous in many third world societies, is the mounting awareness that ethnic affiliation and ethnic identity are overriding other social cleavages and superseding other bases of differentiation to become the master principle and the major identity for purposes of sociopolitical action. This state of affairs therefore raises the possibility that ethnicity (projected upon the old bases of identity in terms of language, "race," religion, and place of origin) as a basis for mobilization for political action has challenged and is challenging the primacy for such mobilization of social class on the one hand and the nation-state on the other. Therefore, in a general analysis, two relevant issues that need to be kept in mind are: to what extent and in what way ethnicity modifies, incorporates, or even replaces class conflict as a major paradigm for interpreting social conflict and change; and also in what manner ethnicity has influenced the aims and activities of nation making and national integration, which were taken to be the principal tasks of the newly founded third world nation-states.

In the transition from the politics of the nation-state to the politics of ethnic pluralism, what I call "the politicization of ethnicity" is the moving force (see chapter 12 for further development of this idea). In a systematic discussion of ethnic conflict, many issues can be brought within the ambit of an interpretive framework that addresses questions of how ethnic groups in an arena see themselves as acquiring, maintaining, and protecting their alleged group entitlements to capacities and "symbolic capital" such as education and occupation, to "life chances" and material rewards such as incomes and commodities, and sumptuary privileges that enable distinct styles of life, and to "honors" such as titles and offices, markers of ethnic and national pride, and religious and linguistic precedence and esteem. These honors are accorded by the state or other authorities that are the principal arbiters of rank. In this proclamation and pursuit of invidious "group entitlements," power, prestige, occupations, material goods, aesthetic judgments, manners and morals, and religious convictions come together and naturally implicate one another.

Religion is not purely a matter of belief and worship; it also has social and political resonances and communitarian associations. Likewise, language is not merely a communicative device but has implications for cultural identity and literary creation, educational advantage, occupation, and historical legitimation of social precedence. Similarly, territory has multiple implications, which go beyond spatial location to include charged claims about "homelands" and "sons [and daughters] of the soil." We have to comprehend an arena of politics in which, as Donald Horowitz puts it: "Fundamental issues, such as citizenship, electoral systems, designation of official languages and religions, the rights of groups to 'special position' in the polity, rather than merely setting the framework for politics, become the recurrent subjects of politics."[2] Quests for group worth, group honor, group equalization, and so on are central foci in the politics of ethnicity and a critical ingredient in the spirals of intense sentiments and explosive violence that ensue.

"COMMUNALISM" AS COLONIAL DISCOURSE

The word <u>*communalism*</u> has come to South Asianists from a special usage under the British Raj. The rivalries and <u>collisions of "religious," "linguis-tic,"</u> "regional," and "racial" groupings were all considered <u>expressions of communalism.</u> In colonial India and Ceylon, and subsequently in postin-dependence India, Pakistan, Sri Lanka, and Bangladesh, this concept has been invoked and used with different affective and evaluative connotations and implications, but overall in a negative and condemnatory sense.

Let us begin with a recent imputation that has had high visibility. In his "subaltern" text *The Construction of Communalism in Colonial North India* (1990), Gyanendra Pandey has powerfully argued that in India the British used the attribution of a Hindu-Muslim communal divide ("com-munalism") as a master narrative to explain all riots and public distur-bances in which Hindus and Muslims (and others) were involved, and moreover, to characterize quite a few incidents in which no trace of "com-munalism" can be found in the historical record.[3] Moreover, <u>when care-fully dissected, what were seen as massive outbreaks of sectarian violence between Hindus and Muslims would seem to show internal competition between Hindu upper and lower castes, and especially the social ambitions of mobile castes espousing religious orthodoxy, to be more salient than a monolithic Hindu-Muslim divide.[4]</u>

Moreover, a long line of historians, politicians, and other commentators have accused British administrators of employing "communal" divide-and-rule tactics to foment local factionalism and thereby wield undisputed authority and maintain magisterial rule. This conspiracy theory no doubt has many persuasive affirmations (although it has also been overextended by some accusers).

But there are also occasions and times when communalism was invoked by the British as a bad thing, which they had to resist, and it was also con-sidered in the same vein by Indian liberals. Especially during the last phase of British rule in India and Ceylon, when the colonies were being gradually prepared—according to the rhetoric of official imperial declarations—for representative government and self-rule, religious and other minorities seeking separate electoral rolls, reserved seats, special quotas, and other forms of protection were often criticized by the commissions sent out from London to hold hearings and to craft new constitutions for subscribing to divisive "communal" interests and jeopardizing democracy (although the commissioners did, in fact, make such special provisions wherever they thought it necessary).

It is particularly interesting for us that South Asian liberal (and social-ist) nationalist politicians clamoring for the end of colonial rule and preparing for the realization of their own nation-states after independence were also by and large forced to face the insistent demands of "communal-ism." They tended to react to them in two ways, one as requiring corrective reform, where they evidenced social injustice for depressed groups, and the other as requiring political criticism and denunciation, where they were perceived as being potentially used by the "bourgeoisie" or the "middle classes" to influence and dupe the masses in order to gather support for policies that furthered their own privileged "class" interests.

A revealing example is Jawarharlal Nehru, whose liberal-socialist position on communalism was followed or supported by the liberal intelligentsia of the colonial nationalist movements. Especially when it came to the "de-pressed classes" (Gandhi's harijans, later also labeled "scheduled castes" and "scheduled tribes"), Nehru and the Congress leaders were convinced that all invidious social and customary barriers that stood in the way of their full development individually and collectively should be removed, and that educational and economic opportunities ought to be provided them in order to get rid of their disabilities as rapidly as possible. Thus af-firmative action in favor of the depressed and backward classes championed by B. R. Ambedkar was much discussed in the constitutional debates and translated into legislative action.

But the attitudes of Nehru and his liberal stalwarts hardened where they perceived that members of a small reactionary upper middle class and bourgeoisie within each community exploited "communalist" sentiments and demands to further their own political interests. Both Nehru and Gandhi did sympathetically see why minorities like the Muslims feared being swamped by the Hindu majority, and honestly tried to teach Con-gress supporters why it was the obligation of the Hindus to be sensitive to such fears and to set the example of showing tolerance.

But it was felt that the demands of communalism must be resisted, es-pecially because religious passions among the people at large could easily be aroused, since they were accustomed to think in terms of religious cleavage and constantly encouraged to do so by communal religious organi-zations and government action, as well as by certain political elites. Nehru observed:

> It is nevertheless extraordinary how the bourgeois classes, both among the
> Hindus and the Muslims, succeeded, in the sacred name of religion, in getting

a measure of mass sympathy and support for programs and demands which had absolutely nothing to do with the masses, or even the lower middle class. Every one of the communal demands put forward by any communal group is, in the final analysis, a demand for jobs, and these jobs could only go to a handful of the upper middle class. There is also, of course, the demand for special and additional seats in the legislature, as symbolizing political power, but this too is looked upon chiefly as the power to exercise patronage. These narrow political demands, benefiting at the most a small number of the upper middle classes, and often creating barriers in the way of national unity and progress, were cleverly made to appear the demands of the masses of that particular religious group. Religious passion was hitched on them in order to hide their barrenness.[5]

A thesis that has had strong support in the past among both left-wing and liberal scholars and politicians and journalists, and that still continues to be voiced by many, is that communalist politics, which involves political parties and organizations, especially espousing religious and caste and linguistic claims allegedly on behalf of their respective masses, is best understood as the instrumental and self-serving pastime of upper-middle-class and mobile entrepreneurial elites, who stand most to gain by riding to power on this electoral platform. And since they are the literate and educated and have professional skills, they profit most from affirmative action and minority entitlements.

It would be foolish to deny that this thesis (and one kind of master narrative) has merit and provides one perspective for deconstructing communalist politics and revealing its basis. And at least to some of us investigating the widespread, almost worldwide, eruptions of conflicts that are currently called "ethnic" or "ethnonationalist," it is also clear that there are more features at work than are simply instrumental (such as ruling-class or elite interest), primordial (in the sense of ingrained natural instincts), or "constructionist" (such as communities persuasively imagined by the new literary intelligentsia). As I have suggested before in referring to the discourse of ethnicity that has today gained the high ground as a viewing perspective, there are more than the abovementioned features at work. There are other processes—communicational, mobilizational, and semiotic—that have to be tracked to understand how and why in the context of competitive democratic electoral politics, the appeal to collective ethnic identity and entitlements, and religious, linguistic, territorial, and caste or "racial" legacies and attributes powerfully impels people to participate with heightened sentiments and aspirations in collective actions, which may be imbued with extreme violence. It is hoped that the following case studies of collective violence will help to convey the complex interactions and interweavings that produce ethnonationalist movements and conflicts.

It is easy when faced with the damage, dislocation, violence, and disturbance of alleged "law and order" that occurs in ethnonational conflicts to view these conflicts in a totally negative way. I have already intimated why this is a simplistic reading: the generation of ethnonationalist and regional conflicts is intimately connected with the failure of the homogenizing and centralizing nation-state-making project, and the monopolizing of state power by a majority in an arena in which minorities and groups distinguished by multicultural differences (territorial, religious, linguistic, and "racial" or "ethnic" in the narrow sense) also coexist. The discourse of ethnicity has elevated to prominence concepts such as "plural society," "multicultural accommodation and coexistence," "devolution of political and administrative powers" to regional or ethnic collectivities, and the rights of "self-determination" of minorities, including those of "resistance" and "secession." Parallel with these developments "organic communities," united by common cultural legacies—language, literature, religion, and customs—have been reformulated in many parts of the world. In order to understand such social and cultural constructions of identity, and the claims related to them, we need to get beyond purely "instrumental" and "utilitarian" considerations.

Finally, it is relevant to bear in mind that there is a spectrum of semantic connotations that extends beyond the gloss and valuation given the words *communalism* and *communal* in South Asia since the time of the British Raj. But in fact, as used in expressions such as "communal sentiments," the word *communal* also carries semantically enriching associations that are collective rather than individual in scope. This sense of *communal* taps meanings from several cognate notions, such as "community" (a people living in a locality having common interests and an administrative unity); and "commune" in the French sense of the smallest political division (cf. also "communalism": the theory that the state should be a confederation of self-governing communes). No doubt we could extend this network of associations to link up with Marx's "communism" (minimally, a community sharing goods according to need), and even with Victor Turner's "communitas" (a heightened, undifferentiated, transcending, "liminal" feeling that participants experience in climactic phases of ritual). In a different vein, Will Kymlicka has recently argued that liberalism, "as a political philosophy often viewed as being primarily concerned with the relationship between the individual and the state, and with limiting state intrusions on the liberties of citizens," can be reconciled with "the virtues and importance of our membership in a community and culture."[6]

In the light of these associations and elaborations, it is wise for us in this study to keep an open mind with regard to the virtues deriving from the co-presence and interplay of communal solidarity and "brotherhood" and collective cultural practices and rights, on the one hand, and, on the other, conflictual, divisive, and destructive tendencies in what are called ethnic conflicts, especially in their impact on the alleged requirements and maintenance of "nation-states" and on the attainment of "national integration."

COLLECTIVE VIOLENCE: DOMAINS OF INQUIRY

A great deal already has been written on the historical antecedents of ethnic conflicts, and on the political, religious, economic, and social circumstances in which many of them have broken out. These accounts include the effects of global processes that stem from the influence of metropolitan centers upon satellite countries, the assumptions and the problems of nation making, and the politics of ethnic and other group entitlement claims in plural societies.

In contrast to this rich literature, relatively little is known about the nature of the destruction and dislocations caused by collective violence during ethnic conflicts. This study is an attempt to broach this complex issue and probe some aspects of it, while at the same time situating it in the larger aforementioned context. The phenomena of ethnic and collective violence entail at least three large domains of inquiry, which can be labeled the anthropology of collective violence, the anthropology of displaced persons, and the anthropology of suffering.

The first, the anthropology of collective violence, is the study of the forms and trajectories of collective aggression, and the characteristics of the aggressors themselves as members of civilian crowds and mobs, or of professional security forces and paramilitary "guerrilla" or insurgent groups. The organization and dynamics of these crowds and groups, their strategies and techniques of violence, and so on, are part of this inquiry.

The second, the anthropology of displaced persons, is the study of the victims of "ethnic cleansing" and violence as displaced persons, and as refugees who have taken to flight and have faced relocation. Their marginal existence, placement in camps, control and manipulation by authorities, asymmetrical relations with the local populace and invidious comparisons with the latter, relegation to the limbo of "nonnationals" if they have breached a frontier, attempts to reconstruct their own identity, and the theodicy of their suffering in mytho-historical terms—these are some of the features of the anthropology of displacement and dislocation. This train of inquiry ultimately merges with the situation of overseas communities established as a result of diaspora and their complex attitudes and relations with their kin at home and their hosts abroad.

The third, the anthropology of suffering, is the study of the experiences and sufferings and coping patterns of the victims and survivors; the trials of suffering torture and witnessing the brutal deaths of husbands, sons, kinsmen, and friends; the traumas of women who have been made widows, of women raped, degraded, and humiliated; the inability of survivors to conduct normal mortuary rites and grieving for their dead; and the loss of homes and property and businesses. These ordeals and the means of coping with them at individual, family, community and collective levels, as well as the social and psychic costs that deter or defeat restoration and rehabilitation—these are some of the features of the anthropology of suffering. The phenomena of collective violence, of displacement and dislocation, and of the suffering of survivors are linked, and any ample study of ethnic conflict must address them.

CROWDS AND RIOTS

This study is limited to only a part of the first domain of collective violence outlined above. It focuses primarily on the phenomenon of civilian riots, the most frequent and dramatic expression of ethnic conflict; it is only marginally concerned with those states and forms of ethnic conflict that have developed into a condition of civil war in which professional armed security forces of the state are engaged in clashes with armed oppositional guerrilla movements and insurgency groups, who in turn, in a triangular contest, may be at war with one another. This radical state of civil war and insurgency is frequently the end process preceded by episodic civilian riots of the kind focused upon in this book.

Although a main submission of the book is its complexity, multidimensionality, and embeddedness in larger contexts, the phenomenon of "riots" enacted by "civilian crowds" needs to be defined briefly here. It is difficult to mark off "riots" as one particular kind of collective violence, distinct from such outbursts as "rebellions," "insurrections," and "millenarian movements." If, by the term riots, we understand collectivities of people, or "crowds," engaging in violent acts such as arson, destruction of property, and physical injury to human beings (including extreme acts of homicide and rape), directed against a designated enemy, whether it be a social group or category or the state or political administration (or a combination of them), then rebellions, insurrections, millenarian movements, peasant wars, political strikes, and so forth, may go through a phase or contain incidents and encounters that have the features of "riots."

It is also true that the word *riots* may have tendentious conservative, illiberal, and authoritarian connotations, and may be the opprobrious label pinned by political authorities, the security forces of the state, or the upper classes and landed aristocracy onto the collective mobilization and political protests and resistance mounted by the so-called lower orders: workers, peasants, lumpenproletariat, and "criminal classes." In such contexts of evaluation and rhetorical use, the crowds are also described as "mobs," implying that the participants are irrational, out of control, out to burn and loot, and therefore deserving of forcible repressive action by the police, the army, and gentlemen vigilantes. There is a genre of writing on popular movements in Western Europe by scholars such as George Rudé, E. P. Thompson, Eric Hobsbawm, Natalie Zemon Davis, Charles Tilly, and others that has commented on these associations and their implications. Yet these authors have also continued to employ the word *riots* in a neutral way to designate the collective violence of crowds, whether it occurs in revolutions, rebellions, religious wars, or other occasions of public disturbance. In the same way, I also neutrally call the phenomenon of collective violence during ethnic conflict "riots."

In recent years, a genre of historical studies influenced in part by literature of the aforementioned kind, and self-labeled "subaltern studies," has tried to describe and interpret various collective actions and movements on the part of Indian peasantry and urban populations during the British Raj. A leading exponent of the subaltern perspective, Ranajit Guha, characterizes official British accounts of these events as dressed up in "the prose of counterinsurgency." Attempts are now being made to write Indian history as a saga of the struggle between the subaltern classes and the elite, and the Indian masses and the British imperial rule. Writing on "the colonial construction of 'communalism,'" Gyanendra Pandey, for example, charges that British administrators reduced a variety of protest movements to the single master principle of an enduring communal divide between Muslims and Hindus and justified the use of deadly force to suppress them by defining them as "riots" threatening law and order.[7]

Well taken though these points may be, the collective ethnic violence on which this book focuses has, except for the 1915 riots in colonial Ceylon, occurred in postindependence India, Pakistan, Sri Lanka, and Bangladesh. The label *riots* is currently widely used in these countries to designate certain kinds of collective crowd action, and witnesses and sources of many kinds have indeed documented acts of violence in the form of arson, loot-

ing, and physical injury. But while the master concepts of "counterinsurgency" and "resistance" may be powerful readings of colonial history
vis-à-vis the alien and exploitative British Raj and its indigenous "collaborators," the same postulates cannot so easily and unproblematically be applied when the aggressors can be shown not solely to be the government or
the ruling classes—although these have been integrally implicated in such
"ethnic" riots—and where the colliding entities comprise a spectrum of social categories, ranging from the educated and affluent to a majority of ordinary, poorer folk.

RIOTS AS CONTINGENT AND RECURRING PHENOMENA

Is there any sense in drawing a distinction between local religious/sectarian
or even caste conflicts that in the main entail small groups, mobilized on
the basis of patron-client ties, acting in pursuance of disputes over sumptuary privileges and ritual precedence, on the one hand, and "communal
conflicts" involving larger ethnic collectivities perceived as united by,
among other things, religious affiliation, mother tongue, homeland, and
economic specialization, on the other? More specifically, has this second
order of communal conflicts expanded and become more ubiquitous and
intense at a time when new nation-states are attempting to order their political lives in terms of participatory democracy and their economic lives
according to varying mixes of socialist welfare and capitalist market-
oriented canons?

A further question, closely linked to the preceding one, is whether these
clashes and explosions of violence are an expression of deep-seated, primordial cleavages based on tendentious historical memories and mythologies and reinforced by economic disparities and political rivalries. Are riots
eruptions that occur repeatedly along such hoary fault lines? Or are they
better seen in more dynamic terms, not as recurring manifestations of
bounded and crystallized identities, but as the responses of collectivities
whose mobilization and membership are partly at least contingent on social, economic, and political circumstances and calculations?

The boundaries and intensities of communal solidarity and identity
change along with the larger political and economic map, and political, economic, and social advantage and privilege underlie the eruption and subsidence of communal riots in modern South Asia in response to revivalist
and reformist religious, cultural, and ethnic stimuli. Such riots are episodic,
recurring events, which may occur after long periods of co-existence, between ethnic communities who have shared many understandings and

conventions, have frequently taken part in one another's cults and attended one another's shrines, and have syncretically borrowed practices from one another.

Why, then, are "ethnic" formations, however temporary and variable, effective for religious, political, and economic competition and conflict in post-colonial nation-states? A heightened politicization of ethnicity and simultaneously an ethnification of politics are marked features of our time, and the power of this discourse invites extensive study, as ideology, as verbal performance, as performative action, and as practice with pragmatic outcomes.

THE COLLECTIVE STANDPOINT

It is clear that many of the communal conflicts that this work focuses on, conflicts engaging large collectivities of people, exploding into violence, and in turn structured by strategies and techniques of violence, are intimately related to the issues of late colonialism and of postindependence times. Whatever their retrospective justifications and rootedness in history, these conflicts relate to present interests and objectives—such as those stemming from representative democracy, mass politics, the distributive policies of the welfare state, world economic processes, the capacities and use of old and new media of communication for mobilization of people, and the divisive interests of groups in plural societies.

So to my way of thinking, no doubt at the risk of simplifying and narrowing my approach, it is important at this stage of my study probing collective violence to go so far as is possible in systematically sketching the collective, interpersonal, and communicative dimensions of ethnic conflict, and not to attempt systematically to integrate those processes with the actors' *individual* genetic, physical, mental, and affective capacities. The latter task is beyond me and outside my ken in any case. The imperatives and justification for a collective, interpersonal perspective as a coherent exercise are provided by these diagnostic manifestations:

1. In the later stages of colonialism and the postindependence era, the search for *collective identity*—whether national, subnational, ethnic, or regional—has been conducted with a sense of urgency. Frequently, the impulse to define and enact a collective identity based in "traditional" religion, language, culture, and homelands is fused with a sense of resistance to the alleged hegemonic march of Western power, which especially in the form of colonial rule has inferiorized peoples who have not attained to its technological and material level, and denigrated their religions and cultural attainments.

2. The people at large have frequently pressed their claims to rights, privileges, and benefits in terms of the argument of *collective entitlements* (not in terms of individual rights).

3. Frequently, the search for religious salvation and congregational solidarity is pursued through participation in public ritual that seeks *salvation for the collectivity*. The rise (or resurgence) of religious fundamentalism and millennial and *bhakti* (devotional) movements is evidence of the collective character of the salvation search.

4. Insurrections, riots, and elections are all actions by collectivities of people *mobilized for public action*. In a larger sense, we are dealing with the activities and interactions of people *in public arenas*—assembled for large-scale ceremonies, for mass politics, for purposes of protest and punitive actions in *public places and sites,* such as main thoroughfares, city centers and plazas, nodes of transportation, schools and colleges, and so on.

5. Finally, viewed as both contingent and recurring volcanic, even demonizing, hostilities, ethnic riots need to be scrutinized and closely examined as collective events, constituted of certain discernible components drawn from a cultural repertoire and public culture, and combined into sequences that form the trajectory and phases of the riots. Some of the components of this repertoire may well be drawn from the forms of everyday ritualized life, and from the ritual calendar of festivities. They may be imitated, or inverted, or parodied, according to their dramatic and communicative possibilities.

6. An entirely different question remains even when all this has been taken into account: Are crowds driven in certain respects by energies, imperatives, and interpersonal communicative processes special to their existence as temporary, volatile, active "masses"? Here we enter the domain of what has been called "mass psychology," the "psychology of crowds," and "political psychology," and it is my view that although we must begin with and exhaust the historical specificities, contextual particulars, and organized purposive features of certain riot episodes in the form of case studies, we must also subsequently ask more general and comparative questions about the constitution and movement of rioting crowds that seem general to these case studies insofar as they exhibit tendencies, patterns, and processes that are shared.

THE LAYOUT OF THE STUDY

This volume was conceived as a diptych. The first part consists of some case studies, which attempt to be detailed and rounded documentations, giving full weight to historical developments and to the political, economic, social, and religious contexts in which certain episodes of collective violence, chiefly in the form of civilian riots, have occurred. They also give details of the riots themselves—their duration, their phases, the identity of the participants (the faces in the crowd) and the victims, the nature of the violence and destruction, the extent to which there is evidence of planning and direction by interested parties, and the actions of the security forces of the state. The illustrations are taken from Sri Lanka, India, and Pakistan, and the documentation and discussion of these issues in "narrative form" are guided by certain patterns and processes that are up to a point shared.

The second part, which is based on the first, attempts to delineate some comparative points that emerge from the case studies, further supplemented by other examples, notably the dispute over the Babri mosque in Ayodhya by Hindu nationalists and the aftermath of riots in Bombay and elsewhere, and to state some issues and processes of general relevance to situations of collective violence and crowd actions. It is hoped that the convergent patterns established and the comparative and theoretical discussions deriving from them may have general relevance to the multitude of ethnic, ethnonational, and communal conflicts occurring in many parts of the globe today, and not simply to South Asia.

My analysis is based on both original and secondary sources, including the writings of many scholars, government records, the reports of official and unofficial commissions of inquiry, newspaper columns and magazine articles, and personal research. All these in one form or another constitute narratives, which have been arranged and structured according to categories and in formats consciously or unconsciously employed by the authors. For me as author, all these sources comprise a body of archival references and information, which I have used to construct, not so much a single unifying metanarrative, but a number of middle-range narratives according to certain categories I have chosen. Where there are general patterns and processes that these narratives share, I have drawn attention to them by intertextual cross-referencing, and even taken the risk of interpreting them by conceptual theorizing. Both deductive and inductive processes are necessarily dialectically deployed.

I have felt throughout my labors as author that I was not so much an outsider as a participant observer attempting to order and arrange the archival information at hand so as to foreground repetitive features as well as differences and inconsistencies. My exposure to ethnic conflict began when as a person of Sri Lankan origins and with experience of life in that country, the riots of 1983 there touched and involved me personally so directly and intensely that as an insider as well as an anthropologist, I felt entitled and indeed compelled to write my version and to make evaluations and proposals, because the people and events I was "representing" were not differently "the other" but intimately my own. Simultaneously, I could accept that my "voice," or representation, was one among other possible "voices" and representations, although they too, insofar as they narrated events that happened, had to refer to a body of archival references and to reported "evidence" that could be tested, challenged, or confirmed according to shared verification criteria. Thus, provided they agree on certain rules of relevance, selection, and confirmation of information cited, a community of scholars can make preferential evaluations among multiple representations or narratives of the 1983 Sri Lankan riots.

I have at the next widening circle of experience and knowledge, a strong sense of being a South Asian: centered as a Sri Lankan, I have cathected a strong identity with and possess a fair knowledge of many things and persons in India, Pakistan, and Bangladesh, an identity that also recognizes preferences, appreciations, dislikes, and critical attitudes. I have approached and treated the various kinds of information concerning events in India, Pakistan, and Bangladesh that were available to me with the expectation of being able to construct coherent narratives that relate to and can be tested against the evidence (even if that evidence is not always factual in some unrealistically neutral or objective sense). No doubt other South Asianists will have the opportunity to pass judgments on the plausibility of my accounts, and their assessments are necessarily an important test.

Aside from being a Sri Lankan and a South Asian, and carrying many other co-existent and situationally arousable identities, I am also an anthropologist, professionally trained in the West, who has interacted for many years with colleagues and students of primarily, but by no means exclusively, Western origin. By experience and knowledge and long residence, I also necessarily participate, but in a selective manner, in Western civilization. As author, I am not only writing in English but also know that I am principally addressing my professional colleagues, fellow academics, and, more widely, certain segments of the reading public in the West and East. I would, however, stoutly resist any suggestion that my accounts in this book are structured by preconceived Western categories of thought contaminated by valuations and perceptions grounded in an allegedly myopic Western milieu. On the contrary, my writings first relate to events witnessed and described, or reported by various sources in "experience near" terms, and they have been attuned to the actors' ways of seeing, hearing, and experiencing events. But they also had to cope with sources of a more tendentious kind. Like every other author, I have exercised my own critical skills in selecting, evaluating, and developing my narratives, which try to "translate" my selections and inferences into a language of representation my readers can understand and, I hope, appreciate.

3   The 1915 Sinhala Buddhist–Muslim Riots in Ceylon

The episodes that triggered the 1915 riots in colonial Ceylon resemble the perennial sources of strife between Hindus and Muslims in India. The tensions started in Gampola, once the capital of a medieval Sinhalese kingdom. There, as in many other towns, Buddhists lived in close proximity to Muslims, who had hitherto made no objections to the *peraheras* (processions) that the Buddhists staged annually at Wesak (the Buddha's birthday and day of enlightenment), during Esala (the month of July-August), and on other occasions.

But things changed after a new mosque was built on Ambagamuwa Street in 1907 by newly arrived "Coast Moors" from India, whom the Sinhalese called "Hambankaraya."[1] The Moors' leaders objected to the Buddhist Esala peraheras that had always passed that way with beating of drums and pipe music. "The Basnayake Nilame (Lay Officer) of the Walahagoda Dewala (temple), from which the procession was organized, pointed out that the route was a 'via sacra' laid out by ancient custom and, he believed, guaranteed by the Kandyan Convention of 1815," Charles Blackton notes. "Each successive year after 1907, however, the Coast Moors registered their protest, with the result that, in 1909, a police decision rerouted the procession in spite of the pleas of the Basnayake Nilame. When this annual argument recurred in 1911, the government agent agreed to a return to the traditional route, provided that the Buddhists' music and drumming cease fifty yards on either side of the Coast Moormen's mosque."[2]

When a newly appointed *basnayake nilame* applied for a procession license in 1912, the government agent issued it on condition that the prohibition on music be in force whenever the procession moved past the Coast Moors' mosque and all other places of worship. Charging that the govern-

ment had deprived them and the Dewala of their rights, the basnayake nilame, backed by the temple servants and tenants, instituted a suit in the district court in Kandy against the attorney general of the colony, ultimately
winning a favorable decision from Judge Paul E. Pieris in 1914. "The attorney general of Ceylon appealed the case to the Supreme Court of Ceylon,
where, on February 2, 1915, Judge Pieris's decision was reversed by Justices
Shaw and de Sampayo. This decision caused wide dissatisfaction among
Buddhists in Ceylon. The case was then appealed further, by Gampola Buddhists, to the Privy Council in London . . . but the frustration evoked by the
Supreme Court decision was felt most intensely in the up-country provinces
where the Kandyan Convention of 1815 was particularly relevant."[3]

The Buddhist plaintiff in the Gampola perahera case based his right on
the fifth provision of the Kandyan Convention of 1815, which was described by his solicitors as a "solemn treaty of cession between the British
Crown and the Kandyan Sinhalese which could not be varied by subsequent legislation." The centenary of the convention fell in 1915, and several prominent Sinhalese Buddhist activists, politicians, and even highly
placed Sri Lankan officials who were loyal to the Crown—such as District
Judge Paul E. Pieris, whose judgment on behalf of the Buddhist plaintiff
had been reversed by the Supreme Court—and Sinhalese Christian cler-
gymen, such as the Reverend J. Simon De Silva, had participated in the organization of the National Day Movement to commemorate that historic
moment, which no doubt was shot through with both pride and ambivalence. On the one hand, the Sinhalese saw in it the passing away of their
last kingdom, which had withstood the colonial powers for quite some time
and had subsequently been romanticized; on the other hand, although the
British had become the overlords, they had signed a treaty in which they
undertook to protect and respect the religion and customs of the people.

Despite the name of the National Day Movement, it did not sport anticolonial sentiments or harbor a "conspiracy" against the Raj. However, it
should not escape attention that many Buddhists did view the Coast
Moors' objections to their processions as flouting their traditional rights
and customs. And it is not fortuitous that a month after the Supreme
Court's adverse judgment, on March 2, 1915, the supposed centenary of
the fall of the Kandyan kingdom, the newspaper *Dinamina* published a
special issue with reproductions of the Lion Flag and photographs of the
last king, Sri Wickrama Rajasinha, and one of his queens.

Indeed, it must have come as a puncturing of Buddhist expectations
when the Judicial Committee of the Privy Council, in confirming the judg-

ment of the Supreme Court, incorporated this passage from the submission of the Coast Moor respondents' solicitors:

> We would point out that after the rebellion of 1818 a proclamation was issued in November of that year, and from that date down to the present time the government of the island has always been administered upon the footing that all persons inhabiting the island should have full liberty of conscience, and the free exercise of all such modes of religious worship as were not prohibited by law, provided they be contented with the quiet and peaceable enjoyment of the same, not giving offense or scandal to the government.

The Privy Council went on to affirm that the administration of laws "must be regarded as liable to such changes by competent authority as in process of time and under changing circumstances the general interests of the colony or the interests of law and order may demand." In practice, what the imperial power was telling its Ceylonese colonial subjects was that it alone had the right and power to administer the country, unfettered by any alleged treaty, and according to its own judgment of what was in the "interests" of the colony. The colonial authorities showed what they meant by their sole right to judge the interests of the colony when they overreacted to the riots of 1915 by letting the armed forces and the police incarcerate and kill many persons in the belief that the riots constituted a conspiracy to terminate British rule.

THE RISE OF SINHALESE BUDDHIST REVIVALISM AND NATIONALISM

During the nineteenth century, especially in its second half, in colonial Ceylon, there were revivalist and reformist developments in Buddhism, the religion of the majority of the Sinhalese (who themselves were and are the majority "ethnic" category in the island); in Hinduism, the religion of the majority of Tamils; and in Islam, the religion of the Coast Moors. To a significant degree these developments were reactions to the proselytizing and propagandist thrust of the Christian missions, which also enjoyed a virtual monopoly of education, especially through the English and Anglo-vernacular schools, which produced the so-called English-speaking elite, the majority of whom were native Christians. Christian missions enjoying colonial favored treatment also denigrated the beliefs and religious practices of the Buddhists and Hindus as superstitious, inferior, and conservative.

These religious movements, especially those that stirred within Buddhism and Hinduism, and that are respectively associated with famous charismatic and innovative leaders such as Anagarika Dharmapala (1864–1933) and Arumuga Navalar, have hitherto been labeled religious "revivalism," religious "reformism," religious "modernism," "Protestant Buddhism," and so on. Their Islamic revivalist counterpart occurred later, toward the end of the century.

Significantly, these three reactions in Buddhism, Hinduism, and Islam were (and are still today) intimately and exclusively linked to different "communities," now described as ethnic groups—the Sinhalese, the Tamils, and Muslims/Moors. The minorities among the Sinhalese and Tamils who had become Christians were the targets of the revivalists. The three revivalist movements were united in their antagonism to the Christian missions, but at the same time, they borrowed features from them. In another respect—and this is crucial to the theme of the relation between religious revivalism and militancy and violence—they also heightened, made self-conscious, and deepened the communal and ethnic consciousness, solidarity, and exclusiveness of the three "ethnic-religious" communities. (In the case of the Sinhalese and Tamils, language added another dimension to their separateness; the Muslims were Tamil-speaking or bilingual.) These developments thus also confirm the general tendency of revivalist (and fundamentalist) movements to become exclusive and separatist, rather than ecumenical and coalescing. In the case I am describing, the three revivalisms became "oppositional" in a dual sense: they were openly oppositional to the Christian denominations, as the latter were to them; and they were open to the possibility of becoming oppositional among themselves if their interests and objectives collided. (Thus Sinhala Buddhists and Sinhala Roman Catholics clashed in 1883; Sinhala Buddhists and Muslims collided in 1915; and in the postindependence years, especially from 1956 on, the Sinhala and Tamils have been ethnic antagonists.)

Of all the revivalist developments in Sri Lanka in the latter half of the nineteenth century and since, the most complex, weighty, powerful, and fateful for the historical trajectory of the country has been Sinhala Buddhist revivalism (up to a point usefully labeled "Protestant Buddhism" by Gananath Obeyesekere). This had its start first among certain educated and anti-Christian preacher monks such as Migettuwatte Gunananda (incumbent of Dipaduttama Vihara at Kotahena) and H. Sumangala (principal of Vidyodaya Pirivena), was then stimulated and given organizational muscle and propagandistic efficacy by the Theosophists, notably Colonel H. S. Olcott and Mme. H. P. Blavatsky, and culminated with the efforts of their protégé Anagarika Dharmapala, a charismatic reformer who extended its reach and intensity to new levels.[4]

The revivalism associated with Dharmapala as its exemplar was a product directly of the encounter with missionary Christianity and secondarily with British colonialism, which provided a protective umbrella for the Christian missions and simultaneously "disestablished" the Buddhist religion and Sangha (order of Buddhist monks), which had enjoyed the protection and patronage of the native Kandyan kingdom conquered by the British in 1815. Buddhist revivalism incorporated some of the Christian (principally Protestant) missions' values, attitudes, and techniques; it was at once an "imitation" and a "repudiation." On the one hand, there was the selective retrieval of some aspects of the philosophical constructs of early Buddhism, as embodied in the *sutta* discourses, and monastic discipline, as set out in the *vinaya pitaka;* on the other, there was a denigration, rejection, and excision of "heathen" elements (seen through missionary eyes), polytheistic "excesses," superstitious ritual practices, and magical manipulations. The need to reform from within has been characterized as a "Protestant" reaction. And the counterattack of Buddhist proselytization consisted of the successful borrowing and deployment of Western and Christian techniques and institutional forms: the printing press, organizations (e.g., the Young Men's Buddhist Association, or YMBA), schools to teach English as well as Buddhism, public debates, and so on.

Buddhist activism critically influenced a constituency consisting of an emergent urban "middle class" (traders, small entrepreneurs, lawyers, lower echelons of the administration) and a village "elite" (vernacular school teachers, registrars and notaries public, native physicians, headmen) that differentiated itself from the rural peasantry. And this constituency was principally the spearhead and carrier of two trends: affirmation of a Sinhala Buddhist "identity" (Obeyesekere) and generation of what might be called a "self-respect" movement—self-upliftment in the face of colonial domination and denigration. As Sarath Amunugama has emphasized, Dharmapala was much taken with propounding a code of lay ethics, paralleling the behavior code for Buddhist monks (*vinaya*) propounded in early Buddhism. In evaluating this preoccupation and its significance, it is useful to note that revivalist (and fundamentalist) streams are generally antipermissive and are intolerant of moral relativism or relaxation of standards of conduct. Dharmapala's *Daily Code for the Laity,* a manual setting out two hundred rules for lay Buddhist conduct, reflected Western norms of cleanliness, politeness, and etiquette, on the one hand, and the orthodox behavior traditionally expected of genteel wives, benevolent masters, and acquiescent servants and employees, on the other. It was also preoccupied with a "puritanical" attitude to sexuality and modesty in family life.[5]

In assessing the reformism spearheaded by Dharmapala, it would be an exaggeration, I think, to view it as responsible for any significant "social reform," outside of the strictures and norms imposed on lay sexuality and on Sinhalese "bourgeois" family conduct. Buddhist revivalism in colonial Ceylon was not marked by a desire for deep social and economic reform. It did not seek to change the established caste discrimination and dominance; to build enduring political organizations; or to motivate people to address themselves seriously to transforming landlord-tenant relations in peasant agriculture and to play an active entrepreneurial role in establishing large-scale capitalist business enterprises. Its organization took the form of multicentric "temperance societies" and local associations, and its rhetorical exhortations to young Sri Lankans urged them, for example, to "learn industries, learn weaving, learn arts and crafts, learn agriculture, learn medical sciences. . . . To be independent we must produce our rice, our own clothes, our own building materials, our own medicines and then will come independence." A pamphlet published in Calcutta in 1922 gives the reader a sense of the range of issues that Dharmapala never tired of repeating in distinctly hectoring rhetoric: it contains advice "to ransack the literature of the science of patriotism [so as] to learn to act as patriots for the preservation of our nation"; it exudes sentimental romanticization of the past, extolling in particular the exemplary hero of the *Mahavamsa*, the righteous Dutthagamani, who "reinvigorated and revitalized the nation"; it fulminates against the British, who "for the sake of filthy lucre opened liquor shops in Ceylon"; it attacks the "Tamils, Cochins, [and] Hambankarayas [who] are employed in large numbers to the prejudice of the people of the Island—sons of the soil, who contribute the largest share"; and at the same time, it exhorts young men to seek scientific and professional education in the United States, Japan, Germany, England, and elsewhere abroad. There is no indication of how these young men, who were to be patriotic and imbued with a sense of the past, as well as with reformed Buddhism, were at the same time creatively to incorporate and adapt to science and technology. Dharmapala was more a propagandist than a creative or profound thinker-reformer.[6]

A problematic reading of the movement emerges when Dharmapala's ethic is christened "this-worldly" asceticism.[7] As an ethic of action justifiable within Buddhism, it simply did not catch on. Dharmapala's role as *anagarika* (a homeless layman who has taken a vow of celibacy and is dedicated to active work on behalf of the Buddhist religion) was not imitated by Sinhalese Buddhists, save for a couple of his associates. Aside from the founding of Buddhist schools and printing activities, which provided avenues of occupational and social advancement and enhanced the sense of identity and self-respect of the rising Sinhalese middle class, the main energies of Buddhist revivalism flowed, not into an active transformation of this world socially, economically, and politically (which is what Max Weber saw as entailed in Protestant Christianity's inner-worldly asceticism), but into quite another project, namely, the promotion of Sinhala Buddhist nationalism and an accompanying critique of the misdeeds of British colonial rule. The phrase used by Richard Gombrich and Obeyesekere, "this-worldly asceticism," although no doubt consciously meant to distinguish it from Max Weber's formulation vis-à-vis the Protestant ethic, nevertheless poses the question of just what lay ascetic actions of a this-worldly kind might simultaneously be meaningful and relate to the Buddhist goal of liberation from this world. It is relevant to note that a substantial number of the emergent Buddhist petite bourgeoisie, traders, and middle class had already emerged by the 1880s, and that Dharmapala himself rose from this seedbed rather than stimulating its formation through his advocacy. This social category no doubt expanded at the turn of the century, endowed temples, observed lay religiosity on *poya* days and at other marked times, and participated in some good causes, such as temperance campaigns.

The limits and appropriateness of the label "Protestant Buddhism" are more relevantly considered elsewhere.[8] A central submission made here is that the marriage of revivalist Buddhism and militant Sinhalese nationalism emerged in the late nineteenth century primarily as a reaction to and legacy of the colonial era.[9] Body will be given later to the judgment that Dharmapala's modern Buddhism was a moralistic and nationalist ideology, mainly a protest (rather than Protestant) Buddhism, appropriate for an educated and increasingly urbanized population: for a middle class of aspiring administrators, clerks, teachers, and professionals; for a village elite of vernacular teachers, ayurvedic physicians, and Buddhist monks; for small entrepreneurs and businessmen (*mudalalis*) competing with rivals belonging to other communities; and ultimately even for an urban working class recently come from villages.

All these categories of population brought into the fold of Sinhala Buddhist nationalism were by the very nature of the colonial and postcolonial economy focused on the filling of state-generated and -financed administrative and professional positions and on the capture of the bounty of the state, the chief controller of resources and distributor of subsidies, rewards, and licenses. Buddhist revivalism fueling Sinhala Buddhist nationalism and majoritarian domination thus in its final thrust became a means of hegemonic capture and exercise of power and wealth, an exclusivist position that promised monopolistic gains to the majority. Wherever local business sprouted, there too the patronage of the state for subsidies, protection, access to resources, and fending off of rivals has been vital. The patronage of politicians and the patron-client networks of mudalalis are involved in a reciprocal exchange of benefits. It could be argued with the benefit of hindsight that the role of the Buddhist schools, the *Mahabodhi Journal,* the YMBA, and the Buddhist press was not so much the implementation of social reform as the forging of an ideology and consciousness of nationalist identity, destiny, and majoritarian privilege.

Treating Sinhala Buddhist revivalism and nationalism as a reaction to British colonial domination and its preferential and discriminatory policies is seeing only one half of the picture. The other half—dialectically and dynamically related to the former, and especially deriving from colonial economic ventures, setting up of administrative and judicial frameworks, and spreading of literacy and education—consists of the processes of internal social and economic differentiation and invidious competition, and of elite formation and "class" fragmentation, among the native peoples. To this were added the rivalries under colonial administration of ethnic communities that found solidarity in religious revival, mytho-historical identity formation, and strategies of collaboration with the British Raj, which in turn had a practiced imperial eye for the costs and benefits of a policy of divide and rule.

In 1915, Sinhala Buddhist revivalism and nationalism came into violent collision with the evolving Islamic consciousness and identity especially of the Coast Moors, whose economic activities and acquisitiveness ran counter to the economic interests of some Sinhala Buddhist "low-country" businessmen and the alleged consumer interests of the Sinhalese public. This episode is attractive as a case study both because it has been more researched and written about than any other subsequent communal or ethnic riot and because it can be placed within the larger political, religious, and economic context, impulsions, and trends of that time. A close look at the details of the episode—the participants in the riots, the creation of public opinion, the course of the riots, the nature of punitive actions—also will permit us to see those features of the collective violence itself that *cannot* be seen as flowing inevitably and solely from Sinhala Buddhist or Muslim religious propensities as such.

DEMOGRAPHIC DISTRIBUTIONS

According to the Census of 1911, out of a total population of 4,106,350, the Sinhalese comprised 66.10 percent (24.30 percent Kandyans and 41.80 per-

Table 1   Population of Colonial Ceylon, 1911

Province	Population	Percentage of Total
Western	1,106,321	26.94
Central	672,258	16.37
Southern	628,817	15.31
Northwestern	434,116	10.58
Sabaragamuwa	408,521	9.95
Northern	369,651	9.00
Uva	216,692	5.28
Eastern	183,698	4.47
North Central	86,276	2.10
Total	4,106,350	

SOURCE: E. B. Denham, *The Census of Ceylon, 1911* (Colombo: Government Printer, 1912).

cent low-country Sinhalese), 25.70 percent were Tamils (half of whom were Indian immigrants and plantation laborers), and 6.50 percent were Muslims or Moors, of whom one in seven were Indian Coast Moors. The remainder included Burghers (the descendants of Dutch settlers), British, and Malays, who although also Muslim were a separate census category.

Colonial Ceylon was administratively divided into nine provinces, whose populations are shown in table 1. It is noteworthy that the five provinces implicated in the 1915 riots—Western, Central, Southern, Northwestern, and Sabaragamuwa—were also demographically the five largest provinces in the island, containing 78.9 percent of the total population.

The Western Province, which had the largest proportion of the population (26.9 percent), also contained the island's only large city: Colombo, the island's capital, with 211,274 people. Jaffna (40,441 inhabitants, mainly Tamil), located in the Northern Province, was the next largest town, followed by Galle (39,960), and Kandy (29,927), the capitals of the Southern and Central provinces. There were also numerous smaller towns, administrative, marketing and educational centers, such as Kalutara, Kurunegala, Gampola, Matale, Negombo, Ratnapura, Chilaw, virtually all of them located in the five most populous provinces listed above.

RELIGIOUS DISTRIBUTION

In 1911, 60 percent of the population of Ceylon were Buddhist, 23 percent Hindu, 10 percent Christian, and 6.5 percent Muslim. Of the Sinhalese population, about 91 percent were Buddhist and about 9 percent Christian. The majority of the Tamils, 87.6 percent, were Hindu, while about 12 percent were Christian. All Sinhalese were either Buddhist or Christian, virtually all Tamils were Hindu or Christian, and virtually all Moors and Malays were Muslim. The island's Muslims spoke Tamil as their mother tongue and shared certain customs with Tamils on the subcontinent.

The proportions of Sinhalese who were Buddhist and Christian in selected provinces is relevant to the issue of Buddhist revivalism and anti-Christian sentiment. For example, in the Western and Northwestern provinces, about 18 percent and 17 percent of Sinhalese declared themselves to be Christian, and 82 percent and 83 percent said they were Buddhist. In strong contrast, about 98 percent or more of Sinhalese in the Sinhalese-dominated Southern, Central, Sabaragamuwa, Uva, and North Central provinces were Buddhist.

In Colombo Municipality, the proportions identified with different religions show a quite extraordinary mix: Buddhists there comprised 31 percent, Christians 28 percent, Muslims 22 percent, and Hindus 19 percent. The capital city is thus an interesting arena for following the relationships between the religious communities. However, in Colombo District, outside of the municipality, the two largest religious groups were Buddhists, 74 percent, and Christians, 21.4 percent.

The Christians, although comprising only 10 percent of the population, were unevenly distributed in the country. The highest proportion of Christians—mostly Catholics—was found in the Chilaw and Mannar districts, where virtually half the population was Christian. Christians came second in numbers in Colombo, Jaffna, Puttalam, and Kurunegala districts, however. The lowest proportion of Christians was to be found in the deep south, especially in the Hambantota district. More than 17 percent of the Sinhalese population of the Western and Northwestern provinces were Christians.

The denominational distribution of the Christians in 1911 was as follows: 83 percent were Roman Catholic, 10 percent Church of England, and 4.23 percent Wesleyan (Methodist), while Presbyterians, Baptists, Congregationalists, and other denominations amounted to less than 1 percent each. Communicants of the Church of England, who numbered about 41,000, were most numerous in the Western and Central provinces, and they also had a presence in the Southern Province. The Wesleyans, numbering about 17,000, also had their largest representation in the Western Province. The Wesleyan Methodist Mission began its work in 1814, the American Missionary Board was established in Jaffna in 1816, and the first missionaries of the Church Missionary Society (Church of England) arrived in 1818. All the Christian missions concentrated their energies on founding schools, and all the principal towns, Colombo, Kandy, Galle, Jaffna, and Matara, had famous schools that taught in the English language. The principal Roman Catholic missions in Ceylon managed 711 schools in 1911, with some 60,000 pupils.

THE MUSLIMS

The census of 1911 calls adherents of Islam "Muhammadans," but following modern usage they are referred to here as Muslims. The census also distinguishes among Muslims by the allegedly "racial" labels "Moors" and "Malays," and it further subdivides the Moors into "Ceylon Moors" and "Indian or Coast Moors," a distribution that plays an important role in the story that follows.

The census figure for all Muslims in 1911 was 283,631, a minority of 6.5 percent of the total population. The largest concentration of Muslims was in the Eastern Province, where they made up nearly 39 percent of the population and lived chiefly in the Batticaloa district. Another concentration was located in the Puttalam district of the Northwestern Province. Neither of these Muslim groups figured in the 1915 riots.

It is noteworthy from the perspective of the discussion to follow that the Moors as a category constituted 21 percent of the Galle Municipality, and 18 percent and 17 percent respectively of the Colombo and Kandy municipalities. Muslims were also found dispersed throughout the rest of the island, and they constituted the second-largest religious group in six districts—Galle, Matara, Hambantota, Anuradhapura, Mannar, and Batticaloa. There was apparently an uncomplimentary proverb among the Sinhalese and Tamils that in translation said: "There is no place where the Moorman and the crow cannot be found."

Let us now probe the implications of the distinction made at that time between "Ceylon Moors" and "Indian or Coast Moors." The former were by far the larger category, making up a total of 233,901. The latter, while numbering only 32,724, had certain conspicuous and distinctive features. They had in the main arrived "from the Coromandel Coast or inner districts of South India as traders or laborers, [and maintained] relations of amity and intermarriage with their friends in South India." Permanent residents among them called themselves "Sonahar as distinguished from the Sammankarar or non-resident population from India."[10] The census report notes: "The Indian Moors are found in the largest numbers in those parts of the Island where their business in Ceylon would naturally take them. There were over 16,000 in the Western Province, of whom nearly 14,000 were enumerated in the Colombo Municipality. There were over 8,000 in the Central Province, where they are largely engaged in trade as shopkeepers, jewelers, and 'curio' sellers in the town of Kandy and as rice contractors and traders in the planting districts. There were nearly 3,000 in the Northwestern Province and 1,800 in the Province of Sabaragamuwa, where they do a considerable gemming business."[11]

BUDDHIST REACTIONS TO CHRISTIANITY

The 1915 riots were preceded by lesser clashes between Buddhists and Christians, the most significant of which was the Kotahena riot of 1883. These incidents disclose some of the motivations and preoccupations of the Buddhist movement.

As has been noted, the Buddhist revivalists borrowed propaganda techniques, institutional forms, and the uses of the printing press from the Protestant missionaries. One well-known episode was the famous two-day debate held in Panadura, a town south of Colombo, in 1873, between the Buddhist monk Migettuwatte Gunananda, of whom we shall hear more, and the Reverend David de Silva, a Methodist, on the relative merits of their respective religions. (Local enthusiasts gave the victory to the monk.) As early as 1862, Gunananda had formed the Society for the Propagation of Buddhism as a counterweight to the Christian missions.

It was during the rising tide of Buddhist reaction to Christianity that Colonel Olcott arrived in Ceylon on his first visit in 1880, and he soon afterwards founded the Buddhist Theosophical Society with the aid of Mme. Blavatsky. The stimulus given by the Theosophists to Ceylon's Buddhist revival, and the emergence of Anagarika Dharmapala under their patronage and tutelage, has been well documented elsewhere. Here the concern is to document the implications and consequences of the anti-Christian reaction insofar as violent encounters and riots resulted. There is no doubt that a local Christian elite—educated in English, the first among the natives to enter the professions and administrative service, and to undertake entrepreneurial activities such as starting coconut and coffee plantations—dominated the political and social life of the country.[12] As Kumari Jayawardena puts it:

> The economic, political and social advantages held by Christians were especially resented by the newly-emergent Sinhala Buddhist bourgeoisie, who financed the movement of Buddhist revival. The Buddhist petty bourgeoisie of small traders, white-collar workers, writers, journalists and teachers, with the

support of the Buddhist monks, also opposed the hegemony of Christians in colonial society. These groups spearheaded the revivalist movement to promote Buddhist education, challenge missionary influence and to arouse national and patriotic feelings among Sinhala Buddhists. Bureaucrats and missionaries were attacked for their religion and the campaign was directed at this time against the "Christian" presence rather than against British colonialism as such. Even if this was a tactic to avoid charges of sedition, it had the effect of arousing Buddhists to a "holy war" instead of an anticolonial struggle.[13]

At the same time, there is the irony that the anti-Christian propaganda was partly at least financed by Buddhists who had made their fortunes trading in arrack (palm spirit), against which Buddhist temperance activists later agitated. Famous examples of Buddhist arrack traders whose fortunes later contributed to conspicuous philanthropy and the founding of many Buddhist schools were Thomas Amarasuriya and Jeronis Dias.

THE KOTAHENA RIOT OF 1883

A violent clash allegedly motivated by "religious" tensions and differences among the local populace in the nineteenth century took place between Buddhists and Roman Catholics in a populous section of Colombo called Kotahena on Easter Sunday, March 25, 1883.[14] Kotahena had a strong Roman Catholic concentration, centered on the cathedral complex of St. Lucia,[15] but it was also a growing commercial and residential center for an increasing Buddhist population, whose self-consciousness was exemplified and stimulated by a vigorous monk, Migettuwatte Gunananda, who belonged to the Amarapura sect and was the presiding eminence at a Buddhist temple located in Kotahena, the Dipaduttama Vihara. Ethnic difference did not figure in this clash, for virtually all participants were Sinhalese.

Gunananda, who was a native of Balapitiya in the south of the island, exemplified the new kind of monk spearheading the Buddhist revival. He was a charismatic preacher and a polemical debater, reputed to have bested his Christian adversaries in the Panadure debate of 1873, as well as an energetic organizer and fund-raiser, who procured a printing press and published tracts and pamphlets as a countermeasure to Christian missionary propaganda, and who founded the Society for the Propagation of Buddhism in 1862 in imitation of the Society for the Propagation of the Gospel. His activities and published views are alleged to have stimulated the arrival of Colonel Olcott in Ceylon to champion the Buddhist cause.

Gunananda quite intentionally prepared the stage for conducting celebrations and processions to mark certain building and decorative achievements in his Kotahena temple. These merit-making processions (*pinkama*) were not merely public expressions of Buddhist piety. They were also displays of Buddhist strength in public space—the streets of Kotahena and Mutwal and neighboring wards. Only a few hundred yards separated the Roman Catholic cathedral of St. Lucia from the Dipaduttama Vihara, founded in 1832, on land purchased with the help of private donations, by the monk Sinigama Dhirakkhanda, whose incumbency had in due course passed to his sister's son, Gunananda, in 1858.[16] "The establishment of the Dipaduttama Vihara at Kotahena met the demand for Buddhist religious services [on the part] of the new business community who migrated to Colombo from the southern province. There were cinnamon, coir, spice and furniture dealers among them, and being southerners they belonged to a number of castes. Most of them were non-Goyigamas. Though there was another vihara in Kotahena, [affiliated with] the traditional and conservative Siyam Nikaya, they did not extend their patronage to it."[17]

Upon completion of interior decorations and other building improvements at the Dipaduttama temple, the most significant of which was the construction of a large reclining statue of the Buddha, Gunananda arranged the staging of a lengthy festival of "unusual magnificence" to mark the occasion, a climactic rite being the ceremony of "opening the eyes" of the Buddha statue (*netra pinkama*). The painting of the eyes ritually animates the Buddha's radiant presence.

In January 1883, under the leadership of their monk, the lay devotees of the Buddhist temple gave notice of a grand festival to be held from February 8th to March 31st. "Arrangements were made for reading *pirit* and preaching *bana* for six or seven weeks, and it was proposed to invite five hundred priests to be present on the 31st March (the last day of the festival) in order that five hundred sections of the 'Tripitaka' scriptures might be repeated by them in one day, and five hundred 'atapirikara' (the eight articles which constitute the personal property of a Buddhist priest), presented to them. These articles were to be brought with perahera [procession] and offered to the vihara by the Buddhist inhabitants of the villages in the neighbourhood of Colombo."[18]

In the meantime, smallpox had broken out in the city of Colombo, and the principal civil medical officer requested the postponement of any ceremonies likely to bring large numbers of people together. It seems that Gunananda at first agreed to comply but subsequently decided not to do so.

Notices, purporting to be issued under the authority of Migettuwatte Unnanse, to bring in offerings with the usual perahera, were sent from Kotahena temple to the villages round Colombo, and Buddhist processions, which seem to have had the general sanction of the police without formal license, came to the vihara almost daily from about the middle of February. . . .

. . . The Roman Catholics first tired of, and then became irritated at, the constant parade of Buddhist rejoicing, which had been going on for days and weeks, and seemed likely to last for months. They saw large processions, accompanied by music, conveying offerings to the temple, daily passing their cathedral during the season of Lent, and at last they realized the fact that if these peraheras continued, they might interfere with their own assemblies and festivals during Holy Week. This naturally aroused their jealousy and anger, and they began to fancy that all kinds of slights and insults to their religion were intended.[19]

From then on a series of moves on the part of Buddhists and Catholics, further compounded by contradictory decisions by the police and civil authorities about who might or might not hold processions during the Christian Holy Week before Easter, inevitably led to a climactic street battle.

As noted, Gunananda, "the chief priest" of Dipaduttama Vihara, had planned for festivities to begin on February 8th and to conclude on March 31st. March 23d was chosen for the climactic ritual of "opening the eyes" of the Buddha statue because, being the day of the full moon, it was an auspicious time. The question has been raised whether Gunananda deliberately chose the month of March for his Buddhist festivities knowing full well, having lived for some years in Kotahena in proximity to the cathedral, that Holy Week, from Palm Sunday to Easter Sunday, was a key period in the Roman Catholic calendar. The month of March is not a time for festivities in the traditional Buddhist calendar.

From the Roman Catholics' point of view, March was the season of Lent, and Holy Week was of particular importance for their religious observances, particularly Good Friday, the day on which Christ was crucified, which fell that year on March 23d, and Easter Sunday, the day of Christ's resurrection, which fell on March 25th. It had been customary for the Catholics to hold processions on Palm Sunday, Good Friday, and Easter Day.

As things stood, the Buddhist festivities at the temple a few hundred yards away from St. Lucia would extend through Holy Week, and although the Buddhists had hitherto been allowed to hold festivities, Catholic sensitivities began to simmer when it became clear that there would be competitive and irreconcilable festivities taking place simultaneously on Good Friday. There was some muddling on the part of the police when they first issued a license for the Buddhists to hold their procession on Good Friday,[20] then took into account the Roman Catholics' customary request for a procession on the same day, as well as their objections to a rival Buddhist procession on that day, and finally persuaded Gunananda to call off his procession. However, the police got the consent of the Roman Catholic bishop for the Buddhists to hold their procession on Easter Sunday between 1:30 and 4 P.M. after the Roman Catholics had completed their services in the morning.

But feelings had been stirred, mischievous rumors had been launched, and the Good Friday buildup had only barely been defused. The compromise of having Christian and Buddhist processions and festivities at two separate times on Easter Sunday did not keep the two sides apart. The Roman Catholics had held their services on Easter morning and had dispersed, but "a little before one o'clock the neighbourhood was alarmed by the sudden ringing of the bells in all Roman Catholic churches in the neighbourhood, and without delay, as if at a preconcerted signal, large bodies of men ready armed with clubs, and marked on the forehead and back with white crosses, began to assemble at St. Lucia's corner."[21] The Catholics were thoroughly enraged by rumors that the Buddhists were carrying a cross with a monkey nailed to it and a statue resembling the Virgin Mary.

The peaceful and unarmed Buddhist procession, with women and children in attendance, became transformed when it reached the canal bridge on Skinner's Road, less than half a mile from St. Lucia's. Upon hearing a rumor that a Buddhist priest had been assaulted, the menfolk rushed into a timber yard close by and took sticks and whatever else could serve as weapons. The police, caught in between, ordered the Catholics to disperse, and on their refusing, made a charge, which was greeted by brickbats and stones. The Buddhists, "in order to force a passage, attempted to drive their carts through the Catholic mob, but the latter seized and killed their bullocks, broke up the carts and burned them and their contents on the public highway." Thereafter, the crowds dispersed. Two people had been killed and about thirty injured, including twelve constables.

The next day, March 26, there were two other Buddhist processions on their way to the Kotahena temple, one from Koratota, a village some ten or twelve miles from Colombo, and the other from Peliyagoda, situated on the city's outskirts. The latter was armed this time with clubs, swords, muskets, and other weapons and was bent on violence. Meanwhile, a Roman Catholic crowd assembled at Kotahena was in an excited state because rumor had it that a Catholic priest had been assaulted. This day, however, not only armed police but also men from the Royal Dublin Fusiliers were on duty, and they managed to turn back the Buddhist processions before any clashes could take place.

The famous "Kotahena riot" was actually a limited episode that lasted one day (or at most two, if the abortive processions on March 26 are counted as a continuation of the violence). Fewer than ten thousand people took part, according to one estimate, and the outbreak was not directed against the British colonial authorities but was part of the infighting for space, influence, and presence among two Sinhalese religious communities competing first of all in Colombo and only secondarily elsewhere in the island.[22]

Outside Kotahena itself, sporadic violence occurred for a few days. On Monday, March 26, a Roman Catholic chapel at Dehiwela, just south of Colombo, was burned, and there were other attacks on Catholic property. At Ratmalana, also to the south of the city, Buddhists paraded a cross after hearing a rumor that Christians were carrying a yellow robe on a pole.[23] Rumors were rife, but violence fizzled out.

The commission that inquired into the riots was composed of F. R. Saunders, government agent, Western Province, Lt. Colonel J. Duncan of the Royal Dublin Fusiliers, and J. H. DeSaram, district judge, Kurunegala. There were no Catholics or Buddhists on it, and all the members were government officials. In summing up, this commission enumerated the following as the causes of the riots:

1. The proximity of the Buddhist temple and the Roman Catholic cathedral at Kotahena.

2. The gradual revival of Buddhism and the controversies consequent thereon.

3. The protracted nature of the Buddhist festival and the grand scale on which it was carried out by so bitter an opponent of the Christian religion as Migettuwatte Unnanse.

4. The continuance of the Buddhist festival throughout Holy Week.

5. The spreading of false reports regarding insults to the Christian religion, which were believed by the Roman Catholics and greatly exasperated them.

6. The apparent inability of the Roman Catholic authorities to control the more ignorant of their flock.

7. The indiscretion and indecision displayed by the police in granting, withholding, and canceling licenses.

8. The insufficiency of the information possessed by the police, defective arrangements made by them, and their failure properly to enforce the

law at the first sign of trouble or to grasp the magnitude of the disturbance until it was too late.[24]

All these were indeed components of the chain of events culminating in the Easter riot at Kotahena. This sequence of events is, as we shall see, typical of the phases civilian riots go through as short-lived, unstable phenomena.

For various reasons, the police force on the spot at times of collective violence linked to "ethnic" conflict (ethnicity itself being broadly understood as implicating allegedly "racial" or "blood" links, linguistic, religious, and territorial bonds, and mytho-historical continuities) is *usually* unprepared and unable to cope with riots and similar civilian outbursts. Usually, too, it is the army, called in later, that is perceived as more effective in restoring order.

A prominent role is played in such disturbances by processions of demonstrators, accompanied by loud music and carrying emblems, flags, statues, and placards, embellished by slogans, insults, and boasts. The timing and presentation of such parades are integrally linked to the religious and civil calendar of festivals and commemorative rites and to other features of public culture. The processions themselves mobilize people for public support and action. Parading through streets, past civil and religious buildings and monuments, and converging and aggregating at squares and parks and *maidans* is a public display of social presence and the taking command of space and territory, some of which belongs to the "enemy," whether it be an ethnic other, the "government," or an opponent "class" or caste. Collective presentation of identity and self, mobilization and show of social support, public staging of protest laced with rhetorical speech and music and, above all, noise: this is how collective causes are to a large extent pursued. At some stage, violence becomes a primary mode of conducting politics and achieving certain objectives.

Another important feature that needs to be recognized is the role of rumors, later found to be false, but which at the time are believed and serve to fuel rioting, inciting people to arm themselves, band together, and be ready to commit violence. At Kotahena, both sides believed that their respective priests had been attacked, and the Catholics believed that their sacred symbols were being insulted. The power of rumor in triggering action should not be underestimated.

The Kotahena riot of 1883 might well be regarded as a manifestation of early Sinhala Buddhist nationalism, which the British authorities failed to recognize at that time. There is no doubt that the Catholics felt that the

Buddhists were invading their sacred space. "The offence on the part of the Buddhists consisted of their taking the images so near the cathedral," Monsignor Pagnani told the investigating commission. Bells were rung to summon the faithful to block the Buddhist procession. "We have no hesitation in stating that we believe the illegal assemblies, both on Good Friday and Easter-day were thoroughly organized and previously arranged by the Roman Catholics, with the express purpose of attacking Buddhist processions," the commission concluded.[25]

It is likely that British official sentiment was prejudiced against the Roman Catholic Church (the colonial government had withdrawn the special privileges it granted the Anglican Church, as an expression of its "religious neutrality," only in 1880), and that the authorities that granted licenses to stage processions did not want to displease the Buddhists.[26] Be that as it may, the Buddhist leaders, now strengthened by Olcott's propagandist abilities, not only felt that they were the injured party, but mounted an agitation whose pregnant significance was missed by the authorities.

Protesting that they were the victims of attacks by Catholic mobs, the Buddhist leaders insistently asked that the rioters who had been apprehended near St. Lucia's on Easter Sunday be brought to court, and that the injuries done to Buddhists and their property be redressed. Absent reliable evidence and the necessary witnesses to prosecute them, the colonial authorities had released those apprehended, however, and they kept evading the Buddhist request. The findings of Governor Longden's Commission of Inquiry did not satisfy the Buddhist leaders. They wanted the Colonial Office to hold a separate inquiry. A Buddhist Defence Committee was formed, both to seek redress and with other objectives in mind. Colonel Olcott, who made his second visit to the island in January 1884, joined the committee and was asked to present the Buddhist case in London.

In addition to raising the question of bringing the rioters to court, Olcott proposed to the Colonial Office that the Buddhist community be empowered to manage property belonging to the Sangha, because the monks were prohibited by the rules of their ordination from "meddling in worldly affairs"; that Wesak be declared a public holiday for Buddhist government employees; that Buddhist registrars of marriage be appointed in Buddhist villages and city wards; that religious processions accompanied by the beating of tom-toms be allowed to resume. "Harsh and unpleasant as the sound of tom toms may be to European ears, yet it is music to the Asiatic, and a festival without it is lifeless and uninteresting to them," Olcott explained to the colonial secretary, Lord Derby. "Discontent and despair are rapidly spreading among the Sinhalese Buddhists," he added, saying that prior to the promotion of the manufacture and sale of arrack by the colonial authorities, the Sinhalese had been "a most kindly, quiet and virtuous nation." Their devotion to Buddhism had survived the bloody policies of the Portuguese and the despicable craftiness of the Dutch, and they now felt "as though the [present] ruling power were secretly willing to deliver them over to the Romish mob, and determined to deny them common protection."[27]

Olcott's intervention did little to achieve redress of Buddhist grievances over the Kotahena riot; but the Buddhist revival had for the first time made its voice heard in London independently of the official colonial channels of communication via the governor.[28] The riot was not merely a religious clash between Roman Catholics and Buddhists. It was also an early stirring of the ambitions of a Buddhist majority whose purposes and future were being shaped by leaders whose religious, political, and economic hopes were beginning to be articulated within the colonial framework, prefiguring organized attempts, not only to win greater concessions and recognition from the British Raj, but also to launch a Buddhist nationalism of the Sinhalese majority, of which Anagarika Dharmapala and his associates would be the chief advocates. In 1915, in the midst of a world war, the British were to misread and grossly exaggerate the anticolonial dimensions and objectives of the "Sinhalese-Muslim" riots, which, although they had ethnic, religious, economic, and sociopolitical strands, were not yet a move in the direction of resistance to colonial rule and emancipation from it.

Although prominent monks like Gunananda and Sumangala were the leaders of the Buddhist revival up to the 1880s, in subsequent years, the most conspicuous defenders of Buddhist interests, and critics of Christian missions, were not ordained monks but laymen. Among them were Dharmapala, who fashioned the new role of the anagarika, and his follower and associate Walisinha Harischandra (1877–1913). Harischandra, a member of the Maha Bohdi Society who campaigned for government protection of sacred sites in the ancient capital of Anuradhapura in the North Central Province, led protests in June 1903 during the Buddhist *poson* festivities to persuade the government to lift the restrictions placed on Buddhist processions. A minor anti-Christian riot ensued in Anuradhapura, during which, among other things, a Roman Catholic church was burned and a slaughterhouse destroyed. Harischandra was arrested for inciting it, but was later acquitted. This antigovernment riot took place during the customary full-moon pilgrimage to the city. "Only a few hundred of an estimated ten thousand pilgrims present. . . took part in the riot. Many Low Country men [people from the southwestern province] were said to be involved. They left town immediately after the riot and managed to avoid arrest."[29]

THE ALLEGED CAUSES OF THE 1915 RIOTS

A widely accepted explanation of the 1915 riots runs as follows: "The riots were the culmination of developing antagonism between the Sinhalese population and the 'Coast Moors,' recent Muslim immigrants from Southern India. The causes for this ill-feeling were mainly economic and religious. The Sinhalese resented the virtual monopoly enjoyed by Muslims over petty trade in foodstuffs. The War with its shortages and high prices caused considerable hardship to the people and it was easy to believe that these Muslim traders were exploiting the situation."[30] But the immediate precipitating or triggering event leading up to the riots was the familiar one of religious processions playing music while passing Muslim mosques.

Rioting broke out in Kandy after midnight on May 28, 1915, and continued intermittently for two days until May 30. By June 1, rioting had spread to Colombo and the Western Province, and by the next day, it had ignited in the Southern, Central, Northwestern, and Sabaragamuwa provinces. The disturbances were more or less brought under control, after some nine days, by June 6, although isolated outbreaks occurred for some days afterwards. In actual area, the space affected, including towns, was about three hundred square miles.

According to one account, at least thirty-nine people were killed by the rioters, and damage to property was estimated at six million rupees.[31] Martial law was proclaimed on June 2 in the five affected provinces, and was withdrawn only on August 30. At least sixty-three people were killed by the military and police in suppressing the riots, and many prominent Sinhalese leaders of elitist connections were imprisoned on charges of sedition.

A second account sums up the damage as follows: "From a communal clash up-country, disorders spread into six of Ceylon's nine provinces, causing the deaths of 140 people, the arrests of 8,786, imprisonment of 4,497 and at a cost of about Rs. 7,000,000."[32] Floggings and shootings by English volunteers mobilized to quell the riots—mainly tea planters and employees of Colombo commercial firms—were worse than anything the rioters did. Governor Sir John Anderson, who replaced Sir Robert Chalmers, would later condemn these atrocities.[33]

The outbreak of World War I had spawned anxieties and suspicions. Suggestions of German intrigue seemed plausible to the British, and perhaps the vague knowledge that Turkey and the Caliphate of Islam were enemies of His Majesty's government, strengthened by the news of the arrest in Egypt of the ex-sultan of the Maldive Islands (a Ceylon dependency) for pan-Islamic propaganda, may have made some of the Sinhalese Buddhists believe that punitive actions against the Muslims in Ceylon would be tolerated.[34] Another indirectly relevant factor contributing to the turmoil may have been the centenary of the Kandyan Convention of 1815, when the last Sinhalese kingdom yielded to British rule, under conditions stated in a treaty. The alleged nonobservance of certain understandings inscribed in this treaty regarding the continued governmental protection and patronage of the Buddhist religion (Article 5) was a matter of bitter complaint among certain segments of the Buddhist clergy and many budding "nationalist" leaders.[35]

But the most decisive and weightiest circumstances that dictated the violent actions against the Muslims, the Coast Moors in particular, but not exclusively, were, according to many commentators, more "economic" in the first instance, although clearly the economic grievances and prejudices were also closely and decisively linked with the emergent commercial and business interests of certain low-country urban Sinhalese, who were also the champions of Buddhist revivalism. For example, the newspaper *Sinhala Jatiya*, edited by Piyadasa Sirisena at this time, not only invoked a Sinhalese "National Awakening" but in tandem also carried anti-Moor stories in its columns shortly before the 1915 riots.

By 1915, World War I had created shortages of food and imported goods and a simultaneous rise in prices. Coast Moor traders, who were prominent in Colombo and the other towns in the retail trade in foodstuffs, and who had already been negatively stereotyped among the Sinhalese, were inevitably accused of creating artificial increases in the prices of necessities. "The charges against the Coast Moors were that they were unscrupulous, alien (some compared them to Jews; others, in 1915, to Germans), and they loaned money at usurious rates. . . . Before the 1915 riots, Sinhalese had boycotted Coast Moormen's boutiques (general merchandise shops and food counters) as a warning to them to desist from attempting to seduce Sinhalese girls."[36]

Kumari Jayawardena has highlighted the powerful economic ingredients of the 1915 riots. In the villages and towns of colonial Ceylon, small shops run by Coast Moors, who came from and frequently returned to South India, provided the foodstuffs and other necessities of life for the poor, and these shopkeepers often acted as pawnbrokers and moneylenders. "Restrictions on trade and a shortage of freight caused a decline in imports and exports in the first year of the war. Several of Ceylon's main products were affected by the slump, and a fall in coconut prices and the depression in plumbago [graphite] and rubber resulted in a reduction of wages and the retrenchment of labor in these industries. There was also an increase in unemployment among skilled workers in the towns. The shortages caused by the war led to a sharp and sudden rise in the price of foodstuffs and other necessities, which were most keenly felt by the poor."[37] In the context of such contracting horizons, it was a general complaint of the time that retail traders were exacting exorbitant prices from poor people. And the Coast Moors were marked out by the Sinhalese public as the embodiment of this rapacity.

Sinhalese newspapers and Buddhist journals led a campaign against minority groups. For example, in 1909, a leading journalist, Piyadasa Sirisena, advised the Sinhalese to "refrain from having transactions with the Coast Moor, the Cochin and the foreigner." In the same year, the *Mahabodhi Journal,* published in English by Anagarika Dharmapala, denounced the "merchants from Bombay and peddlers from South India" who traded in Ceylon, while the "sons of the soil" abandoned agriculture to "work like galley slaves in urban clerical jobs." *Sinhala Bauddhaya,* also run by Dharmapala, was most vociferous in its attacks. "From the day the foreign white man stepped in this country, the industries, habits and customs of the Sinhalese began to disappear and now the Sinhalese are obliged to fall at the feet of the Coast Moors and Tamils," it complained in 1912. "A suitable plan should be adopted to send this damnable lot [the Coast Moors] out of the country," a Sinhalese-language newspaper, *Lakmina,* declared in 1915, when the hostility between Buddhists and Muslims had increased. Another paper, *Dinamina,* spoke of "our inveterate enemies, the Moors."[38] Some of the editors of Sinhalese newspapers that carried inflammatory letters making complaints against Moor traders were charged under martial law in 1915, and papers like *Sinhala Bauddhaya* and *Sinhala Jatiya* were banned by the government.

RIOTING BEGINS IN KANDY

Although the most violent foci of the riots were in the low country, and in Colombo and its suburbs in particular, they did not begin there, but upcountry in Kandy, preceded by the controversy in the town of Gampola about the objections of the Coast Moors to noisy Buddhist processions passing their mosques, which had been simmering for years (see map 1).

In February 1915, after much legal wrangling, the Supreme Court of Ceylon ruled against the Buddhists in Gampola. Charles Blackton describes what followed:

> Within a fortnight, clashes took place between Buddhists and Moors in Kandy, Kurunegela, and Badulla. Piyadasa Sirisena's *Sinhala Jatiya* (March 9, 1915)

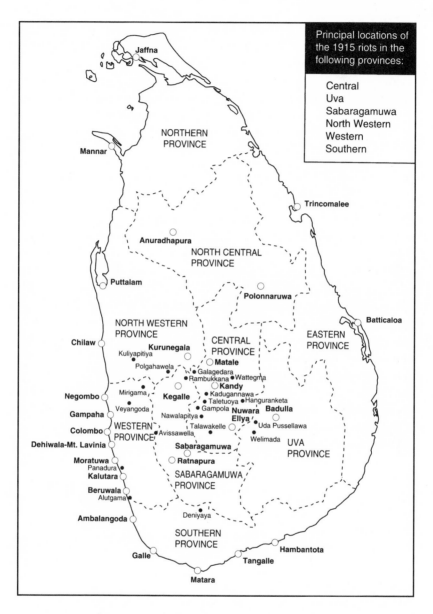

Map 1.   Sri Lanka

reported on the "outrages" by Moors against Buddhists in Kurunegela. The governor, Sir Robert Chalmers, cited an attempt by Buddhists in Kandy to block the pavement in front of Moormen's boutiques "at a spot where Buddhist processions had of recent years been accustomed to halt and distribute alms," a hint that Buddhists were setting their faces against Islam. Coast Moors and Afghans were reported to have attacked a Hindu procession in Kandy near the Castle Hill Street mosque where the riots were soon to begin. It had become a more than usually troublesome spring. Yet, as Wesak (May 28) approached, when thousands of pilgrims from all across the island would pour into Kandy to revere the Buddha on his birthday, there was no apprehension of riots, other than a police directive to make certain that no trouble developed during the procession in the vicinity of the Castle Hill Street mosque.[39]

In general, it is true to say that when riots actually explode, they come as a shock to most of those caught up in them; but it is also true that after the event, many retrospectively recognize the buildup of tensions and the warning signals. The Coast Moor shopkeepers and traders of Kandy had only recently rebuilt their chief mosque, which they had inaugurated with festivity in March 1915. The mosque stood prominently on Castle Hill Street, one of the main streets of Kandy. Wesak, the day on which Buddha was born and on which he later attained enlightenment, fell on May 28, and in anticipation, several Buddhists had applied for licenses to set up alms stalls (*dansalas*). In this particular year, some Muslim traders had objected that these stalls would cut into their trade, but licenses were issued when Sinhalese municipal councilors intervened.

Next, the issue of processions increased the growing tensions. A. P. Kannangara describes the escalation as follows:

> For the previous twenty-five years or so it had been the practice on Wesak night for parties of Buddhist "carol singers" and musicians to tour the streets of Kandy in bullock carts. In April 1915 some prominent Coast Moors in Kandy told the superintendent of police of their fears that this time the "carol-procession" would lead to disturbances. He declined to forbid the processions, but specifically prohibited them from playing music while passing any mosque. Nevertheless he was later persuaded to give permission for the carol-parties to play at the house of a prominent Buddhist businessman, although it stood only a few yards away from the mosque. The understanding was that the performance would take place after midnight by when prayers there would have ended for the day. At midnight on 28th May, when the carol-carts each with a crowd behind it were moving towards the Buddhist businessman's house, they found the mosque lit up and a crowd of Muslims watching them from within. As trouble seemed likely, the police inspector on duty tried to divert the processions. But he failed. There was a clash, the procession broke up, and the mosque and some nearby Muslim shops were damaged.[40]

Blackton gives a somewhat different account, but there is no doubt about the time—the early morning hours of May 29—and place of the clash that led to the attack on the mosque in Kandy. The city was thronged with crowds, consisting both of locals and of pilgrims and sightseers from other provinces. A procession consisting of seven elephants, led by the Dalada Maligawa's giant tusker bearing the Buddha's tooth in a jeweled casket, made a stately circuit of the town, escorted by drummers, dancers, and torchbearers.[41]

> The procession went according to normal plans until it neared the new mosque in Castle Hill Street. The singers had apparently agreed to be silent as they passed this place of worship. The crowd, however, had grown to great size and so the police decided to divert the procession away from the mosque entirely. The procession directors agreed to this but, as one account puts it, as the procession turned back "some Moormen outside the mosque jeered and hooted as if they had bested the Buddhists after all. So they later returned, attacked the Moormen and wrecked the mosque, going on to attack their shops."[42]

The events in Kandy are vividly described by the Reverend A. G. Fraser, principal of a boys' school called Trinity College, who marshaled some of the masters and students of the school to restrain the rioters. Around 3 A.M. on the morning of May 29, Fraser wrote, there was "an attack on that mosque, which had been most aggressive in its objections to *dansala* and processions." It was an empty shell next morning. "No one had been killed or hurt, and the Moors had brought the attack on themselves, by their religious intolerance." By evening of the same day, a Saturday, crowds began to collect, and "mischief was afoot." Fraser "went down in dinner dress" at about 9 P.M. to see for himself and found "the crowd were armed with clubs and had great beams to use as battering rams." Led by "Low-Country Sinhalese—a much less religious, and more deliberately dangerous set of men than were in evidence the previous night," they had smashed up a jeweler's shop and assaulted the superintendent of police. More attacks were launched against Moor shops and houses on orders given "by one of these leaders," and at one end of the street, a Sinhalese was shot by a Moor. "Meantime, too much arrack was being drunk."[43]

In Kandy the police never mastered the mobs during their first outburst. W. T. Stace and his small police force dispersed mobs only to have them reform around the next corner and begin looting there. The police seem to have been unable to arrest any of the original disturbers. Given the panic mood and the inflated size of the population, police with truncheons constituted an inadequate force. Fraser writes that later that Saturday night, crowds began to move from Kandy toward the adjacent localities of

Katukelle and Gatembe, where the crowd had burned the local mosque by 4 A.M. on Sunday morning (the 30th).

By Sunday afternoon, the crowds had formed again in the central streets of Kandy. On Trincomalee Street, Fraser saw "a crowd of about a thousand, armed with knives and clubs attacking a Moor house. Two Moors were killed, and a Sinhalese man lay bleeding and stabbed in front of us."[44] Similar things happened on the 31st, and reports were received that crowds were committing arson in Kadugannawa, ten miles away, and that Punjabi troops sent from Colombo were charging them. On June 1, the governor arrived in Kandy, and martial law was declared the following day (June 2).

Fraser's account tallies with those provided by other sources. On the evening of the 29th, crowds moved down the Kandy-Peradeniya road, reaching Gatembe in the dawn hours. A British observer found "the street littered with piles of burning loot and ashes, the village mosque burned out."[45] During the morning, rumors flew in Kandy that gangs of Moors were coming to destroy the Dalada Maligawa (the Temple of the Tooth) in retaliation for mosques wrecked. In fact, a group of twenty-five to thirty Moors did travel up by train, but they were intercepted by police at Kadugannawa. By evening, however, Sinhalese gangs were loose in Kandy's streets, and the governor, notified of this second outbreak, ordered the sending of more police from Colombo and one hundred troopers of the 28th Punjabi regiment, garrisoned in Ceylon. The reinforcements arrived in Kandy at dawn on Saturday, May 30th. This draining-off of police from the Western Province may inadvertently have set the stage for the mass looting in Colombo.

After Inspector General Dowbiggin took charge in Kandy, "reports came in of disturbances in the direction of Kadugannawa to the west, Gampola to the south, Teldeniya to the east, and Panwila to the north of Kandy." Dowbiggin personally led a force toward Kadugannawa, while sending parties by car to these danger points. He saw much damage and disarmed some Sinhalese. Halfway to Kadugannawa, there was a mêlée. Having collected a crowd, F. P. Walgampahe, the basnayake nilame of the Gadaladeniya Devale, appeared, in Dowbiggin's words, "brandishing an open knife." Walgampahe was injured and died before reaching hospital. This case was to be revived by the Sinhalese mission in London in later days.

Let us now pause here for a moment and take in the intriguing significance of Fraser's pointed reference to "Low-Country Sinhalese" leading and directing the mob just twelve hours after the first outburst in Kandy. "The mass of rioters were out against Mohammedans pure and simple on economic and religious grounds, and without design against British Rule, some indeed believing an attack on Mohammedans would be popular as the Empire was fighting Turkey," Fraser wrote D. B. Jayatilaka (who was in London with E. W. Perera to ventilate the grievances arising from prosecutions for alleged participation in the riots) on August 25, 1917. He averred that in his opinion, there was "no doubt that the riots were organized in advance, that there was a small clique of men hostile to Government and representing the opinion of a man like Dharmapala, whose articles were read and who was flattered and well received, and this clique exploited the hatred of the Mohammedans by directing attention to them, and probably in organizing and starting the first chief riot outbreaks. But they were not typical of the people as a whole or of the nation." In a postscript to this letter, he added: "That there was a planned start and some organization I as living in Kandy can have no doubt."[46]

In a subsequent letter to Jayatilaka, dated September 5, 1917, while firmly denying that "there was any conspiracy on the part of the Cingalese against the Government," Fraser reiterated that he found it "difficult to believe that there was no organization in advance. For one thing I knew that the riots were going to take place before they took place and warned the authorities to be on their guard in order that there might be no trouble."[47]

EVENTS IN THE KANDYAN AND NORTHWESTERN PROVINCES

The disorders at Gampola occurred on May 30, only a day behind those in Kandy, when the town began to fill with strangers. J. R. Walters and his police could not move them on. As darkness fell, a *bhikkhu* (Buddhist monk) addressed the crowd, shouts of "Sadhu!" (Holy!) were raised, and a gang rushed several Moor shops. Walters phoned for help and intervened until all but four of his men had faded away, some injured. The Moors defended the mosque with guns, but it was almost gutted. By the time Walters, "despairing of reinforcements," distributed rifles and dispersed the mob, most Moor premises had been sacked, and the Moors had fled. Walters reported his view that this riot had been planned. The Moors returned on June 1, and the troubles moved on again.

Similar events were taking place at Matale on the same day. The assistant government agent (A.G.A.) there doubted any local plot and blamed outsiders. North and east of Kandy in the Pata Dumbara–Uda Dumbara area, the A.G.A. reported that lootings were organized by priests, headmen, and notaries, backed by schoolmasters and low-country traders and stirred to action by persistent rumors that the government wanted the

Moors expelled, Moors were planning to attack Buddhist temples, and "British rule ended on the 27th; Buddhism is reviving."[48]

Further up-country at Nuwara Eliya, energetic measures, warning of Moors, banning of processions, closing of drink shops, and conferences with communal leaders contained the rioting within a few days. During the worst outburst at Nuwara Eliya, all Buddhist houses showed lighted paper lanterns, presumably to ensure their owners freedom from molestation by looters. Of these areas, remote Uva Province suffered the least disturbance. There, as elsewhere, Kandyan chiefs helped British officials keep the peace. In North Central Province and the two Tamil provinces, no riots were reported.

Sabaragamuwa and Northwestern Province, between Kandy and Colombo, through which rioters and pilgrims moved westward in the days after the Kandy riots, became an area of severe disorders. Fierce action was reported from Rambukkana and Kegalle (June 1–2) and Ratnapura (June 2–3). Officials at Kurunegala reported a new factor: gangs moving eastward across the Maha Oya, precipitating widespread looting of Moors on the approaches to the low country. *Goondas* (thugs) were replacing the frightened villagers. False proclamations and rumors undermined the effectiveness of small police detachments until Punjabi infantry put the gangs down with point-blank fire. Similar patterns took shape in Puttalam-Chilaw, in Siyane Korale East (where one gang engaged the police while another struck its target), and in the Veyangoda area, locus of the most persistent violence.

RIOTING IN COLOMBO

The proximate beginning of the riots in Colombo is recorded in the diary of J. G. Fraser, the Western Province government agent, who was presiding at a meeting of the Sanitary Board on May 31 when, at about 4:00 P.M., he was called away by J. H. Daniels (the senior police officer in Colombo since the inspector general had been ordered up-country). Sinhalese railway fitters, alleged to be chronically unruly, had clashed with Moors near the factory yard, and Daniels asked Fraser to call out the troops. Fraser, with several Sinhalese leaders, went to the yard, and after a conference, the workers dispersed sullenly. Fraser later recalled that returning home, he "did not . . . like the appearance of the people on the streets and began to connect the incident in Colombo with events in Kandy." Acting on his intuition, he alerted the military, and half an hour later, at 6:30 P.M., a phone call told him rioting had broken out in the Pettah commercial district. He sent police patrols into the Maradana and Borella areas, only to find the police "worse than useless," perhaps because they were few and only armed with truncheons against very large, if uncertain, mobs. Police leadership had been sent off to Kandy with the best constables. Only the troops brought some calm by midnight, as Fraser—cruising by car with the mayor—observed.

The governor, Sir Robert Chalmers, had reached Kandy when, on May 31, he heard that rioters were on the streets in Colombo. He had already ordered General H. H. L. Malcolm to Colombo. Stubbs, the colonial secretary, arrived in Colombo the next morning and reported the rioting to Chalmers as "sporadic." The next day Stubbs wrote a private note to a friend at the Colonial Office in London describing events in more ominous terms: looting all day, the police ineffective, "the scum of Colombo have seized their opportunity," troops too few to cope with the shifting, regrouping gangs. The troops were attacked about 9 P.M., and they fired on the mob, clearing the streets. Stubbs, having worked himself into a "Sepoy Mutiny" state of mind, warned that having "tasted loot," the mobs might attack European bungalows, and that martial law was now imperative.

Still at Kandy, the governor proclaimed martial law in several provinces, including the Western Province, on June 2 and then returned to Colombo. He described Colombo as quiet but perturbed after much destruction, numerous murders, and shooting by troops. When Stubbs wrote his Whitehall friend again on June 8, he suggested that the governor's dispatches failed to show the full scope of the damage and danger. The military command, on June 2, reported that armed parties advancing upon Colombo from four directions that afternoon had been dispersed. Most of the violence in the city was over by then. But numbers of Moors had fled with their families to India or had taken refuge in the Colombo municipality.

EVENTS IN THE WESTERN AND SOUTHERN PROVINCES

Moors and property were attacked in about six hundred villages in the Western Province. The commissioner for Kalutara, Festing, declared: "Each village appears to have turned out en masse for the destruction of Moorish property in its vicinity and to have furnished a detachment to march with the nucleus of rioters from such centers as Colombo and Siyane Korale East upon the next center to be attacked." This view became the basis for the later theory that every village in riot districts should pay compensation, except those that were not Buddhist or could prove their innocence.

The whole Panadura-Kalutara area, immediately south of Colombo, was preplanned for uprising, Festing felt. Property owners manipulated "street-leaders," who stirred up the masses with stories of assaults on Sinhalese women and attacks on Buddhist temples. He had seen some pamphlets of an "inflammatory" nature handed out during the past year at meetings in Buddhist schools, where the ringleaders were "Buddhists of Fisher Caste." He regretfully noted that most minor headmen "were in it." Abdul Rahiman and other prominent Moors toured the stricken areas shortly after the riots and, although intensely prejudiced, their reports turned up data that sometimes corroborated other sources—details of damaged communities, desecrated and dynamited mosques, smashed bazaars, looted shops, burned homes, and the inadequacy and occasional complicity of the police. There had been some anti-British speeches. A month before the riots, the president of the village tribunal of Welitara had publicly threatened to expel the Moors for their dishonesty. Nationalist cards and slogans appeared. In Atulugama, weeks before the riots, a series of meetings were allegedly held in Buddhist schools, and Moors were sternly excluded "from even the neighborhood" of these sessions. Abdul Rahiman's report ended on a vengeful note, "for the insult hurled at Islam some visible and abiding mark must be put upon Buddhist temples, if for no other reason, at least to preserve the prestige of the British Raj."[49]

FACES IN THE CROWD

Recalling George Rudé's citations of Taine and Burke, who characterized the participants in the French Revolution as "mobs" made up of criminals, vagabonds, and assassins,[50] Kumari Jayawardena notes that some Ceylonese writers have similarly described the rioting and looting that took place in Colombo as the work of "street rowdies, looters, habitual criminals and their henchmen."[51] But in actual fact the mobs "were composed of the urban workers and city poor" and were led "by skilled workers, in particular the railway locomotive men who struck work in 1912." Taking her cue from Eric Hobsbawm's observation that the movement of food prices was an almost "infallible indicator" of popular unrest in Paris during the French Revolution, Jayawardena remarks that "much the same was true of the Colombo poor, who faced a growth of unemployment and a rapid rise in prices after the outbreak of the First World War."[52] And the Moor traders were targets because they were accused of taking advantage of the situation and raising the prices of necessities.

People of working and laboring status in the Colombo of 1915 were "not an organized working class in the modern sense," but they were militant and had staged a series of agitations, culminating in the strike of 1912. Moreover, as Jayawardena surmises, the workers "were no doubt readers of the Sinhalese language press, which at that time was conducting an aggressive campaign against Indian traders and Indian workers in Ceylon." And it was specifically the Sinhalese railway workers who had shown hostility to Indian immigrant labor as competitors and potential blacklegs. "In 1910, for example, the locomotive workers had protested against the influx of South Indian workers on the railways, and in 1913, in presenting their grievances before the Railway Commission, they complained that Indian Tamils and Malayalis were employed in preference to Sinhalese."[53]

Jayawardena gives us a vivid account of the buildup of tensions and the gathering of a crowd in an ugly mood that first broke out in rioting in Colombo. Her description of the behavior of the crowd, its targeting of shops, arson, and destruction of property accompanied by looting rings many bells for those familiar with other urban riots. I can do no better than quote her in extenso, while noting that her explanations are couched primarily in economic terms:

> The details of the riots that occurred in Colombo are of significance in assessing the nature of the disorders. On May 31, some of the railway workers quarreled with the Moor proprietor of a teashop located opposite the locomotive workshop in Maradana. The issue was the increase in the price of a cup of tea, and the workers, having made allusions to the rioting against Moors in Kandy, returned to their work yard and pelted the shop with stones. The police were summoned and at the end of the day the railway men were asked to pass through the gate in single file so the culprits could be identified. They refused to comply and showed signs of unrest. When the workers were eventually allowed to leave, many of them had missed their last train home. The railway workers used their enforced detention in the city to contact other groups of urban workers, and it was reported that the ranks of the workers were joined by "the idlers, the unemployed and the habitual criminals." The shops of Moors in the neighborhood of the railway workshops were attacked, and rioting and looting, which spread to other parts of Colombo, lasted three days. The railway locomotive men threatened to strike and a number of them stayed away from work.
>
> From several eyewitness accounts and from the governor's dispatches and police reports, it is apparent that (1) the rioting in Colombo had hardly any religious motives, (2) the targets for the attack were the shops of the Coast Moors and other Muslims, (3) there were very few assaults or killings of Moors or desecration of their mosques, and (4) the rioting was not led by the criminals of Colombo but by members of the working class, who were joined by the floating population composed of the unemployed and urban poor. The rioting in Colombo seems to have followed a similar pattern in all parts of the

city. The crowds were mainly unarmed, and those who were armed carried sticks or crowbars. It has been recorded that the procedure of rioting was for the crowd to raise a cry of "loot" near a Moor shop, thereby causing the owner to run away; "the ruffians would then enter the shop and throw goods to the pavement. . . and the needy men and women who were about would carry the things away." The "mob" would then move to another part of Colombo and attack the Moor shops in that area. A police inspector, describing a group of rioters who came from Maradana to Borella in a tram, said, "I observed the poorer classes of the residents in the neighborhood including Sinhalese, fishmongers, dhobies and rowdies making for the junction. . . looting began. . . it was the men who came in the tramcar who broke open the boutiques [shops], and immediately the resident rowdies rushed in and looted the goods."

Although there were instances of killing or assaulting Moors and of attacks on mosques in other parts of the country, it is noteworthy that the "mob" in Colombo was not bent on attacking the Moors themselves or pillaging their places of worship on religious grounds, but rather on plundering the Moors' shops, which symbolized the hardships caused by profiteering and unfair trade practices. In parts of Colombo, where the Moors were strong in numbers, there was fighting between Sinhalese and Moors, but eyewitnesses were generally agreed that the crowd in Colombo aimed at destroying the Coast Moor shops rather than injuring the Moors and that "actual death from violence by the mob was small." The governor admitted that the riots in Colombo were a "sympathetic but independent outbreak, which while retaining the anti-Mohammedan stamp of the original Kandy outbreak was essentially more turbulent and criminal in character, actuated by little or no religious impulse and bent on plundering and on wounding or killing the Moor traders. The reaction of the government to the Colombo outbreak can best be understood in the context of the economic and political events preceding the riots. For, whereas religious riots could be swiftly controlled, a working-class uprising presented a far more serious prospect of economic dislocation and social upheaval. . . .

A government report on the riots in the Western Province most definitely pointed the finger at the railway workers: "The foci of disturbance on the first of June—viz. Colombo, Angulana, Veyangoda and Mirigama—point to the intimate relation between the Railway and the Riots. The leaders realized to the full the advantage to them by a means of transport which permitted their emissaries being distributed rapidly throughout the district."[54]

It is essential to keep in view the spatial and demographic locations of Colombo's commercial centers, railway shops, port facilities, and residential places of shopkeepers and workers. Pettah, Maradana, Kotahena, and Dematagoda were the main locations of work sites, shops, and working-class habitation. And in the interstices of these complexes, many new Buddhist temples had been built and peopled by monks newly come from the provinces to service the rural migrants turned workers.

POLITICAL AND ECONOMIC FACETS
OF BUDDHIST REVIVALISM

As we have seen, the Colombo riots initially began opposite the locomotive workshop in Maradana after a quarrel between some railway workers and a Moor teashop owner. But the mob attacks spread from Maradana to Borella, and they found their best targets in the Pettah, the "native" commercial center of Colombo, whose retail shops selling cloth, rice, groceries, imported dry goods, and so on, were at the beginning of the twentieth century dominated by Natukottai Chettiars, Muslim traders from the Malabar and Coromandel coasts and from Gujarat (e.g., the Borah and Khojas). The island's import trade was, of course, dominated by British firms, but the Pettah trade and local distribution of goods were primarily in the hands of Indian "aliens." Their dominance was most keenly felt by the nascent and growing class of Sinhalese low-country Buddhist merchants and traders, whose most prosperous leaders and vocal rhetoricians combined religious revival and modern interests in pleading the cause of the Sinhalese "sons of the soil." Some members of the most famous of these Pettah merchant families—H. Don Carolis who dealt in furniture, N. S. Fernando, in stationery, and D. D. Pedris—were charged by the British with being implicated in the riots. Edmund Hewavitarana, son of Carolis and brother of Anagarika Dharmapala, died in jail in penal servitude after his death sentence was commuted; Pedris's only son was court-martialed and shot for inciting rioters to attack Muslim shops; and Fernando's son, Albert Wijesekera, who was also Pedris's son-in-law, had his death sentence commuted to life imprisonment and died in jail shortly afterwards.[55]

It is difficult to resist the conclusion that if one were to search for leaders behind the scenes who fanned the flames of the riots—and were perhaps even openly involved in pointing out rival businesses as targets—obvious candidates would be found among the Sinhalese Pettah merchants, whose Buddhist enthusiasms were interwoven with their economic interests and political aspirations. The ideologues and advisers of this rising class were the leaders of Buddhist revivalism and the Sinhalese national cultural renaissance, among them Anagarika Dharmapala, the novelist and newspaper editor Piyadasa Sirisena, and prominent monks such as Migettuvatte Gunananda and Hikkaduve Sumangala. Verses by Dharmapala depicting the Sinhalese as victims of foreign exploitation appeared in his paper *Sinhala Bauddhaya,* accompanied by a cartoon showing the helpless Sinhala in the grip of alien traders, moneylenders, and land grabbers. To get an idea of the rancor fueling Dharmapala's nostalgia for a lost, pristine

Buddhism and a vigorous, just, and noble ancient Sinhala civilization, one must, however, read the letter he wrote to the secretary of state for the colonies from Calcutta on June 15, 1915, demanding a Royal Commission on the causes of the riots and assailing the Muslims.[56] "The present terrible destruction may be traced to economic causes," Dharmapala said, blaming the British for not observing the promises made in the 1815 treaty. A couple of pages later, however, he added, "The causes are economic and spiritual." Noting that there had been looting of German shops in West Ham, Liverpool, and elsewhere in England, he said, "What the German is to the Britisher that the Muhammedan is to the Sinhalese. He is alien to the Sinhalese by religion, race and language." He commended the Dutch for protecting the Javanese from aliens and asked for similar protection for, and discriminatory policy in favor of, the Sinhalese: "Aliens without a history and sons of the soil with a history should not be judged by the same standards."

Their heritage of "communal laws" and communal landholding had given the Sinhalese a "religious democracy" for twenty-two centuries, Dharmapala said, but it had not survived in the face of British colonialism, which had destroyed native industries and impoverished the Sinhala peasantry, whom it debased by traffic in liquor and even turned into plantation coolie labor. He lashed out at the Muslims as British-protected foreigners who were exploiting the vulnerable Sinhalese:

> The Muhammedans, an alien people who in the early part of the 19th century were common traders, by Shylockian methods became prosperous like the Jews. The Sinhalese, sons of the soil, whose ancestors for 2358 years had shed rivers of blood to keep the country from alien invaders . . . today they are in the eyes of the British only vagabonds. . . . The alien South Indian Muhammadan comes to Ceylon, sees the neglected, illiterate villagers, without any experience in trade, without any knowledge of any kind of technical industry, and isolated from the whole of Asia on account of his language, religion and race, and the result is that the Muhammadan thrives and the son of the soil goes to the walls.[57]

Kingsley de Silva gives an unvarnished summation of Dharmapala, which appears plausible: "Dharmapala grasped as few of his contemporaries did the political implications of the Buddhist resurgence and he never lost sight of the need to set this latter within the wider framework of the rise of nationalism in Asia . . . his blending of religious fervor and national pride, of a sophisticated internationalism with a coarse insularity served as a model for the Buddhist activists of post-independence Sri Lanka."[58]

There remains the issue of the culpability of the Sinhalese leaders of Buddhist temperance societies for inciting mobs against designated Muslim victims.[59] Although the temperance societies voiced criticism of certain imperial policies, there seems to be no good reason for the British to have imprisoned the leaders of these societies on the charge that they motivated or participated in the riots. Those imprisoned wrongly for a while included D. S. Senanayake, the future first prime minister of independent Sri Lanka; his brother, F. R. Senanayake, a vigorous nationalist, who died prematurely; and D. B. Jayatilaka, another important Sinhala Buddhist leader in the 1930s and early 1940s. As leaders of the Ceylon National Congress, formed in 1918, these men became constitutionalists, collaborating with the British in a plan for slow devolution of powers, and separated off from the slogans of the traditional cultural renaissance and political nationalist Buddhism flaunted by the likes of Dharmapala, Piyadasa Sirisena, and John de Silva (1857–1922).

The last-named deserves special mention. As Jayawardena remarks, there was "political content" in de Silva's plays about heroic Sinhalese kings, *Sri Wickrema Rajasinha* and *Duttugemunu,* and in "the provocative anti-British dialogue" of his modern satire *Sinhala Parabava Natya,* which portrayed the decadence of the Sinhalese as a result of foreign influences.[60] If Anagarika Dharmapala and Piyadasa Sirisena were the foremost ideologues of the Sinhalese nationalist revival, de Silva can be regarded "the founder of the Sinhalese nationalist theatre," Sarath Amunugama observes.[61]

De Silva was born in the suburbs of Colombo into an affluent Goyigama-caste family with strong Buddhist connections. He was, however, educated at a Christian mission school (like Dharmapala) and later at the Colombo Academy. After teaching for a while, he entered the Colombo Law College and became an accredited proctor (the equivalent of a British solicitor). His true love was the theater, and he led the way in forging a new syncretic urban tradition of *nurti* plays compounded of elements taken from the folk tradition and from itinerant visiting Indian dramatic groups. In content and message, these plays either dramatized and glorified nationalist historical themes or as social criticism castigated the Westernized Sinhalese elite for forsaking traditional ways and aping the manners and customs of the British. (They also contain stereotyped slurs against Muslims, Tamils, and alien elements.) *Sri Wickrema Rajasinha* and *Duttugemunu* are examples of the first theme; *Sinhala Parabava Natya,* which deals with the decadence and downfall of an affluent Sinhalese family that has adopted a Western style of life, is a pro-temperance play in the second mode.

Although de Silva and his backers belonged to the Sinhala bourgeoisie, for whom the Buddhist revivalist nationalist movement was the high road to political prominence, the principal audience for his plays was drawn from the railway, harbor, and factory workers of Colombo. "The main Sinhalese playhouses were located in the Pettah, Maradana and Slave Island, in close proximity to the working class districts," Amunugama notes.

> Plays were staged on Saturday nights when the workers were enjoying their weekend holiday. Special attention was paid to plays put on after pay days. "Nurti" plays were advertised at work places, where itinerant musical bands were paid to play snatches of the songs which had achieved popularity. De Silva's players were also drawn mostly from the working class. Among them were sailors, wine waiters, arrack sellers and harbor workers. And his plays included a couple of working class roles to which were assigned risque songs and rude comments slighting the ways of the upper classes.[62]

ISLAMIC REVIVALISM UNVEILED

Muslim sentiments and preoccupations in Ceylon in the nineteenth century have been studied by Vijay Samaraweera and Ameer Ali.[63] Ali reminds us that 1915 was the first time that anti-Muslim riots had taken place in Ceylon, and that they were not simply precipitated by local disputes over processions in Matale and Kandy, or by the commercial practices of the Coast Moors. He also reminds us that not only the Coast Moors but all Muslims were potential victims, and that not only Muslim shops but numerous mosques too were destroyed. "A total of 25 Muslims were murdered, 189 were wounded and at least four of their women raped. In addition 4075 Muslim shops were looted, 350 houses and 17 mosques were set ablaze, and another 86 mosques suffered some sort of structural damage," he notes.[64] In monetary terms the damage was over 5.5 million rupees (Blackton puts the figure at 7 million), a very considerable sum in those days. The majority of the victims were Ceylon Muslims and not the Coast Moors. When the riots ended, four days after the imposition of martial law (they lasted for nine days in all), a total of 412 persons, mostly Sinhalese, were charged. Of these, 34 were sentenced to death, and the rest were given prison sentences of varying length.

Paralleling the Buddhist revivalism spearheaded by Dharmapala and the Hindu Saiva-Siddanta reformism championed by Arumuga Navalar among the Ceylon Tamils, a heightened pan-Islamic consciousness was felt by all Muslims in Ceylon toward the end of the nineteenth century. Ali wonders whether the growth of the pan-Islamic sentiments did not contribute to the isolationism of Muslims in colonial Ceylon, and whether the heightening of their collective identity through participation in an Islamic brand of revivalism and purification did not in fact raise an exclusivist and separatist image of the Muslims among the Sinhalese, who were at that same time in the grip of their own religious and nationalist and cultural revival.

Islam, too, in Ceylon was moved to counter the aggressiveness and criticisms of a proselytizing Christianity and its missionaries. The lack of charismatic leadership among the Muslims of the kind represented by Dharmapala and Navalar was remedied by the arrival of the Egyptian political exile Arabi Pasha in 1883. There had been in the nineteenth century "a continuous and intimate cultural flow between the Muslims of Ceylon and those who lived in South India via religious teachers (*ulema*) and schools (*madrasas*)." Arabi Pasha was an ardent Egyptian nationalist, and his arrival stimulated the Muslims of Ceylon to establish direct cultural contact with the Middle East after an interval of centuries.[65]

The new pan-Islamic sentiments found local enthusiasts in Siddi Lebbe and I. L. M. Abdul Azeez, who came under the direct influence of Arabi Pasha. Journals like the *Muslim Necan* and the *Muslim Guardian*, published in Ceylon between 1883 and 1915, showed increased interest in the affairs of Muslim countries. Muslims were invited and urged to subscribe funds for the construction of the Hejaz Railway, an Arabian project. The Ottoman sultan, Abdülhamīd II, who was then also caliph of Islam, was adopted as a figure of veneration; and a special request was made by local enthusiasts like Azeez to the ulema to recite the sultan's name on Fridays at the congregational sermons in mosques. Finally the *turukki topi*, or fez, worn by the Egyptian exiles was adopted by many local Muslims as their "national" headgear; and a Muslim lawyer even won the right to wear a fez in the law courts in place of the traditional wig.

Even after Abdülhamīd was deposed by Kemal Atatürk and the Young Turks in 1909, the Ceylon Muslims continued to be interested in Turkish affairs. Since Turkey declared war on Britain and her allies in 1914, there was an air of plausibility to the rumors circulating at the time of the 1915 riots that the British wanted the Muslims to be punished and even removed from the island.

Aside from pan-Islamic consciousness of this type, the Muslims of Ceylon were also exposed via South India to the kind of Islamic revivalism with puritanical and purificational tendencies represented by the fundamentalist Wahhabi movement, which spread through Muslim North India in the early part of the nineteenth century and began to have an impact on Muslims in the south in later decades.[66] There the movement appears to have initiated attempts by some Tamil Muslims to rid themselves of "non-

Muslim accretions" that had sullied Islamic orthodoxy. These included some neo-Hindu social observances and Tamil names, although attempts to replace the Tamil language with Urdu did not succeed. In fact, in Ceylon, Abdul Azeez, while in favor of discarding non-Islamic accretions, insisted that the ulema preach in Tamil, which the people could understand. Pan-Islamic trends and revivalism seem to have come to a head in the first decade of the twentieth century.

The Muslim revivalist and reformist movement championed by Siddi Lebbe and Abdul Azeez also stimulated considerable progress in education among the Muslim community in Ceylon. Ali notes that "the increase in the number of Muslim scholars in Government and Grant-in-Aid Schools from 1,663 in 1880 to 3,443 in 1901 and to 8,839 in 1915; the opening of the first Anglo-Mohammedan School . . . in 1884; the establishment of the Colombo Educational Society in 1891; the funding of Al-Madrasatul Zahira in 1892, which later emerged as Zahira College, the premier Muslim educational institution in Ceylon, were all the result of Muslim revivalism in the last quarter of the nineteenth century."[67]

The South Indian Muslims who came to be known as the "Coast Moors" began to arrive in large numbers from the last quarter of the nineteenth century onwards, and as the carriers of Wahhabi-inspired fundamentalism and of their own "fanatical" religious practices, they were the first to come into collision with Sinhala Buddhists over the hoary issue of processions playing music passing mosques.

Already in South India, the Madras suburb of Triplicane had become notorious for clashes on account of cow slaughter, beef consumption, and the rival processions of Hindus and of Muslims (especially the latter's Muharram processions to commemorate the martyrdom of Hassan and Hussain). Kayalpatnam, a Tamil-speaking Muslim village in the Tinnevelly District, had been active in the movement to rid Islam of neo-Hindu observances and non-Islamic accretions.

It was these same Muslims, new migrants and settlers in Colombo and in many interior towns as traders and shopkeepers, who, as builders of their own mosques or as supporters of established ones, became confrontational (unlike the older, assimilated Muslims) over Buddhist processions playing music while passing their mosques. We thus return to our opening story. The Ambagamuwa Street mosque at Gampola and the Castle Hill Street mosque at Kandy that precipitated the riots in 1915 were built, run, and patronized by Indian Muslims. And these mosques now challenged the traditional routes taken by Buddhist processions, which in origin predated them. So rather than treating the Gampola and Kandy incidents as purely "local" and "parochial," it is necessary to see them as outcomes of a larger religious wave and enlarged pan-Muslim consciousness that had touched all the Muslims, and the Coast Moors in particular.

The feeling that music was abominable (*makruh*), and that processions with blaring music were repugnant to orthodox Muslims, if originally pressed by the South Indian Moors, was soon adopted by other Muslims as well. "The protests in the fall of 1902, in Hambantota in 1911 and in Balangoda in 1914 were raised almost entirely by the Ceylon Muslims and in the communal clash in Kurunegala they were also partly involved," Ali notes.[68]

> At a time when feelings of nationalism were running high within the majority community, the attempt by a local Muslim minority not to identify itself with the home country, to ally instead with another minority which was not only alien to Ceylon but also thought to be an economic encumbrance and above all to defend that minority's economic activities in the name of religious and racial connections was to invite the majority community to an open confrontation. It is therefore not surprising that the initial distinction which the Sinhalese made between the Indian and Ceylon Moors began to fade gradually and to disappear completely when violence broke out in 1915.[69]

THE SCOPE OF THE RIOTS

Once Colombo itself was affected, the rioting radiated to its environs, especially along the coast going north, engulfing Puttalam, Chilaw, and the Siyane Korale, but also rolling south, inundating Kalutara and then spreading all down the coast to Galle. A. P. Kannangara has traced the pathways of the spreading conflagration as follows:

> In the minds of many officials, though there were notable exceptions, the belief that the riots had been pre-arranged went together with the assumption that they had taken place simultaneously everywhere. But from the official reports themselves, as well as from other sources, it is possible to trace the spread of the riots from bazaar to bazaar along the railways and the main roads leading out of Kandy. . . and finally to Colombo. From Colombo the rioting spread along the Kelani valley as far as Ratnapura, and southwards along the coast as far as Matara, where it turned inland and went as far as Deniyaya. Along these main routes it also took to lesser roads where it proceeded at a slower pace, which accounts for the fact that bazaars along these roads were affected several days after the attacks on Muslims in the main centres had ceased.[70]

Four thousand and seventy-five Muslim shops were sacked and looted, 350 houses and 17 mosques were set ablaze, and another 86 mosques were damaged. The monetary value of damage was 5.5 million rupees to 7.5 million rupees.[71] According to one account at least 39 persons were killed by the rioters, and at least another 63 persons were killed by the military police in suppressing the riots. A second, probably more correct, records 140 deaths, the arrest of 8,786 persons and the imprisonment of 4,497. One account, relating to Muslim victims only, states that a total of 25 Muslims were murdered, 189 wounded, and at least 4 of their women raped.[72]

"Looting was often a secondary motive," Kannangara says. "The crowds which attacked the Muslim shops either set fire to the goods or threw them out on the road, from where other people often picked them up later." He cites a special commissioner, J. Devane, as remarking: "In many places bonfires were lighted. The loot was publicly burned. This seems to show that many, at all events, of the villagers did not loot for the sake of pure loot. They looted as a kind of protest against some real or imaginary grievance."[73]

One stereotype can thus be laid to rest: the riots were not solely, or primarily, the work of criminals, vagabonds, and lumpen elements. The participants were clearly a cross-section of the urban and rural populations. But there is a lack of systematic information about the faces in the crowd.

Although the riots began in Kandy, there seem to be no adequate descriptions of the social status of the participants there; the same applies to Gampola, where the dispute about processions passing mosques began. Both towns, being commercial centers, had shopkeepers of Sinhalese, Moor, and other origins. Both, being administrative and educational centers, would have had a range of government officials, clerks, teachers, and students. Both also had many Buddhist temples, with resident monks, and some mosques in the midst of Muslim enclaves. In Kandy itself, the Wesak perahera must have drawn crowds from both the town and its surrounding region. Thus what the assistant government agent reported of Pata and Uda Dumbara may plausibly have had a wider significance: looting, he said, was organized by "priests, headmen, and notaries backed by school masters and low-country traders stirred to action by persistent rumors." Another official report (by Festing) said this of the Panadura-Kalutara belt, on the coast south of Colombo: "Property owners manipulated the 'street leaders' who stirred the masses with stories of assaults on Sinhalese women and attacks on viharas." He also reports that "most minor headmen were in it." However, the commissioner for Kalutara asserted that gangs radiated out from Colombo inciting local rural and urban populations to participate: "Each village appears to have turned out *en masse* for the destruction of Moorish property in its vicinity and to have furnished a detachment to march with the nucleus of the rioters from such centers as Colombo and Siyane Korale East upon the next center to be attacked."[74]

The police reported that the looting of Moor shops in Colombo was "not the work of habitual criminals." Colombo's railway workers were the most likely leaders of the "gangs" that moved about the city and streaked out to the suburbs, attracting other inhabitants. They knew the strategic importance of using the railway as a mode of transport. Both the Kandy-Colombo railway line and other lines in the Western Province provided speedy transport for large numbers of rioters: "The foci of disturbances on the 1st of June—viz. Colombo, Angulana, Veyangoda and Mirigama—point to the intimate relation between the railway and the riots," Jayawardena quotes from a report.[75] The tramcars in the Maradana-Borella-Pettah chain were likewise used by gangs.

KANNANGARA'S THESIS

Kannangara argues, with considerable citation of the writings of British officials and other sources, that it was certain segments of "the lower orders," to use a label from Rudé, or, to use Kannangara's label, "poorer members of the subordinate [Sinhala] castes," who were especially susceptible to participation in the riots. These people were concentrated in villages near the urban centers, which had mushroomed as a result of the social, administrative, legal, and economic changes introduced by the British Raj and the construction of major road and railway networks primarily feeding a commercial sector focused on large capitalist plantations. "New towns and townships had arisen and old ones had expanded, with law courts, police stations, government offices, lawyers' and notaries' offices, and densely populated bazaars containing a variety of shops, warehouses, artisans' workshops, taverns and so forth," Kannangara notes.

> The communities in the villages upon which these urban centres arose and those of the villages which stood nearby or along the main roads and railways were thus transformed. . . . Economic and other processes which were enriching some people were impoverishing others; the lands they held were being reduced, taken away altogether or their tenures made more precarious. . . . Among those who were thus deposited at the bottom of the social heap in urbanized areas there were, as already indicated, significant differences. . . . But what they all had in common was poverty and the struggle in insecure and often dangerous or demeaning occupations, in a new environment where they often felt the forces of the law as well as the social order itself weighing down upon them.[76]

Kannangara does suggest as a subtheme that some of the members of the newly mobile castes, such as the Duravas, Karavas, and Salagamas, may have felt resentment of the elite members of the Goyigama caste, especially its superior headmen (*mudaliyars*), whom they could not contest frontally, and that they may have been prone to displace this caste resentment onto people of other races and religions. But it is really the poorer members of still lower castes, especially the Vahumpara and Batgama castes, that he singles out as the typical participants in the riots, "partly because the incidence of landlessness was greater in these castes than in the dominant caste—partly perhaps because the traditional tenures on which the majority of cultivators belonging to these castes held land may have been weaker and therefore more vulnerable to the new economic conditions."[77] But there were other suggestive reasons why the Vahumpara and Batgama castes, which were the most numerous of the subordinate castes in the interior of the country, were predisposed "to answer the call of race and religion in danger."

> In at least two of the anti-British uprisings with a markedly Buddhist colouring which took place in the Kandyan Provinces in the first half of the nineteenth century, including the major rebellion of 1848, the leaders who were alleged to have set up as pretenders to the Sinhalese throne were *vahumpuras*. . . . In 1848 proclamations were issued by the rebels alleging that the English queen intended to destroy the Dalada Maligawa, and that certain Kandyan headmen of the highest rank were traitors, some of them Christians and others of European blood. *Vahumpuras* from Peliyagoda and elsewhere were involved in considerable numbers in the clash which took place on Easter Sunday 1883 in Colombo. . . . On the day after this clash an armed crowd from Peliyagoda crossed the Kelani river into Colombo—as they had done in 1846 and were to do in 1915—with the evident intention of confronting the Catholics. *Vahumpuras* may have entered Colombo in 1883, and Colombo and Kandy in 1915, out of loyalty to rich fellow-members of their castes who were active Buddhists in the bazaars of these towns. But their traditions of religiopatriotic militancy probably carried as much weight with them. So also with the rioters from the *batgama* caste. This caste had traditionally been the soldiers of the Sinhalese kings. Their deference to *goyigama* headmen may have been weakening but not their memories of a martial past, which may indeed have been quickening in response to various changes in their social and economic position. It was these traditions no doubt as much as the call of the local village headmen of their caste which drove them at the beginning of the 1915 riots to set out from their villages and go to nearby towns.[78]

Many of those who were involved in the riots also stood low in the hierarchy of caste. They came from localities near the bazaars which were traditionally inhabited by concentrations of the subordinate castes. . . . *Vahumpura* men from Wanawahala and other villages around Peliyagoda, near Colombo, were present in Kandy on the eve of the riots. They had been got down, a shrewd observer suggested, by the organizers of the carol-procession in anticipation of trouble with the Muslims. . . . Men from the same caste and area were in the van of the crowds which, when the riots started in Colombo, tried to enter the city. . . . An official reported seeing five hundred *vahumpuras* from Peliyagoda marching towards the Maradana junction with a Buddhist flag at their head. . . . In the Panadura bazaar the most prominent element in the crowds was formed by people from the village of Pinwatte, a considerable number of whose inhabitants belonged to those sections of the *salagama* caste which were traditionally its most disadvantaged and also most combative.[79]

Kannangara suggests that those who had left their villages or saw their villages transformed by urbanization included workers in the graphite mines of the interior and in the railway workshops, municipal services, and graphite sheds of Colombo. Buddhist loyalties may have stirred these men to action when they were led to believe that temples, including the Dalada Maligawa, were about to be attacked by Coast Moors, whom they further- more associated with the wartime increases in unemployment and food prices. Neither the temperance movement inaugurated in 1912 nor the Buddhist revivalists and budding politicians such D. S. Senanayake and D. B. Jayatilaka, who led it, were responsible for the outbreak or the course of the riots, he insists. The movement was not "seditious" in intent or a conspiracy against British colonial rule, as British officials believed when they over- reacted and incarcerated many temperance workers and killed some of them.

However, Kannangara also tries to argue that the ideas and prejudices and slogans of Buddhist revivalist activists and champions of a Buddhist "nationalism," such as Dharmapala and Piyadasa Sirisena, and the propa- ganda they transmitted through newspapers, journals, the theater, and public speaking, did not integrally link up with the promotion and ad- vancement of the interests of Buddhist businessmen. The Buddhist publi- cists, "who understandably wished to further the interests of businessmen who financed them," had in mind "to boost not the profits but the social prestige of their patrons, who were a relatively new group in Sinhalese society, drawn largely though not exclusively from the non-*goyigama* castes."[80] Kannangara would like to mute the links between Buddhist re- vivalism and commercial interests to the extent that they imply any direct connection between the Buddhist merchants and antagonism to the Coast Moors and their economic success. But I have already cited other evidence as to why and how some of the prominent members of the newly success- ful and socially mobile Pettah merchant families could have fused their re- vivalist religious enthusiasm with a Sinhala nationalism that at this time spoke for the cultural and economic interests of the Sinhala people at large, many of them in precisely that deteriorating, déclassé condition that Kan- nangara so vividly describes as existing in or near the new bazaar towns.[81] Moreover, it is significant that temperance leaders were encouraging local temperance societies to improve the lot of the peasantry by establishing trading cooperatives, rural savings banks, and so on, and thereby to extricate the peasants from debt, poverty, and the clutches of traders.

Kannangara's attempt to dissociate the 1915 riots from the larger religiopolitical context, and from any organized direction both before and after the riots broke out, leaves us perilously close to the theory that the riots broke out "spontaneously" and spread simply by "contagion," unaided by design or organization. Kannangara suggests, however, that the crowds were assembled simply by the force of rumors that the Moors were coming to attack Sinhalese temples, interests, and people. Whether this is a sufficient explanation, readers must decide for themselves.

WERE THE RIOTS PLANNED?

After attempting to trace the evidence for the degree of planning and the identity of the organizers and perpetrators of the riots as far as possible, Michael Roberts comes down in favor of two hypotheses, between which he is unable to make a final choice. He posits a distinction between a "national elite," composed of affluent individuals and families with nationwide prestige, power, and authority, and "local elites" whose members belonged to influential kindreds (*pelantiyas*). His first hypothesis is that "common causal and background factors resulted in anti-Moorish communal riots which revealed some common patterns and which involved some uncoordinated preplanning on the part of either the national and/or the local elite." The second hypothesis, while positing "common causal and background factors," rejects the idea that the riots were to any degree preplanned, but asserts that they show common patterns and "threw up riot leaders who were, in part, associated with similar organizations [associations such as temperance societies] and were centred in the local elite."[82]

What emerges from Roberts's documentation, which focuses mainly on the provinces and little on Colombo, is that segments of the "local elite," local notables such as middle- and lower-ranking headmen, and members of local associations (concerned with temperance and/or religious welfare) participated, led, or colluded in the riots. It is probably not very helpful to pose the question in either/or exclusionary terms as regards preplanning, the degree of coordination of mob attacks, and the degree of spontaneity of outbreaks, for at different sites, there were different combinations of features, predisposing circumstances, and contingent chain reactions.

The riots were purposive and instrumental in their logic rather than simply or solely an expression of crowd mentality run amok in the context of anomie, widespread hardship, or incidental provocation. The Coast Moors first, and the Muslims at large, were purposely targeted, and the crowds knew what they were about when they attacked their shops and their mosques. But the behavior and energies of riot crowds are not exhausted by considerations of design, prior purposes, or prearrangement.

When the Wesak merit-making activities, carols, and processions in Kandy were frustrated and challenged, it was in the cards that they would be transformed into attacks on Muslim establishments, as the police realized and as A. G. Fraser has stated. But the collective excitement and frayed tempers of the moment dictated the timing and the details of the attacks.

Two concepts that may be employed to describe the trajectory of such riots are *focalization* and *transvaluation*. These are linked processes by which a series of local incidents and small-scale disputes, occasioned by religious, commercial, interfamilial, or other issues, and involving people in direct contact with one another, cumulatively build up into larger and larger clashes between growing numbers of antagonists only indirectly involved in the original disputes. This progressive involvement of the ethnic public coincides with their coming under the sway of the rhetoric of propagandists and the horror tales of rumormongers, who appeal to larger, deeper, certainly more emotive and enduring—and therefore less local-context-bound—loyalties and cleavages, such as race, religion, language, nation, or place of origin. To sum up: focalization progressively denudes local incidents and disputes of their contextual particulars, and transvaluation distorts, abstracts, and aggregates those incidents into larger collective issues of national or ethnic interest. The case studies that follow confirm and elaborate the relevance of the processes of focalization and transvaluation, and others that will be identified.

4 Two Postindependence Ethnic Riots in Sri Lanka

Between 1948, the year Sri Lanka achieved independence, and 1983, there have been some seven occurrences of mass violence unleashed by segments of the majority Sinhalese, who constitute 74 percent of the population, against the Tamil minority, who make up about 18 percent. The Tamils are subdivided into Sri Lankan Tamils (12.6 percent) and Indian Tamils (5.6 percent), but both groups have from time to time been victims of violence initiated by Sinhalese and have sometimes responded in kind. The most significant of these riots took place in 1956, 1958,[1] 1977, 1981, and 1983. In this chapter, I shall briefly deal with the first and last of the series: the riots that took place in 1956 are significant because they signaled the stirrings of the first postindependence conflict fueled by issues of official language and land-settlement policy as they affected ethnic group interests; the riots of 1983 are notable as the most violent and extensive of the occurrences, and they figure in the context of the early stages of the conflict that was escalating into a civil war between the armed forces of the state, dominated by the Sinhalese, and the Tamil insurgents, who had resorted to armed retaliation. The 1983 riots are also distinctive as the last instance so far of collective civilian violence; the ethnic conflict has since then developed into warfare between the armed forces and the insurgents, with the civilian population caught in between.

1956: THE FIRST ERUPTION

My own firsthand and indelible experience of ethnic riots happened in June 1956, when as a twenty-seven-year-old social scientist, recently returned from graduate studies in the United States, I took a team of thirty-three students (twenty-six Sinhalese and seven Tamils) to conduct a sur-

vey of some newly settled peasant colonies in Gal Oya Valley.[2] The Gal
Oya Multipurpose Scheme was Sri Lanka's first and largest postindependence development project, whose tasks were flood control, provision of
irrigation for cultivating the "maximum acreage of land possible," and
generation of electricity for domestic and industrial use. The Gal Oya Development Board, appointed by the Sri Lankan government in 1949, was
modeled on the Tennessee Valley Authority and the Damodar Valley Corporation, but was actually more circumscribed in its structure and powers
than these two giant corporations. The largest component of the board's
agricultural plan was the settlement of landless peasants from depressed
villages with families and some agricultural experience on small paddy and
highland allotments. (Provision was also made for larger-scale cultivation,
marketing, and processing of cash crops by cooperative agricultural and industrial undertakings.)

From 1950 to 1958, about 43 village units were created in what was referred to as the Left Bank, where most of the settlement had thus far taken
place. The total number of colonists given allotments of land was 5,859. Of
these, about 50 percent came from the board's "area of authority" in the
Eastern Province, consisting of local Muslims and Tamils from the east
coast and Sinhalese or Sinhalized Veddahs from the interior jungle villages, who had been displaced by the dam and reservoir. The next major
group consisted of "Kandyan" Sinhalese villagers from the Central Province
(25 percent), the majority coming from the Kandy and Kegalle districts.
The remaining 25 percent came from other areas, such as the Southern (8
percent), Western, and Sabaragamuva provinces, and they were all Sinhalese. Although the colonists were ethnically mixed, the Sinhalese colonists
were spatially separated from the local east coast Tamils and Muslims. The
former were settled on the favored upper reaches of the Left Bank, immediately below the dam, and the latter were allotted less well irrigated lands
at the ends of the irrigation channels contiguous with their original settlements.

A phalanx of officials, bureaucrats, and experts running the development program were locally housed in comfortable government-built bungalows in the administrative center, the fast-growing boomtown of Amparai, which was also the locus of a bustling bazaar of shops and of the
rooming houses and shacks that accommodated hundreds of construction
workers and transport personnel (who, if married, had left their spouses
and families behind), as well as casual laborers and other young men in
search of employment or making a living because the local mudalalis
(small businessmen) and other traders needed their muscle.

The Gal Oya scheme was located some 150 miles by road from Colombo, the island's capital, in a region that had previously been a jungle sparsely populated by slash-and-burn cultivators. By Sri Lankan reckoning in 1956, it was situated in the deep interior, and it was relatively inaccessible because of poor roads and transport facilities. Except for telephone and radio communications, available primarily to the elite officials and administrative offices, the valley had the air of being sealed off. The residents irregularly got news via the Colombo newspapers and from bus and truck drivers, traveling traders, and passengers in transit.

The 1956 riots—which, as we know now, were only the first and smallest in a series of Sinhala-Tamil civilian clashes from that time to the most recent in 1983—were the first ethnic riots in the island after Sri Lanka attained independence. There was a long gap of forty-one years separating these riots from the riots of 1915 between the Sinhalese and Muslims (discussed at length in chapter 3). Although the last decades of British rule and the early years of independence since 1948 had seen labor disputes and trade union strikes, thuggery at elections, and other disturbances of the public peace (ranging from vendettas between traders and merchants and their respective retinues to armed robbery and homicide), there was nothing that in scale, explosiveness, and novelty matched the 1956 eruption (for 1915 was by then only a memory trace).[3]

Prior to the 1956 riots, S. W. R. D. Bandaranaike had been under mounting pressure from his own Sri Lanka Freedom Party to bring in a "Sinhala Only Bill," and it had been announced that such a bill would be introduced. Bandaranaike had said that provisions for the "reasonable use of Tamil" would come later, but he had also in his speeches maintained that unless a "Sinhalese only" policy were adopted, the Sinhalese "race, religion and culture would vanish."[4]

From the point of view of Tamils, certain ominous events that accompanied this projected legislation foreshadowed worse to come. In the same year, the government announced that the leading teacher training college in the country would be reserved for Sinhalese teachers only. Around the same time, the Eksath Bhikkhu Peramuna (United Front of the Monks) demanded that persons educated in English or Tamil be prevented from taking public examinations until the year 1967.

The Federal Party, whose leader was S. J. V. Chelvanayagam, had made a strong showing in the elections of 1956, especially in the north, emerging as the dominant Tamil party. This result was in strong contrast to its poor showing in the 1952 elections. Its mounting success among the Tamils was because it advocated that the Tamil language should have "parity status" with Sinhalese. What distinguished the Federal Party from other Tamil political parties, besides its advocacy of a federal constitution, was its launching of a campaign of noncooperation and civil disobedience along the lines of Gandhian satyagraha to exert pressure on the government. The most effective of these civil protests was staged in June 1956.

The Official Language (or "Sinhala Only") Bill, specifying that Sinhala would henceforth replace English as Sri Lanka's official language, was introduced on June 5, and the Bandaranaike-led MEP government passed it on June 14, 1956, by a vote of 56 to 29.[5] The debating of the bill caused a buildup of tensions on both sides and the eruption of violence. James Manor notes:

> Federal Party Leaders had whipped up feeling against the bill for weeks and on 5 June, the day that it would be introduced in Parliament, a complete "hartal" (suspension of normal business) was held in the Tamil-majority areas. The day before Chelvanayagam had written to Bandaranaike, "members of Parliament belonging to our party will lead a batch of about 200 *satyagrahis* to sit on the steps of the western entrance to the House of Representatives and there they will remain fasting the whole day. . . . I write to you asking you for your cooperation . . . to ensure that the *satyagrahis* are not disturbed."[6]

On June 5, the Tamil satyagrahis, who had been refused entry to Parliament, which had been cordoned off with fences and was guarded by policemen, staged a sit-down demonstration nearby, and this led to their forcible ejection and signaled the riot. Some 200 Tamil protesters, including leading politicians, took part in this satyagraha rally on Galle Face Green. A crowd of Sinhalese collected, and several Tamil leaders and volunteers participating were physically injured and had to be taken to hospital.[7] Meanwhile, small bands of Sinhalese roamed through the city, looting shops and destroying a few vehicles. The next morning, more serious looting was perpetrated in the Pettah shopping zone. The official estimates of damage done during two days was 87 injuries to persons and 43 lootings of shops. Some 113 people were arrested.

The Tamil sit-down demonstration "led to bitter riots in which over 100 people were injured. In a few days, they had spread to Eastern Province, where Tamils and Sinhalese lived intermingled; in Batticaloa and the Gal Oya Valley there was such violence that between 20 and 200 persons were killed, depending on which side was doing the tallying," according to W. Howard Wriggins.[8] "Sinhalese toughs—inspired as always by fantastic rumors—seized government cars, bulldozers and high explosives and for a few days terrorized the Tamil minority in the colony," Manor writes. "Scores of Tamils, certainly well over one hundred, were massacred and hundreds more were driven into hiding. The army was sent to quell disturbances."[9] In Batticaloa, a mass demonstration by about ten thousand Tamils was fired on by the police, resulting in at least two deaths. In the Gal Oya Valley, violence on a scale hitherto unknown broke out some five days after the turmoil in Colombo, setting a precedent for even more destructive violence two years later.

If one wonders what the relationship between the official language controversy and ethnic violence in the Eastern Province might be, why the rioting leapt from urban Colombo on the west coast to Gal Oya, a bustling enclave of hectic development activity and peasant resettlement, the answer is that around this time, the language issue was also becoming interwoven with the government's policy of peasant resettlement in the less populous parts of the island. Just as the first issue had implications for the educational and employment prospects of the Tamils, so the second would be construed as causing demographic changes in Sinhalese and Tamil (and Muslim) ethnic ratios in the Eastern Province, and therefore as bearing on the politics of territorial control and of "homelands." In fact, on the occasion of the inauguration of the Federal Party in December 1949, its leader, Chelvanayagam, had warned that the government's colonization policy, whose beginning was evidenced by the Gal Oya Scheme, was even more dangerous to the Tamil people than the Sinhala-language policy. "There is evidence" he said, "that the government intends planting a Sinhalese population in this purely Tamil-speaking area."[10]

Like the officials and colonists we were interacting with in Gal Oya Valley, my students and I had virtually no intimation of the events taking place in Colombo, or any inkling of the explosion about to happen in our midst. After finding ourselves trapped in Amparai, we were quickly shipped out by the Gal Oya authorities as soon as the violence showed signs of subsiding. Upon my return to the campus at Peradeniya, the vice-chancellor of the university, Sir Nicholas Atygalle, requested that I write him a report on the happenings of Gal Oya as soon as I could, including if possible statements by students who were contactable—this was the period of the long vacation—because the riots in question were a new phenomenon and many people were uncertain as to what to make of them.

I submitted a speedily composed memorandum (together with statements by some of the students) to Sir Nicholas. A few years later, in 1960, I left Sri Lanka, and in the course of several changes of residence and workplace in three countries, Thailand, England, and the United States, I managed to lose my copy of the memorandum. In 1992, to my thankful surprise, Professor Kingsley de Silva of Peradeniya University sent me a copy of the document, which he had received from another professor, who had come across it in the university's archives. The student reports were not retrieved.

I have decided to reproduce my 1956 memorandum here with minimal changes, despite some interpretive shortcomings. One of its virtues in its pristine state is that it quite self-consciously conveys that the "narrative" was constructed out of various kinds of fragments—my own encounters and conversations, reports from students, newspaper accounts, reports of reports, and so on—which were arranged to provide a connected story. The authorial work is transparent.

A second virtue is that the narrative singled out themes such as the central role of rumors in triggering the violence and also in generating anger and panic among the participants, the slowness to action of the police (themselves drawn from the majority community), and the critical faces in the crowd—in this case, the mobile and volatile labor force and construction workers who unleashed the violence. More than three decades later, when I began my comparative study of riots, I would find these themes to be of recurring import. Some obvious prejudices about "the criminal classes" expressed in this text have been allowed to stand, since a text written many years ago is being reproduced.[11]

The third significance of this report, which is not underscored in the original writing, because it was taken not to be unusual for those times at the university, is that a lecturer of Tamil ethnic origins was able to lead a team of students, the vast majority of whom were of Sinhalese ethnic origin, to Gal Oya for sociological research. Moreover, it is a mark of the tolerance, friendship, and mutual trust of those times that when the riots broke out, the Sinhalese students took good care to protect me and the seven other Tamils in the team from any possible victimization. The university campuses are much different today.

THE GAL OYA RIOTS: A REPORT
FROM A YOUNG ACADEMIC TO HIS VICE-CHANCELLOR

In writing about the Gal Oya riots, it would not be possible to give a meaningful and chronological account of the happenings if one were to confine oneself to only what one *saw* with one's own eyes. I am taking the liberty of presenting an account based on direct knowledge as well as indirect information elicited from persons. However I shall carefully specify and differentiate between statements based on events witnessed by me and statements based on accounts given by others in the valley at the time of the riots. Care will be taken to state the sources of the facts narrated.

The Gal Oya disturbance cannot of course be treated as an isolated phenomenon. It must be viewed in the general context of communal tensions and political differences existing in the country and also as a continuation of disturbances that started in Colombo during and after June fifth. The account given here however deals only with incidents that happened in the Eastern Province.

The trouble started in the Gal Oya Valley itself on June 11 at Amparai. I remained in the valley for four days (June 11–14) and was evacuated to Batticaloa on the night of June 14. The events related here are those that happened during those four days; however, certain events in the Eastern Province that happened before the eleventh will be referred to to provide the necessary background.

EVENTS IN GAL OYA AND THE EASTERN PROVINCE PRIOR TO THE
11TH THAT HAVE A BEARING ON THE RIOTS

1. The setting fire to a Sinhalese shop in Batticaloa: a Sinhalese person inside the shop shot with a gun three Tamil persons in the crowd that had gathered to watch the fire (newspaper account).

2. Subsequently, the Tamils in Karativu on the Batticaloa-Amparai road stoned Gal Oya Board trucks. On the ninth I saw in Amparai town three trucks which had damaged windshields caused by stone throwing.

3. In Gal Oya Valley itself, the Danish Equipment Company engaged in construction work had labor trouble. From officials I gathered that they were on strike and that their work was discontinued (hearsay).

Comment. *These Events Indicate That:*

(a) Communal tensions (Sinhalese versus Tamil) had by now spread to the Eastern Province.

(b) Because the main supply route to Gal Oya was the Batticaloa-Amparai road, and because there were large numbers of Tamils concentrated in Batticaloa and in the colonized areas of the valley, and a large number of Sinhalese in the Gal Oya Valley, what takes place in Batticaloa and its hinterland would have repercussion in the Valley and vice versa.

(c) Because of labor trouble, there were certain elements in the Valley who would prove dangerous during riots.

THE FIRST DAY OF THE RIOTS—MONDAY, JUNE 11

The Attack on the Tamils in Amparai

At about 2 P.M. the University team left the hospital where they were housed to do field work in the colonized areas. The team was divided into two groups: (a) about 26 Sinhalese students travelling in a converted lorry and working in Unit 32, and (b) about seven Tamil students travelling in a land rover and conducting investigations in Unit 14.

On this particular day I went along with group (b), and returned to the hospital with them at about 10 o'clock in the night, when students came rushing to me and informed me about the communal clashes that took place that evening. Leslie Gunasekere, who was in charge of team (a) on the eleventh, reported that at about 8:30 P.M. when their bus was returning from the field, it was stopped by a mob who asked whether there were Tamils in the bus. On being told there were none, they were allowed to proceed (see Leslie Gunasekere's account).

Immediately they returned home the Sinhalese students fearing that their Tamil friends in the team who had gone separately were in danger, formed in groups and stationed themselves at points on various roads to warn us of the danger. One such group of students who scouted the Amparai-Uhana road witnessed a mob setting fire to a canteen run by a Tamil (see P. N. M. Fernando's and A. Andarawewa's and T. D. J. Vitharana's accounts).

Another group of three students reported that in the evening while they were having tea at Miranda's (a restaurant and store run by Indian Tamils), a mob gathered outside and stoned the place (see M. L. Wijesekera's and Manopala's accounts of incident).

That night victims of physical assault by the mob were brought to the hospital for medical attention. Because the doctor was short of staff, the university students lent a helping hand. I personally saw four victims—all of them were Tamils and two were dangerously clubbed on their skulls.

The Rumor of the Raped Telephone Operator

The next morning (Tuesday) I was told by various persons about the incidents of the previous afternoon. Karunaratne and Podisingho (drivers of the land rover and lorry detailed for our use) said that on Monday afternoon one of the truck drivers whose vehicle had been stoned by Tamils on the Batticaloa-Amparai road, had come to Amparai and propagated the story that a Sinhalese telephone operator (girl) in Batticaloa had been raped and stripped and sent naked along the streets. (This story was later pronounced as untrue by the police and Government Agent—Newspaper account.) This rumor believed by the common people in Amparai inflamed their passions against the Tamils— hence the retaliations. Throughout the riots havoc and panic were created by rumors and in trying to understand the violence one must bear in mind that rumors of atrocities done by one group against the other created panic and fear in the people thus inciting them to retaliatory acts. The rumor of the raped girl is the first of the series.

On Tuesday morning Mr. Kuruthumpala (the Senior Statistical and Public Relations Officer) told me about the incident at the Chinese Cafe the previous night. Some of the Board Officials including Mr. Kuruthumpala—all members of the Y.M.C.A.—were celebrating at the Chinese Cafe. According to him, a mob collected outside and demanded that the Tamil officials and their wives inside be delivered to them, and that the Sinhalese officials refused to do so. Podisingho (driver of our lorry) told me that three Tamil ladies inside the cafe were stealthily taken through the back of the cafe to safety. According to Mr. Kuruthumpala, when he emerged out of the cafe he was assaulted by the mob, and the cars of the officials were stoned. I also met Mr. Wirasekera (Assistant Commissioner of Local Government) on Tuesday morning, and he said that the mob entered his house, where Mr. Rajavarothiam also lived, assaulted the latter and stole some goods. In general, the assaults on Monday night were against Tamils in Amparai and less frequently against Sinhalese officials who protected Tamil officials.

In discussing the happenings on Monday with various persons I was told
that the mob was spearheaded by irrigation and construction workers and
truck drivers, etc., living in Amparai and nearby construction sites such as
Pallang Oya. I also got the impression that the police made no attempt to
prevent the assaults and looting, and that they had looked on. The police force
at Amparai and in the Valley was woefully small, but it appears that officers
did not intervene where they were actually present at scenes of assault and
looting. I must emphasize that this statement is hearsay.

THE SECOND DAY—TUESDAY, JUNE 12

On Tuesday morning the Acting Resident Manager, Mr. Abeyawardene,
phoned me that because of the previous day's troubles we should not go out
into the field, and he requested me to come to the Circuit Bungalow. (This is
the house in which top officials of the Board and other members of the
Government reside during their periodic visits from Colombo.) I went there at
about 10 A.M. and found the Chairman of the Board, Mr. Kanagasundram, and
the other top officials conferring with persons who I was told were the ring
leaders and spokesmen of the Amparai workers. From the conference
proceedings that I overheard, I gathered that the latter were demanding that
about 50 odd families of Sinhalese workers in Amparai were residing in
Batticaloa and that the women and children there were in danger of attack by
Tamils, and that therefore they should be transported from Batticaloa to
Amparai. I heard the Chairman telephone the Government Agent, Batticaloa,
and making arrangements with him for the transportation of the families.
Soon afterwards I left for the hospital.

The Siege of the Circuit Bungalow

In the evening started the siege of the Circuit Bungalow. After the previous
day's incidents in Amparai, I gathered that the Tamils in Amparai had gone to
the police station and to the Circuit Bungalow to seek refuge. By the evening
therefore the Circuit Bungalow was full of Tamils. This site had also become
the headquarters of the officials who were dealing with the riots. Therefore it
was a strategic place.

I have already referred to the chairman's agreement to transport the
Sinhalese families from Batticaloa to Amparai. I gathered that the actual
transportation was delayed, for what reasons I am not sure. By evening, a large
mob had encircled the Circuit Bungalow which was under police protection.
From Father Wickramanayake (who subsequently gave evidence to the
Magistrate with regard to the shooting at the Circuit Bungalow) and Mr.
Gooneratne (Agricultural Officer, Extension) I gathered that the police had
used tear gas to disperse the mob but were unsuccessful. Then when the mob
tried to stop a jeep bringing a bren gun and assaulted the driver, the police
opened fire. One man was shot dead through the bowels, another shot through
the shoulder (he subsequently died) and the third was shot in the arm. All
three were Sinhalese. Then the mob cut off the electricity and water supply to
the bungalow, and a group broke into a dynamite dump at Inginiyagala and
stole dynamite with the intention of blowing up the bungalow. Fortunately

they could not lay hands on the detonators. The military arrived about 11 P.M. and with their arrival the mob dispersed. Early in the morning (3:30 A.M.) the mob set fire to Miranda's restaurant, and I saw the fire from the hospital.

THE THIRD DAY—WEDNESDAY, JUNE 13

On Wednesday morning I gathered that the Tamil refugees in Amparai were sent under escort to Batticaloa that morning.

I had repeatedly gotten in touch with the authorities requesting transport for us to get out of the valley, but they said they were unable to do so. On Wednesday morning at about 10:30 A.M. I went to the Amparai Police Station to make further requests. At about 11:30 A.M. when I was about to return to the hospital a lorry arrived with Sinhalese refugees from Bakiela, who said that they had been attacked by Tamil Colonists.

The Mythical Tamil Army

By noon, started the biggest scare which caused pandemonium in Amparai. The rumor spread like wildfire that a Tamil army, 6,000 strong, armed with guns and other weapons were approaching Amparai, having laid waste Uhana, and killed women and children there. Neither the Police nor the Army were able to counter in time this rumor or check its veracity. The panic was so great that a mass evacuation and flight of persons from Amparai took place.

The Seizure of Vehicles and Flight from Amparai

Many of the looters and rioters went to the workshop, took over the vehicles—lorries, mandators, euclids, etc. Some of the vehicles filled with armed men and carrying dynamite went to meet the mythical army which was supposed to be advancing. The others packed with men, women and children evacuated the valley through the Inginiyagala-Moneragala road. (From newspaper accounts we know the subsequent history of these escaping vehicles—many of them were seized by the police all over the country, and some of the looters caused trouble all along the coastal route of the Southern and Western Provinces.)

Fighting Spreads to Colonized Areas

As mentioned before, many rioters got into vehicles and went into the colonized areas. At the same time, the Tamil colonists had taken the offensive in retaliation. *That is to say that on the third day the fighting had spread to the colonized areas which had hitherto been peaceful.* The marauding gangs in vehicles looted and attacked the colonized areas. The Tamil colonists retreating to their parent villages returned in large numbers armed with guns. Pitched battles began to take place in Bakiela, Vellai Valli, Village Units 11, 16, 14, etc. In Amparai town the Cooperative Stores were looted. (See A. S. Jayawardene's account of men in vehicles on the rampage and the injured man brought to hospital in a mandator.)

With this turn of events the Sinhalese colonists now found themselves in great danger and started to flee in the direction of Amparai. On Wednesday night, four Tamil students and I slept in the Circuit Bungalow, which was chockful of Sinhalese colonists seeking refuge there.

The Flight of the Officials

Another paralyzing effect of the panic created by the myth of the murderous Tamil army advancing on Amparai was the flight of many of the Board Officials from the valley. I gathered that many of them left the valley in the Board's landrovers. Thus after the evacuation of the Tamil officials and the flight of most of the Sinhalese officials, the civil administration was literally reduced to a handful of remaining officials.

THE FOURTH DAY—THURSDAY, JUNE 14

On the fourth morning I was present at the Circuit Bungalow where a conference between the police and all remaining board officers was held. The bungalow grounds were swarming with Sinhalese refugees from the colonized areas. Since an armed escort was leaving for Batticaloa I was able to send away the Tamil students. In the afternoon the Sinhalese students were removed to the Technical Training Institute. They left for Badulla in a mandator the next day, and from there returned to their homes by trains.

Batticaloa became the scene of a reverse scare and rumor. The G.A.'s bungalow was mobbed by many residents of Batticaloa who said that a Sinhalese army from Amparai, armed and in possession of dynamite and travelling in Board vehicles was going to attack the town. They requested the G.A. to issue them with rifles and to give them permission to blow up the bridges. The basis of this scare was the fact that earlier in the day a marauding party from the valley was sighted 10 miles from Batticaloa. No army invaded Batticaloa that night.

ON THE BREAKDOWN OF THE ADMINISTRATION

Various press reports and statements by politicians refer to the breakdown of the Administration, implying that the riots were not handled properly by the officials. Such an allegation is a difficult one to examine, and the reader should take these comments as being purely personal.

The question arises whether the Board could have foreseen the riots, the atrocities and mob passions. Did the government foresee the Colombo riots? Should the Board have anticipated riots in the Valley, after what happened in Colombo a few days previously?

When the riots started the civil administration lost control, but then no civil administration of officials is competent to deal with this kind of sudden violence. A civil administration is ultimately dependant on the police force to maintain law and order and meet violence with force. The police force in Amparai was unpardonably inefficient on the first night. A show of force and might might have made a difference, as vigorous action in Colombo demonstrated, and as the army's toughness in Gal Oya proved. But then, on the other hand, the police force in the valley was pitifully small and understandably fearful of intervening against hundreds banded into mobs.

Regarding the flight of the officials, it is objectively true that many officials deserted their posts. The Tamil officials were evacuated from Amparai and many of the Sinhalese officials had left by the third day. Anyone who had been in the valley would understand the terror aroused in many and the havoc created by panic. He would be a brave man who was willing to endanger his life and the lives of his wife and children for the sake of national interest. To my mind the question arises as to under what conditions must a civil officer stick by his post. Must a civil officer stick to it if he has reason to believe that his life is in danger? It could be argued that where there is no security of life, there ends occupational responsibility. Whether the flight of the officials was understandable or reprehensible, the fact is that their flight in a sense paralyzed the administration, for they themselves were the administration. Their flight meant that there was no possibility of a volunteer force being organized, and a serious lack of persons for organizing refugee work.

One serious error committed by both civil officers and the military was their failure to demobilize the vehicles in the workshop. The fighting spread to the colonized areas because rioters were able to seize vehicles and travel in them. Marauding gangs were dangerously hostile and difficult to seize once they were in possession of vehicles which enabled them to move and operate in a large geographical area. The failure to demobilize the vehicles would seem to be an administrative mistake and an error of strategy.

The Gal Oya flareup is a superb study of rumor—the panic it creates and its magnification as it passes on from person to person. It is true that neither the civil nor military and police agencies were able to make an effective and timely denial of these rumors and to pacify the terror stricken people. It is of course debatable whether panic stricken and therefore at that moment irrational people would believe official denials, when in this country official denials are based on questionable veracity. Furthermore it is necessary to remember that a rumor to be denied must first be investigated and proven false, and this involves time; the time gap may be necessary but at the same time fatal as we have witnessed in Gal Oya on the third day when the rumor circulated that a Tamil army was advancing. I would like to convey to the reader my own feeling that a more constructive approach to the riots is not to try and see the rights and wrongs but to first understand the phenomenon of civil strife. The rumors and their consequences clearly portrayed that in times of civil strife normal methods of communication are useless and the assumption of a reasonable man unreal. Furthermore, whereas the civil officials are usually not trained to cope with riots, the military and police, though presumably trained in war and defense, were for the first time engaged in actual warfare, and therefore where there is no experience it might be too much to expect precision and speed in action.

I have already referred to the probability that the rioting, assaults and looting were spearheaded by irrigation and construction workers and that subsequently the truck drivers joined in the fray. It is also suspected that a lot of I.R.C.s (Island Reconvicted Criminals) had found their way into the valley. The former persons if not criminal in background were criminally inclined during the riots. They might not have been directly concerned with the language issue, but the political issue and the wave of emotionalism prevailing in the country provided the opportunity and context for these elements to exploit the situation. The recent Colombo riots and the Riots of 1915 showed that civil unrest could be exploited by criminal elements. Furthermore it is very plausible that irrigation and construction workers and truck drivers have a special stamp and possibly a special psychological make up. In the valley, unlike the colonists who are a permanent population, they are transient and move with their mobile jobs. They are footloose, used to working in jungles, cut off from normal family relationships, and therefore prone to violence. Amparai is an explosive town because it is very much like the boom town of the American West. Under these circumstances, foresight demands that these workers be *carefully screened and selected.* I am not aware of the system of selection practiced by the Board, but a more scrupulous system is recommended. Also, in the presence of such an inflammable population it is strange that a better policing system and a larger police force was not stationed in Gal Oya. Better police action at the initial stages would possibly have squashed the rising or at least mitigated its worst features.

Lastly, the riots demonstrated in sharp relief the geographical isolation of the valley and the paucity of roads leading in and out of it. The difficulty of rushing in police and army reinforcements was a grave problem. Since the major road is from Batticaloa through Kalmunai, which is a Tamil area, there was no possibility of sealing off and isolating the Tamil and Sinhalese areas during the earlier stages. Obviously several other roads leading into the valley and an air service are needed. Civil strife in a fringe area poorly fed with roads is naturally difficult to control.

THE COLOMBO RIOTS OF 1983: A SYNOPSIS

The course of the Sinhalese riots against the Tamil minority in Sri Lanka in 1983 has been documented by me elsewhere.[12] Here let me summarize what we know of the locations at which the arson and violence took place and the kinds of participants—"the faces in the crowd."

The 1983 riots began in Colombo on July 24 and lasted until August 5. They spread to other parts of the country from this point of origin, especially to the towns of Gampaha and Kalutara in the southwest; Kandy, Kegalle, Matale, Badulla, and Nuwara Eliya in the central tea plantation districts; and Trincomalee in the Eastern Province. Although the official death toll was about 470, it has been estimated that about 2,000–3,000 people were murdered, many of them in a brutal manner. Thousands were displaced from their homes, most of them ending up in about a dozen makeshift refugee camps. "Within the city of Colombo almost a hundred thousand people, more than half the city's Tamil population, were displaced from their homes, and many never returned to their neighborhoods or to their workplaces. Outside the country, it was estimated that there were about 175 thousand refugees and displaced persons."[13] In this account I shall limit myself to happenings in Colombo.

One feature of these riots that I want to underscore is their actual beginning, which bears some resemblance to the inception of the Delhi riots of 1984, in that an incident of violent death had traumatic and emotionally heightening effects on a crowd and worked as a triggering event for acts of crowd violence, which escalated rapidly into large-scale, spreading ethnic riots.

The conventional story is that the most proximate triggering event was the ambush of an army truck and the killing and mutilation of thirteen soldiers at Tirunelveli, a place in the heart of Sri Lankan Tamil territory in North Sri Lanka, which had been under the occupation of a Sinhalese army for some time. The ambush was the work of Tamil insurgents belonging to the Liberation Tigers of Tamil Eelam (LTTE). This was certainly a moment of escalation in the ethnic conflict. India had begun to supply the Tigers with the Claymore land mine as a way of enabling them better to withstand the Sri Lankan Army (overwhelmingly Sinhalese in composition). Although skirmishes had taken place before, never before had so many Sinhala soldiers been killed at once. On July 23, certain elements in the army decided to bring the corpses in their mangled state to Colombo at the central Kanatte cemetery in Borella before giving them a military burial.

The preparations for the burial were complicated and plagued by adventitious and uncontrollable factors. One of the soldiers killed was a young second lieutenant, who had apparently been a popular student at Ananda College, a premier Buddhist school, located in Maradana. Many pupils of this school, together with their parents and teachers, gathered at the cemetery and awaited the arrival of the bodies.

In the meantime, the plane transporting the bodies to Colombo from Jaffna was delayed, and the waiting crowd, increasing in size, also became increasingly restless. After arrival, the bodies were to be taken to a funerary home next to the cemetery for preparation, but the delay also caused the police and army troops who had gathered in numbers at Borella to become emotionally agitated. And, as might be expected, the Sinhala media added further fuel to the mounting grief and rage. (There are separate Sinhalese and Tamil newspapers, radio, and television channels in Sri Lanka.)

In the end, the long delay in the arrival of the bodies at Ratmalana airport, the unruliness of the packed crowd at the cemetery, and the demand of the grief-stricken relatives of the dead that the bodies be handed to them so that they could conduct their own rites forced the authorities to cancel the official burial at Kanatte. The bodies were taken to army headquarters.

The crowd then erupted in spontaneous violence and surged into the streets.

Reviewing the trajectory of the riots, it seems plausible to suggest that they went through two phases. The first phase began in the vicinity of the cemetery in Borella, more or less as an overflow of heightened emotions on the part of the crowd gathered there—the schoolboys, friends, and relatives of the dead, some of the security forces, plus some of the local populace in Borella.

Soon after the mortuary rites, street thuggery, stopping of traffic, and physical attacks broke out in Borella, Thimbirigasyaya, Nugegoda, Wellawatte, and Bambalapitiya, and almost a whole day passed before the army and police were called upon to intervene. This first phase of violence lasted one day; it was only after a short lull that crowd violence resumed in a form that was decidedly more destructive and homicidal, showing firm evidence of planning and direction, the participation of certain politicians (especially from the ruling party) and government employees (minor staff, laborers, technicians), and the use of government vehicles and buses.

A conspicuous feature of the 1983 riots was that the mob violence, especially in its second phase, was organized and for the most part purposive. The crowds came armed with weapons such as metal rods and knives and carrying gasoline, which was frequently confiscated from passing motor vehicles. Evidence of the rioters' prior intent and planning was the fact that they carried voter lists and the addresses of Tamil owners and occupants of houses, shops, industries, and other property. Moreover, the gangs frequently had access to transportation; they arrived mostly in government-owned trucks and buses or were dropped off at successive locations by the Colombo coastline trains.

Affirmation of these incidents comes from a senior official in the Sri Lankan Ministry of Foreign Affairs, Ambassador T. D. S. A. Dissanayaka, who has written a detailed and graphic account of the rioting in Colombo and elsewhere. He writes: "In the afternoon [of July 25] the violence took a different turn. There was organized violence by gangs which were obviously trained and who operated with military precision. Their targets were the economic bases of the Tamils in Colombo and their homes."[14]

This kind of organized violence first occurred in Ratmalana, on the southern periphery of Colombo, which had the largest concentration of factories in Sri Lanka, and then it moved northwards into the city. It coincided with another organized operation: a train traveling from Galle was made to make unscheduled stops in Ratmalana, and then at each stop into the city, at Dehiwela, Wellawatte, and other places, "squads were discharged. . . . They demonstrated remarkable skill in destroying homes. . . . Tamil homes were identified with pinpoint accuracy using electoral lists. In attacking shops, the trained squads responded to three commands in Sinhala: 'kada [break], adha [haul],' and 'gini [set fire].' "[15] At this phase of the violence, there was little looting of property, only systematic destruction of Tamil property and the eradication of the alleged affluence.

A well-informed friend of mine has pointed out to me that the "liberalized economy" introduced from 1977 onwards had opened up new commercial and business opportunities. Many shops selling imported and local goods had opened. New business premises and houses had been constructed in Colombo, and higher rents had become possible. At the same time, this had aggravated competition, and the riots gave some Sinhala businessmen an opportunity to wipe out their competitors, enabled some landlords to get rid of unwanted tenants, and so on. It has also been suggested that Cyril Mathew, the chauvinist minister of industries, was vociferous that Tamil businessmen in Colombo were working both sides of the street—collaborating with the government in Colombo and with the Tamil insurgents in Jaffna—and that they therefore deserved to be "taught a lesson." Matthew's ministry was a repository of knowledge about businesses, including details of their locations and owners. Its employees also provided the manpower for the government union called the Jatika Sevaka Sangamaya, which was involved in punitive actions and thuggery. It was also the source for vehicles that were used for political purposes.

In a retrospective look at the manner in which events unfolded, it is plausible to suggest that there was a deadly confluence of two separate but complementary streams. Certain segments of the government, particularly Minister Matthew and his agents and client cohorts, had gathered information and made plans for punitive action against the Tamils in Colombo, and the ambush and killing of the thirteen Sinhalese soldiers in the north and the subsequent events at the Kanatte cemetery afforded the occasion for the prepared pogrom. That the army authorities and the minister of defence handled the deaths of the soldiers and their mangled corpses in polythene bags in a manner that would, whether intended or not, inevitably excite the emotions of the Sinhalese public at large is made even more problematic by the fact that news of the army's retaliatory violence on July 24 in Tirunelveli and Kantharmadu (in Jaffna), which resulted in an estimated 50 to 70 Tamils being killed, was suppressed from the media, both newspapers and radio, which in the meantime transmitted the inflammatory news of the dead Sinhalese soldiers and the conveyance of their dismembered remains to Colombo.

Ambassador Dissanayaka, who, I presume, had access to official records by virtue of his high position, reports that by Monday, August 1, when the riots had virtually subsided, the following number of incidents had taken place in Sri Lanka overall: 471 deaths, 8,077 cases of arson, and 3,835 cases of looting. Colombo district topped the list with 227 deaths, 2,720 cases of arson, and 1,712 of looting; Kandy district suffered 31 deaths, 1,065 acts of arson, and 132 of looting. Other districts where much violence occurred were Badulla (52 deaths, 838 cases of arson, and 630 lootings), Matale (3 deaths, 1,131 acts of arson, and 838 lootings), Kegalle (24 deaths, 390 cases of arson, and 195 lootings). Leaving aside Colombo district, one may reasonably conclude from the location and demographic profile of the other districts, which are mostly located "up-country," where tea planta-tions and the towns servicing them are located, that not only Sri Lankan Tamil but also Indian Tamil business establishments, and the Indian Tamil labor working in the plantation sector were targeted.

It may also be noted that Trincomalee district in the Eastern Province, in which there has been tension between the Sri Lankan Tamil residents and the allegedly newly arriving Sinhalese settlers, experienced 634 incidents of arson, and Jaffna district suffered 70 deaths, the second-largest number, primarily owing to the security forces taking punitive action against Tamil civilians as a sequel to the killing of 13 soldiers of the Sri Lankan Army in the north on July 23, 1983.

The following is list of the locations and the kinds of property method-ically burned, destroyed, and looted in Colombo:

1.   Tamil houses in Colombo's middle- and lower-class residential wards of Ratmalana, Wellawatte, Dehiwela, Bambalapitiya, and Kirillapone.

2.   Tamil shops—groceries, textile shops, tea boutiques—lining Col-ombo's principal waterfront thoroughfare, especially in Bambalapitiya, and also in well-established residential and business zones such as Borella and Kotahena. In the densest shopping district, Pettah, Tamil shops and the shops of Indian merchants, principally selling cloth and wholesale foodstuffs, were targeted. Moreover, shops located in the city's newer and expanding residen-tial areas such as Timbirigasyaya and Nugegoda were also affected.

3.   Textile mills, garment factories, rubber-goods factories, and coconut-oil processing plants at Ratmalana, Grandpass, Ja-ela, and Peliyagoda, at the edges of the city, owned and managed by Tamil entrepreneurs and large businessmen.[16]

4.   The Indian Overseas Bank, the principal bank for Sri Lankans of In-dian origin and Indian citizens in Sri Lanka.

The victims in Colombo were Tamil shopkeepers; Tamil homeowners, especially of the middle class and administrative/clerical/professional categories; Tamil large business capitalists and entrepreneurs, and Indian merchants, both Tamil and non-Tamil.

These facts clearly indicate that the locations affected were central market and business zones, sites of new industrial development stimulated by the economic liberalization initiated by the new government of J. R. Jayewardene in 1977, and middle-class residential areas. There was practically no arson in slums and working-class residential zones.

At the most general level, the rioters on the Sinhalese side were all male and virtually all drawn from the urban population of Colombo and its suburbs. Those who actually committed murders, inflicted bodily harm, and engaged in arson, property destruction, and looting were typically drawn from the urban working class. A more detailed enumeration would include the following categories: wage workers in government and private factories and mills; transport workers, such as bus drivers and conductors, and workers in railroad yards and electrical installations; petty traders and market workers, including fish sellers and porters; small shopkeepers and salesmen in government corporations; hospital workers; high school students and the students of technical and tutorial institutes, including recent school leavers. The literacy explosion and the poor employment prospects of school graduates and leavers were potent factors in motivating the last category. Finally, there was the urban underclass of unemployed and underemployed shantytown dwellers.

It would be a mistake to exclude from the list of participants those whose involvement was less visible but nonetheless crucial to the hatching, organization, and direction of the riots. Certain Sinhala politicians and their local agents, organized crime figures and smugglers, and small businessmen seeking to eliminate rivals were all involved in directing and manipulating the violence. Some of these might be described as "riot captains" who were experts at "raising a mob" (to use expressions current in England in the nineteenth century). In addition, some militant Buddhist monks played a role in inciting crowd action, sometimes as supportive witnesses and orators. Finally, it has been well attested that many members of the police force and security forces stood by during the 1983 riots—unwilling to restrain the rioters, showing sympathy for their actions, and in a few instances actively participating in the work of destruction.

An intriguing question that some interpreters have grappled with is why, after a hiatus of some nineteen years since the last Sinhala-Tamil riots of 1958, a crop of riots of mounting violence should have occurred at short intervals in 1977, 1981, and 1983. Since the last three upheavals took place on the watch of the United National Party, it has been asked to what extent the "liberalized open economy" and capitalist, market-oriented policies introduced by President Jayewardene created economic dislocations injurious to segments of the Sinhalese population, who might have sponsored, supported, and even participated in varying degrees in the spate of riots against the Tamils.

The Tamils were targeted for a combination of reasons: they were perceived as privileged and a suitable object of redressive action on behalf of the majority Sinhalese population, especially its poorer segments; because they were convenient victims, against whom aggression that could not be directed at the state could be displaced; and because Tamil business interests could be dispossessed or eliminated to the advantage of Sinhalese small-scale entrepreneurs and traders, who suffered most in the changeover from the state-regulated welfare and protectionist policy of the previously ruling Sri Lanka Freedom Party to the capitalist, market-oriented, free-trade policy heralded by the UNP in 1977.

In sum, the 1983 riots were a kind of pogrom, which was motivated, purposive, systematic, and organized. Politically and economically, they were a punitive action against Tamils. Those who stood to gain most were, firstly, middle-level Sinhala entrepreneurs, businessmen, and white-collar workers, and, secondly, the urban poor, mainly through looting. Many of the latter were recent migrants from rural areas, whose living conditions had deteriorated as the open economy created and widened disparities of wealth and income distribution. Despite rising wages, their real incomes had declined as a result of inflation, urban housing scarcities, and the issuing of food stamps in place of the former subsidized rice program. Moreover, the measures taken to create an open-market economy caused short-term internal dislocations and imbalances, which were aggravated by pressure from the World Bank, the International Monetary Fund, and other international organizations.[17]

5   Sikh Identity, Separation, and Ethnic Conflict

This chapter is primarily concerned with documenting the Hindu-Sikh riots that engulfed Delhi in 1984 and highlighting aspects of them that illustrate and illuminate the phenomenon of collective violence generated in the course of ethnic conflict.

The history of the Sikhs, the conspicuous changes and transformations in their religion from their first guru, Nānak (1469–1539), to their tenth and last guru, Gobind Singh (1666–1708), and thereafter; their golden age under Maharaja Ranjit Singh (1780–1839), who constructed the Sikh empire in the Punjab, with its capital at Lahore, and who is alleged to have realized the cry "The Khalsa shall rule!" (attributed to Guru Gobind Singh, who created the Sikh warrior order called the Khalsa); their shifting fortunes under the British; all this and much else has been treated by many scholars. It will suffice here as a backdrop to the riots of 1984 if I point to a few landmark developments in the religious and political affairs of the Sikhs in India, especially in the Punjab, from the 1920s onwards.[1]

THE SUCCESSIVE PARTITIONS OF THE PUNJAB

One set of developments to bear in mind is the succession of "partitions" that the Punjab has undergone. A unitary Punjab under British rule was first partitioned in 1947 with the formation of Pakistan. It is well to remember that the creation of India and Pakistan in 1947 was done at a huge human cost: about half a million people died and around fifteen million people changed residence through migration. The Punjab as a whole felt the worst effects of the turmoil of Partition. There were twelve million refugees from the Punjab alone, and possibly two hundred thousand of its people were slaughtered. The killings began in March 1947, when Muslim mobs killed Sikhs in large numbers in Rawalpindi. In turn, Sikhs in east and central Punjab began to arm and retaliate in kind against the Muslims, and these deadly exchanges led to the transfer of massive numbers of refugees.[2] In the newly created Indian Punjab, the population distribution in 1951 was 62 percent Hindu, 35 percent Sikh, and less than 3 percent Muslim.

In 1966, the Punjab was divided again, when the Hindu majority areas, where Hindi speakers predominated, were separated off to form the new state of Haryana. Chandigarh became the joint capital of the two states. The Sikhs had campaigned for a Punjabi-speaking state, based both on linguistic grounds and on memories of the Sikh empire of Ranjit Singh. Reduced in territory to some 50,000 square kilometers, the new Punjab had a population of 11 million, about 60 percent of whom were Sikh.

The linguistic state of Punjab was not achieved without dispute and contest. Although most people spoke Punjabi in daily life, it was a written language only for the Sikhs.[3] And throughout the 1950s, in the face of Sikh propaganda, especially under the Akali Dal leader Master Tara Singh, for the right of self-determination for Sikhs, together with their espousal of the Punjabi language and "Gurmukhi culture," the Punjabi Hindus by and large educated their children in Hindi and affirmed that Hindi was their mother tongue. "The shift of Punjabi-speaking Hindus," Paul Brass has written, was "more dramatic" than any linguistic choice previously made in Punjab, "because it was an overt and deliberate political act."[4] Although the Indian government had consented to the creation of many linguistic states in the 1950s, there was resistance to the creation of a Punjabi-speaking state, despite Tara Singh's campaign.[5] Punjabi Suba was achieved in 1966, after the deaths of Tara Singh and Nehru.

Since the late 1980s, we have witnessed attempts by extremist Sikhs, especially the militant followers of the late Jarnail Singh Bhindranwale, to effect a third partition through a secessionist demand for an independent state of Khalistan. The demand and its denial have led to the worst phase of internal violence that India has faced since independence.

THE POLITICS OF THE AKALI DAL MOVEMENT

The question of the separate identity of Sikhs, firmly distinguished from Hindus, seems to have come into prominence in the 1920s. At the very time of the Gandhian nationalist movement, the Sikhs, conscious of their own nationalist stirrings, took decisive steps to form two organizations, the Akali Dal ("army of the faithful") and the Shiromani Gurudwara Parbandhak Committee (hereafter referred to as SGPC), which have played the most crucial roles in Sikh politics to this day.

In November 1920, an estimated 10,000 Sikhs met in Amritsar to establish a committee to draft new rules for the management of the Golden Temple there. It was this committee that became the SGPC. Soon afterwards, the Akali Dal was formed as a central organization to coordinate and direct local *jathas*, which were attempting to take control of the Sikh *gurudwaras* (temples) from the traditional *mahants*. The SGPC led by the Akali Dal activists forcibly took over shrine after shrine, and by 1925 the SGPC had gained formal ownership of some of the gurudwaras. The British colonial authorities recognized and legitimated the SGPC and made it "the Religious Parliament of Sikhs," a position and a role that it claims to this day. The Sikh Gurudwaras and Shrines Act of 1925 placed more than 200 temples under the control of the SGPC, which was to be elected by all adult Sikhs living in Punjab. Controlling large funds—in the 1980s about Rs 70 million—the SGPC became a magnet for Sikh politicians. "In the Sikh-majority Punjab formed in 1966 the SGPC became an organization which could create and destroy governments."[6]

Although the Akali Dal decided to support the Raj in World War II, and succeeded in persuading Sikhs to join the British Indian Army, it had not yet forged a clear policy regarding the future of the Sikhs in the postwar world in 1947. Although there had been talk by Tara Singh of an independent Sikh state if the country were to be divided, there was no effective hooking up with the rounds of deliberations between the British, the Indian National Congress, and the Muslim League. And in the face of the violence of Partition and vast displacements of people as refugees, the Akali Dal consented to the partition of Punjab as inevitable.

POLITICAL CONTESTS, 1947–1984

In many ways, the most critical factors cumulatively leading to a politics of escalation, as well as of factionalism, were those that issued from a complicated but calculated contest between the political parties that controlled the federal government in Delhi and those that wielded power in Punjab State.

In Delhi, the parties that would crucially compete for power, especially in the 1970s, were Congress (I), which ruled most of the time, and the Janata Party, which briefly came to power in 1977. In Punjab State, the political stakes were contested by Congress (I) on the one side and the Akali Dal and Janata in coalition on the other.

The most critical feature of the dialectics of contest, which led to a fraught and spiraling trajectory of divisive violence, culminating in the extreme acts of Jarnail Singh Bhindranwale and his fundamentalist militants, was the intersection and interference of federal politics with the politics of

Punjab State. For instance, it is said that it was Indira Gandhi and Congress (I) that originally set up and sponsored Bhindranwale as a rival to the Akali Dal, the political grouping that the local Congress (I) feared in Punjab, and that was led by a triumvirate of Sikh leaders, namely, Parkash Singh Badal, a former Punjab chief minister; Harchand Singh Longowal, a respected religious leader; and Gurucharan Singh Tohra, who headed the SGPC. This tangle was further aggravated by the personal differences between Zail Singh, then union home minister, and Punjab's Congress (I) chief minister, Darbara Singh. In the end, the politics of divide and rule turned out to be a nightmare for the government of Indira Gandhi, whose death they brought about.

The wrestling between Congress and the Akali Dal goes back to the early days of independence. Then, too, there was an antagonistic pairing between Partap Singh Kairon, a Jat, who was Congress chief minister of Punjab and an ally of Nehru's, and Master Tara Singh, a Khatri, a leading figure in the Akali Dal, and several times president of the SGPC. Both leaders had been part of the Gandhian nationalist movement, but Tara Singh had already in the early 1950s accused the Hindu majority of trying to absorb the Sikhs, and advocated Punjabi Suba, a new state that would safeguard the Punjabi language and the interests of the Sikhs. After 1960, Tara Singh and the Akali Dal had decisively terminated friendly dealings with Congress, and Tara Singh led a campaign of civil disobedience for the creation of Punjabi Suba. Since the time of Tara Singh and since the creation of Punjabi Suba, there have been three significant interrelated developments in the politics of the Punjab.

First, there was the rise of the Jat Sikhs,[7] with their power base located among the Sikh peasantry in rural areas, and their domination in time of the Akali Dal. It is generally recognized that the Sikhs in Punjab are divided into three categories: (a) the Khatri, who are urban in origin and have traditionally practiced commercial, trading, and clerical occupations, and who produced not only all ten gurus but also Master Tara Singh, the most forceful of the modern Sikh leaders; (b) the Jats, rural agriculturalists who constitute up to 60 percent of the Sikhs, and from whose ranks came Sant Fateh Singh, Master Tara Singh's successor; and (c) the minority of "low castes," namely, the Mazhabis (untouchables), and the Ramgarhias (artisans).

Second, especially in the 1960s, many Jat Sikhs changed their political affiliation from Congress to the Akali Dal, a change facilitated by the fall of P. S. Kairon in 1964. In the elections of 1967, the majority of MLA's of Akali designation, about twenty-four in number, were Jat Sikhs.

Third, there was the intensification of the already ingrained factionalism of Punjab politics, which was laced with violence, the latter being in some commentators' eyes a mode of enacting politics brought with them by the Jat Sikhs.[8]

Congress's loss of control of Punjab politics and the increasing factionalism and violence of Indian politics in general went hand in hand. In February 1967, the United Front, made up of non-Congress parties and led by the Akali Dal, took office. And the next five years were turbulent, with shifts of control and two dramatic interventions by the federal center. The United Front gave way after a few months to a Congress-supported minority "Janta Party" in November 1967, whose rule was superseded, again after only a few months, by president's rule (August 1960–February 1969). President's rule gave way to Akali Dal–Jana Sangh coalitions, which lasted till about June 1971, to be replaced again by president's rule with the collapse of the Akali Dal government and the beginning of the third Indo-Pakistan War.

During the next five years (1972–77), there was Congress rule in Punjab, with Giani Zail Singh as chief minister: but while a state of emergency imposed on the whole country helped Zail Singh continue in office, a sustained and powerful opposition to Congress rule was mounted by the Akali Dal, staged from the gurudwaras. The elections of March 1977 saw the triumphant return of the Akali Dal, which formed a coalition government with the Janata Party. The humiliated Congress did not win a single seat. Parkash Singh Badal was now enthroned as chief minister, but his coalition collapsed two years later, amidst a mounting tide of violence that would progressively engulf Punjab.

The Congress Party, led by Indira Gandhi, lost the national elections of 1977 as well, and gave way to a Janata Party government, which, however, torn by internal dissension and factional politics, was dissolved in January 1980. Although the Congress Party lost the election in Punjab in 1977 and was out of power in Delhi, it had set in motion the old strategy of splitting the Akali Dal and promoting factionalism, this time with diabolical results.

As Robin Jeffrey explains, "the technique developed was to encourage dissatisfied Akali factions to start a campaign 'for complete autonomy of Punjab' and to accuse their own government of failure to look after Sikh interests. This would anger Hindus in the Janata Party, put Akali ministers in the position of having to qualify their devotion to their religion and thus divide Parkash Singh Badal's government. In the ensuing disarray it might be possible to 'bring in a Congress (I) government.' "[9]

It is these political strategies and tactics that help explain the temporary crossing of the interests of Indira Gandhi and Jarnail Singh Bhindranwale, a Jat Sikh from southern Punjab, who was a charismatic and dynamic young Sant. Bhindranwale's call for a revived Sikhism, dedicated to the old militant ideals and aggressive masculinity of Guru Gobind Singh's Khalsa (the order of the pure), and in due course an autonomous state of Khalistan, reminiscent of the glories and trials of the eighteenth century, gathered a following especially of young Sikhs disenchanted with the worldly politics and compromises of their elders.[10] On April 13, 1978, Bhindranwale had made his mark when he and his followers staged a march and broke up the annual convention of the Sant Nirankaris held at the holy city of Amritsar on the grounds that this group was actually heretical, reprobate, and anti-Sikh, because, contrary to Gobind's ruling that he was the last guru, this religious group believed in a living guru, and contrary to Gobind's ruling that the canon was thereafter closed, this group made additions to it.[11] The Nirankaris were also accused of being lax in some of their practices, notably the worship of the sandals of Baba Gurbachan Singh, their spiritual head. This encounter was marked by armed violence—three Nirankaris and a dozen Sikhs lost their lives—and it was an omen of things to come. "Baba Gurbachan Singh was shot dead in April 1980. His death was followed by mass killings of Sant Nirankaris in Punjab."[12]

It has been alleged that Indira Gandhi and her circle of advisers saw in Bhindranwale an agent who could be used to challenge the Akali Dal leaders in Punjab. Their calculation was that Bhindranwale's aggressive promotion of exclusivist Sikh claims would help loosen the Akali's bonds with urban Hindus.

In August 1978, a Dal Khalsa had been founded in Chandigarh, pledged to achieve an independent Sikh state, and it is alleged that Congress (I) and Zail Singh (the former chief minister) had helped finance the first meeting.[13] It would seem that Congress had actively tried to undermine the Akali Dal's candidates' chances of winning the 1979 elections to the SGPC, and that although it was unsuccessful in its aim, it did manage to sow the seeds of dissension within the Akali Dal. Bhindranwale's faction was one that emerged as a prominent presence, dedicated to extremist causes and to the purification of the faith.

In January 1980, Indira Gandhi and Congress (I) won the general elections, but Punjab politics had reached such a state of turmoil, and the violence practiced by Bhindranwale and his armed gangs had helped destabilize Punjab to such an extent, that Indira Gandhi seized the opportunity to dissolve Parkash Singh Badal's government and call for fresh elections at the end of May. The escalation of violent acts and the slide toward "terrorism" can be gauged from this enumeration of murders and vendettas:

On April 24, 1980, Gurbachan Singh, the leader of the Nirankari Mission, was assassinated in Delhi. Bhindranwale's involvement was suspected.

On September 9, 1981, Lala Jagat Narain, head of the *Punjab Kesari* chain of newspapers, an ally of Partap Singh Kairon's, was submachine-gunned by three Sikh motorcycle riders. Two days earlier, the Akali Dal had organized a peaceful and orderly procession of some 100,000 Sikh marchers. The Akali's new president, Harchand Singh Longowal, played a prominent part in advancing Sikh claims—for example, that Amritsar be declared a holy city—and in affirming the nationhood of Sikhs within the Union of India. The murder of Narain was attributed to Bhindranwale, and a warrant was issued for his arrest; a gun battle ensued, but Bhindranwale managed to elude the chase and took refuge at his headquarters at Chowk Mehta in Punjab, before giving himself up in the presence of a crowd of 50,000 people. "Then the rioting began; before it was over the police had opened fire and eight people were dead."[14] The police in fact had no hard evidence against Bhindranwale, and he was released. This episode confirmed his ascendance as the charismatic leader of the extremists in Punjab and made him a sworn enemy of the government, dedicated to winning Khalistan, if necessary by violent means.

The arrest and release of Bhindranwale triggered a barrage of violent incidents in the following months, the like of which had never happened before. On September 22, a submachine gun sprayed bullets in Jullundur Market; an Indian Airlines plane was hijacked a week later; two policemen were killed and their weapons stolen; a bomb exploded in Bhindranwale's own headquarters, killing three; and a number of other assassinations took place, the most conspicuous being that of Santokh Singh, "the most powerful Sikh in New Delhi, closely connected to the Congress (I) and a regular associate of Bhindranwale" on December 21.[15] In short, shootings and killings were being directed by multiple actors, including agents of the state, at one another. It was difficult to discern who was doing what to whom and why. As public order deteriorated, the menace of violence hung in the air. Violence rather than being an aberration was becoming the routine form of enacting politics. Finally, on October 5, 1983, a massacre of bus passengers, all Hindu, prompted the declaration of president's rule in Punjab.

On February 27, 1984, Parkash Singh Badal, twice chief minister of Punjab, publicly burned the Indian Constitution and proclaimed his support for the aims of Bhindranwale's crusade, showing that highly placed

Sikhs disenchanted with government policy were being drawn toward an extremist position.

At the last stages of his marked career, Bhindranwale, fearing arrest by the government, occupied the Akal Takt in the Golden Temple complex in Amritsar with a number of his followers and fortified it. Trained and equipped with modern weapons, they prepared for what they must have suspected was to be their last siege. The Punjab police were as deeply divided as civil society. The fateful storming of the Golden Temple by the Indian Army, code-named "Operation Blue Star," occurred on June 6, 1984. A thousand people were killed, pilgrims among them, along with Bhindranwale and his followers, and the buildings were extensively damaged (see figure 1). This show of force by the Indian government was viewed as an outrage by the majority of the Sikh community—even among those far removed from the politics of both the Akali and Bhindranwale—and provided the impetus for a further escalation of violence and terror.

On October 31, 1984, Prime Minister Indira Gandhi was herself assassinated by her Sikh security guards, and a tornado of violence devastated Delhi (and other places, such as Kanpur, Bokaro, and Indore). Delhi's intellectuals plunged into an anguished search for understanding. "Why did this kind of horror—and it's a qualitatively new type of horror in our body-politic—erupt at all, tearing apart a 500 year history of spiritual and symbiotic relationships?" Darshan Singh Maini asked.[16]

Rajni Kothari has sketched the prevailing mood among the Hindus, especially in North India, who felt "that the Sikhs were more like enemies than friends, that they were the cause of national disintegration, that they were responsible for large scale murders of Hindus in Punjab (actually more Sikhs were killed by the extremists than Hindus), that they were an aggressive and violent people, loyal to Bhindranwale and other extremists, on the whole out to undermine Indian unity. All this got reinforced by wild rumours and press censorship."[17] Mounting resentment of the Sikhs was compounded by the perception that they were disproportionately prosperous and economically successful.

Following Indira Gandhi's assassination, the predominantly Hindu population of Delhi unleashed a massive orgy of violence against the minority Sikhs. The vast majority of the victims were Sikh inhabitants of "the settlement colonies" on the fringes of the city, who were by origin not drawn from the ranks of the Punjabi Jats or Khatri, but were either Sindhi Sikhs, a residue of the refugee exodus at the time of Partition, or "low-caste" Mazhabi Sikhs living on the edge of poverty. Neither of these slum populations had anything to do with the involuted and explosive politics that

Figure 1.   Sikh militants guarding the Golden Temple in Amritsar before Operation Blue Star. Pramod Pushkarna (*India Today*).

counterposed the Akali Dal activists, Bhindranwale's militants, and Congress (I) politicians. What features of the urban landscape of Delhi itself, its distribution of power, disposition of space, congested contiguity of peoples, electoral strategies, slum landlordism, and municipal politics contributed to the rampage of the crowds? How do we differentiate the issues and strains of the wider political scene from the particular demographic and spatial ecology of the metropolis of Delhi, and then relate the two?

THE ANTI-SIKH RIOTS OF 1984 IN DELHI

In 1984, Hindus comprised 83 percent of Delhi's total population of about 6.2 million people. Estimates of the Sikh population ranged from 6.3 percent to 7.5 percent (an estimated 300,000–500,000 people). A majority of them had settled in Delhi after Partition (1947), before which the Sikhs were only 1.2 percent of the city's population.[18]

The riots occurred in many different parts of the city but were at their worst in localities such as Munrika in the south, Mangolpuri and Sultanpuri in the west, Trilokpuri and Kalyanpuri in the east, and Jahangiripuri in the north. The literature refers to these poorer sections of Delhi as the trans-Jamuna colonies and resettlement colonies.

Whatever the previous history of Hindu-Sikh relations, and their exchanges of violence, one thing is clear about the riots that occurred in Delhi between October 31 and November 4, 1984: "This violence was essentially one sided, namely, the non-Sikhs attacked the Sikhs and damaged, looted, and burnt their properties, . . . [and] Gurudwaras, and killed a few thousand of them."[19]

The authors of *Who Are the Guilty?* observe that their own individual experiences as well as extensive interviews with varied persons (victims, their neighbors, police officers, political leaders, army officers) "suggest that the attack on the Sikhs followed a common pattern, whether they took place in Munrika in the South, or Mangolpuri in the West, or Trilokpuri in the East. The uniformity in the sequence of events at every spot were masterminded by some powerful organized groups. . . . Newspaper reports suggest that this pattern [was] similar in all Congress (I) ruled states."[20]

The authors of a second report, *Report of the Citizens' Commission*, affirmed a collective purposiveness behind the carnage: "The remarkable uniformity in the pattern of the crimes committed, with some local variations, strongly suggests that at some stage the objective became to 'Teach the Sikhs a lesson.' "[21] It is certainly noteworthy that the announcement of the Indian Parliament on April 26, 1985, concerning the formation of an official commission—which came to be called the Misra Commission, taking the name of its chairman, Justice Ranganath Misra—to inquire into the riots stated that the commissioners' task was "to inquire into the allegations in regard to *the incidents of organized violence* which took place in Delhi following the assassination of the late Prime Minister" (emphasis added).

Although the Delhi administration itself denied "the allegation of organized violence and stated that all possible steps were taken to quell the riots at [the] shortest time possible," and although advocates on the Sikh and Hindu sides exaggerated or underestimated the degree of directed violence, it seems a fair judgment to say that the riots in some of their phases showed patterns of organization.[22]

Naturally, the parties making representations to the Misra Commission differed in their accounts of what took place. Thus for instance, the Citizens' Justice Commission (CJC), representing Sikh interests and containing retired justices, judges, military officers, and advocates made the forceful and extreme charge that "the violence in Delhi was premeditated, organized and was perpetrated methodically. . . so as to lead to the irresistible conclusion of central direction, guidance and control. The task was without doubt performed with the complicity, connivance and active involvement of the administration as well as the members of the ruling party." The CJC later withdrew from the hearings, alleging partiality on the part of the Misra Commission.

A radically opposite submission was made by the Nagrik Suraksha Samiti, representing the Arya Samaj point of view. It denied that the riots were "the handiwork of any organized group of people," asserting that they "were all sporadic and spontaneous and . . . erupted [because of] grave provocation and anger on account of the tragic assassination of the late Prime Minister . . . which aroused a sudden and tremendous feeling of shock, distress, and uncontrollable anger amongst the people." The Samiti also reminded the Misra Commission that the assailants "had in their mind the events that had taken place in Punjab earlier and had known the atrocities committed by some members of the Sikh community as extremists."

THE TRAJECTORY OF THE RIOTS

The rioting began in the evening of October 31, 1984, and had more or less abated by the end of November 4. It may thus be said to have lasted from three to four days.

First Day: October 31

Indira Gandhi was shot on October 31, 1984, at 9:15 A.M. by two of her Sikh security guards. She was rushed to the All India Institute of Medical Sciences (AIIMS) for treatment. By 11:00 A.M., All Indian Radio (AIR) reported that she had been attacked; by 2:30 P.M., the evening editions of several papers in the capital carried the news of her death, identifying Sikhs as the assailants.

Crowds had been gathering at the AIIMS, and there were stray incidents of assaults on Sikh passers-by. Soon after All Indian Radio announced Indira Gandhi's death, gathering crowds "went on a rampage in several parts of Delhi adjacent to the AIIMS, namely Safdarjung Enclave, Laxmibai Nagar, INA Market and South Extension."[23]

The Misra Commission's version is that the rioters, forming different groups in the vicinity of the AIIMS, proceeded toward the Defence Colony, RK Puram, Prithviraj Road, and Hauz Khas, indulging in violence and arson on the way.[24] Word spread quickly, inciting attacks in various places in the city, although the main incidents were reported from the places in South Delhi where the riots had begun (see map 2).

"By the late evening [of October 31], outbreaks occurred in areas as far afield as New Friends Colony, Lajpat Nagar, Karol Bagh and New Delhi. Gurudwaras, houses, shops, factories, workshops and other property belonging to Sikhs were looted and damaged or destroyed. Sikh pedestrians and passengers, dragged out of cars or buses, were assaulted."[25] Another account reports "the arrival of young people in tempo vans, scooters, motorcycles or trucks from the night of October 31" at places such as Munrika, Saket, South Extension, Lajpat Nagar, Bhogpal, Jangpura, and Ashram in the south and southeast; at the Connaught Circus shopping area in the center, and later, at the trans-Jamuna colonies and resettlement colonies in other areas in the north.[26] Indira Gandhi's son Rajiv Gandhi, who was sworn as prime minister at 6:50 P.M., made a broadcast to the nation appealing for calm, but it was ineffective, as were AIR and television (Doordarshan) broadcasts of an order prohibiting the assembly of five or more persons and the carrying of arms in the Union Territory of Delhi.

> The rumors were three. First, Sikhs were distributing sweets and lighting lamps to celebrate Mrs. Gandhi's death. . . . The second rumor was that trainloads of hundreds of Hindu dead bodies had arrived at Old Delhi Station from Punjab. Third, water was poisoned by the Sikhs. As for the latter two rumors, we came across evidence of policemen in vans touring certain localities and announcing through loudspeakers the arrival of the train and the poisoning of water. In certain areas, we heard that police officials had rung up residents

advising them not to drink the water. These rumors (the last two were officially repudiated later) contributed to the shaping of a public mind that acquiesced in the attacks and murders that took place soon after.[27]

Second Day: November 1

This day was critical in that the wave of rioting that had begun around the All India Institute of Medical Sciences, where the stricken Mrs. Gandhi was taken, spread in widening ripples through various parts of the city proper already named, reaching its maximal virulence and destructive fury in the resettlement colonies, such as Sultanpuri and Mangolpuri in West Delhi, Trilokpuri and Kalyanpuri, trans-Jamuna colonies in the east of Delhi, and other places such as Gandhi Nagar, Janakpuri, and Palam Colony.

I shall in a later section deal with the collective violence directed against the Sikhs in these settlements on Delhi's periphery, whose inhabitants were mostly of the "lower social orders," the urban working class, artisans, small businessmen, and lower ranges of the Congress (I) Party hierarchy, and their clients, thugs, and retinues ("the criminal elements"). All the sources available to me amply document the experiences and views of victims and neighbors of these settlements, and most of them unambiguously establish that certain identified Congress (I) leaders, workers, and activists mobilized and directed the arsonists, and that local block leaders (*pradhans*) and activists actually identified Sikh houses, shops, businesses, gurudwaras, and schools for the mobs.

The chief administrators of Delhi, the lieutenant governor and the home minister, responded tardily to requests that the police force be more effectively deployed and dragged their feet about the need to call in the army when the evidence of police indifference to the pleas of victims for protection and collusion with the arsonists in the destruction of property and even the killing of Sikhs was submitted by several members of Parliament, distinguished citizens, social workers, journalists, and the like. The same administrators did not think it necessary at that time to set up camps for refugees. An indefinite curfew was imposed at 6:00 P.M. that day.

Third Day: November 2

Violence and terror continued unabated. Reports appeared of an increase in the orgy of arson, rape, and murder; of Sikh passengers on trains being murdered; and of trains approaching Delhi being forcibly stopped by crowds in outlying areas in order to enable them to attack Sikh passengers. "As a large number of victims who had been rendered homeless fled in terror, no less than eighteen unofficial camps came into being."[28] In other

Map 2. Delhi

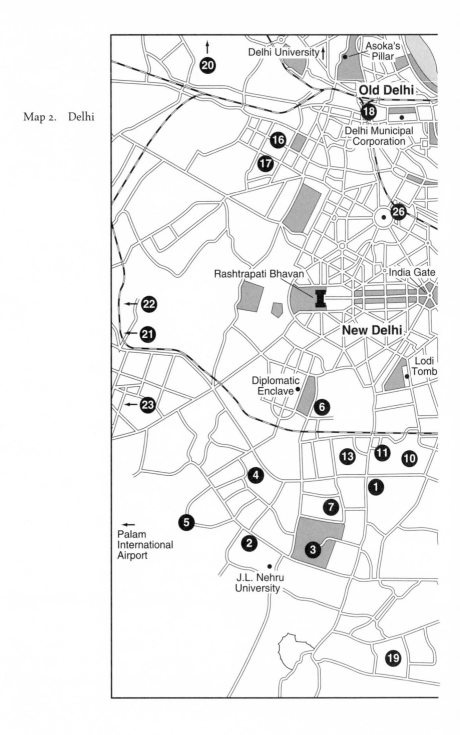

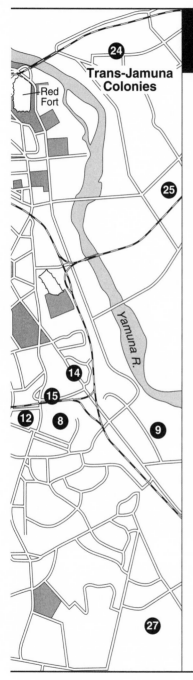

KEY: Locations that Figured in the 1984 Hindu-Sikh riots

1. All India Institute of Medical Sciences
2. Munirka
3. Hauz Khas
4. Ramakrishna Puram
5. Vasant Vihar
6. Chanakyapuri
7. Safdarjang Enclave
8. Lajpat Nagar
9. Friends Colony
10. South Extension
11. Ina Market
12. Defence Colony
13. Lakshmibai Nagar
14. Bhogal
15. Jangpura
16. Karol Bagh
17. Krishna Nagar
18. Sadar Bazar
19. Saket
20. To Ashok Vihar
21. To Janakpuri
22. To Delhi Cantonment
23. To Palam
24. Gandhi Nagar
25. Shakapur
26. Connaught Circus
27. Tughlakabad

NOTE: The following areas on the periphery of Delhi where much of the violence took place are not marked on this map; Mangolpuri and Sultanpuri in the west, Trilokpuri and Kalyanpuri in the east (Trans-Jamuna Colonies) and Jahangiripur in the north.

words, it was only on the third day that voluntary agencies and concerned citizens, faced with governmental sloth, endeavored to provide as best they could for the displaced, both in terms of material care and emotional solace. Prime Minister Rajiv Gandhi made a second broadcast in the evening, reiterating his government's commitment to restoring and preserving communal peace.

Reports mounted of trains approaching Delhi being invaded by mobs assembled at railway stations. Sikh passengers were attacked and frequently beaten to death and set afire on the spot, sometimes while alive. The logic of this was that immediate burning of the bodies prevents the identity of the dead from being known. Cutting of hair and shaving off the beard, thereby removing the most obvious marks of Sikh identity, preceded the burning.

As Kulbir Singh, an eloquent victim, remarked: "All the attacks took place in the Hindu belt, and [they] certainly occurred in those states where the Congress (I) was in power. . . . In those places where there were non-Congress parties but which I'd call communal [they] didn't happen." For example, the attacks did not occur "in the trains going towards Bombay or in the Bombay region." They happened on trains coming toward Delhi, which was clearly within the Hindu belt. "And the fact that they took place on the 1st [of November] suggests that they had enough time to think and plan."[29] This informant, Kulbir Singh, a twenty-eight-year-old businessman, was on his way home to Bihar after a business trip to Delhi. He was pulled out of the train on November 1 at Gawa Road Station, beaten up, and left for dead. He found his way to the local hospital, where he was given little care ("It's Sardars [Sikhs] so let them just die . . ."), until he was rescued by a Hindu friend.

A middle-class Hindu woman named Ratnabehn, who was traveling toward Delhi from Baroda, reported that when the train—the Janata—arrived at Tughlakabad Station at about 10:30 or 11:00 A.M. on November 1, gangs armed with iron rods and cycle chains and carrying kerosene attacked and killed some Sikh passengers, all male. Before this train, two other trains, the Rajdhani and Deluxe, had also been stopped and attacked, so that the mobs had been at work all morning. It was estimated that about twenty-four to twenty-five Sikhs had been killed. Ratnabehn recalled:

> We gathered from the other passengers that the crowd was attacking Sikhs and so the people in the compartment quickly locked the doors and pulled down the shutters. . . . When the doors remained closed [the crowd] threatened to burn the bogey so the passengers had to open the doors. A group of about eight or ten young men, between the ages of twenty and twenty-five, armed

with iron rods came into the compartment to make a search for Sikhs. Some of the non-Sikh passengers tried to hide the four or five Sikhs in the compartment but the mob managed to search them out and then they began to drag them [away].

Among the passengers was a *sanyasini* (an ascetic holy woman), who in particular, along with other passengers, "pleaded with folded hands and requested them not to attack the Sikhs. They even argued that killing or attacking the Sikhs was no way to react to Mrs. Gandhi's assassination . . . [saying,] 'Is this how we are showing Indiraji that we respect her?'"

"For a while the attacking group was temporarily halted . . . and the attackers began to leave the compartment. But immediately afterwards the first attacking group was replaced by a more militant group which did not show any feelings for the pleas of the passengers. They just ruthlessly hunted down the Sikhs without any mercy." An old man was dragged out, his hair was first burnt, then he was doused with kerosene and set on fire. Two other younger men tried to run away but they were caught. "The old man who had been set on fire . . . continued to burn screaming with agony and remained alive right through the time the train remained halted at the station."[30]

On November 1, too, Doordarshan television coverage of mourners filing past Mrs. Gandhi's body lying in state at Teenmurti Bhavan, broadcast shouts of "Khoon ka badla khoon!" ("Blood for blood!"). Although at the time many blamed the television authorities for irresponsible conduct, the Misra Commission, after its inquiry a year later, reported the director general of Doordarshan's explanation that the shouts were transmitted because the telecast was live, and that the coverage was terminated when the incident took place. The Misra Commission stated without comment: "When the cassette [of the relevant portion of the televised program] was played, the Commission found that the shout had been repeated eighteen times spread over 37 seconds."[31]

Fourth Day: November 3

This was the day of Indira Gandhi's cremation. The national media, Akashvani and Doordarshan, covered the event in detail. Aside from the thousands lined up to watch the cortege, many more viewed it on television. It is very likely that the cremation was a cathartic climax to the national tragedy, and that it probably also foreshadowed the inevitable subsidence of the rioting.

Large contingents of the armed forces, in addition to performing their ceremonial duties in connection with the funeral, were also by then a visible presence in many parts of the city, doing a much better job of surveillance and riot control than the police force had done hitherto. The curfew was also being more effectively enforced than before.

Fifth Day: November 4

As observed earlier, communal riots mercifully do not last at any given location for more than a few days. As the cathartic violence of the crowds is spent, the agencies of the state and the security forces, which shock or collusion had initially made inert, increasingly begin to assert their regulatory and preventive authority. Soldiers on the streets and strict imposition of curfew are the signs of a return to (uneasy) normalcy. Thus, while sporadic incidents of violence continued to occur here and there in Delhi, it had by and large dawned on the administration and civilian leaders that the visible problems of the displaced, the refugees, the injured, and the bereaved demanded relief.

Time and again, these tasks constitute the aftermath of communal violence and ethnic riots. Figures of the numbers killed, maimed, and arrested, and estimates of the havoc done, the houses, vehicles and other property destroyed, damaged, and looted, are publicized, confirmed, and contested. Overviews of the disaster, postmortems by official and unofficial commissions of inquiry, are begun, and reports are composed with an eye to their timeliness and relevance to a public that must retrospectively digest and come to terms with the outburst.

THE SCALE OF THE DESTRUCTION

The *Report of the Citizens' Commission* describes the havoc wrought by the riots thus:

> During the four days of mob rule over large areas of Delhi, the loss of life and property was staggering. According to responsible estimates, well over *two thousand were murdered*, leaving behind over a thousand widows and numerous orphans (emphasis added). Sikh educational institutions, several large gurudwaras and many Sikh houses were burnt. Trucks, taxicabs, three-wheeler scooters, cars, motorcycles and scooters were burnt in their hundreds. Movable property, cash and jewelry were stolen and destroyed. Factories and business premises, together with machinery and stock-in-trade were looted, damaged or destroyed.[32]

The home minister announced in Parliament that the number of Sikhs killed in Delhi during the 1984 riots was 2,141, and that another 586 persons were said to have been killed in other parts of the country during that period. The Misra Commission reports that the Delhi administration filed with it a list of 2,212 persons "upon whose death payment of compensation had been admitted and given to the next of kin."[33] The Delhi administration subsequently filed a statement that the number of deaths caused by the riots was 2,307. The Citizens' Justice Commission, however, representing Sikh interests, submitted a list of 3,879 deaths to the Misra Commission, which concluded that the correct figure had to be somewhere between the higher figure of the committee and the lower figure conceded by the Delhi administration.

The killings were carried out with a pitiless frenzy that strains interpretation. "It is in evidence that hundreds of people so killed were burnt while they were half dead or while they were in an unconscious state or had already died. The DSGMC [Delhi Sikh Gurudwara Management Committee] has specified in written arguments the names of 73 people who were burnt alive after they became unconscious and thirteen persons who were burnt after they died. There is evidence that hundreds of charred bodies were recovered."[34]

The damage and looting to property was extensive and thorough. The Delhi administration reported to the Misra Commission that a total of 180 gurudwaras spread over different parts of the city had been subject to arson, looting, and burning, and that about eleven educational institutions, all founded and run by Sikh groups, had been damaged in a similar manner.[35] The purposiveness of these acts of destruction and appropriation did not escape the guarded and oblique prose of the Misra Commission: "From the fact that so many *gurudwaras* and educational institutions had been damaged, it is reasonable to hold that the rioters not only had the Sikh populations as their targets but also kept an eye on their religious institutions."[36]

There was a definite pattern in the choice of victims. Both the Sikhs who were killed and their assailants were predominately males aged 20–50. However, in those areas where there was most arson and lynching, such as the resettlement colonies, women and children as well as old persons were also victimized or burned alive. Some women were raped. The documentation by Uma Chakravarty and Nandita Haksar in *The Delhi Riots: Three Days in the Life of a Nation,* based on detailed interviews with victims, leaves us in no doubt that although Sikh males were the first target in these areas, the brutalities and arson frequently became indiscriminate and knew no restraints (see figure 2).

A chartered accountant, a non-Sikh and a resident of New Friends' Colony, gave an eyewitness account, which the Citizens' Commission reports as follows: "The crowd was armed with lathis, crow-bars and iron rods.

Figure 2.   Arson committed during the anti-Sikh riots in Delhi in 1984.
Pramod Pushkarna (*India Today*).

Figure 3.   Property destruction during the anti-Sikh riots in Delhi in 1984. *India Today.*

They did not see any firearms, either with the crowd or with the beleaguered Sikhs. . . . In New Friends' Colony, they saw several Sikh-owned shops which had been set on fire. Intervening shops belonging to Hindus had not been touched. . . . Two trucks parked nearby were set on fire. The crowd then invaded the gurudwara opposite the shops. They ransacked the rooms in the gurudwara compound and set fire to the buildings" (see figure 3).[37]

Here is how another witness described the burning of the Sikh-owned Khalsa Middle School, situated in Sarojini Nagar (in this case the destruction worked against the interests of the Hindus themselves, since the majority of the students belonged to their own community):

> On the afternoon of 1 November, at about 3:30 or 4 P.M., a mob of about 250–300 men came to the school which has 525 pupils of whom 65% are non-Sikhs. The mob first set fire to the tents and the school desks. Thereafter, they demolished the boundary wall of the school. They then entered the building and broke open the steel cupboards and looted them. They stole the school typewriter, instruments belonging to the school band, utensils, etc. Two desks and seven steel cupboards were seen being taken away. They destroyed the library and scientific equipment in the laboratory. The school building was burnt as also the Headmaster's scooter.[38]

It may be suggested that, leaving aside the massive destruction of human life, the burning of homes, property, goods, and vehicles of all kinds is a double action that expresses as much the attacking mob's own sense of relative "deprivation" and inaccessibility to worldly goods as it does the mob's purposive reduction of the enemy's affluence and its demotion to a lower level.[39] The bonfires, the public destruction of property by fire, are a reversal of the paradigmatic potlatch of the Kwakiutl. In the potlatch, the possessors destroyed their accumulated surplus wealth in a public display of conspicuous waste in order to shame their competitors and enhance their status. In the communal riots, it is possessors who are despoiled by a mob that burns their possessions—and loots them as well—in order to level down and equalize poverty.

ORGANIZED VIOLENCE IN THE SETTLEMENT COLONIES

"The killings which were widespread, especially in the outlying colonies, were the result of the instigation of local political cadres who mobilized some political workers and criminal elements and hoodlums *from neighboring villages as well as from the neighborhood itself.* In some areas, especially the congested and poor, women were raped and molested" (emphasis added).[40] These observations have been confirmed by all the sources consulted, and direct our attention to the distinctive circumstances prevailing on Delhi's periphery, which may shed light on this extreme manifestation of violence.

The outlying settlements such as Trilokpuri, Mangolpuri, and Sultanpuri had a special relation to Congress (I). These settlements were initiated by the Congress (I) as part of its urban resettlement program. The resettlement program, begun in 1960, has progressively spawned more and more colonies, which dramatically proliferated in the Emergency period (June 1975–February 1977) in particular. By 1984, there were some forty colonies, with densely packed populations ranging from 30,000 to 300,000 in each. The inhabitants of these colonies were thus beholden to Congress (I) and were considered its strong support base and constituency, providing not only votes but also participants in political rallies. "There exists in such areas an established organizational network through which masses are mobilized for demonstration of Congress (I)'s ostensible support."[41] A veteran Delhi politician is reported as describing them as "the best kept women" (*rakhel*) of Congress (I). It is therefore in line with this setup that these settlers should willingly have lent their muscle (and at the same time indulged their greed for loot) when they were beckoned by the local political bosses to take punitive action against the Sikhs.

But there is also a tragic irony to this story of political patronage. Many of the Sikhs who had been given allotments in these settlement colonies had also been thankful to Congress (I), had been its supporters, and had voted for it. Hence the chagrin of these Sikhs that their local Congress (I) activists, block leaders (*pradhan*), and elected Congress officials should have directed the attacks on them. "Sufferers from Trilokpuri and Mangolpuri . . . whom we met looked dazed and uncomprehending when they said to us: 'We were allotted their houses here by Indiraji. We have always voted for her party. Why were we attacked?' "[42] The authors of *The Delhi Riots* record the pathos of the feelings of abandonment by the Congress (I) and its agencies of state expressed by the Sikhs of Trilokpur and Sultanpuri, who had served as traditional vote banks of the ruling party.

The story of Nanki Bai, who lost both her husband and fourteen members of her extended family, tells it all. Her husband ran a mat-making business in Kalyanapuri, which employed some workers. He was a good provider. Nanki Bai had led a sheltered life, and the family had saved money and jewelry as dowry for their daughter. Nanki Bai spoke obsessively of her husband, who was burnt alive. She felt guilty that he had died on an empty stomach. "He had not eaten anything because he was mourning Mrs. Gandhi's death."[43]

The family had shut themselves in a house. The crowd broke open the door, and struck down Nanki Bai's husband with a *lathi* (staff). Then "the rioters tore open a part of the ceiling and set the room on fire. When the people tried to escape they were stoned and pushed back into the burning room." As another victim said of people who were killed in similar fashion, they died "like goats in a slaughter house."[44] Nanki Bai reported that on November 2, she counted thirty-two bodies, which were removed in her presence by the police. The bodies were piled in a truck and taken away.

The politics and dynamics of riot behavior in the resettlement colonies cannot be fully comprehended without taking into account the populations of the villages at the periphery of the colonies. The participation of Jats and Gujjars from the so-called urban villages of Delhi substantially added to the numbers of rioters and contributed to the riots, murders, and looting. They were particularly dominant in West and South Delhi. Most of these villagers had once owned land in Ber Sarai, Munirka, and Mohammadpur, which had been taken away for the urban expansion of New Delhi. Their remaining land was generally unirrigated and of very poor quality. For this reason the villagers in these areas had to augment their resources through nonagricultural means, not the least of these being brigandage. Many invested in transport companies and brick-kilns, while others constructed houses on their remaining lands for the purpose of renting them. They thus controlled some economic resources and acquired political clout. It is a known fact that if one is to make any headway in an election in Delhi, the Gujjars and Jats of these areas have to be on one's side. Unfortunately, much of the police force stationed in this area and round about was drawn from these communities. For this reason, there had on various occasions been noticeable complicity in these areas between the criminals and the police. This truth was brought home starkly during the riots. The authors of *Who Are the Guilty?* note:

> As for the Scheduled Caste communities who were displaced due to the acquisition of land for urban expansion those from the Valmiki community utilized the benefits of the reservation policy and came into the city where they found jobs in the police, UPSC, etc. The Bangis went into the Corporation, while the third-major group, the Dhanaks, considered the lowest caste, are engaged in a variety of odd jobs. Among the Scheduled Caste communities living in the resettlement colonies, the Valmikis are predominately supporters of Jagivan Ram, while the Bhangis are solid supporters of Congress (I). Information gathered by us from the trouble spots in these areas suggests that the Bhangis—many of them working as sweepers in the corporation—comprised the bulk of the local miscreants who attacked the Sikhs.

It is this background and context that makes comprehensible this observation: "In some areas, like Trilokpuri, Mangolpuri and the trans-Jamuna colonies, the arsonists consisted of Gujjar or Jat farmers from neighboring villages, and were accompanied by local residents, some of whom, were Congress (I) activists. In these areas, we were told Congress (I) followers of the Bhangi caste (belonging to the scheduled caste community) took part in the looting."[45]

Events that took place in one settlement colony, Trilokpuri, reveal much about the perpetrators of the communal violence. This is a story of how certain influential politicians, with the police acting as their accessories, were able to mobilize mobs and enact a reign of terror for more than forty-eight hours, while immobilizing the forces of law and order. In this settlement, between October 31 and November 2, at least 400 Sikhs, mainly young men, were burnt alive, with the connivance of the local police and active participation of an organized group of miscreants led by a Congress (I) councilor (see figure 4). These brutalities were preceded by circulation of the kind of rumors described earlier about the diabolical doings of the Sikhs to celebrate Indira Gandhi's death.

> The beginning of the tragedy could be traced to the night of October 31 when reportedly the Congress (I) Councillor Ashok Kumar, a doctor who runs a clinic in Kalyanpuri, one kilometer from Trilokpuri, held a meeting at the latter place. The violence that broke out immediately following the meeting

Figure 4. Widows and children of Sikh men killed during the anti-Sikh riots in Delhi, 1984. Raghu Rai (*India Today*).

reached its climax next morning, when Gujjar farmers from the neighboring village of Chilla landed at Trilokpuri, and accompanied by a group of local inhabitants (described by the residents as Scheduled Caste people) raided Blocks 28, 32, 33 and 34 and systematically attacked Sikh houses, dragged out the young men, killed and burnt them and set the houses on fire. In some cases, the assailants hit the victims with iron rods on their heads before pouring kerosene on them.[46]

The authors of *Who Are the Guilty?* report that when they visited Trilokpuri on the morning of November 3, many of the survivors informed them that the local Congress (I) councilor, Dr. Ashok Kumar, had instigated the mob, which had a free run for two full days until the arrival of the troops. The police too were alleged to have behaved in line with the objectives of Dr. Kumar's onslaught. This same Congress politician and local bigwig was also the subject of bitter complaints by survivors interviewed by the authors of *The Delhi Riots*.

Nanki Bai described how Ashok Kumar directed his thugs, while keeping at a distance himself. He got the sweepers to do the dirty work. "He gave them *daru* (liquor). He had the killings done by the *kanjars* [a group of sweepers] and the *bhangis* [another group of sweepers]. The educated can't do this kind of thing—only the *neech-log* [low-caste people] do things like this. And all around us we've got them. . . . He [Ashok Kumar] stood on the *kotha* [roof of his house] and was watching from up there." When the Sikh women went to complain to him, he shouted, "Go! Go!" and ordered a *kanjar* called Tara, a mob leader, to bring sheets (*chadars*) and give them to them to use as shrouds. "Tara is with Ashok, they're all his *chamelias* [flunkeys]." "Some of the participants were shopkeepers who supplied kerosene to the arsonists. Some others among the neighbors of the victims were petty traders like milkmen, mechanics, or dealers in cement. The majority of the victims were poor Sikh-merchants, artisans, and daily wage laborers."[47]

The behavior of the police was remarkably lax and partial.

The sanctioned strength of the police on the Kalyanpuri police station, under which Trilokpuri falls[,] is 113, including one Inspector (who is the Station House Officer) and around 90 constables among others. The SHO reached Trilokpuri at about 2:30 P.M. on November 1 when the plunder and killings were taking place. The first thing he did was to remove the head constable and another constable from the spot, allowing the criminals to escape whatever little detection there was possible. It was a continuous spree of arson, rape, and murders after that. Later inquiries conducted by a senior police official revealed that at least four women, their ages ranging from 14 to 50 were gang raped. Later seven cases of rape from Trilokpuri were officially reported by the J. P. Narayan Hospital, Delhi.[48]

In spite of the mounting reports of carnage and burning of entire blocks of houses, the headquarters police grossly underrepresented the number of deaths and declared that Trilokpuri was peaceful, while it was being reduced to cinders and practically all its menfolk had been killed and the women and children were fleeing for their lives.

FACES IN THE CROWD

Although many neighbors and friends, both Hindu and Muslim, gave shelter, refuge, and protection to the beleaguered Sikhs to the extent that it was possible and safe for them to do so, there is ample evidence that colony residents in the shape of Congress (I) activists, block leaders (*pradhan*), and higher officials of the Congress (I) Party were involved. Local Congress offices were frequently the sites for mobs assembling, for burning bodies, and for launching raids. Representatives of Congress (I) mobilized their local clients and thugs, provided them with liquor, and directed vendors of kerosene, the sale of which is restricted to permit holders, to distribute it. They also provided information about the targets—Sikh houses, business establishment permit holders, schools, and gurudwaras. Along with Gujjars and Jats from the villages bordering the settlement colonies, who had their own scores to settle, local "low-caste" supporters of Congress (I), such as Bhangis and Chamars, appear to have been readily available to form such organized mobs.

Another set of participants, willing or forced, were bus drivers, such as those who worked for the Delhi Transportation Corporation (based in South Delhi). The evidence is solid that public vehicles were used to transport rioters from place to place. These mobile gangs, spreaders of rumors, shouters of slogans, instigators of violence among the public, acting as strike forces, were a critical element in the rapid sparking and spread of violence at key junctions of the city.

The evidence is firm, too, that in the settlement colonies some police officers, especially station house officers, and police constables, were implicated in the riots, their collusion extending from inaction to absence.

> In the resettlement colonies, the police . . . directly participated in the violence against the Sikhs. We were told by survivors that at the first signs of tension those who felt threatened personally went to the nearby police stations to seek their intervention. But the police did not respond. In Trilokpuri, the police reportedly accompanied the arsonists and provided them with diesel from their

jeeps. The Station House Officer (SHO) of Kalyanpuri police station under which Trilokpuri falls, withdrew the constables who were on duty there when Sikh girls were being raped. Much later, the higher authorities took action against the SHO and his two colleagues by suspending and arresting them for a criminal negligence of duties. In Sultanpuri, the SHO, one Bhatti, is alleged to have killed two Sikhs and helped the mob in disarming those Sikhs who tried to resist the mob.[49]

Who Are the Guilty? lists the occupations of some of those identified by informants as participants in the rioting, arson, and murder in the settlement colonies. Most were ordinary gainfully employed citizens, who constitute the majority of the local populace: a shopkeeper; a railway worker; a tailor; a mason; a dealer in cement; a TV shop owner; a video shop owner; a teashop owner; a furniture dealer; a Congress (I) pradhan; a Congress (I) worker; a meat shop owner; a dairy owner; a shoemaker; a grocery shop owner; a cloth and *chappal* (footwear) seller; a liquor seller; a sweeper; a rickshaw repairer; a milkman; a teacher; a cloth and tailoring shop owner; a landowner and *goala* (milkman); an auto-rickshaw driver; a kerosene seller; a property dealer; a carpenter; a mechanic; a vegetable seller; the owner of godown; a flour mill owner; a paper seller; a barber; the owner of three-star hotel; a *dhoby* (washerman); an opium dealer; a local *goonda* (thug).

Lower-echelon Congress (I) workers, kerosene sellers, sweepers (low caste), and shopkeepers are the types that occur several times. All told, the riot participants, the vast majority of them Hindus, were a cross-section of the inhabitants one might expect to find in a settlement on the periphery of one of India's large cities.

THE ROLE OF CONGRESS

The parts played in the 1984 Delhi pogrom against the Sikhs by lower-echelon Congress Party (I) activists, pradhans, and supporters, and in one case by a higher-level politician, Dr. Ashok Kumar, who orchestrated the Trilokpuri horrors, have already been described. Kumar was by no means a maverick or an exception. There is evidence of the involvement of some members of the upper echelons of the Congress Party, including members of Parliament, members of the Delhi Metropolitan Council, and members of the Metropolitan Corporation. The *Report on the Citizens' Commission* asserts:

> Many who came forward to relate their experiences and provide eye-witness accounts to the Commission, have specifically and repeatedly named certain political leaders belonging to the ruling party. These included several MPs in

the outgoing Parliament, members of the Delhi Metropolitan Council and members of the Municipal Corporation. Scores of political functionaries in local areas or blocks and area *pradhans* were also named. They have been accused of having instigated the violence, making arrangements for the supply of kerosene and other inflammable material and of identifying the houses of Sikhs. Some of them have also been accused of interceding with the authorities to obtain the release of their followers who had been arrested for various crimes.[50]

The authors of *Who Are the Guilty?* report the following evidence given by the residents of the settlement colonies whom they interviewed:

We were told both by Hindus and Sikhs—many among the latter were Congress (I) supporters—that certain Congress (I) leaders played a decisive role in organizing the riots. Residents of Mangolpuri told us they saw Mr. Ishwar Singh, a Congress (I) Corporator among many others [whom the text mentions in an annex] actively participating in the orgy of violence. All these people were described by the local residents as lieutenants of the Congress (I) MP from the area—Sajjan Kumar. Similarly in Anand Parbat, Congress (I) councilors like Bhairava, Mahendra and Manget Ram, considered to be loyal followers of the Congress (I) MP, Mr. Dharamdas Shastri, were named as the main culprits. In Prakash Nagar, Congress (I) people were found carrying voters lists to identify Sikh households. In the Gabdhinagar area again, a local Congress (I) councillor, Sukhanlal, was identified by the victims as the main leader of the assailants. Escapees from the area who we met at the Shakarpur relief camp on November 6 blamed their Congress (I) MP Mr. H. K. L. Bhagat for having masterminded the riots.[51] On November 1, Satbir Singh (Jat), a Youth Congress (I) leader, brought buses filled with people from Ber Sarai to Sri Guru Harikshan Public School at Munirka and burnt the school building and buses, and continued looting and assaults on Sikhs the whole night. Another group of miscreants led by Jagdish Tokas, a Congress (I) corporator, joined the above group in looting and assaults. In the Safdarjung–Kidwai Nagar area of South Delhi, eye witness accounts by those who stood in front of All India Medical Institute from where Mrs. Gandhi's body was taken out in procession on the evening of October 31, confirmed the presence of the Congress (I) Councillor of the area, Arjan Dass, at the time when the attacks on Sikh pedestrians, bus drivers, and conductors began.

The allegations against these individuals repeatedly voiced by the residents of the respective localities which we visited, cannot be dismissed as politically motivated propaganda, since many among the Sikhs who accused them of complicity in the riots, had been traditionally Congress (I) voters.[52]

The official Misra Commission's indictment of "anti-social" and "criminal" elements as the main perpetrators of the riots and assessment of the role of the ruling Congress Party (I) have to be evaluated in the light of this kind of evidence. The Misra Commission report is a rich document to deconstruct on this issue of culpability because at different points, it implicates different agents, while inadvertently disclosing its own preferences. Perhaps out of a sense of loyalty, it seeks not only to absolve higher-level members of the Congress Party but also to attribute an unconvincing "split personality" to those lower echelons of the party who joined ranks with the "anti-socials." The report takes care to absolve the party as an institution and distinguish it from its low-level members.

On the question of whether the riots showed "organized violence," the Misra Commission report is unambiguous: "It would not be wrong to say that there was organized violence at Delhi, and that it was done by the anti-social elements, and [that] in the riots, thousands of people who do not really belong to the classification of anti-socials did participate. Many of these participants were people from the lower ranks of the Congress (I) party and sympathizers." The commission was careful to specify that it could not "draw a conclusion inferentially from the fact of participation of party workers and sympathizers or some leaders at local levels that the Party was involved in organizing what has been rightly called a carnage."[53] Having examined the relevant affidavits and cross-examined the accusing deponents, the commission concluded: "All the material on the record in the ultimate analysis is not evidence of that type relying on which the Commission can record a finding that the Congress (I) Party or some leaders in that party had organized the violence which manifests in the shape of the riots." The report points out that the "Congress (I) Party denounced the riots by regular resolutions adopted at official meetings of the party" and that it had urged that "the unity of India must not only be preserved and strengthened through tolerance and communal harmony but also good neighborly relations."[54]

The report then advances this extenuating argument: "If the Congress (I) Party or some of its highly placed leaders had set the rioters to operate, one would expect the Sikhs with Congress base and affinity to have escaped the depredation." (This plea seems to be of dubious value, because in the Sri Lanka riots of 1983, the mobs destroyed the businesses and industrial properties and homes of Tamils in Colombo who were clearly well-known patrons of the UNP and had access to high-level UNP politicians. In fact, under the stress of the riots, the whole community of Tamils was the undifferentiated target, although some possible victims were saved by the protection money they had paid.)

The Misra Commission's report resorts to tendentious sophistry when it comes to explain the motivations of the lower-level politicians and agents of the Congress Party. Admitting that it received plentiful written evidence alleging that persons associated with the Congress (I)—such as workers, local leaders, and numbers of the youth wing—had been named as organizers of riot violence, the report is not only concerned once again to exonerate the party, but also resorts to the maneuver of splitting the party from the individuals belonging to it, and of differentiating between the "public" and "personal" involvements of the accused: "These details supplied by DSGMC [the Delhi Sikh Gurudwara Management Committee] fortify the conclusion that some of the Congress (I) party on their own had indulged and participated in the turmoil for considerations entirely their own." Not everyone who takes a dip in the Ganges is purified. Similarly, not everyone in Congress (I) is a Mahatma Gandhi. "The party label . . . [does not] take away the individual element."

The report, in this respect following conventional stereotyped allegations, repeatedly resorts to condemnation of so-called anti-socials, out for loot and impervious to the national tragedy, as the main culprits. "The mob was jubilating and dancing," it observes. "There was no sign of sorrow and grief on their faces. There were no mourners of the Prime Minister." It then gives this explanation for the crowd's euphoric and boisterous behavior: "Anti-social gangsters obviously had no mourning to observe. The troubled atmosphere provided them with the opportunity to plunder and otherwise satisfy their animal desires and, therefore, the conduct exhibited . . . shows that the constituents of the mobs were the anti-social ruffians and usually not the people of Smt. Gandhi's camp or party who ordinarily were likely to exhibit mournful conduct."[55]

At one point, the report forgets the evidence the Misra Commission had collected, charging that: "The change in the pattern from the spontaneous reaction to organized riots was the outcome of the take-over of the situation by the anti-social elements."[56] Such blanket denunciations miss the significance of the fact that a good cross-section of the ordinary population of Delhi participated; the report also does not know how to interpret the crowd euphoria, a problem that will be tackled later.

THE CONDUCT OF THE POLICE

The Misra Commission did not flinch from taking to task the Delhi Police Force for its poor communication, tardiness in acting, and at times active connivance. "There is abundant evidence before the Commission that the police on the whole did not behave properly and failed to act as a professional force," the report notes.[57]

The metropolitan city of Delhi is administered by the Home Ministry of the central government. The lieutenant governor is the chief administrator and the police commissioner and police force are under his control. (There seems to be a sort of dyarchy, in that the home secretary of the Delhi administration appointed by the Home Ministry also shares in the administration of the city.) The strength of the police force in Delhi at the time of the riots was 22,000 constables, 3,000 head constables, 1,400 inspectors and sub-inspectors, and some 242 higher officers, culminating in the police commissioner.

While it is widely recognized that the police force as a whole was inadequate in size to service the needs of a densely populated and growing city, it was not so thinly distributed that it could not have acted more positively than it did. The city was divided into five police districts, and it had sixty-three police stations and twenty-five police posts. The population of Delhi was roughly 6.5 million, and there was one policeman to roughly two hundred people.

The Misra Commission records that the lieutenant governor of Delhi, the chief administrator of the city, testified: "I am inclined to agree that there was a failure in the channel of communication between the local officers and the police and the district administration as also [at the] Commissioner's level."[58] It is noteworthy that the lieutenant governor during the riots, Shri Gavai, was chided by Rajiv Gandhi for not acting "more swiftly in calling the army," and was thereafter removed from that position. Shri Gavai's answer was that a large number of members of the public who were bystanders would have been shot by the army as curfew breakers, and that this was politically unwise.[59]

Although apparently clear instructions had been given by the higher police authorities to those below, who were manning the police posts, with regard to the necessity of patrolling, inactivity and stonewalling were widespread among those so instructed. When contacted by telephone by the besieged Sikhs, police stations did not respond. "The behavior of most policemen was [so] shabby that they allowed people to be killed, houses to be burnt, property to be looted, ladies to be dragged and misbehaved [with] within their very presence. Their plea was that they were few and could not meet the unruly armed mob [consisting] usually of hundreds or thousands."[60]

Two major charges against the police were substantiated, despite the Delhi administration's stubborn attempt to defend police conduct and paper over its shortcomings. The first was the poor communication from the lower levels of the force on the ground to their superior officers, situated in allegedly nodal information-receiving and order-transmitting offices. The police commissioner, Tandon, told the Misra Commission that there had been a failure on the part of the lower echelons of the force at local police stations to report the mob destruction and killing to their five district police control rooms, let alone to higher levels. Other superior officers made the same charge. One of the worst areas of arson, looting, and slaughter was Kalyanpuri (of which Trilokpuri is a section), twelve kilometers from police headquarters. On the night of November 1, more that two hundred people died there. But the additional commissioner of police for the area (there are six such officers immediately below the police commissioner) claimed that he did not hear about this massacre until sixteen to eighteen hours afterwards (that is, 7:00 P.M. on November 2).

Such poor information, usually underestimating and underreporting the extent of the disorder and destruction, was only reluctantly passed up to the highest levels, with grievous consequences. In due course, the commissioner of police reported to the lieutenant governor of Delhi that only 20 to 30 deaths had taken place in Trilokpuri, and only 30 to 40 in Palam Colony, when the actual numbers were more like 260 and 300, respectively. Behind this story of tardy misreporting lurk these structuring forces: the hierarchy of social distance and powers that separates constables from officers; the fear of underlings reporting bad news that might reflect their inefficiency; and the bonds of sympathy that must have existed between the lower ranks of the police and their civilian public.

The second major substantiated charge against the Delhi police involved instances of police collusion with the rioters, by acts both of omission and commission. In addition to the condemnations in the Misra Commission Report already cited, one further charge was that the police systematically attempted to take away licensed firearms from Sikhs, while not similarly disarming Hindus. The weaker minority group was thus exposed to the full armed strength of the rioters (see figure 5).[61]

The report also lists these allegations, which it did not attempt to contradict: that police stood by and did not clear the way when mobs blocked fire engines; that police in uniform marched behind or mingled with the hostile crowds; and, worse still, that the police method of recovering looted materials was to invite the culprits to pile up their loot and leave, a procedure that not only exonerated looters who voluntarily surrendered goods but also caused a great mix-up of property, as well as further stealing from the standing piles. The farce of allowing recovered stolen property to be stolen again was only bettered by one last charge—that in some instances uniformed policemen participated in the looting.

The police at higher levels did not participate in the riots, the report concluded, and cited instances of heroic and courageous actions by officers in

Figure 5. Police chasing a Sikh truck driver accused of driving his vehicle into a crowd and killing some people at the Bangla Sahib Gurudwara in Delhi during the 1984 riots. Bhavan Singh (*India Today*).

rescuing Sikhs or helping them to escape. But it summarily dismissed the defensive pleas of the police authorities and the Delhi administration that the extant legislation (such as the Delhi Police Act of 1978, which incorporated older and outdated provisions contained in the Punjab Police Rules of 1934) was inadequate to deal with major disorders. It remarked that the so-called "spontaneous national outburst" after Indira Gandhi's death had not manifested itself in most parts of India, and that the Delhi police force of some 30,000, although insufficient, was not totally inadequate to deal with the riots. Furthermore, since such riots had taken place before, the plea of surprise and unpreparedness could not be invoked: "By October 1984 riots had become too frequent in India, and under the excuse or cover of every possible plea based upon economic, religious, political, and social issues, society was being victimized by riots. . . . Delhi and neighboring places had seen riots on more than one occasion."[62]

The higher levels and superior officers of the Delhi police force were not taken off the hook altogether. The Misra Commission recommended that the conduct of delinquent police officers should be officially investigated by the Delhi administration and the police force. It also wryly recalled that the Marwah inquiry, launched by the Delhi administration to identify incidents of severe failure to act and negligence by police officers, had been derailed by officers of the highest rank (a couple of deputy and additional commissioners of police) who were in charge of South and East Delhi.

Allegations had been made by various parties that buses belonging to the Delhi Transportation Corporation were seen transporting armed mobs, especially during the first two days of the riots.

The DTC is a large organization. In 1984, it had about thirty depots for buses, distributed all over the city; its Central Communication Centre was located close to Pragati Maidan. In addition to the thousands of buses it owns, the DTC also uses private buses whenever the need arises.

On November 1, when the greatest amount of destruction and violence took place, most DTC buses were plying the usual routes. By November 2, it seems, once the news of bus takeovers and diversions had become known, the DTC's buses were taken out of service. The verdict of the Misra Commission speaks for itself:

> Though the Corporation does not admit use of its buses for movement of rioters, the Commission is prepared to accept the material collected by the Investigating Agency and its conclusion that the route buses were forcibly diverted by the mobs to facilitate their movements and when the drivers found any opportunity to escape, they returned to the depot. There is no material to hold that the Corporation had extended any assistance to the rioters by allowing its buses to transport the rioters.[63]

THE TALE OF THE AFFIDAVITS

Appendix 3 of the Report of the Misra Commission is labeled "Classification of Affidavits Received in Delhi." Printed without comment, it invites commentary and some speculation. Table 2 shows the number of affidavits filed by Sikhs on behalf of Sikh victims and by non-Sikhs against Sikhs for selected areas, according to the police station/area of the city in which these affidavits originated, as well as the number of people alleged to have been killed. Some fascinating features emerge when these affidavits are scrutinized.

We should remember that the Sikh population of Delhi (as estimated by the Misra Commission) was only 393,921, or 6.33 percent of a total population in the Union Territory of Delhi of some 6,215,406 (with 5,763,200 classified as urban and 452,206 as rural). The question arises of what relation we might expect between this demographic distribution and the number of affidavits presented by *both* sides to defend and rebut each other's charges.

Table 2   Affidavits Filed in Connection with the 1984 Riots,
Selected Areas of Delhi

Police Station/Area	By Sikhs*	By non-Sikhs, against Sikhs	Total Affidavits	Number of people killed
Ashok Vihar Nimri Colony	9	38	47	1
Mangolpuri (Rohuri Complex)	29	81	110	60
Sultanpuri	33	66	99	108
Jahangiripuri	13	37	50	26
Ganathinagar	11	189	200	9
Nand Nagri	20	5	25	441
Kalyanpuri	68	144	212	196
Shakarpur	29	299	328	57
Krishna Nagar	20	242	262	22
Karol Bagh	19	50	69	—
Pahar Ganj	1	64	65	1
Delhi Cantonment Sagar Puri; Palam	49	48	97	149

SOURCE: Based on information in *Report of Justice Ranganath Misra Commission of Inquiry* (New Delhi: S.N., 1986), appendix 3.
    Sixty-nine police station/areas are enumerated by the report, from which the above areas were selected. A total of 2,894 affidavits were received, of which 628 were submitted by Sikhs on behalf of victims and 2,266 by non-Sikhs against the riot victims. The total number of people killed was 2,894.

    *On behalf of Sikh riot victims, alleging killing, arson, shooting, etc.

Another fact to bear in mind is that the Misra Commission was autho-rized to be constituted in late April 1985, some five months after the riots had occurred. Its hearings, which actually began later, were not concluded with regard to Delhi for another year. The affidavits show that even after a time lag of this length, both Sikhs and non-Sikhs, victims and aggressors, were still disputing as to what had happened in the 1984 riots. The antago-nisms had obviously not withered away.

    In those areas of Delhi where the Sikhs had suffered most in terms of killing, arson, and looting—areas such as Mangolpuri, Sultanpuri, Kalyan-puri, and Shakarpur—the number of affidavits filed by non-Sikhs *against* Sikhs, contesting their charges and making countercharges, was larger by a proportion of three or four to one than the number of affidavits filed by the Sikhs against the aggressors. Delhi Cantonment, a disaster area, where the numbers of affidavits filed by both sides were roughly equal, is an exception.

In some areas, such as Ganathinagar and Pahar Ganj, which I take to be overwhelmingly non-Sikh, a great number of affidavits were filed *against* Sikhs, while only a very few were filed by Sikhs. Moreover, there were hardly any instances of killings and arson in these areas. This suggests a determination on the part of non-Sikhs, through organizational representations, to resist being cast as culpable aggressors, to reduce the blame attachable to them, and, indeed, to turn the tables and even represent the victims as the aggressors. It is disturbing to think that dominant majorities can carry on such campaigns of vilification against vulnerable minorities and seek to erase the record and deny the nature of their collective violence.

CONCLUDING COMMENTS

Even when the suddenness and the emotional trauma of Indira Gandhi's assassination are taken into account, the evidence is clear that at least from November 1 on, the destructive actions of the mobs at various points in the metropolis of Delhi, and especially in its settlement colonies on the periphery, were encouraged, directed, and even provisioned by Congress (I) politicians, activists, and supporters, and indirectly aided by an inactive, co-operative police force.

The distinguished political scientist Rajni Kothari, who was on the spot during the riots, maintains that there was a "large measure of advance planning and rehearsing," and that "soon after Operation Blue Star and the extremist response thereto in parts of Punjab, a plan of identifying Sikh targets ranging from households to commercial establishments to Gurudwaras had been undertaken, including the planning of logistics and the techniques to be employed. Both a psychology and a technology of 're-venge' had thus been blue-printed before the assassination provided the moment to carry it out." To substantiate this charge, Kothari points to evidence of an organized system for distributing kerosene, gasoline, and combustible chemical powders to all parts of the city with which to burn bodies and set ablaze trucks and buildings. "There was evidence of men on scooters locating the places followed by mobs who carried out the killings and the arson, in many areas supervised by higher-ups moving in Ambassador cars from one place to another. . . . The synchronization of logistics and the striking similarity of technique" points to a large measure "of advance planning and rehearsing."[64]

Kothari was admittedly an outspoken critic of the Indira Gandhi regime. Much in what he says is reminiscent, however, of the 1983 riots in Colombo, about which evidence has been steadily mounting of prior collection of vital information, organizing of gangs, and so on, pointing to governmental involvement. In Delhi, the police either absented themselves from scenes of violence, passively looked on, or even directly participated; moreover, they handled the rioters whom they arrested leniently and connived in their early release. One writer has alleged that most of the lower cadres of the Delhi police were "drawn from Haryana Jats who have all along been anti-Sikh."[65]

In South Delhi, DTC buses were used by mobs to move from place to place igniting acts of violence; the participation of bus drivers and the use of government vehicles are prima facie evidence of either administrative assent or inability to take preventative action.

Finally, the official media transmitted inflammatory information and news, thereby adding to the heightening of collective passions that demanded "blood for blood."

Who Are the Guilty? points an accusatory finger at the highest officers responsible for the administration of Delhi, such as the home minister and the lieutenant governor, for foot-dragging in regard to calling in the army, for propagating inaccurate information concerning casualties, for claiming the situation to be under control prematurely, and for delayed action in regard to relief measures. "The Congress (I) High Command's reluctance to probe into the allegations against their own councilors and other leaders further lends credence to the suspicions voiced above. Even Prime Minister Rajiv Gandhi seems to dismiss the serious charges being levelled against his party men."[66] In any case, there seems to have been little coordination between the Delhi administration, the police, and the army. "Surprisingly, there was no central control point. The Administration functioned from Old Delhi, the police from Indraprastha Estate and the army from the Cantonment."[67]

Since Indira Gandhi's death raised the problem of succession and the necessity of going to the polls soon afterwards, the "managers" of the state, the technocrats, and the ruling party's politicians seem to have exploited the assassination and the ensuing conditions by directing and staging organized violence against the Sikhs, thereby ensuring a Hindu vote in their favor. "Hindu ekta Zindabad" (Long Live Hindu Unity), "Khoon ka badla khoon" (Blood for blood) and "Hindu-Hindu bhai bhai" (the brotherhood of Hindus) were potent slogans.

In the ensuing elections, Rajiv Gandhi was elected in a landslide vote to succeed his slain mother. In July 1985, he signed an accord with one of the

Akali Dal leaders, Harchand Singh Longowal. But by August, Longowal had fallen to the bullets aimed by Sikh "extremists" at Sherpur gurudwara, near Sangur in Punjab. The accord promised the transfer of Chandigarh to Punjab, with a corresponding transfer of certain areas—Fasilka and Abo-har—to Haryana.

In the Punjab assembly elections in September 1985, the Akali Dal-L, headed by Surjit Singh Barnala, was handsomely elected to power, but there was no progress toward implementation of the terms of the accord. The Akali Dal itself was riven by factionalism, and groups opposed to the ruling section formed their own Unified Akali Dal. The continuing strife and violence gave reason for president's rule to be imposed on Punjab once more in May 1987.

BHINDRANWALE'S FUNDAMENTALISM AND MILITANCY: RELIGION, POLITICS, AND VIOLENCE

To what extent is the Sikh religion as such integral to the Sikh politics reviewed above, and a contributor to the "ethnic conflict" between Sikhs and others, whether these be Hindus, non-Sikh Punjabis, Congress politicians, or the Indian government?

Before going any further, it is important to specify that there have been and are Sikhs who do not think religion and politics should mix (the "secularists," by one Indian definition associated with Nehru), or who have not participated in separatist politics. What I have to say therefore can apply only to those who have been close adherents of the Akali Dal movement, and of fundamentalist movements such as the one led by Jarnail Singh Bhindranwale.

It should be evident that the makeup and course of Sikh history enacted by those identified earlier as the primary actors in recent times demonstrates (in the same way my writings on Sri Lankan Buddhism have maintained) that it is not possible or meaningful to disentangle or differentiate a domain of exclusively "religious" concerns from the political, social, and economic concerns of the Sikh community and the preoccupations of individual Sikhs with issues of identity and self-respect.

Bhindranwale's movement, informed by his distinctive brand of religious fundamentalism and militant politics, might be an instructive phenomenon to scrutinize as an example of the entwining of religion and politics to form a total complex. Such scrutiny also sheds light on the efficacy and moral accountability of collective violence inspired by radical concerns as a mode of political action and political discourse.

Bhindranwale's fundamentalism fused religious and political concerns and aspirations on behalf of the Sikh community, whose identity and destiny were taken to be inseparably linked with its commitment to the Sikh faith and its practices.[68] Harjot Oberoi has recently made the significant observation that the Punjabi word *mulvad* is a linguistic equivalent of "fundamentalism," and that "Sikh journalists, essayists, and politicians, in discussing contemporary religious and political movements, now constantly use the term mulvad, connoting a polity and society organized on the basis of religious (particularly scriptural) authority."[69]

Before describing Bhindranwale's movement, let me specify what I see as some of the main ingredients of "religious fundamentalism" in the modern context. They are (1) a selective emphasis on and a univocal exegesis of certain precepts tendentiously taken from a canonical corpus that is usually more complex, more multivalent, less bounded, and less narrow than the fundamentalists' reading of it; (2) an exclusionary, separatist, and antagonistic attitude, rather than a coalescing and tolerant stance, toward other sects and traditions within the same religion, let alone other religions; and (3) the advocacy of a set of practices and a program of objectives that fuse the congregation's religious concerns of faith and salvation with its sociopolitical existence and interests as a "nationality" or "ethnic group." These concerns and objectives also imperatively demand separation from and vigilance against other such religiopolitical communities, which are seen as threatening the purity of customs and endangering the well-being of the community in question. In the contemporary context, there is also a strong rejection of, and antagonism toward, the corrosive and deracinating influences of "modernization" and "modernity," which are seen as accompaniments of Western industrialism and imperialism and global capitalism. Consumerist values, changes in clothing and hair styles, and in forms of recreation, ranging from the cinema to dance halls, smoking, and drinking to easy interaction between the sexes—these are taken to be the visible behavioral indices and traces of a deeper malaise. This rejection of modern consumerism is usually coupled with an attack on the urbanized middle classes, who have been most influenced by Western ideas, technology and "secularist" attitudes, and, simultaneously, with an espousal of the cause of the poor and the oppressed.

Fundamentalist movements that envision a new society on earth become focused on charismatic leaders who embody and preach the message of revival and reform, and who advocate commitment to struggle and martyrdom in order to strive for the ideal order. A rhetoric of uncompromising struggle for this pristine order is deployed.

Mark Juergensmeyer has culled extracts from Bhindranwale's speeches and sermons that eloquently convey his orientation to the world as inspired by his distinctive commitment to the Sikh religion. When the press and other critics accused him of being an extremist, Bhindranwale explained what sort of extremist he was: "One who takes the vows of faith and helps others take it; who reads the scripture and helps others do the same; who avoids liquor and drugs and helps others do likewise . . . ; who says, 'respect your scriptures, unite under the flag, stoutly support the community, and be attached to your Lord's throne and home.'" External enemies posed an ever-present danger: "In order to destroy religion, on all sides and in many forms mean tactics have been initiated." Sikhs must defend the faith: "Young men: with folded hands, I beseech you. . . . Until we enter our home, until we have swords on us, [the *kaccha*—warrior's knee-length drawers] on our bodies, Guru's word on our tongues, and the double-edged sword in our hands, we shall get beatings." Fully conscious of the fact that the Sikh religious tradition applauds nonviolence and forbids the taking of human life, except in certain extreme circumstances, when social or spiritual justice is at stake, Bhindranwale asserted: "For a Sikh it is a great sin to keep weapons and kill anyone . . . [but] it is an even greater sin to have weapons and not seek justice." There could be "no deliverance without weapons" being used, he said: "It is a sin for a Sikh to keep weapons to hurt an innocent person, to rob anyone's home, to dishonour anyone or to oppress anyone. But there is no greater sin for a Sikh than keeping weapons and not using them to protect the faith."

Bhindranwale's sermons powerfully moved his followers because he simultaneously inspired and aroused guilt and tension and the urge to act at two levels—at the level of the interior lives of individuals who had betrayed norms or become lax about religious practices, and at the level of the Sikh collectivity, which had let itself be "enslaved" by the Hindu majority, by the Delhi politicians (although he did not spell out in detail the nature of this slavery). The renovation of the self was indissolubly linked to the redemption of the community. Reminding his audience that a great Sikh martyr had said, "Even if I have to give my head may I never lose my love for the Sikh faith," Bhindranwale railed against Sikh officials and modernized youth: "I am sorry to note that many people who hanker after a government position say instead, 'even if I lose my faith, may I never lose my position.' And our younger generation has started saying this: 'even if I lose my faith, may a beard never grow on my face' . . . If you find the beard too heavy, pray to God saying . . . 'we do not like this Sikhism and manhood. Have mercy on us. Make us into women.'"[70]

In underscoring the special and separate identity of the Sikhs, proclaiming the inseparability of politics from religion, and envisaging a separate state for the Sikhs alone, Bhindranwale espoused causes that had also been voiced by many Akali Dal leaders, and before them by the Tat Khalsa and Singh Sabha advocates of the late nineteenth century. His distinctiveness and the powerful impact he had on his followers, especially the insecurely placed youth, who saw the doors of establishment closed against them, had to do with the manner in which he revived certain militant traditions associated with the sixth guru, Hargobind (1595–1644), and the tenth guru, Gobind Singh (1666–1708), and made them the vehicle of internal religiosity, personal identity, and collective Sikh destiny. In 1699, Guru Gobind Singh had instituted the Khalsa (the purified or the chosen) as the order of baptized Sikhs; they were to call themselves Singh (lion) and wear the five "k's"—kés (unshorn hair), kangha (wooden comb), kada (steel bracelet), kaccha (knee-length drawers worn by warriors), and kirpan (sword). These physical markers of separation from Hindu and Muslim and the badges of a brotherhood of right practices would have a remarkable imprinting role in Bhindranwale's campaign to purify the Sikhs and to enable them to regain faith.

As T. N. Madan puts it: "The religious beliefs that were singled out by Bhindranwale above all others were, first, the inseparability of religion and the state on politics, tracing this teaching to the sixth guru, Hargobind, and second, the indivisible or corporate character of the Sikh, deriving it from the praxis of the tenth guru, Gobind."[71] These elements selectively emphasized militancy as righteous action, and comprised a narrow part of the Sikh religious doctrine, whose first five guru propounders never handled arms. But the elements chosen were reminders of a time in the past when Sikhs had been besieged, and they were seen now as necessary instruments for them to preserve and protect their boundaries in the present time of similar danger.

Bhindranwale seems to have both enlivened and energized the charged imagery of the two swords and more deeply inscribed it on the very bodies of his followers. Tradition has it that the sixth preceptor, Guru Hargobind, who challenged the hegemony of the Mughal state, "broke with the convention that the guru should concern himself solely with spiritual pursuits. He tied round his waist two swords, one to symbolize miri (politics) and the other piri (spirituality)."[72]

The doctrine of miri-piri pronounces "the indivisibility of religious and political power, and of the spiritual and the temporal" and gives "legitimacy to the political organizer from within Darbar Sahib" (the Golden

Temple). "*Miri piri* is indeed so fundamental that it receives material concretization in the *nishan*, or Sikh emblem, in which the double-edged sword representing the purity of faith is shielded by two protecting *kirpans* (swords)."[73] This emblem has in time incorporated other additional values.

"Sikhs often interpret the two edges of the sword as symbolizing spiritual and worldly foes, and they say that the battle sword (*kirpan*) . . . that Sikhs are supposed to wear at all times symbolizes an awareness of these same enemies."[74] It is noteworthy that at the last stages of his career, Bhindranwale wore two swords in the manner of Guru Hargobind, thereby metonymically indexing the emblem to his body, and perhaps even iconically imaging it. The concept of miri-piri similarly justifies Sikh support for an independent political party,[75] and ultimately also the goal of Khalistan as a separate religiopolitical sovereignty.

There are two additional components of the Bhindranwale message that so compellingly attracted his following from 1978 to 1984, which, although composed of a variety of persons of different economic, cultural, and political backgrounds, was predominantly drawn from those who were, as Oberoi puts it, "at the bottom of the social ladder." One component was the exciting promise of a Khalistan that would eradicate social inequalities, disallow the exploitation of the weak, especially those living in "the backward village community," erase "segregation of humanity, based upon caste, jati [subcaste], birth, locality and colour," and forbid "cruel and distasteful practices" prevailing between Sikh males and females. These were some of the objectives proclaimed by the Panthic Committee that announced the formation of the Sikh homeland of Khalistan on January 26, 1986. In the 1980s and early 1990s, other fundamentalist organizations, such as the Damdani Taksal, which was at this time led by Bhindranwale, made similar critiques of inequalities in the distribution of wealth and resources. At one public meeting in 1986, jointly sponsored by the Damdani Taksal and the All-India Students Federation, the collective resolution passed by the assembly enthusiastically asserted the need to break "the chains of slavery" that shackled the Sikhs, namely, internal social inequality, exploitation whereby the produce of the poor was sold at low prices, while the goods they bought were high-priced, and domination by the external Hindu majority, which inferiorized them.[76]

The goal of an egalitarian brotherhood of Sikhs was coupled with a millenarian vision. Oberoi states that "for much of their history, at least since the rise of the Khalsa, Sikhs have opted to deal with major social crises—state oppression, economic upheavals, colonialism, collapse of semiotic categories—by invoking the millenarian paradigm," and that central to this propensity has been "a prophetic figure of extraordinary charisma with the will to establish an alternative social system in which oppression would cease and people would lead a life of harmony, purity, and good deeds. Bhindranwale was heir to his cultural tradition."[77]

Bhindranwale knew little about economics or parliamentary politics, but he phrased the complex problems faced by Sikhs in terms of a crisis resulting from "the religious depravity now prevailing among the Sikhs and the ever-increasing Hindu domination over the Sikhs," and called on the faithful to participate in the *dharma yuddha* (righteous battle, holy war) in which good was pitted against evil and only one side could be victorious. This apocalyptic vision—a final solution that was a leap into an unrealistic transcendental future—was apparently voiced in an eighteenth-century millenarian quatrain that asserted: "The army of the Guru will sit on the throne of Delhi. . . . The Khalsa will rule, their enemies will be vanquished." Bhindranwale echoed this vision of future deliverance—an unrealistic fantasy for a minority that constituted only 2 percent of India's population—in his sermons.

Bhindranwale's admonitions, accusations, and urgings combine a beleaguered sense of Sikh vulnerability, and a corresponding need for vigilance, with an empowering activist sense of martial and spiritual conquest as the road to salvation. Other gurus of the past championing Sikh objectives had been slaughtered by the Moghuls. The glory of Ranjit Singh's empire had been brief. There is a disquieting theme that woefully reveals itself as one follows the path of Bhindranwale's cause. Bhindranwale senses that he will be a martyr. While his martyr's cause is couched in the compelling language of an ultimate struggle against an imperfect world, it is also driven by the rhetoric and the actions of a beleaguered and trapped animal, whose resort to desperate armed violence has turned him into an irredeemable criminal, guilty with his followers of arbitrarily, impulsively, and vengefully killing many Sikhs and Hindus. The dharma yuddha had turned into a demonic bloodbath, in which hero and villain could not be differentiated. If this was the dissolution of a *yuga*, where were the signs of a regenerative new world cycle?

The Golden Temple of Amritsar, so named after its gold-plated dome, had in time become a complex with a dual ordering. The Golden Temple itself, standing in the middle of a sacred tank, was originally built around 1606, by Guru Arjan and his followers. It is a place for congregational praying and for listening to readings from the Sikh holy book, the sole object of worship in a religion opposed to idolatry. Arjan's son and successor, Guru

Hargobind (1595–1644) built a second temple, the Akal Takht (the throne of the immortal God) facing the Golden Temple and standing outside the sacred tank and made it his political headquarters for challenging Mughal power.[78] The Akal Takht houses the traditional weapons associated with the sixth and tenth gurus. Inside the Akal Takht, "instead of chanting hymns of peace, the congregation heard ballads extolling feats of heroism, and instead of listening to religious discourses, discussed plans of military conquests."[79] The rituals and recitations of the two temples thus enact the two strands of the Sikh heritage, which are continuously reenacted in worship and enduringly shaped in stone and space.

Bhindranwale and his followers, armed to the teeth, occupied the Akal Takht, the repository and reminder of Sikh martial deeds. They turned it into a fort of last resistance and were destroyed there by the Indian Army. Among the generals directing the attack were two Sikhs. But the attack on the temple horrified the vast majority of Sikhs, including those who did not condone or participate in Bhindranwale's politics. Spurning the repairs to the Akal Takht made by the Indian government, Sikhs have demolished it in order to rebuild it with their own labor. The two temples of the complex will no doubt stand again to proclaim the duality and complementarity of the Sikh legacy and its orientation to the world. But what do we infer from the failure of Bhindranwale's pursuit of Sikh spiritual and political deliverance through fundamentalist violence? And to what extent is the emergence of the juggernaut of so-called Hindu nationalism dialectically related to militant Sikh separation?

SIKH IDENTITY AND THE BOUNDARY PROBLEM

The Sikh community or collectivity, popularly called the Panth in the Punjabi language, is by no means monolithic: they have been, and are even today, "divided by geography, ethnicity, social hierarchy, sects, ritual practices, and individual preferences. Consequently, when it comes to political participation, Sikhs have never been represented by a single political party."[80] The two major political parties that Sikhs have supported are the Congress Party and the Akali Dal (which is exclusively Sikh); the religious and political agendas of other organizations, such as the SGPC, the Dal Khalsa, and the Damdani Taksal, have, however, further crosscut and differentiated the Panth. Even as a religious collectivity, the Sikhs have had no "organized vertical hierarchy" to bind them, and several texts have functioned in the past as manuals of conduct (*rahit-nama*). In manifesting different subtraditions, Sikhism participated in the religious milieu characteristic of other Indian religious collectivities. Moreover, Sikh transactions have been regulated and adjudicated according to Punjabi customary law, and further supplemented and amplified by Anglo-Saxon law as it was applied and interpreted piecemeal during the colonial and postcolonial periods.

These are some of the features that point to a Sikh predicament articulated from time to time by various Sikh leaders—the lack of unambiguous markers of Sikh identity that would set them apart, especially vis-à-vis the Hindus, whom they see as "threatening" to incorporate or assimilate them. In the late nineteenth century, the Tat Khalsa movement coped with this issue and tried to stipulate the practices, rituals, and markers of an exclusive Sikh identity. An important thrust of Bhindranwale's campaign was also to erase these ambiguities.[81] Sikh fundamentalists would like to see a code of Sikh personal law enacted, although in practice this has proved to be difficult. Bhindranwale urged all Sikhs to undergo the Khalsa *amrit* ceremony and to uphold the five *k*'s. He toured the countryside extensively, urging the youth to be initiated and saying, "Only people without ambiguity in their heart have the right to call themselves Khalsa." And his punitive action against the Sant Nirankaris can also be interpreted as an attempt to stamp out a sectarian tendency that diluted religious practice in the direction of Hindu worship.

While Bhindranwale was the most recent reiterator of the Sikh identity issue, the issue itself is an entrenched one, and is likely to be a major ongoing concern to the Sikh collectivity. This concern is most likely exacerbated by the recent upsurge of Hindu nationalism and the campaign to demolish the Muslim Babri Masjid in Ayodhya and to build a temple to Ram in its place.

POLARIZED VIOLENCE AND THE PASSAGE TO CIVIL WAR

In 1989–90, in the southern, southwestern, and central parts of Sri Lanka, polarized violence—that is, violence committed by armed gangs or groups, paramilitary agents, official security forces, and insurgents battling one another in the midst of a bewildered, fear-ridden, helpless civilian population—had reached a climax.[82] Happenings similar to those in Sri Lanka were a continuing nightmare in the Punjab in 1990–91. In Sri Lanka, both the security forces of the state and the insurgents, the JVP, employed death squads, as well as unidentifiable gangs, to conduct assassinations. They would leave the corpses burning on the street, floating down a river, or tied to lampposts. This signifies organized violence as the order of the day and as a principal mode of enacting politics, through which power is produced, acquired, and employed in a theatricalized and repetitive manner.

Violence took the form of revenge killings. Some killings were targeted in the sense that certain known opponents were singled out and ambushed; others were arbitrary, in that they were randomly carried out against innocent civilians, who by virtue of the contagion of being fellow villagers or relatives of the enemy were punished or killed just to spread intimidation. The killers justified these acts as "preventive" measures against anticipated collusion on the part of the victims.

Violence spread like an epidemic, infecting and killing without warning and seemingly at random. The population at large frequently did not know whether the kidnappings, disappearances, and killings were motivated by public political calculations or reasons of private vendetta. When a JVP suspect was killed, a net of guilt by association was cast, endangering the lives of his associates, his kinsmen, his fellow villagers. A report written on behalf of International Alert entitled *Political Killings in Southern Sri Lanka* documents instances of "the total helplessness created where there is an assumption that the threat comes from some section of the guardians of law and order themselves, at times under cover of curfew."[83]

On the one hand, this state of chronic public violence breached the bounds of civil order: there was no right of complaint or of litigation; no possibility of appeal to habeas corpus or judicial procedure. But on the other hand, in becoming routinized and normalized, this violence constituted a new arena of social action, a theater of violence, with its signals and its semiotic logic, its raids, shootings, hangings, shamings, warnings, and threats posted on walls and shop doors. The people at large surreptitiously recognized the messages but did not publicly discuss them; they responded to the call to strike by staying away from work and by shutting shops. The threats of violence and punishments thus produced nonviolent compliance among the civilian populace.

THE REIGN OF TERROR IN THE PUNJAB, 1990–1991

In the Punjab in 1990 civilians, both Hindu and Sikh, were victimized by the police, the army, and the Sikh militants. Some of these last were no different from criminal gangs, looting and killing in the name of holy war, but making of that war a parasitic mode of livelihood. V. S. Naipaul's poignant and empathetic account of the grieving condition of Sikh families, in a state of shock, and caught up in the crossfire of intrigue, divided loyalties and shifting alliances is worth citing:

> When terror became an expression of faith, the idea of *seva* [service, one of the good and poetic concepts of Sikhism] was altered.

Now five years after the assault on the temple, the terrorists lived only for murder: the idea of the enemy and the traitor, grudge and complaint, were like a complete expression of their faith. Violent deaths could be predicted for most of them: the police were not idle or unskilled. But while they were free they lived hectically, going out to kill again and again. Every day there were seven or eight killings, most of them mere items in the official report printed two days later. Only exceptional events were reported in detail.

Such an event was the killing by a gang, in half an hour, of six members of a family in a village about ten miles away from Mehta Chowk. The two elder sons of the family had been killed, the father and the mother, the grandmother, and a cousin. All the people killed were devout, *amritdhari* Sikhs, that is, Sikhs who were initiated into the *Khalsa.* [The taking of *amrit* (nectar) is supposed to make you a member of the brotherhood of pure Sikhs, who will henceforth reject food not cooked by *amritdharis;* the initiation is said to help control the five evils: lust, anger, covetousness, ego, family attachments]. The eldest son, the principal target of the gang, had been an associate of Bhindranwale. But a note left by the gang, in the room where four of the killings had taken place— the note bloodstained when it was found—said that the killers belonged to the "Bhindranwale Tiger Force."[84]

The intergang warfare among the Sikh militants is itself seemingly an "inevitable" phase among insurgents today. In Sri Lanka, the Tamil militant groups, divided into a number of competing factions, turned on one another in the same way Sikh militants have done. But what Naipaul fails to record is the parallel violence of the security forces. Barbara Crossette, writing in the *New York Times,* vividly reports the dilemma of "Punjabis, sandwiched between Sikh rebels and New Delhi":

> Despite what Punjabis call "police raj" or armed rule in this state, where about 60 percent of the population is Sikh, thousands of people have died this year. A militant campaign of intimidation of state government employees and the press is daily more audacious, officials are assassinated, criminal gangs flourish and, most wrenching to the hard-working Sikh community, Sikhs have begun killing each other as divisions among them deepen.
>
> Up to 95 percent of the dead are Sikhs: militants, policemen, suspected informers and ordinary men, women and children.

Crossette reports that "Jagjit Singh Aurora, a retired lieutenant general and critic of Government handling of Punjab . . . who heads the civil-rights group, the Sikh Forum, blames government officials and the militants symbolized if not led by an underground organization called the Panthic Committee. 'The villager doesn't want to get robbed and killed by militants or criminals. . . . But the villager is also getting robbed and killed by the police.' Further militarization of the state, he said, will only create 'an actively hostile population.'

"Sikh leaders say many families have already been alienated by officially sanctioned death squads and extortion by policemen who abduct young people and threaten to book them as terrorists if ransoms are not paid. Reports of torture and death in police custody are common."[85]

The story of the widespread and endemic violence in Punjab did not stop here of course. The internecine and factional violence among the Sikhs, compounded by the police and army counteractions against the Sikh militants and civilians, was itself a smaller component of the larger scene, in which Sikh militants were constantly attacking and killing Hindu civilians. The following excerpt from a *New York Times* report typified hundreds of similar incidents:

> The authorities imposed an indefinite curfew today on a town in Punjab state after Sikh separatists shot 15 Hindus to death there in a new surge of political violence in India.
>
> The police in Chandigarh, the Punjab state capital, said 15 bodies were found in Jullundur after militants rode through the town in a car on Sunday firing assault rifles at Hindus. . . .
>
> In Jullundur, the curfew was ordered after Hindu crowds started gathering at a hospital to prepare for the cremation of the 15 bodies, the Chandigarh police said. They said that only a limited number of people would be allowed to attend the cremation rites.
>
> Sikh men [more accurately, many Sikhs] are easily distinguished by their full beards and turbans from the Hindus, who make up three-quarters of India's population of 850 million but are a minority in Punjab.
>
> The police said the attack may have been intended as a protest against the roundup of more than 300 Sikh politicians to prevent them from meeting on Sunday at Anantpur, near Chandigarh.
>
> More than 3,500 people—policemen, militants, politicians and ordinary citizens caught up in violence—have been killed so far this year in the Punjab violence.
>
> Chandra Shekhar, India's new Prime Minister, said today that he was willing to talk to any leader to try to ease India's political violence. He said the Sikh meeting in Punjab had to be banned because it would have increased religious polarization.
>
> New Delhi dissolved Punjab's state assembly three years ago and put the state under direct rule by a governor and bureaucrats in a vain attempt to quell the separatist violence.[86]

THE INDIAN ELECTIONS OF 1991 AND GENERALIZED VIOLENCE

With rebellions convulsing Punjab, Assam, and Kashmir, and with political parties, the security forces, and militants all resorting to armed violence, the Hindu nationalism of the Bharata Janata Party (BJP) and the caste politics of V. P. Singh's National Front were explosive. The elections of 1991 were unanimously rated by journalists as the most violent in India's postindependence history as a democracy. A spate of killings culminated in Rajiv Gandhi's assassination outside Madras, allegedly by Sri Lankan Tamil militants, as a result of which the elections were postponed, with the uncertain expectation of their being resumed a few weeks later. James Clad has sketched the violent context of the electoral campaign in India in late May 1991 as follows:

> Another election promises only further paralysis in which no one party wins a majority.
> Yet elections and parliamentary instability only hint at India's torn fabric. Topping the list are rebellions, convulsing the Punjab and Kashmir. . . . In Kashmir, especially, the degree of alienation between the 4 million Kashmiris and the security forces positioned in the beautiful valley is profound.
> I detected no shred of common ground between the populace and what has become an occupying force. Yet the retention of Kashmir, India's only Muslim majority state, remains an article of faith for all Indian parties and politicians. . . . Nothing unites Indians more than the determination to "hold" Kashmir; nothing unites Kashmiris more than a desire to be rid of India, a tragic impasse that results mostly, but not entirely, from India's manipulation of Kashmiri politics during the last three decades.
> In the Punjab, a different logic yields the same grim result. . . . an original demand for a separate state for the majority Sikhs has now become a fratricidal rebellion in which Sikhs belonging to a score or more groups butcher each other. Predominantly Sikh policemen create new groups to fight the older groups. . . .
> The Bharatiya Janata Party, or BJP, India's Hindu revivalists, want to revive "Hindu-ness," a glorious time before the Muslim and Christian invaders, but the prospect frightens the country's 110 million Muslims (after Indonesia, India is the most populous Muslim nation). . . .
> While the fracturing of national politics proceeds, so does the unraveling of civic peace. Riots between dominant Hindus and the big Muslim minority have ravaged communal harmony in recent months. Indian observers say the unrest is the worst since the 1947 Partition which split British India in two. . . .
> Many longstanding social issues have resurfaced with new bitterness, such as ethnic quarreling over retention of the English language; and the vexed issue of caste, fanned by controversial plans last year for an affirmative action program giving many government jobs to "backward castes," a category distinct from caste "untouchable." . . .
> . . . India remains wedded to perhaps the best legacy of British rule—the ballot box. Although politics have become deeply criminalized in some Indian states, governments change in Delhi and in its states through elections, not (as in Pakistan) through overt or disguised military coups. When observing elections I have seen both a mixture of textbook civics and ballot-box hijacking reminiscent of the Philippines. Still, it beats periodic shows of bayonets in the capital city.[87]

APPENDIX: CONSTRUCTING A SIKH IDENTITY

One has to go back at least to the eighteenth and nineteenth centuries to fully comprehend Bhindranwale's religious impulsions and the cultural and religious capital he was drawing on and elaborating. Sikh history is characterized by a series of highly complex ruptures, rapprochements, and transitions. The concept of an exclusive Sikh identity, and of the Sikh collectivity as a separate one with definable boundaries, was not there from the outset. It was not fully dominant even in the latter part of the eighteenth century and in the early nineteenth century, at the time of Ranjit Singh's empire. The territories in which Sikhs lived, the languages they spoke, the agrarian festivals in which they participated, the ritual officiants they patronized, and the universe of their rites of passage—all these were shared with the other communities amongst whom they lived in the Punjab. This is not, of course, to deny that under the guidance and teachings of the Sikh gurus, certain identity markers and distinct practices and places of worship did develop:

> The initial Guru period, following the death of Nanak, provided significant axes of identity to the embryonic Sikh faith: allegiance to the person of Guru Nanak and his nine successors; identification with their teachings (*bani*); the foundation of congregations (*sangats*); the setting up of elaborate pilgrim centres at places like Goindwal and Amritsar; the convention of a communal meal (*langar*); and the compilation by Guru Arjan of an anthology, commonly known as the Adi Granth, which ultimately acquired the status of a major sacred text of the Panth.[88]

This text compiled by the fifth guru, Arjan, in one sense turned the Sikhs into a "textual community," and by the late sixteenth and early seventeenth centuries, pious Sikhs were characterized by "the centrality of belief and abiding faith in the person and utterances of the Sikh gurus; the need to visit the dharamsala [a monastic establishment or place for reading and singing scriptures]; and the repeated emphasis on the sangat as a body of practitioners in faith."[89]

But even so, at this time, the category "Sikh" was flexible and problematic, and the Sikhs were still in the process of growing and evolving. The collation of the Adi Granth did not create a firm separation of the Sikh Panth from other religious traditions. The voluminous hagiographical narratives (*Janam-sakhi*) of the life of Guru Nānak borrowed liberally from Puranic stories, Sufi hagiographies, and Buddhist Jatakas.

The initial Guru period came to a sudden end with the execution of Guru Arjan by the Moghuls in 1606. "A continuous Jat influx into the Sikh movement throughout the seventeenth century alongside a protracted conflict with an increasingly hostile Mughal state gradually gave rise to new Sikh cultural patterns." One major development was the institution of the Khalsa by the last Sikh guru, Gobind Singh, in the last decade of the seventeenth century. "The Khalsa [order or brotherhood] was instituted to finally end the ambiguities of Sikh religiosity," and the distinctive identity of the Sikh was "inscribed through a complex cultural repertoire made up of inventive rituals, codes of conduct, mythical narratives and a whole new classificatory code regarding the body."[90] Initiation into the Khalsa involved the famous *khande ki pahul* rite of drinking sanctified water into which a double-edged sword was dipped. However, not all Sikhs became Khalsa; many, including Sikhs who were drawn from the Brahmin and Khatri castes, resisted Khalsa initiation and identity.

The Khalsa continued its work of securing religious boundedness, and forged its own dharma (moral code), which it called Rahit. Oberoi underscores the importance of texts called Rahit-namas, which developed the Khalsa conception of selfhood by codifying five areas: life-cycle rituals, tabooed behavior, the implications of transgressions, and the constitution of sacred space. Since they were produced in the first three-quarters of the eighteenth century, the Rahit-namas serve to refute the idea that Khalsa identity only became dominant in the late nineteenth century under British sponsorship.

By the second half of the eighteenth century, a distinctive Khalsa order had thus emerged. The Adi Granth assumed the status of the voice of an eternal guru, who was no different from God; and the Sikh gurus' teachings were the "voice" of God—they brought God and man together. The doctrine of Guru Granth was conjoined to the notion of Guru Panth: the guru was present wherever the Sikh congregation assembled. When, in 1708, at the death of Gobind Singh, there was no guru to succeed him, the Panth turned into his collective successor.

During the course of the eighteenth century, tens of thousands of Sikhs, many of whom belonged to the "lower social orders," embraced Khalsa identity, partly because of the Khalsa's campaign to displace the Mughal state in Punjab. By the 1770s, Khalsa Sikhs, who had formed regional political units called *misls*, which controlled certain territories and distributed hereditary land rents to functionaries, controlled the Mughal *suba* of Punjab and large portions of the provinces of Multan and Shahjahanabad. The solidarity infused through the rituals of *gurmatta* (resolutions passed by the faithful in the presence of the Adi Granth) and *sarbat-khalsa* (meetings of corporate bodies) was "a crucial ingredient in the making of these Khalsa Sikhs."[91]

But on the other hand, at the same time, the Khalsa was attaining greater control, there was acceptance in many circles that there were alternate ways of being a Sikh, and that "the Sikh Panth was not coterminous with the Khalsa and it was possible to be a Sikh without being a Khalsa."[92] The Sikhs who did not turn into Khalsa Sikhs were by no means numerically insignificant, and in the mid eighteenth century, they were often referred to as the Sahajdharis (this label included Nānak-panthis as well as Udasis).

In many ways, the Sahajdhari Sikhs inverted Khalsa categories of thought and practices and "transgressed" Khalsa religious boundaries. They cut their hair, did not undergo initiation, obeyed no norm to obligatorily carry arms, smoked tobacco, and had a radically different version of the line of succession from Guru Nānak. While "Khalsa Sikhs began to recognize the Adi Granth as guru, Sahajdhari Sikhs were not given to accept a text as guru and favoured living human gurus."[93] But they recognized Nānak as their guru and read and recited from the Adi Granth.

The Udasis, perhaps the most conspicuous and numerous segment of the Sahajdharis, were organized in a number of major orders, managed shrines across north India, and set up their own establishments at major pilgrimage centers such as Amritsar, Hardwar, and Banaras. They did not consider the Khalsa Rahit-namas to be binding, and rather than the five *k*'s, their outfit included a cap, a rosary of flowers, a cotton bag, a vessel made of a dried pumpkin gourd, a deerskin upon which to perform Hatha Yoga, and so on. There was a distinct difference in worldly orientations and involvement between the Khalsa and Sahajdhari Sikhs: the former thought of salvation as attainable while they pursued their pragmatic worldly objectives within the encompassing framework of religious beliefs and practices; the latter declared that secular pursuits were not compatible with the goal of human liberation, which required world renunciation.

It is not surprising therefore that "the Khalsa principalities, numbering more than two score in the last quarter of the eighteenth century, did not seek to dissolve preexisting social hierarchies. . . . Their main aim was to absorb the local segmentary lineages and found an empire on them."[94] The processes of state formation that culminated in the Lahore state of Maharaja Ranjit Singh (1780–1839) consisted of multiple accommodations: between the Khalsa Sikhs and the lineages and caste organizations; between the Khalsa and Sahajdhari Sikhs; and between Khalsa notions of exclusive Sikh identity and a more inclusive identity incorporating rituals associated with Hinduism and Hindu ritual specialists. "It is this extraordinary fusion of Khalsa and non-Khalsa identities which marks out Sikh tradition in the eighteenth century from what was to follow under colonial rule."[95]

By the early nineteenth century, there had crystallized what Oberoi calls the *Sanatan* Sikh tradition, which embodied a rapprochement between Khalsa and Sahajdhari identities. Although by the early twentieth century, this Sanatan tradition had lost its dominance, its complex intermingling of trends and rich hierarchized diversity make it noteworthy. The main text of the Sanatan tradition was the Dasam Granth, whose "intertextuality" was linked to the Puranas and Hindu epics such as the Mahabharata. Under its umbrella, Hindu priests publicly worshipped images within the precincts of the Golden Temple, and it was considered legitimate to worship living gurus, whose descendants inherited their charisma. The lineages descended from these Sikh gurus became known as Bedis, Trehans, Bhallas, and Sodhis.[96] Members of these guru lineages served as custodians of Sikh shrines, established monastic establishments, imparted religious instruction, dispensed charity, and took care of their family relics.

But side by side with the saintly lineages who inherited charisma, there was also a lively tradition of holy men—the Bhais, Sants, and Babas—who achieved and earned their holiness in their lifetime. These holy men, recognized for their piety, were credited with powers to perform miracles, heal the sick, and succor the distressed.

Sanatan Sikhism also included ascetic orders, such as the Udasis, Nirmalas, Gianis, Dhadis, and many others. In the mid nineteenth century, there were over 250 Udasi *akharas* (establishments). Although smaller in scale, the Nirmalas were an especially significant ascetic order, and many of their akharas engaged "in meditation, yoga and in the study of the Adi Granth, the Vedas, the Mahabharata, the Ramayana, the Puranas and the Sastras."[97] The Udasi and Nirmala establishments were second only to the famous guru lineages among the recipients of religious grants from the Sikh state; they also undertook the task of propagating the faith and establishing branches and pilgrim centers on the periphery of the Sikh world. Their central establishments were famous for studying, creating, and diffusing both sacred and secular knowledge pertaining to the scriptures, literary classics, rhetoric, astrology, and medicine.

Oberoi regards Sanatan Sikhism as primarily a "priestly religion," whose dominance derived from its being "the religious universe of Sikh elites"; but it was an "official religion" closely aligned with the Sikh kingdom of Lahore, and it progressively lost strength and validity once the British annexed Punjab.

The era of the loss of Sikh empire and the establishment of British Raj saw the spawning of the organizations called Singh Sabhas. The first of these was the Sri Guru Singh Sabha, formed in Amritsar in 1873. Although responsive to the changes injected into Punjabi society by British rule, it sought to preserve traditional cultural values and attempted to answer questions about Sikh identity, the differences between the Sahajdhari and Khalsa traditions, the place of low-caste Sikhs (e.g., Mazhabi and Chamar Sikhs) within the Sikh collectivity, and orthopraxy in the externals of physical appearance.

The affluent intellectuals who led most of the early Singh Sabhas (the one at Lahore was formed in 1879) were pluralistic and inclusive in their attitudes and inclined toward Sanatanist tolerance of a variety of traditions. There was a phenomenal expansion of Singh Sabhas in the late 1880s (about 115 were formed between 1880 and 1900, the majority of them in Punjab), related to the increasing number of Sikhs responding to educational opportunities, the expansion in communications, commerce, and services, and the rise of new market towns and trading networks that also penetrated the rural economy. Physical and social mobility and expanding opportunities also brought new members into the ranks of the elite.

Oberoi underscores the enormous transformation involved in the tolerant pluralism of Sanatan Sikhism giving way to the three "core doctrines" of the Tat Khalsa, guru, Granth, and gurudwara, which became "the litmus test of authentic Sikhism" and came to be widely accepted by the Sikh public in the early twentieth century. Arising in opposition to the prevailing Sanatan Sikh tradition and popular religion, the Tat Khalsa conducted persistent campaigns against the cult of saints (*pirs*), local festivals and agrarian fairs made merry with music, folk songs, and dance, and the worship of gods, local shrines, and ancestral spirits. "Underwriting the Tat Khalsa's authoritative discourse were a series of factors: the colonial state, the British army, the collapse of customary culture, and the new political configuration in the localities," Oberoi observes.[98]

In the late nineteenth century a growing body of Sikhs took part in a systematic campaign to purge their faith of religious diversity, as well as what they saw as Hindu accretions and as a Brahmanical stranglehold over their rituals. The result was a fundamental change in the nature of the Sikh tradition. From an amorphous entity it rapidly turned into a homogeneous community. And of all the competing entities, symbols and norms that went into constituting the long history of the Sikh movement, it was the Khalsa sampradaya that succeeded in imprinting its image on the "new" community. . . . The Udasis, Nirmalas—a motley complex of traditions referred to here as Sahajdharis—came to be seen as deviants. With the active displacement or subordination of many of the Sikh sub-traditions, a single Sikh identity began to crystallize in the first decade of this century.[99]

The Tat Khalsa's drive to impose and inscribe an exclusive Sikh identity and to achieve a separatist collective identity shorn of Hindu influences and practices merits detailed consideration, especially the moves by which many strands of Sanatan Sikhism were displaced and inferiorized, thereby making the Tat Khalsa the clamorous center of Sikh tradition. "Between 1880 and 1909 the body was made a principal focus of symbolic concern and a central means of projecting ideological preoccupations."[100] Although Guru Gobind Singh may have been the first within Sikh tradition

> to recognize the semiotic potential of the body to manifest the power of a corporate imagination, it took an interval of almost three centuries and a decisive intervention by Singh Sabha activists before this sign-vehicle was fully harnessed. . . . Scriptural truths and corporeal existence were made isomorphic and pointed to the same objective: Sikh corporate identity and the independence of the Sikh religious community. . . . The oft-repeated rhetorical statement "Ham Hindu Nahin" (We are not Hindus) now had a subjective basis; what it lacked was supplemented by further innovation.[101]

Oberoi shows how the Tat Khalsa combined its attempts to elevate the spiritual condition of its adherents with the strict regulation of their bodies. The Khalsa sought to impose a distinct physical appearance and identity on its followers by rigidly enforcing external symbols of identity, particularly the five *k*'s, and formalizing new life-cycle rituals, especially those pertaining to Khalsa initiation. In its rewritten hagiographies of martyrs, its popular tracts, and the new novels written by its literary members, the Khalsa emphasized how the heroic figures of the eighteenth century had been "punished, tortured and killed for desiring to retain their cultural markers," and how "the ideal Sikh modes of bodily comportment" were exemplified by them.[102] "Only those who stuck to the glorious heritage of the heroic epoch deserved to be called Sikhs. In other words those who were minus the Five K's—for instance the Udasis, the Nirmalas and the Sahajdharis—were not Sikhs. They had failed to live up to the high standards of the past and therefore should be stripped of their rights to community membership."[103] Bhindranwale's sermons some seven or eight decades later even more trenchantly restated these messages in colloquial idiom.

The ways in which Sikhs belonged to the larger Hindu culture, especially their marriage practices, *biradari* (clan) norms, and life-cycle rites, such as weddings and funerals, and whether these customs put them in danger of being assimilated and encompassed, created a recurring problem for Sikh identity. In direct contrast to the Sanatan Sikh tradition of tolerance of diverse Sikh local family, kinship, and caste practices, the Khalsa Sikhs deliberately set out to declare "Hindu" (and "Muslim") adhesions unorthodox. They worked to forge and invent new rituals, at whose core was the Adi Granth, the sacred object to be circumambulated and to be recited as sacred formulae.

The great majority of Sikh households in the late nineteenth century and the early decades of the twentieth "performed their rites of passage according to the long-established conventions of customary culture or the respective customs of their biradaris and caste groups." Moreover, as may be expected "there was an immense variation in ceremonial, not only among the different castes of Sikhs but also within caste groups and among Sikhs of different localities." The village *nai* (barber) and the local Brahmin *purohit* (priest) figured in Sikh life-cycle rites. "Much as with marriage ceremonial, Sikhs lacked any distinctive mortuary rite that could be described as a charter of corporate identity." In the eyes of the Tat Khalsa, these practices "were completely anti-Sikh in nature; they had brought about the degeneration of Sikhism and its increasing assimilation into Hinduism."[104]

Between 1884 and 1915, many manuals were published on how Sikhs ought to arrange their life-cycle rituals. These new specifications, which played a fundamental role in etching Sikh cultural boundaries, while dispensing with earlier "Hindu" ritual functionaries, sought to standardize rituals for all Sikhs—Jats, Khatris, Mazahbis—shorn of any caste or biradari associations; made the Adi Granth the central sacred object (for example, replacing the fire in marriage rites) and sole text for recitation; and focused on the wearing of the five *k*'s. These newly devised purified ritual injunctions were in due course inserted into the Rahit-namas, which sought to stipulate Khalsa conceptions of moral duties and proper ritual practices.[105]

In addition to these radical changes in life-cycle rituals, other innovations were introduced by the Tat Khalsa with regard to dress, language, the annual calendar and appropriate festivals, dietary taboos, and so on to strengthen the distinctions and socioreligious boundaries between Sikhs and non-Sikhs.[106] A critical step taken with far-reaching implications was espousing the Punjabi language and the Gurmukhi script, in which the Adi Granth was written, as emblems and vehicles of Sikh identity.[107] (The appropriation of Punjabi, with its implications for educational instruction, employment recruitment and administration, and its distinctness from Urdu and Hindi, the markers of Muslim and Hindu identity, inevitably fed into issues of linguistic nationalism and the carving out of linguistic states, which came to a head in postindependence times. The second partition of Punjab took place in 1966, with Haryana hiving off to form a separate state.)

Oberoi has convincingly argued, especially against Richard Fox's thesis in his *Lions of the Punjab* (1985), that Sikh identity as we know it today was not primarily or solely a creation of and reaction to colonial policies of the Raj. There was an anterior trend and legacy in precolonial Sikh tradition, especially as it came alive in the eighteenth century in the Rahitnama literature and ritual prescriptions, which enunciated a Sikh identity "similar to the one promulgated by the Singh under the Tat Khalsa (what Fox terms the 'Singhs' or the 'Lions')" and insisted that the Khalsa Sikh must "maintain the external symbols of his faith."[108]

This antecedent Khalsa legacy was reactivated and reformulated in the late nineteenth century, and the Sikh internal dialogue and tensions between Sahajdhari nonacceptance of the Khalsa code and the tolerant pluralistic Sanatan tradition, on the one hand, and the reformist, "rationalizing" drive of the Tat Khalsa, on the other, cannot be reduced to the stimulus of British rule. The profound social and economic changes experienced by Punjabi society (and in India in general) under British rule also generated the rise of new elites. As in other British colonies, these new elites learned from the rulers and their agents and imbibed some of their values. At the same time, however, they reacted against and resisted colonial domination and inferiorization, transformed old traditions, and invented new ones. As Oberoi puts it:

> The Dalhousian revolution in communications, the commercialization of the rural economy, the rise of new market towns and trading networks, the establishment of schools and colleges to train native collaborators in British modes, the new civil codes based on legal codes instead of customary sanctions, the unprecedented irrigation projects to turn barren lands into granaries—all these transformations dramatically altered the nature of Punjabi society. Punjabi school-boys were made in their curricula to memorize the new changes as the blessings of the British Raj.[109]

These changes did not immediately produce significant urbanized, educated, commercially prominent Sikh elite groups. The majority of Sikhs being agriculturalists, the commercial and governmental service advantages first went to those Hindu groups long resident in the cities. So did the rewards of local government and municipal politics. But the Sikhs in turn generated their own mobile elites, and these were also the promoters and advocates of a homogeneous Tat Khalsa identity and of preferential educational policies on behalf of depressed Sikhs. A multitude of Singh Sabhas in the cities and towns of the Punjab gave evidence of new Sikh elites organizing in associations to promote their interests.

The recruitment policies of the British Indian Army, which favored Sikhs, based on stereotypes of Sikh military prowess and loyalty, no doubt directly affected the development of Khalsa doctrines and disciplinary codes. The trickle of Sikh peasants into the Indian Army after the first

Anglo-Sikh war in 1846 turned into a regular flow following the annexation of the Punjab. Governor-General Lord James Dalhousie encouraged the recruitment of Sikhs, and the Sikhs' loyal fighting side by side with the British during the 1857 Indian Mutiny reaped rich rewards. "Thus was Punjab turned into the army barracks of the Raj, and Sikhs made the most formidable human resource within the imperial fighting machine."[110] Of interest to us is that the British military authorities required a Sikh recruit to undergo the initiation rite, and to exhibit the external symbols of his faith, and employed "grunthees" (readers of the Granth and gurudwara functionaries) to conduct Sikh rituals. Thus, ignorant or unmindful of the complex array and diversity of Sikh practices, "army commanders enforced an extremely narrow, functional and mechanistic definition of the Sikh faith." Since the army's sponsorship of a particular image of Sikhism accorded so well with that upheld by the Tat Khalsa, it is no wonder that Sikh soldiers became the staunchest supporters of the latter's project.[111]

SIKH PROTEST POLITICS AGAINST THE RAJ

Where Oberoi leaves off is an apt place to review the submissions of Richard Fox in *Lions of the Punjab*. Fox attempts to fit together the ethnographic and historical particulars of what he calls the "Punjab puzzle," which consists of two questions. First, "Why did followers of Sikhism, specifically those called Singhs or 'Lions,' engage in a mass rural protest against British rule that shook early twentieth-century Punjab?" (The protest in question took place between 1920 and 1925 and was part of a vigorous political activity mounted by the Akali movement.) Second, "Where did the Sikh identity that provided the cultural meaning for the social movement come from?"

Let us take the second question first. Fox's answer is that "British rulers, in pursuit of their colonial interests, through means dictated by their cultural beliefs, foreshadowed, even constructed, the Sikh identity which was later espoused by the Singh Sabhas." By "cultural beliefs," Fox has in mind nineteenth-century British "orientalizing beliefs" predicated on notions of racial divisions of humankind, which in India took the form of treating certain Indian religious communities, castes, or regional populations as so many distinctive and bounded species. The primary agent of this identity-shaping process was the British Indian Army, which nurtured the orthodox, separatist, and martial identity of the turbaned and unshorn Singh among Sikh rural recruits to its regiments and companies.[112]

This claim has, as we saw earlier, been refuted by Harjot Oberoi, who has convincingly sketched the Tat Khalsa's forging of this specialized identity in the eighteenth century. Others have supported this critique.[113] But all are agreed that the British Army played an intensifying and sustaining role in that kind of Sikh identity formation adopted and reworked by the reforming urban middle- and lower-middle-class Sikhs who led the Akali movement.

Fox's discussion of the roots and direction of the urban and rural protest movements of the early 1920s sets the stage for understanding the Akali politics that precedes the final shift to the fundamentalist extremism of Bhindranwale's militancy. It is stated that the penetration of capitalist world economy into the Punjab under the aegis of British colonialism generated certain internal contradictions characterized by the differences between the economy of the petty commodity-producing small peasantry, dependent on well irrigation, in the central Punjab, and the more mercantile and prosperous economy of the canal colonies. These two zones came into competition with each other, and the small producers of the central Punjab became increasingly disadvantaged even as they intensified their labor inputs to the point of self-exploitation in order to compete with the labor-saving benefits that canal irrigation provided the colonists. In other words, unequal exchange resulted, value flowing from the former to the latter. "When the Punjab's rural economy deteriorated after World War I (a collapse precipitated by the contradictions of colonial exploitation), peasants, imbued with the Raj's image of the militant Singh, joined with urban reformers, who broadcast a similar identity. The upshot was a mass religious protest that was also a political uprising; it lasted for five years and was only put down at great cost to the British."[114]

Fox's interesting submission is that the Akali movement began as "religious reformism in Punjab cities and ended as anticolonial revolt in Punjab villages."[115] He attempts to show that the protest began at urban sites where a spirit of "reformed" Sikh consciousness as a struggle for cultural identity, political power, and economic privileges had developed, especially among lower-middle-class Sikhs. From these urban centers, especially in the immediate postwar years, the movement spread to and inducted an aggrieved rural population in the central Punjab, and then the better-placed rural lower middle class of the canal colonies, climaxing as a movement of mass protest that "equally expressed religious intent, anti-colonialism and agrarian protest."[116]

The Akali movement dynamically moved through three successive confrontations. The identity consciousness of the Singh Sabha movement was in its first phase a response to the Hindu revivalist and reformist militancy of certain Arya Samaj enthusiasts, whose threat of incorporating or converting Sikhs elicited not only an affirmation of separate identity but also a struggle by the Akalis to gain control of Sikh shrines.[117] At the same time, as we saw in Oberoi's account, there arose a contest on the part of the Tat Khalsa Sikhs (Fox's "Lions") to dominate, marginalize, and inferiorize the Sanatan (and Sahajdhari) traditions of non-Khalsa Sikhs. This was an internal war among the Sikhs. Ultimately, a struggle between the Singhs/Khalsa Sikhs and the British Raj broke out. The struggle of these urban reform Sikhs to take control of Sikh shrines managed by conservative mahants and ritual officiants tolerant of Sanatan eclecticism brought the Singhs into conflict with the British colonial authorities, who supported managers in place and suspected the Singhs of hatching an anticolonial subversion. The actual techniques and strategies of induction of the rural lower middle class and peasantry deployed by the Akali leaders were similar to those used by British army recruiters among rural Sikhs, while the protest campaigns often resonated with military overtones.

According to Fox's account, while Amritsar, the home of the first Singh Sabha, organized in 1873, was dominated by the rich landed gentry, by the orthodox, who were loyal to the Raj, and by their temple functionaries, the rival Singh Sabha in Lahore, founded six years later, was more egalitarian, espoused the separatist identity advocated by Guru Gobind, and represented the inclinations of the growing urban lower middle class. "The battle between Lahore and Amritsar, between Sikh and Singh, between temple functionary and lower-middle class served as the agency for turning the contradiction in British domination into an anticolonial confrontation."[118]

In 1880, the Lahore and Amritsar associations cooperatively formed the Khalsa Diwan to coordinate the various Singh Sabhas, but their differences were more or less smoothed out by the time the Chief Khalsa Diwan of Amritsar was formed in 1902 to succeed it. "The Chief Khalsa Diwan preached an unequivocal Sikh identity and came increasingly to labor for the religious equality of the low castes." It was led by persons drawn from the ranks of teachers, professionals, merchants, and government servants. In the early years of the twentieth century, more rural Jats joined the movement as urban Khalsa advocates successfully invoked the Singh image, which was concordant with Jat traditions of "militancy, organized protest, and when necessary violence."[119]

Ian Kerr avers that because Fox does not give full value to pre-existing Jat dispositions, such as the use of violence in factional politics, he exaggerates the role of the urban reforming Sikhs in imparting a militant identity to the rural Jats.[120] Be that as it may, the important point for us (and this links up with Oberoi's documentation) is that the Tat Khalsa urban reformers increasingly collided with temple authorities and shrine functionaries, who from their point of view tolerated caste inequities and Hindu practices. Although the Chief Khalsa Diwan had been pro-reform in some matters, such as removing Hindu idols from the Golden Temple and passing the Anand Marriage Act in

1909 (which legalized a non-Brahmanical ceremony for Singhs), it was viewed by the younger and more radical reformers as harboring pro-British attitudes. The Khalsa/Singh radicals severed their connection with the Chief Khalsa Diwan and in December 1919 formed the Central Sikh League, which became the left wing of the Shiromani Gurudwara Parbandhak Committee (SGPC) and the major support of the Akali Dal in the 1920s.

As the Raj itself progressively came to see the reformers as subversive of imperial interests, it abandoned its earlier espousal of the army recruiter's stereotypic image of the militant and loyal Singh. Meanwhile, "the Central Sikh League called for jathas [demonstrations by volunteers] against temple functionaries and noncooperation with the government at one and the same time. . . . By 1920 at the latest—with the creation of the SGPC and the Akali Dal—both the colonial government and the Singh reformers had become conscious of what their confrontation had always objectively involved: religion, identity, and power."[121]

Kerr has drawn attention to the considerable role of the revolution in communications in the Punjab—the expansion in roads, railways, the print media, and telephone and telegraph systems—in promoting social mobilization by the Akali movement.[122] No less important were the campaigns "conducted in the typical format of Akali *morchas* evolved during the Sikh Gurudwara Reform movement in the early twenties," Attar Singh observes. "Organized essentially as a regular display of collectively nonviolent defiance of state authority, these *morchas* came to be associated with sending out bands of volunteers known as *jathas* every day over a considerable period of time to attract public notice and make dramatic impact." This required both a safe assembling point for the volunteers, from which they would also proceed, and a safe sanctuary for the organizers who were in charge of making camping arrangements.[123] This legacy of demonstrations would be put to effective use in later times, although there would be a shift to violence as in the case of the 1982 Dharam Yudh morcha begun by Bhindranwale and the Shiromani Akali Dal.

This historical account has covered the dynamic developments among the Sikhs, their internal sectarian religious disputes, their continuous attempts to define their identity and to erect boundaries vis-à-vis the larger Hindu society, the increasing dominance of the militant Tat Khalsa, and the organized resistance they mounted against the Raj. It meaningfully connects with the issues with which we began this chapter, "The Politics of the Akali Dal Movement" and "Political Contests, 1947–1984." It helps us better understand the emergence of Bhindranwale and the roots of his revivalist, purificatory, separatist movement.

6   Ethnic Conflict in Pakistan

Pakistan's peculiar ethnic and provincial complexity, and its dynamic shifting politics conducted in a tense regional environment in which India, Afghanistan, Iran, China and the former USSR were bordering countries, generated many kinds of internal conflicts, as well as stressful relations with India. Ayesha Jalal has vividly enumerated the country's wounds and scars:

> Painfully carved out of the Indian subcontinent—ostensibly to provide a homeland for the Indian Muslims—Pakistan has been remarkable more for the tensions between its dominant and subordinate regions than for the purported unities of a common religion. Of the forty-two years since its creation, Pakistan has seen military or quasi-military rule for twenty-five; it has been governed under six different constitutions and has been at war with India on three separate occasions. In 1971 Pakistan lost a majority of its Muslim population with the breakaway of its eastern wing and the establishment of a new country, Bangladesh—the only successfully secessionist movement in a newly independent state. A civil war in which Muslim slaughtered Muslim might seem to have exploded the notion that religion alone was sufficient cement to hold Pakistan together. There have been continuing tensions in its remaining provinces in the west.[1]

Like those of India next door, the cities and towns of Pakistan have known many communal riots as intermittent events, involving different antagonists. For example, Karachi "has seen anti-Qadiani [Ahmedi] riots in the early fifties, anti-Pathan riots in 1965, anti-Qadiani riots again in 1969–70, Sindhi-Muhajir riots in 1972–73, and a yearly encounter of Shia-Sunni sectarian riots before the Orangi troubles of 1985."[2] Since then clashes between Pathans and Biharis have occurred in October and December 1986 and February and July 1987, and between Muhajirs and

Sindhis in May, September, and October 1988, and again in May–June 1990.

This ominous listing of outbreaks can be roughly divided into three types. The Shia and Sunni have clashed in Karachi since before independence "with ritualized regularity during the religious month of Moharrum, on the occasion of Ashura, when both sects take out processions."[3] Very little documentation is readily available to say more about this classic example of religious processions on festival days acting as triggering events for clashes between sectarian groups concentrated in different localities of the city, and possibly directed by local leaders and their retinues. With the difference in religious affiliation may go other ingredients, such as competition in trade and crafts, control of urban territory, and the wielding of local power. The processions themselves may performatively image and contest questions of sectarian, caste, and neighborhood precedence and position in a hierarchy of prestige.

Parts of Pakistan, the Punjab in particular, are famous for the purges mounted by orthodox and activist religious-cum-political parties, such as the Majlis-i-Ahrar and Jama'at-i-Islami, against the Ahmedis, who are considered by them to be traitors and fifth columnists (*munafiqeen*). The pious assailants, champions of the cause of "Islamization" of the country, and watchdogs against Hindu infusions, have mounted periodic collective violence against this religious minority, who have scarcely retaliated in kind.[4] The fact that members of this minority are by and large educated and prominently placed in branches of the professions may have incited their conspicuous targeting. They are also branded by some assailants as British collaborators. Postmortems on the riots have studiously ignored the issue of religious tolerance; the authorities have treated them as simply a law-and-order issue. "A cumulative presence resulted in the Ahmedis being declared non-Muslims during Bhutto's tenure, and more recently other such measures were taken by Zia's regime."[5] We should recall that during the 1980s, a government-sponsored "Islamic revival" led to fierce debates about the form of government, Islamic or secular, that Pakistan should adopt. Especially since the Ahmedi heterodoxy is a convenient and combustible issue that can be exploited by religiopolitical groups wanting to muster strength quickly, one cannot say when and how anti-Ahmedi riots may explode again.[6]

Aside from the two categories discussed above, the religion of Islam as such has not figured as an issue—in terms of orthodoxy—in the "ethnic" conflicts that have taken place in Pakistan in the 1980s. The two major kinds of conflict involving riots and other kinds of violence, by both civilians and government security forces, concern two pairs—the Muhajirs (literally "refugees") versus the Pathans (especially in Karachi), and the Muhajirs versus the Sindhis (especially in Karachi, Hyderabad, and certain other urban sites in Sind Province). Ethnic identity in these clashes has primarily invoked essentialist links with language, home territory, and tribal or other communal ties in variable mixes; the issues raised as integral to collective ethnic interests have to do with educational opportunities and attainments; employment opportunities at all levels; both local and national political power; control of urban space, real estate, and communication facilities; and migration of people from other provinces into one's own, or from India and Bangladesh into Pakistan.

In this chapter I focus on the Muhajir-Sindhi and Muhajir-Pathan clashes and seek to place them in their larger contexts.

MUHAJIRS AND SINDHIS

With 60 percent of the country's population, the Punjab is clearly the "dominant" Pakistani province today. Punjabis constitute about 80 percent of the army and dominate the central government.

But in the early history of the founding of Pakistan, the Punjab did not occupy the limelight. For Pakistan was founded, not by Punjabis, but largely by North Indian Urdu-speaking Muslims, under the leadership of Muhammad Ali Jinnah (a Cutchi-speaking Khoja Ismaili from Bombay), Liaquat Ali Khan (an Urdu speaker from Oudh), and Fazh-ul-Haq (a Bengali Muslim). Only gradually, in the 1950s and afterwards, did Punjabi politicians come into their own.

The political scientist Anwar Syed has this to say about the perception by non-Punjabis of Punjabi domination: "The regime they maintain, mainly through their predominance in the military and the higher bureaucracy, has traditionally been authoritarian. Politicians in the minority provinces, who are not only excluded from power but persecuted, seek relief by diminishing the arena—the central government—from which the Punjabis operate their repressive and allegedly exploitative system of rule. The talk of nationality and autonomy is thus part of the counterelite's defense against the ruling elite's oppression and repression."[7]

Punjabi dominance in contemporary Pakistan's politics is one of the factors in the discontent of certain provinces and lies behind the stress on the need for provincial autonomy and for keeping the federal government in check. Punjabi dominance is the inevitable backdrop to any study of Pakistan's ethnic conflicts (a prominent instance is the figure of President Mohammed Zia ul-Haq). The bulk of my account relates to Sind, and the Punjabi factor is part of the landscape.

REFUGEES IN SIND PROVINCE

The changing fortunes and role of the refugees (*muhajirin*) who at Partition left north India to settle across the border in Pakistan are integrally linked to the shifting course of ethnic politics and conflict there.

The first wave of refugees, many millions in number (they made up 8 percent of Pakistan's population in 1951), and still labeled Muhajirs, were Urdu and Gujarati speakers. Most of them emigrated to the port city of Karachi, and because of their high literacy rate, educational attainments, and political involvement in the creation of Pakistan, they have played a conspicuous political role in the governance of the country and enjoyed economic success. "In the elite Civil Service of Pakistan, the Muhajir share remained disproportionately large throughout the 1960s," Theodore P. Wright, Jr., notes.[8]

Karachi, the national capital until 1958 and now the provincial capital of Sind Province, remains Pakistan's most populous and industrially most developed city. But it is not a Sindhi city in population, wealth, power, or culture. Wright observes that although linguistically homogeneous,

> prepartition Sind, somewhat like united Bengal, was sharply split communally between an urban and modernizing Hindu minority and a largely rural and feudally dominated Muslim peasantry. Thus, after Pakistan's independence, when most of the Hindu Sindhis emigrated to India, they were replaced in the cities and modern occupations by a huge influx of equally advanced Urdu-speaking Muslim refugees (*Muhajirin*) from northern India and Delhi and by Gujarati-speaking businessmen from Bombay and the west coast of India. Sind as a province, with 23% of the country's population, soon contained a disproportionate 60% of its industry, and a per capita income 40% higher than the Punjab's. Muslim Sindhis, however, were left at a disadvantage in their own province; only ten per cent were literate, compared to seventy per cent of the newcomers.[9]

The Sindhis were thus in the position of being the depressed indigenous people in a relatively prosperous province.

The Muhajirs (joined after 1971 by Bihari refugees from what became Bangladesh) are "ethnically" diverse and have no "homeland" to which they can territorially relate. Their initial dominance in the cities of Sind, primarily in Karachi, but also in Hyderabad, and in national politics has been diminishing over time, and they have progressively come to fear being marginalized or peripheralized. Their strategy has therefore been to try and gain recognition as a "fifth nationality" (the others being the Punjabis, Sindhis, Baluchis, and Pathans), and to coalesce as a political movement. Some older Muhajirs may still be loyal to the political party dedicated to Islamization, the Jama'at-i-Islami, but many young Muhajirs, especially those who are educated, unemployed, and seeking redress from "discrimination" by governments favoring Sindhi and Punjabi interests, have formed the Muhajir Qaumi Mahaz (MQM, or Refugee Nationality Movement), which has become militant while forging ahead in national and provincial Sind politics.

The countermovement of Sindhi politics and mobilization has followed a course that has resulted in political parties sponsoring exclusively Sindhi interests, such as the Pakistan National Party and the Sind National Alliance, or Sindhi interests in coalition with other regions feeling marginalized, such as the Sind-Baluch-Pakhtun Front. One strand of Sindhi politics has eventually turned militant and even terrorist, in the form of the Jiye Sind movement, keeping pace with and mirroring the extremist wings of the MQM, the militant arm of the Muhajirs.

Sindhi regionalism is fueled by many felt grievances that have accumulated since the founding of Pakistan. "In some ways Pakistan's Sindhi problem and India's Sikh separatism bear comparison: both peripheral groups are fearful of becoming minorities in their own provinces; both are the most prosperous provinces in their respective countries but with wealth unequally distributed between and within ethnic groups; and, most ominously, both are located on the sensitive borders of hostile states always tempted to 'fish in troubled waters,' " Wright observes.[10]

After Partition, "the bulk of non-Punjabi migrants who came to West Pakistan from India arrived in Sind and settled in the urban centers of Hyderabad and Karachi," Farida Shaheed notes. "The Muhajirs were culturally distinct from the Sindhis and, though composed of various ethnic groups, gravitated towards the Urdu-speaking culture of central India, so that Urdu became the *lingua franca* of Karachi."[11] The dominance of the Sindhi language was in due course tested in all the major cities of Sind. Other government policies made the indigenous Sindhis feel that they were being discriminated against and being swamped by the newly arrived outsiders.

> The situation in Sind was further complicated by land policies. To compensate for their losses in India, refugees were given land, while the government also continued the British policy of allotting land to armed-forces personnel. Since there were virtually no Sindhis in the armed forces, both policies resulted in the province's land being progressively acquired by non-Sindhis. Finally,

unbalanced economic policies discriminated against all provinces in favor of Punjab and the city of Karachi. The latter, though situated in Sind, was dissociated from the province and monopolized by non-Sindhis (and initially dominated by Muhajirs). Sind was thus deprived of its greatest asset: Karachi.[12]

In time, especially under the government of Zulfikar Ali Bhutto (1971–77), a sizeable Sindhi educated class was able to compete with the Muhajirs, although it sharply resented the usurpation of its land and employment opportunities by outsiders.

THE SINDHI PREDICAMENT

The frustrations and beleaguered worldview of the Sindhis are eloquently expressed by Anwar Syed:

> In all of Pakistan the Sindhi-speaking people, also called the "old Sindhis," harbor a most anguishing sense of deprivation. They . . . have been reduced to a minority in their cities and larger towns. They fear that they may soon become a minority in the province as a whole. The Muhajirs have attempted to impose their own language and culture on the Sindhi-speaking people in the name of Islam and Pakistani patriotism. They and other settlers have taken economic resources and opportunities that would otherwise have gone to the Sindhi-speaking people. The old Sindhis are virtually absent from Pakistan's armed forces and they are poorly represented in the federal bureaucracy. Many high-ranking positions even in the government of their own province have been filled by Muhajirs and Punjabis either because they have established residence and obtained Sindhi domicile certificates or because they have been sent in by the central government. The old Sindhis regard this state of affairs as unmitigated oppression and they want to put a stop to it.[13]

Additionally, Sindhis see a confirmation of their view of the Punjabi interests backed by Punjabi domination of national politics in their attempt to implement the Kalabagh dam project, which would divert water from the Indus for the benefit of the Punjab and to the detriment of Sind agriculture. The blocking of this project has been one of the major causes of the Pakistan National Party, which convened a Sind National conference at Bharot in October 1987 to discuss "provincial autonomy, demographic change in Sind, the Kalabagh dam, and the 'machinations of imperialism' in Sind."[14] The major concerns of Sind provincial politics were articulated in a lengthy resolution of the conference, which Syed summarizes as follows:

> 1) stop migration from other provinces into Sind; 2) expand employment in these provinces to keep their people at home and to induce those working in

Sind to return home; 3) exclude non-Sindhis from employment and businesses in Sind; 4) deny non-Sindhis the right to vote and contest elections in Sind; 5) reconstitute electoral districts in a way that old Sindhis will fill at least two-thirds of the seats in the Provincial Assembly and two-thirds of Sind's quota of seats in the National Assembly; 6) define a Sindhi as a person who was born in Sind or has lived in Sind for twenty-five years; 7) require adequate proficiency in Sindhi of all persons working in Sind; 8) limit the central government to only four subjects (defense, foreign affairs, currency, and communications); 9) abandon the Kalabagh dam project; 10) confiscate large landholdings, control multi-national corporations operating in Pakistan, and launch a struggle against imperialism.[15]

Scrutinizing these resolutions, one is inevitably led to ask how they relate to the interests and future of the Muhajir population of Sind, who are settled mostly in the urban centers of that province and form the majority of its urban population. For example, while the criterion of 25 years residence will admit "the old Muhajirs" who settled in Sind at the time of partition and their descendants, what about newer migrants? And how will the Muhajirs, whose principal language is Urdu, take to the proposal that they show proficiency in Sindhi?

THE JIYE SIND MOVEMENT

Aside from the PNP, a second Sind thrust has been launched by the Jiye Sind Movement. President Mohammed Ayub Khan's move in 1955 to create the "One Unit" of West Pakistan, thereby merging Sind with the other provinces, as a counterbalance to East Pakistan, did not go down well with Sindhis. The campaign to reverse this unification—which was later achieved—is a critical part of the story of Sindhi politics. In order to advocate Sindhi interests, G. M. Syed formed the Sind United Front in 1967 and the Jiye Sind Mahaz in June 1972. "The Mahaz demanded 'maximum' provincial autonomy, . . . allowing the centre only defence and foreign affairs. Demands included adoption of Sindhi as the *only* official language of Sind, and a *twenty-five* percent Sindhi quota in the armed forces and the federal civil establishment, and the return to Sindhis of all agricultural land in the province previously granted or allotted to outsiders."[16] Provoked by the Bhutto regime's repression, G. M. Syed went so far as to advocate an independent state of Sindhu Desh and guerrilla warfare to achieve liberation. The Jiye Sind Students Federation (JSSF) and an organization of Sindhi professionals, the Sind Graduates Association (SGA), both affiliates of the Mahaz, committed themselves to spreading Syed's aim to ordinary as well as educated Sindhis. In the Jiye Sind Movement, we thus see two familiar components: those most committed to the objectives of provincial autonomy and protection from outsiders were educated students and middle-class professionals who adopted the politics of collective entitlements, meaning quota systems in employment, in higher education, and in the army and civil administration.

In the 1980s, it seemed as if the Jiye Sind Movement might be becoming more accommodative. Syed was succeeded as leader by Dr. Hamida Khunro in 1980, and she and her associates have muted the advocacy of Sindhu Desh in favor of the idea of a confederation of provinces with a center of limited powers, and have also tried to accommodate the demands of the Muhajir Qaumi Mahaz for national rights for the Muhajirs (see below).

Other developments that have to some extent restrained the violent expression of Sindhi parochial interests include the formation of the Pakistan People's Party (PPP), the ascendancy to power as prime minister, after Ayub Khan's fall, of its leader, a Sindhi, Zulfikar Ali Bhutto, and, after his execution, the continuance of his legacy by his daughter, Benazir Bhutto, at the head of a popularly elected government committed in principle to the "restoration of democracy," which succeeded the regime of General Zia ul-Haq. In time, the Sindhi Muslims have generated their own literati, educated professionals, and successful politicians. Ali Bhutto and the PPP, while stressing Islamic socialism instead of Sindhi separation, simultaneously signaled a time of increased recognition of Sindhi interests, as well as increased participation of prominent Sindhis in provincial and national politics and their appointment to administrative posts. But Sindhi frustrations mounted when Zia's Punjabi-backed and -led military regime displaced Bhutto in 1977 and executed him in 1979 for alleged involvement in murder. Benazir Bhutto brought the PPP back to life and revived favored treatment of Sindhi interests, but her defeat and the trajectory of divisive politics in the late 1980s exacerbated ethnic and urban conflicts, especially between militant Muhajirs and Sindhis.

Before she was elected prime minister, Benazir Bhutto spoke sympathetically of the familiar Sindhi grievances and proposed measures to redress them and defuse secessionist sentiment, such as liberating Sindhis in rural areas from repressive feudal rule and the depredations of dacoits; securing a more equitable distribution of provincial resources among cities, small towns, and rural areas; containing migration into Sind from other provinces by carrying out development in all provinces; jettisoning the Kalabagh dam project and providing for equitable water rights among the provinces. At the same time, however, she advised acceptance of all those presently living in Sind as full Sindhis, with full rights, and the recognition of both Sindhi and Urdu as languages of the province. Sindhis and Muhajirs clashed during Benazir's first tenure, from 1988 to 1990, especially in the cities of Hyderabad and Karachi.

THE RISE AND DECLINE OF MUHAJIR FORTUNES

"Urdu-speaking Muhajirin have gradually slipped from dominance (1947–51) to partnership with the Punjabi elite (1951–71) to subordination under Zulfikar Ali Bhutto (1971–77) and General Zia ul-Haq (1977–88) without even a province of their own, to tentative attempts at a return to partnership under Benazir Bhutto (1988 to 1990)," Wright notes. "It is this decline which has produced the militant [MQM] since 1984. . . . The gradual awareness of the peripheralization of the Muhajirs from an increasingly Punjabi-dominated Pakistan was led by the youth, particularly from the lower middle class." Young educated Muhajirs saw their job prospects shrinking both during Ali Bhutto's regime, which awarded job quotas to Sindhis, and during Zia's martial-law rule, which favored Punjabis. "Consequently, in 1979 Altaf Hussain, a Muhajir student at Karachi University, founded the All Pakistan Muhajir Students Organization (A.P.M.S.O.) to compete with the other ethnic student groups, as well as the *Jama'at-i-Islami* youth group, *Jamiat Tulaba*, on campus."[17] In March 1984, Altaf founded the MQM on a wider basis when Zia banned all student organizations.

Before we take up the more recent violent collisions between Muhajirs and Sindhis in Sind Province, let us backtrack a little to the so-called Urdu-Sindhi language riots of 1972. In actual fact, these riots were a product of linguistic, political, economic, and demographic developments, which cumulatively brought the beleaguered Sindhis into collision with the Muhajirs.

Jinnah, and after him Ayub, had both been in favor of Urdu being the national language, and in their time, the Sindhi language had even been dropped as a medium of instruction. After Partition, the largest influx of refugees and immigrants into Pakistan were Punjabi-speaking, but Punjab had also accepted Urdu as its literary language. In Sind itself, Sindhi was in danger of being superseded by Urdu, especially in urban areas, in terms of numbers speaking and using it as their mother tongue.

But Mumtaz Bhutto, the chief minister of Sind, was a champion of Sindhi interests, and in line with the pleas of the Jiye Sind Movement, he succeeded in pushing a bill that made Sindhi the official language of the province through the Provincial Assembly in 1972. Bloody riots followed, and it was left to his cousin Prime Minister Zulfikar Ali Bhutto to award equal status to Urdu.

Although Muhajirs and Sindhis had fought bitter battles over the language issue in 1972, leading to the acceptance of Urdu and Sindhi as official languages, they also recognize that, as the older residents of Sind Province, it is in their interest to close ranks against newcomers such as the Pathans and Punjabis, who take over businesses and compete for jobs. The MQM has advocated that employment quotas in federal and provincial establishments be reserved for Muhajirs and Sindhis, and that their status and numbers be determined by census taking. Thus the Muhajirs and Sindhis both want to stop further migration and also think that "the jobs and other economic opportunities would become theirs if Karachi, and preferably all of Sind, could somehow be rid of the Punjabis and Pathans."[18]

The MQM, with Altaf Hussain as its chief exponent of these objectives, was able to win majorities in December 1987 in municipal elections in Karachi and Hyderabad. Moreover, and this is where hardliners on both Sindhi and Muhajir sides have met, they both want to contain migration from other provinces and deny recent migrants voting rights and access to employment and business opportunities. If implemented, this policy will have the effect "of disenfranchising and disestablishing hundreds of thousands of Punjabis and Pathans, which they are not likely to accept without a fight."[19]

The MQM advocates voting rights for and affirmative action on behalf of those Muhajirs who have been domiciled in Sind by virtue of living there for twenty years, excluding non-Sindhis and non-domiciled Muhajirs. It also advocates assigned places for Muhajir students in colleges on the basis of their population ratio. The basis of ethnic group conflict in demands for collective entitlements is transparently demonstrated in this politics of affirmative action. The MQM has also urged that Pakistanis who have left or want to leave Bangladesh should be allowed to settle in Pakistan, thus making common cause with the Bihari immigrants settled in the slums of Karachi. To cap it all, the MQM has demanded that the Muhajirs be recognized as a separate, fifth nationality in Pakistan. Although internally differentiated by sect, by territory of origin, by language, and by customs, the Muhajirs thus seek to aggregate themselves into a homogeneous nationality in a political arena that recognizes at least four other such ethnic labels.[20]

Additional demands are that only squatter settlements established before 1978 be recognized, that heavy trucks be banned from city streets and driving licenses be denied illiterate persons (measures obviously aimed at

Pathans), and that all Afghans be placed in refugee camps and be denied the right to buy property or establish businesses in Sind.

But as we shall see, whatever the contingent and contextual sharing of interests between Muhajirs and "old Sindhis" vis-à-vis newer migrants, they themselves are competitors and antagonists on crucial issues of education and employment and political control in Sind.

CASE STUDY 1:
MUHAJIR-SINDHI COLLISIONS, 1988–1990

Between the end of September 1988 and the end of May 1990, several violent clashes took place between Muhajirs and Sindhis, principally in the cities of Karachi and Hyderabad, but not without splinter effects in the small towns and rural areas of Sind. These collisions have deepened the divide between the two collectivities (whatever their internal differentiations). Commentators and journalists speak of a "polarization" that threatens to bifurcate the province. Violent exchanges in the two cities and the quick spread of the conflagration to neighboring areas have become almost routine. Thus, for example, on September 30, 1988, "over 250 persons, mainly Muhajirs were killed when about a dozen gunmen, allegedly led by [Sindhi militants] Dr. Qadir Magsi and Janu Arain, opened indiscriminate fire on unarmed people in Hyderabad." Magsi was arrested, which greatly agitated his followers in the Jiye Sind Movement, and on October 1, 1988, about 60 people, mostly Sindhis, were killed in an apparent "backlash by Muhajir militants in Karachi."[21] The *New York Times* noted:

> The reported death toll in the two cities was at least 208.
> Doctors said by telephone from Hyderabad that 162 people, most of them from the Muhajir immigrant community, were slain when unidentified gunmen sprayed bullets at crowds Friday evening. At least 200 people were wounded, and hospitals issued urgent appeals for blood donors.
> In Karachi, hundreds of Muhajir militants reacted violently, burning stores and cars and attacking police officers, witnesses said. Doctors in Karachi said that at least 30 bodies had been brought to hospitals and more were expected. At least 46 people were known to be dead in the violence in Karachi. Fifty people were injured.
> The authorities sent in troops to enforce a curfew overnight in Hyderabad, 110 miles to the east, and extended it to about a third of Karachi this morning. It was the worst explosion of violence in southern Pakistan in nearly two years. Ethnic riots have now taken about 500 lives in the region since 1986.[22]

This exchange of violence exacerbated the antagonistic separation of the two collectivities, as shown in the results of the general elections held in

November 1988, when Sindhis ranged behind the PPP and Muhajirs showed solid support for the MQM. Negotiations followed, and on December 3, 1988, the PPP and the MQM signed the "Karachi Declaration," a 59-point document, designed to heal the tensions. In May 1989, however, the MQM ministers in the Sind cabinet protested the nonimplementation of the agreement, only to be rebutted by the Sind government of Qaim Ali Shah. After threats of resignation by the MQM ministers, and intervention by federal ministers, a temporary settlement was reached, with the release of large numbers of MQM activists and promises of accord implementation.

Then, in early July 1989, some Muhajir student activists at the University of Karachi were shot dead. In response, the MQM broke the accord and staged a strike. Further killing of Muhajirs resulted, with widespread violence throughout Karachi. Prime minister Benazir Bhutto's move to change the chief minister of Sind did not help matters. Protests against the PPP mounted, and Najib Ahmed, a militant leader, was shot. Fresh riots thereupon broke out in Karachi, and the army was called in to patrol the city in tanks.

On May 27, 1990, first in Hyderabad, and then in Karachi, a spasm of violence erupted, whose course will be charted on the basis of extensive cover stories in the June 1990 issue of the monthly newsmagazine *The Herald*, entitled "Massacre in Sindh" and "Hyderabad: A Tale of Two Cities." In Hyderabad, on May 27,

> the police force, comprising the Eagle Squad and other reserves from Sindh's interior, went berserk in the city—reportedly in response to an armed clash in Pucca Qila a day earlier, in which two policemen, along with a dozen civilians, were killed. A demonstration led by Muhajir women and children was brutally crushed by the police leaving scores of people dead. Among the 60 persons killed and more than 250 injured in police firing on two demonstrations were at least a dozen—in some accounts many more—women. The killing of unarmed women demonstrators was one unprecedented event, and one that gave the entire situation a new dimension.[23]

According to the *Herald*, some informants said that the processions of women and children had been staged for a purely local reason: the restoration of water supply in the Fort area, which the authorities had cut off. Women carrying the Qur'an on their heads and chanting "Ya Ali madad!" (Ali is our help!) and "Yazidi hukumat murdabad!" (Death to the Yazidi government!) were the centerpiece of these allegedly peaceful processions of unarmed men, women, and children. (It is interesting to note that the same slogans were shouted against the shah by the Iranian Islamic revolutionaries, and that they have been adopted and translated in Pakistan).

But the *Herald* also reported that "the latest orgy of violence" was no surprise: apparently many "informed persons in Hyderabad" had had a strong feeling before the violence "that a new round of disturbances would break out on the last day of the matriculation examinations." And, in fact, on May 14, some thirteen days before the police fired on the procession on May 27, attempts to stop students from sitting for the last paper at certain examination centers led to clashes that spread to the entire market area and old city of Hyderabad. Three people died on that day, and a curfew was enforced in the troubled areas. (How student examinations fed into the ethnic conflict is clarified when we realize that Muhajirs felt that the Sind government discriminated against Urdu-speaking Muhajir students by allocating special admission quotas for Sindhi students. One may therefore guess that the disruption of the examinations was conducted by Muhajir activists of the MQM.)

It is significant that on May 27, the police were deployed and ready to deal with the procession in the Fort area and other demonstrations elsewhere. For example, three jeeps carrying policemen drove at great speed into the Fort procession, making the people give way. And, apparently the women, when challenged to stop, dared the police to open fire, "because we are carrying the Holy Quran on our heads." The police—one policeman is reported to have shouted, "They are prostitutes"—did open fire, causing a stampede, the shrieking women and children rushing into the Abdul Wahab Shah Jilani Shrine for shelter and the men running toward Station Road.[24] Ambulances arrived and carried off the dead and the wounded to nearby hospitals, first to Bhitai Hospital—which had only "one small operation theatre," so that the surgeons were obliged to operate in the corridors—and then to the St. Elizabeth and Mohammadi hospitals. All these frenzied events were taking place to the deafening noise of voices over the loudspeakers installed in various mosques, screaming, "Come out of your homes, Muhajirs are being killed"; "Please arrange cots and bedding for the injured"; "Rush to the hospitals and donate blood." In response, "volunteers put up *shamianas* [tents] in the hospital compound, while women queued up to donate blood."

Two things are reasonably clear from the reports. First, the most conspicuous aspect of the violence of May 27, which consisted of many incidents in different parts of Hyderabad City, is that it was contingents of the local police force that unleashed the worst killings by firing on crowds. The bloodshed was compounded by the simultaneous and poorly coordinated action of the "six different agencies" on duty, which did some infighting of their own.

Secondly, this overreaction by police and local security agents, which was expected to quell Muhajir demonstrations by force, was an extension of the killings on a smaller scale that had taken place for some months before the May 27 explosion. Moreover, it is evident that the Hyderabad police contingents were virtually all Sindhi in identity and in sympathy with the Sindhi cause; hence, they were antagonistic to the Muhajir demands championed vociferously by the MQM. While Sindhi nationalists openly congratulated the police, the Muhajirs demanded, not only that a state of emergency be declared, but that the national army be called in to protect them. Two days later, on May 29, Muhajir crowds awaiting the arrival of the chief of army staff, Mirza Aslam Beg, at Pucca Qila Chowk, the scene of the shootings, unfurled large banners "bearing slogans in praise of the army, and posters of the former military ruler," Zia. How could these banners and posters have appeared out of nowhere, unless the Muhajir agitators had already prepared them for their campaign against the civilian government of Sind and its police force? The desperate call to the army by the Muhajirs to save them from the police prompted a journalist to ask, "Why have the Muhajirs of Hyderabad finally bid farewell to democracy?"[25]

The news of the violence in Hyderabad triggered a spate of violence in Karachi on May 28, with this difference: the Muhajirs of Karachi, "the bastion of Muhajir power," went after the vulnerable Sindhi residents there. "Fierce clashes broke out between the armed militants and contingents of police and the para-military Rangers in the city's Muhajir strongholds. The clashes were followed by a grim series of target killings, in which scores of people were gunned down—most of them Sindhis."[26] Altogether the violence lasted about ten days in Hyderabad and about six in Karachi. In both cities the clashes took a familiar form once they got under way: armed battles between the police and Muhajir militants, attacks on Sindhi and Muhajir localities by gunmen belonging to the rival ethnic group, and widespread incidents of arson and looting, along with the occasional rape.

It is common knowledge that communal riots displace people and create a refugee problem. But another feature pertaining to displacements of people—forced evacuations by burning homes, intimidations, targeted killings—is that the abandonment of localities in populous cities is also the capture of the same territorial space by the winners (usually the larger of the rival groups living in the locality in question). In Hyderabad, for example, where the Muhajirs were in strength, Sindhi refugees were forced out of Sathi Para, near Choti Gilti, where they had lived peacefully for a long time, and from other inner areas of the city, and they found shelter in Qasimibad Township outside the city. They were put in camps and vacant houses there by the Qasimabad Welfare Associations. But the Muhajirs in nearby farming areas, such as Muso Bhurgiri (where they claimed to have settled since the time of partition), and from suburban localities, such as Matiari and Tando Mohammed Khan, were forced to abandon their homes and gravitate toward the inner core of Hyderabad, where they were given shelter by pro-Muhajir organizations. Thus there were reverse movements between the core and periphery of the city. In Karachi, an ironic thing happened: the Baluchi, who are thought to be some of the city's oldest inhabitants, left their enclaves and sought refuge with their compatriots in Karachi's Lyari area, or went long distances all the way back to Lasbela in Baluchistan. Similarly, many Sindhi families in Karachi packed up and left for the interior of Sind Province. It is not clear how many of these refugees returned to their old home sites and how many permanently abandoned them to be appropriated by the victors and by slum landlords with henchmen at their disposal.

The increasing availability of the modern technology of violence—a special curse of our time—was in evidence in Karachi and Hyderabad. The clashes between Sindhis and Muhajirs showed that there were large quantities of arms in the hands of the "ordinary" members of the two communities, let alone the "professional militants," some of whom used rocket launchers. And in these circumstances, householders began to acquire arms to protect their homes and families. "Perhaps it was for this reason that once the trouble started, it went out of control of the armed militants. The people, once armed, seem to have made their own decisions," one analyst observed.[27] This seems to have been especially true of the strife-torn Liaquatabad and Nazimabad localities of Karachi, where, it is reported, with some poetic license, "almost every second person on the streets was openly displaying a deadly weapon." Large sections of the population appeared to have risen against the state administration itself. It is no exaggeration to say, moreover, that the explosions in Hyderabad and Karachi sent splinters in all directions, which in time reached the remotest corners of Sind.

PAKISTAN'S POLITICAL ARENA AND ITS TENSIONS

Compared to those in India and Sri Lanka, Pakistani political analysts and journalists relate the periodic and endemic ethnic violence and riots in their country directly and emphatically to the weaknesses and inadequacies of the civilian political authorities and institutions at both the provincial and national levels. Pakistan's heritage of military takeovers weighs heavily on many commentators. "The current crisis of the state in Pakistan originates in a state structure inherited from the colonial period in which the military bureaucratic oligarchy is overdeveloped relative to the institutions of civil society," Akmal Hussain observes. "This dominance of the military bureaucratic oligarchy has systematically constrained the development of the political process, thereby preventing the emergence of issue oriented parties with institutionalized grass-roots support."[28]

Owing to the nature of the process by which Pakistan gained independence, the bureaucracy and the army, the pillars of the Raj, were transferred intact and have continued to determine the parameters within which political and economic change can occur. The failure of the political system to subordinate the army and the bureaucracy lay in the inability of the Muslim League in the pre-Partition period and the Pakistan People's Party in the 1970s to tranform themselves from movements into structured organizations able to wield the power of the people and to domesticate the army and bureaucracy.

In her analysis of the forces and factors that have shaped the martial Pakistan state, Ayesha Jalal relies, not on "the common view" that the weakness of political parties is the *main* variable explaining military intervention in Pakistan (especially the fateful takeover of state authority by Ayub Khan in 1958), but on mapping the complex dynamics and precarious internal political balance, the difficulties of the regional and international setting, and Western security calculations that enabled the bureaucratic and military institutions to rise to a position of dominance in the process of exercising Pakistan's sovereignty. The provincial parties' lack of effective organizational machinery is part of this story, as is the county's struggle to establish a party-based system of parliamentary democracy. Jalal shows "the different ways in which the interplay of regional and international factors influenced domestic politics and economy, *distorting relations between the centre and the provinces in particular* and the dialectic between state construction and political processes in general."[29]

Pakistan has "not been able effectively to integrate its provinces or distribute resources equitably between the dominant Punjab and the subordinate provinces of Sind, the North West Frontier Province and Baluchistan as well as between the diverse linguistic groups within them," Jalal observes. "The institutional dominance of a predominantly Punjabi army and civil bureaucracy within the state structure has exacerbated regional grievances, especially since representative government, which might have provided a better balance between the provinces and linguistic groups within them, has been kept in abeyance for long periods of time."[30] Representative government has not had a chance to realize itself largely because the military and bureaucracy have been unprepared for the divisiveness, polemics, and combativeness of political expression.

As noted earlier, in terms of "ethnic" identity, Pakistan's army is dominated by Punjabis, and the civilian bureaucracy by Punjabis and Muhajirs (with the latter's control declining). The central power is at odds with the demands and interests of the provinces, and the "weaker" provinces, the North-West Frontier Province, Baluchistan, and Sind, feel that the state's assets are unequally distributed and that those in power help to sustain this inequality. The increasing provincial nationalism of Sind is fraught with the likelihood of continuing communal conflict. With their demographic strength decreasing in Sind, the Sindhis, who are no more than 50–55 percent of the province's population, want to contain further migration into it, to exclude non-Sindhis from electoral rights, to limit their employment opportunities, and to reserve two-thirds of the seats in the Provincial Assembly and a favorable quota in the National Assembly for themselves. A Sindhi is defined as one who was born in Sind, has resided there for twenty-five years, and uses the Sindhi language. The presence in Sind of Muhajirs, Punjabis, and Pathans makes it very unlikely, however, that these Sindhi demands can be satisfied. The Sindhi-Baluchi-Pakhtun Front, an attempt to confederate the embattled provinces, may have some impact on national policy in achieving more evenhanded distribution of resources and implementation of projects.

There is one final complication to be taken into account in Pakistan's struggle to establish a party-based system of democracy. Some political analysts feel that "only by inducting its citizens into decision making and by evolving democratic institutions can the state hope to reduce or eliminate the authority of sub-state entities."[31] This view is much influenced by what such commentators see as the divisive nature of provincial interests, and perhaps even more important, by their seeing provincial politics in particular as intimately tied to and controlled by ruling elites composed of big landlords and tribal chiefs, who on the one hand challenge the "intrusions" of central authorities and on the other hand engage in the segmentary politics of "autonomous" competitors unwilling to be subordinated, while at the same time holding the majority of lesser folk in the grip of their "feudal" machinery. "With a large number of the state's citizens dependent on the local tribal chief or feudal landlord, this system cannot be challenged through an electoral process unless the state affords some measure of protection to those who oppose the local power structure."[32] With the present dispensation in place, provincial demands, however genuine, in the end benefit mainly the ruling elites.

Starting with the divisiveness of provincial interests and local power structures, the political analysts of Pakistan see as the main issue the question of how to forge a national identity of free and equal citizens ruled by a central authority founded in representative democracy. In contrast, some prominent Indian political scientists see the divisiveness and contentiousness of Indian politics today as a reaction to the excessive control exercised and homogenization imposed by the project of nation-state making and federal control.[33]

THE ROLE OF ISLAM IN COMMUNAL CONFLICT

It is true that at the levels both of ideological theorizing and political practice, Pakistan has progressively faced the task of aligning and "reconciling its self-professed Islamic identity with the imperatives of a modern state structure."[34] Islamic ideologues are basically at odds with the conception of Pakistan as a secular nation-state defined by its territory and a common citizenship. It is also true that "Islamization" is a clarion call that has support among various sections of the population and the Jama'at-i-Islami.

It was in the years following the death of Liaquat Ali Khan that the proponents of a strictly Islamic order began to gain some prominence. But the religious groups sponsoring this objective were divided especially on the question of leadership and united action. Allama Mashriqi who had led the paramilitary Khaksar movement in pre-Partition India, and had organized the Indo-Pakistan League, had a narrow following "among petty shopkeepers, lower ranking government servants as well as the upper ranks of industrial labor."[35] Another group was the Majlis-i-Ahrar, which notwithstanding its dubious credentials attained some notoriety because it spearheaded the movement and riots against the allegedly heretical Ahmediyya community. The biggest threat to a secularist stance on politics was mounted by the Jama'at-i-Islami. Led by Abdul Ala Maududi, its main support came from the Punjab. Although it had poor electoral success in the early 1950s, it was a movement that enjoyed the loyal support of small shopkeepers and the lower echelons of the army and civil service, and was capable of mounting large meetings and demonstrations.[36]

One became keenly aware in the 1980s, especially during the military rule of Zia's government, of the emotions, rhetoric, and polemics that the cause of Islamization can generate, and what that would entail with regard to the shape and content of government and its laws. And more than in any province, it is in the most populous and dominant province of the Punjab that Islamization has gathered its main supporters. Some skeptics have averred that talk of Islam as the cement that holds Pakistan together is loudest in the Punjab because it is a rhetoric that suits its domination of the country.

Pakistan has its religious parties and its *ulama* (Muslim clerics), and some of its prime ministers, such as Liaquat Ali Khan, and ministers, such as Fazlur Rahman, have been committed to instilling Islamic values into Pakistani society, while some later leaders, such as Zia, have gone so far as to advocate the rule of *shari'ah* (Islamic law). At the national and international levels, it seems to have been ideologically necessary, even imperative, for Pakistan to affirm its allegiance to Islam. By and large, however, neither the bulk of the civilian bureaucracy and army (especially their upper echelons), the majority of politicians operating in the national arena, the majority in the upper and middle reaches of urban society, the big landlords of the Punjab and Sind, nor the tribal chiefs of Baluchistan have ever taken it upon themselves to transform their society to fit the injunctions of the Qur'an. Whatever the predilections of Islamic "ideologues" and "reformers," it would be difficult and impracticable to write a history of independent Pakistan in which Islam provided the main thread of the story of the course of internal and external politics. Given the fact that Punjabis, Sindhis, Muhajirs, Biharis, Baluchis, and Pathans have over time interwoven and fused provincial territorial claims and participations, local cultural practices and social codes, distinctive languages and speech styles, distinctive clothing styles, and variant kinship systems with their parochial versions of Islamic traditions, it does not seem plausible to identify and reify a common set of Islamic practices as the core that gives all Pakistanis a national-religious identity. In public debate, there are those who remind their fellows that the Muslim League in 1940 passed a resolution in Lahore, the so-called Pakistan Resolution, that proposed that each of the independent Muslim states forming Pakistan would be "autonomous and sovereign," and that six years later, in 1946, the league's working committee affirmed this assurance. Indeed, there are some political groups in Pakistan today, notably the Tehrik-i-Istqhalal, who, while conceding that Islam is the country's common religion, say that the Pakistani "nation" is compounded of five different "nationalities," each with its own historical, ethnic, cultural, and linguistic traditions and roots, which are older than the concept of Pakistan. One cannot deny the voices of the ulama and mullahs who say that Islam invests Pakistan with its collective identity; it is noteworthy, however, that they are predominantly of Punjabi origin.

The problem of unity versus diversity, and the threat of separatism, has been an entrenched problem from the moment Pakistan was created. Before 1971, two different notions of Pakistan were held respectively by the Muhajirs who were refugees from India and those who by origin were Bengalis. For the former, "Pakistan represented a state that was to serve as a reference point for all Muslims in the subcontinent, in which Indo-Islamic culture would be fostered and protected (especially through the establishment of Urdu as the state language). This viewpoint was a logical extension of the public arena rhetoric on behalf of a Muslim community developed in Uttar Pradesh, an area already considered outside the likely borders of Pakistan." By contrast, "the Bengali vision of Pakistan focused on the working of relational alliances that would enable Muslims to escape domination by a Hindu elite." At the heart of the dispute between East and West Pakistan was a conflict over language. The Bengalis, of course, spoke a language with a venerable literary tradition; but for Punjabis and Biharis, "Urdu represented in the words of Jinnah, 'a language that has been nurtured by a hundred million Muslims of this continent. . . and above all, a language which more than any other provincial language, embodies the best that is in Islamic culture and Muslim tradition, and is nearest to the language used in their Islamic countries. When these two positions proved irreconcilable, . . . the problems of the relationship of the state to the minority was solved through geographic separation and creation of the nation state of Bangladesh."[37]

As we have seen, Pakistan has continued to generate separatist movements whose expression of regional and linguistic differences and identities challenges the counterproposition that reformist Islam and Urdu are what constitute Pakistan as a unity. The Urdu-centered Indo-Islamic culture is the unifying charter that Punjabi Muslims continue to advocate, and this does not recognize or meld with the regional, linguistic, and local religious traditions of the people of the North-West Frontier Province, the Pathans, the Sindhis, Baluchis, and so on.

This set of tensions coexists with another, related conundrum: how to reconcile Islamic identity and norms of conduct derived from shari'ah with the imperatives and norms associated with a modern secular state. "A conflict between a resurgent Islamic clergy and an urban, Western-educated elite undermines efforts to forge a consensus on how Pakistan will approach the 21st century," Edward Gargan has pointed out. However, this seemingly clear-cut opposition is muddied and made more complicated by the politics of the moment. Prime Minister Nawaz Sharif's government took steps to make Pakistan's economy a liberalized open-market-oriented one, which entailed the dismantling of state industry and many state-run banks, as well as lifting restrictions on foreign investment and holding foreign exchange—measures lauded by many of the capitalist-oriented elite (although rumors of corruption in high places abound). Western-educated Pakistani intellectuals were alarmed, however, by Sharif's "steady accession to the aggressive demands of Pakistan's religious right for a more rigid Islamic society. Indeed, the first public hangings and floggings under sharia, Islamic law, have been announced in recent weeks," Gargan noted in November 1991.[38]

CASE STUDY 2: BIHARI MUHAJIRS AND PATHANS IN KARACHI'S SQUATTER SETTLEMENTS

The ethnic riots that exploded in Karachi in April 1985 and October and December 1986 involved Muhajirs and Pathans. But the majority of the Muhajirs in question were Urdu-speaking Bihari refugees from the newly proclaimed nation of Bangladesh. They were especially concentrated in the poor settlements on the northwestern fringes of Karachi, in particular the township of Orangi, Karachi's largest squatter settlement (*katchi abadi*), with an estimated population of about one million. "Ethnically speaking, the township has representations from every ethnic group in Pakistan, but is dominated by the Biharis and Pathans, each of whom constitutes approximately 25 percent of the population. The remaining 50 percent of the population is a mixture of Punjabis, Sindhis, Baluchis, Bengalis, Muhajirs, and the more recently arrived Afghan refugees."[39]

Karachi had had a large Muhajir presence since Partition. Then, in the early 1970s, Biharis who had supported Pakistan in the Bangladesh secession war started to arrive in Sind. Some of these were later repatriated, but many others were left in limbo in refugee camps, because Sindhis feared they might lose their linguistic majority. Subsequently, the city's demography changed again, especially with the large influx of Pathans from heavily populated parts of the North-West Frontier Province, who migrated in search of work in Karachi's industrial plants and used the city as a transfer point and conduit for reaching job opportunities in the Middle East.

The most spectacular and fateful niche seized by the Pathans has been the monopoly control of Karachi's transport and trucking sector. With the onset of the Afghanistan war in 1979, Afghan refugees flooded the slums and squatter settlements of Karachi, bringing in their train the trade in narcotics and in arms. The Afghans and Pathans have interwoven their trading, transport, and smuggling interests. It is estimated that a total of three million Afghan refugees found their way to Pakistan, and of these about one hundred thousand drifted to Karachi. The narcotics and arms smuggling activities of the Afghans are interwoven with the interests that monopolize transport, and both in turn have their deals with and pay protection money to segments of the police and administration:

> Heroin arrived with the Afghan refugees and the lucrative profits of the trade rapidly transformed the traditional poppy-growing areas of Pakistan's north into the golden crescent of heroin. The massive aid provided to the Afghan refugees by the United States in the form of arms and ammunition quickly found its way into the local markets to provide narcotics dealers with armed backup. The two are inextricably linked, and recent years have seen the emergence of a powerful narcotics-arms mafia, accompanied by the growth of a smuggling-transport-police nexus. The fact that the arms and heroin flow into Karachi from the Frontier, combined with the high profile of Pathans in the transport business, creates the impression that the Pathans are in the forefront.[40]

And indeed they are. Certain Pathan settlements in Karachi have become the centers of the trade in arms and narcotics, and as may be expected, they are both at the nodes of the transport system and at critical entry and exit points. For example, Sohrab Goth and Quidabad are controlled by the narcotics-arms mafia and slum landlords.

As populations living contiguously in densely peopled space, there are no two groups in Karachi more different from each other than the Pathans and the Biharis. Pathans speak Pushto, while the Muhajirs, including the Bihari, speak Urdu. The ethnically diverse Muhajirs are city dwellers of long standing and have lifestyles and communicative codes utterly different from those of the Pathans, with their tribal heritage and rural background. Muhajirs also have a strong sense of their old homelands, where kinsmen have been left behind. These remain their ethnic point of reference. Most Muhajir of Bihari origin have been and are poor, although by virtue of their artisanal and small-shopkeeping skills, many of them have been able to establish themselves on a firmer economic basis, provoking the envy of even poorer and newer refugees.

The politics of real estate development and territorial control is a crucial ingredient in the periodic explosions in the squatter settlements, which now harbor close to 40 percent of Karachi's population. Although officially illegal, these settlements have been a source of tidy profits. State officials collude in the illegal occupation of land by developers, who then subdivide and sell plots to the poor. The officials receive commissions and themselves profit by speculating in choice plots. The developers at the next remove are able to lobby for amenities and services, and also for protection from eviction.

In the era before the Afghanistan war, these developers were Muhajirs and Punjabis, whose power and wealth were legitimated by their joining prominent political parties, such as the PPP. But it would appear that the fortunes and power generated by the Pathan- and Afghan-run heroin and arms trade affected real estate politics and the control of space and movement in Karachi in the late 1970s and the 1980s. "New patterns of illegal land development emerged; new systems of informal banking came into being; the transporters mafia expanded to control the city roads and the old squatter settlements came under attack."[41] The transporters' competitive and reckless driving terrorizes the streets, and their retaliatory strikes and stoppage of transport can immobilize a populous city with little public transport.

THE PATHAN-BIHARI RIOTS OF APRIL 1985

Akmal Hussain identifies "transport problems" in Karachi as "the immediate context" making the Pathan and Muhajir communities "vulnerable to being emotionally manipulated into ethnic conflict." Most of the private minibuses linking the various districts of Karachi are owned and operated by Pathans. Owners of fleets of minibuses lease them out at high rates to individual drivers, who are among the poorer members of the Pathan community, and they in turn drive at breakneck speed to beat competitors in picking up passengers, thereby causing frequent accidents. The vehicles, locally dubbed "yellow devils," are notorious killers. Most of Karachi's population, which has grown at a staggering rate, lacks basic public services such as water, housing, and transport, which are scarce, poorly distributed, and subject to frequent breakdowns. "For most citizens, the emotional trigger is early pulled," Hussain says. "Thus, even relatively minor incidents can spark off a riot: A traffic accident, a murder, or a kidnapping." *Between January 1986 and August 1987 alone, there were 242 incidents of rioting in Karachi.* The largest number of deaths (188) occurred as the result of politically motivated bomb explosions, which led to 76 riots; accidents caused by "the transport problem" resulted in 78 deaths and triggered 17 riots.[42]

It was a traffic accident that triggered the 1985 riots in Orangi. Official reports put the death toll at 50, but it was closer to 100 by unofficial estimates. Most of those killed were from Orangi, but the precipitating accident itself occurred elsewhere. The riots took on an ethnic coloring in Orangi only, and that is what has to be explained.

In the early hours of April 15, a girl called Bushra Zaidi, attending Sir Syed College, was killed by a bus, which, racing another bus, jumped the red light, hit a parked vehicle, and careened into a group of students standing inside the College. Angered by Zaidi's death, her fellow students from Sir Syed College and the adjacent Sind Government College for Girls took to the streets to protest the incident, and they were supported by the public at large.

Regular and riot police arrived on the scene and mismanaged the incident. When a female student climbed onto a parked police jeep to address the demonstrators, the police reacted by starting the jeep and driving into the crowd, toppling her, and injuring many students. They followed this with teargassing and baton-charging the demonstrators, and scores of students had to be treated at the Abbassi Shaheed Hospital. The brutality inflicted by the all-male police on the young girls provoked many spectator males to join the fray. Within minutes the main road called Nazimabed became a battleground in which the police fought a "male public"—which included many students who were alleged to belong to a well-organized right-wing student union, the Jamiat-e-Tuleba, and who were accused by the police of staging the protest. The firing by the police into the crowds caused at least ten deaths that day, plus scores of wounded.

In the next phase, the disturbance "spread like wildfire," engulfing the entire Nazimabad area and spilling over into other areas of Karachi (see map 3).

> Buses and other transport vehicles were stopped, pelted with stones and set on fire, streets were barricaded by the police but also by demonstrators who burnt boardings and car tires. Skirmishes took place between members of the public and the police and transporters. Within hours of Bushra Zaidi's death, what had started as a spontaneous reaction to an accident escalated into widespread rioting which continued for several days and was only brought under control by the imposition of strict curfew in large sections of the city, including Karachi's West District, which houses two million inhabitants in the largest squatter settlements of the country (the largest being Orangi and Baldia).[43]

We should note that although the riot was "unplanned," it erupted in a context of general public grievances, which included the transport problem. There is evidence that the protest against the transporters and the police (who were bracketed together) was spearheaded by (male) students who were better organized and also able "to mobilize and sustain protest in other areas over the next few days." For example, a cavalcade of forty youngsters on twenty-five motorbikes rode through the streets urging "the entire Nazimabad commercial area stretching along the main road where the accident occurred" to close down in protest on the day following the accident (April 16). The shops responded.

The next event in the saga on the same day was the response of the now "victimized" Pathan transporters, who called "a lightning strike paralyzing

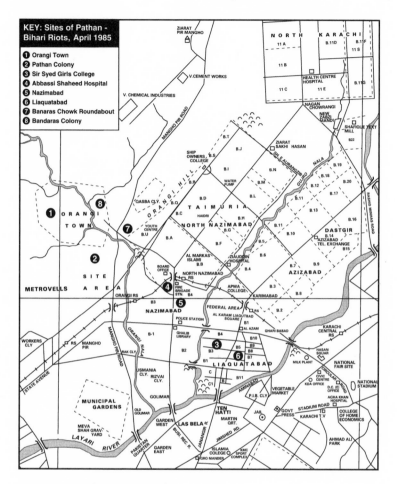

Map 3.   Part of Greater Karachi.

the city," to protest the burning of their buses, minibuses, and some trucks, and to demand police protection and state compensation for the losses they had sustained. The transporters (many of whom were Pathan) also "retaliated against the public by ransacking a dozen houses and setting fire to police cars and motorcycles (the latter being associated with students) in the northern parts of Karachi." The army was called in by 4 P.M. on April 16 to patrol the Nazimabad and Liaquatabad areas, and the soldiers also cordoned off many of the roads leading from the city center to the west and north of Karachi.

It was at this same time of army intervention (April 16) that the severe eruption in Orangi Township began, when a bus loaded with students on their way to attend funeral prayers for Bushra Zaidi, which were to take place in her house in Nazimabad, was forced to make a detour and arrived at the Banaras Chowk roundabout. The Chowk happened to be the only entry point into Orangi, which it also links to Karachi via Nazimabad. A group of Pathan transporters gathered there pelted the bus with stones, and a scuffle ensued between the Pathans and the students.

In order to understand the rioting's final displacement and crystallization as a Pathan-Muhajir ethnic conflict, we need to note that approximately 250,000 of the estimated 1.5 million Pathans living in Karachi are concentrated in Orangi. Furthermore, because of their involvement in the transport business, Pathans tend to congregate around bus and truck depots, auto-repair shops, and bus terminals. Banaras Chowk is a bus terminal for several transport routes, and thus a center for all those activities involved with transport and its ancillary needs, ranging from repair shops to eating places. It was an ethnic stronghold of the Pathans.

So after the incident with the students, the Pathan belligerents, inflamed and thirsting for more action, proceeded to the Abdullah Girls College, situated a short distance from Banaras Chowk. "Once there, the rowdy group entered the college premises, smashed the laboratory equipment, disrupted classes and generally intimidated the students."

Still in a belligerent mood, the group of Pathans returned to Orangi and ended up in Bokhari Colony, where they continued to give vent to their anger." (Bokhari Colony is a non-Pathan settlement in close proximity to Banaras Chowk; it contains Urdu-speakers and a varied population of Muhajirs, but it is not a Bihari settlement.) The Pathans "attacked and set fire to a dozen shops as well as burning down half a dozen shacks in the locality, causing the death of six or seven persons including one woman who was burnt to death." Although the Muhajirs of Bokhari Colony did not retaliate, news of the rampage circulated fast, embroidered with unfounded rumors, and intensifying the free-floating tension.

On April 17 (the third day), a small contingent of from thirty to forty policemen arrived in Orangi to maintain law and order. They told shopkeepers—both Pathans and Muhajirs—located in sectors 5 and 10 and in Urdu Chowk to close up shop. Members of the crowds roving the streets also took it upon themselves to urge the shopkeepers to comply. But the recalcitrant owner of Quetta Bolan Hotel in Sector 10, who happened to be a Quetta Pathan, refused to do so. This made the crowd more insistent. Surrounded by a hostile crowd, the owner panicked and fired, injuring four students. The hotel was reduced to ashes, starting "a general bout of rioting in which the steel and crockery shops in the vicinity were attacked and looted." The crowd then moved to Urdu Chowk and dispersed from there.

However, the news, orally transmitted, distorted and reinterpreted in the process, took an ominous shape in the form of talk of an ethnic conspiracy and collision. "The bus incident at Banaras Chowk thus found itself *transformed into a Bihari-Pathan confrontation although there were no Bihari boys amongst the students*. Whether the Pathans or Bihari were blamed for initiating the violence depended on who was doing the telling. Moreover incidents which were not in fact causally linked, became so as news spread. So that, for example, the *Quetta Bolan Hotel incident was reported to have been a Bihari retaliation against the Pathan attack on the bus*."

These distortions spread, unchecked by a silent state-controlled television and radio and a news blackout by the official press. Groups of people gathering on the streets to exchange information were in danger of being perceived as gangs forming for attack and defense. And newspapers on April 17 reported incorrectly that clashes between Pathans and Biharis had taken place the previous day.

In the late morning of April 18, two truckloads of Pathans armed with axes and pistols toured the streets of the largely Pathan Afridi and Rahim Shah colonies. This caused much alarm, and rumors spread that these Pathans "were harassing non-Pathan residents and that two Bihari girls had been dragged out of their homes and mistreated. Consequently, people from other sectors, including a large number of Biharis, congregated on the scene. *It was at this stage that the confrontations, hitherto opposing the Pathans to everyone else, became a Bihari-Pathan affair*." By now full-fledged clashes were occurring between Pathans and Biharis. "If the Pathans were armed with pistols and axes, the Biharis retaliated with stones and bombs fashioned out of petrol, bulbs and metal piping. As the bombs exploded, fires broke out everywhere adding to the general state of chaos." By 12:30 P.M., rival crowds of Biharis and Pathans, about three to four hundred on each side, were engaged in pitched battle. Moreover, the political leaders of the locality (that is, the councilors of local bodies and newly elected members of the Provincial Assembly, mainly of Bihari affiliation) who were present, "far from trying to control the fighting and bring about a reconciliation . . . *were apparently inciting members of their respective communities to greater militancy*."

A contingent of both regular and riot police was immediately ordered into the area. High officials such as the district commissioner (west) and the sub and deputy martial law administrators converged and toured the area, discovering "wholesale arson in several areas in every sector of the township." After cordoning off the main road and using tear gas to disperse the warring factions, the police "finally managed to dislodge those agitators who, carrying firearms and other weapons, had taken up positions on the hill tops. Despite the presence of a large number of police and army patrol units, skirmishes and rioting continued throughout the day spreading to encompass an area of three square miles." Fire brigades were kept busy extinguishing fires in Mominabad and al-Fateh colonies, where the houses of both Pathans and Biharis were burnt. Even fire engines were attacked.

Despite the widespread clashes and extensive damage to property, it was not a case of large gangs deliberately forming and seeking out victims in the other community (the large clash in the Pathan area referred to earlier was exceptional). Violence typically broke out "in areas of mixed populations and places where small groups of either community happened to come into contact such as bus stops and terminals. Furthermore, rioting took place in a very uneven manner so that even in some of the areas of mixed population such as Sector 5, there was *apparently more looting than carnage* and the unruly elements were brought under control by the local residents." There was no large-scale abandoning of homes either.

Although the ethnic conflict was not so much a generalized explosion involving the rival communities in toto as it was a number of dispersed, discontinuous, encounters of small bands, the damage done to life and property in three days was quite considerable: by the evening of April 19, forty-one people had died, hundreds had been injured, at least three hundred shops and houses had been set ablaze, and a toweling factory and a silk factory had been destroyed. Since the rescue and hospital facilities were meager, many people died simply from loss of blood.

On April 20 and 21, army patrols were intensified, and a complete curfew imposed for thirty-six continuous hours. And many politicians and public figures began to disentangle themselves from their immediate involvements in the riots in order to address the implications of the Orangi incidents. However, rather than acting to cool down their ethnic constituencies, members of the banned political parties blamed the riots on their having been prevented from participating in the elections in March 1985, and charged that the unrest "had been instigated by those elements who also wanted to impede the return of a civilian government and democracy in the country."

In the meantime, the government acceded to the transporters' demand for compensation, thus putting an end to the five-day transport strike. The decision was unpopular with the general public, mainly on the grounds that giving in to the transporters' demands indirectly condoned their reckless driving, and that since vehicles were required by law to be insured, their owners should not be compensated by the government.

From April 22 onwards, things quieted down; the intermittent lifting of the curfew and the resumption of transport enabled people to go to work, especially in the industrial areas. Essential goods flowed into Orangi, and relief camps intensified their work. Orangi remained under partial curfew until the first week of May. Despite the uneasy calm, however, there had been a breakdown of communication between the Pathans and Biharis. The attempts of "peace committees" to discuss matters with assemblies composed of members of both communities were a failure; consequently, representatives of the communities were met separately.

The discrimination and punitive measures they suffered at the hands of the police and security forces were one of the Bihari community's major complaints. As Senator Javed Jabbar put it in a report to the governor of Sind: many citizens of Orangi, particularly the Biharis, feared that "due to the ethnic affinity between the composition of law-enforcing agencies and the other community [the Pathans], their own security is threatened. . . . It appears that the members of one community are being persecuted and victimized by units of law-enforcing agencies acting on the bequest of [*sic*] some representatives of the other community."

This kind of accusation by a victimized ethnic group against the security forces of the state is commonly encountered when the latter belong to an aggressor community, especially if it is the major ethnic group in the region. In the case of the Orangi disturbances, there is good ground for suggesting that the Pathan community and the police force and army had interests and prejudices in common. The army and police are recruited mainly from the Punjab, and in Karachi, it seems, a substantial proportion of the transport business is owned by police officers either directly or through their relatives.

THE TRAJECTORY OF COMMUNAL RIOTS: FURTHER ELABORATION OF THE PROCESSES OF FOCALIZATION AND TRANSVALUATION

We have seen how the original issue of the death of a schoolgirl ballooned into a more general protest against the inequities of the public transport system and that, again, into an anti-Pathan backlash. But there are more twists and turns to the story. Mischievous and distorted rumors circulated, unchecked by the government and its media; and armed, angry Pathans took to the streets in their locality in Orangi, where concentrations of Biharis, their alleged enemies, also lived. Neighborhood boundaries were breached, clashes proliferated, deteriorated, and narrowed into a stark Pathan-Bihari bloodbath. Thus, incidents that took place in the part of the city called Nazimabad came to roost in the Orangi slums many miles away; and the Biharis who had nothing to do with the original events—neither the schoolgirl who died nor her schoolmates were Bihari—were drawn by processes of "distorted" communication, rumors, and prior ethnic sensitivities into violent clashes with the Pathans.

The trajectory of the 1985 Karachi riots illustrates focalization and transvaluation, two processes already mentioned toward the end of chapter 3, in connection with the 1915 riots in colonial Ceylon. Through focalization and transvaluation, local incidents and small-scale disputes occasioned by domestic, business, neighborhood, or other particular issues, and involving people in direct contact with one another, cumulatively build up into larger and larger clashes between growing numbers of antagonists who were only indirectly or peripherally involved in the original disputes. This progressive involvement of the ethnic public coincides with their coming under the sway of propagandists who appeal to larger, more emotive, more enduring (and therefore less context-bound) loyalties and cleavages of race, language, religion, or place of origin. By *focalization,* I mean the process of progressive denudation of local incidents and disputes of their particulars of context and their aggregation. *Transvaluation* refers to the parallel process of assimilating particulars to a larger, collective, more enduring, and therefore less context-bound, cause or interest. The processes of focalization and transvaluation thereby contribute to a progressive polarization and dichotomization of issues and partisans, such that climactic acts of mob violence quickly become self-fulfilling manifestations, incarnations, and reincarnations of allegedly irresolvable communal splits between Pathans and Biharis, Sikhs and Hindus, Sinhalese and Tamils, or Malays and Chinese.

Thus, many phenomena that are linked, amalgamated, and labeled as "ethnic riots," occurring between named communities during a specified period of time, are constituted of complex processes, which shape the escalating course of events. At first, there is a distortion and inflation of the substantive nature of micro-events. Progressively, there occurs a denudation of the specificity of events occurring in their local contexts and their translation and assimilation to more context-free, allegedly enduring master principles of ethnic or communal identity, interests, and entitlements. The outcomes are seen as confirmations of ancient injuries committed by the enemy, and of furtive demographic swamping and economic displacement by the intruder, even unto extinction.

Thus, civilians and "ordinary folk," originally drawn into altercations and grievances because of breaches of kinship norms, *mohalla* or neighborhood loyalty, or business trust, and harried by daily worries about employment for adults, educational opportunities for children, and the keeping of business clients, find themselves caught in a snowballing process and end up as particles of a large, homogenized, and energized avalanche. The difference is that as human masses, they respond to mytho-historical clarion calls that recall their past, explain their present, promise a rosier future, and justify and exonerate punitive violence.

FROM EPISODIC RIOTS TO CONTINUOUS CIVIL WAR

The ethnic riots thus far discussed were bursts of collective violence with a beginning and an end, and lasting two weeks or less. Such eruptions may recur spasmodically over a period of time to form a sort of series. But this discontinuous picture can change when the conflict between two ethnic communities becomes chronic and they move toward a state of continuous strife lasting several years, as for example happened in Northern Ireland and in Lebanon.

When these dynamics are operative, several things are likely to happen. First, aside from fighting with or resisting the ethnic enemy, the embroiled groups may also simultaneously find themselves engaged in warfare with the security forces of the state, initially the police and paramilitary units, and subsequently the army. The Muhajirs and Sindhis were perilously near this condition in 1991 (and the conflict has since worsened). Second, although civilians may participate in riots or in attacks, armed resistance groups or guerrillas increasingly become the defenders of the ethnic collectivity. The MQM of the Muhajirs and the Jiye Sind Movement of the Sindhis represent this phase of the ongoing crisis. (Similarly, the Tigers in Sri Lanka, fighting for Eelam, and the militant groups among the Sikhs fighting for Khalistan represent more mature developments, when episodic ethnic conflicts give place to a civil war.) Third, the conflict sets in motion conspicuous and massive relocations of people. Intimidation, arson, and killings cause a frightened exodus of refugees; then the expectation and fear of future violence pushes out more people, helped by staged threats, bullying, stone-throwing, and ethnic slurs painted on walls and shopfronts. People leave marginal areas or localities where they are a minority and move back to their centers, enclaves, or ghettos. The abandoned space,

houses, and buildings are taken over by the aggressors, and property developers, slum landlords, and businessmen striving to monopolize trade or
evict competitors all have their share in the way collective violence re-
structures urban space and ecology. The final stages of these processes
crystallize and cordon off ethnic groups in their enclaves, with barricades
separating them, and with spaces that are empty or filled with rubble or
dotted with the ruins of buildings, the "desolate interface zones" where
sniping is done, where code words are needed to leave and enter, and from
which further campaigns "for colonizing the outer margins of community
space" are launched.[44]

ISLAMIZATION AND ITS IMPLICATIONS
FOR NATIONAL UNITY

How far has the policy of Islamization succeeded in giving Pakistan a coherent national identity and unity?

Muhammad Ali Jinnah and the Muslim League used Islam to mobilize
support among the Muslims of the subcontinent, and Partition established
Pakistan as a Muslim homeland in 1947.[45] Jinnah saw Islam as providing a
common cultural heritage and identity for the Muslim majority, and it was
in this sense that Pakistan was a Muslim state. But for many others, Pakistan was meant to be, and imperatively needed to be, an Islamic state in
the sense that its legal system and institutions were based upon Islam. The
strong advocacy of renowned interpreters such as Muhammad Iqbal and
Maulana Maududi had their supporters among many ulama, and already
in the constitutional debates of the late 1940s and the early 1950s, strong
religiopolitical parties and pressure groups had formed, which, resisting
Jinnah and the Muslim League, clamored for an Islamically committed
state.[46]

Muhammad Iqbal (1877–1938), a poet-philosopher and renowned interpreter of Islam in South Asia, differed from Jinnah in regarding Islam
as an encompassing religio-social order and holding that Islamic law
(shari'ah) should be the law of Pakistan. He rejected the secularist program
of Turkish nationalists and wrote uncompromisingly: "The religious ideal
of Islam . . . is organically related to the social order which it has created.
The rejection of the one eventually involves the rejection of the other. . . .
In Islam God and the Universe, spirit and matter, Church and State, are organic to each other. . . . All that is secular is therefore sacred in the roots of
its being."[47]

Maulana Maududi, the leader of the Jama'at-i-Islami, whose ideas inspired the Pakistani model of Islamization, also took a moralistic and regulative view of the goals and obligations of an Islamic state:

> Unlike a Secular state, its duty is not merely to maintain internal order, to defend the frontiers and to work for the material prosperity of the country. Rather its first and foremost obligation is to establish the system of *Salat* [prayer] and *Zakat* [alms tax], to propagate and establish those things which have been declared to be "virtues" by God and His Messenger, and to eradicate those things which have been declared to be "vices" by them. In other words, no state can be called Islamic if it does not fulfill this fundamental objective of an Islamic State. Thus a state which does not take interest in establishing virtue and eradicating vice and in which adultery, drinking, gambling, obscene literature, indecent films, vulgar songs, immoral display of beauty, promiscuous mingling of men and women, co-education, etc., flourish without let or hindrance, cannot be called an Islamic State. An Islamic Constitution must declare the above mentioned objective as the primary duty of the State.[48]

Although claimed essentially to charter a Western-inspired parliamentary democracy, Pakistan's first constitution in 1956 reflected an uneasy and unclear compromise between liberal modernists and Islamic enthusiasts. "Islamic provisions were inserted in response to the demands and concerns of those who pushed for a clearer articulation of Islamic identity. The title of the state was the Islamic Republic of Pakistan, the constitution required that the head of state be a Muslim, no law was to run counter to the Qur'an and Sunnah of the prophet."[49] The establishment of the Islamic Ideology Council to advise the government on its laws and policies, and of the Islamic Research Institute, in no way, however, meant a commitment to systematic thoroughgoing implementation of Islamic law, and the question remained as to what such a task implied and whether it were pragmatically feasible. Tensions and contending interpretations between liberalizing modernists and neotraditionalists characterized the regimes of Ayub Khan (1958–69) and Zulfikar Ali Bhutto (1971–77). These problems were further compounded by continuing disagreements among the ulama themselves, and between the Muslim sects (for example, Sunni versus Shiite, and, within the Sunni, different emphases among schools of thought such as the Deobandi, Wahhabi, and Barelvi). While ulama of Sunni and Shiite persuasions could agree on who could be excluded from the Islamic fold— as we have seen in the case of the Ahmedis—among themselves they lacked unanimity concerning Islamic tenets and their interpretation, and there was no central teaching authority to turn to for the orthodox version of truth.

When Ayub Khan, who has been characterized as a Western-oriented Muslim "primarily concerned with establishing a strong centralized government and fostering rapid socio-economic change," established the first martial-law regime in 1958, he reconstituted the Islamic Research Institute and the Council on Islamic Ideology and directed them "to define and interpret Islamic belief and practice in a rational and liberal manner and thus bring out its dynamic character in the context of the intellectual and scientific progress of the modern world."[50] But his appointment of modernist lay Islamic scholars and his modernizing changes were resisted by the ulama. A case in point was their opposition to changes in marriage, divorce, and inheritance practices proposed by a majority of the Commission on Marriage and Family Law Reform. "Although Ayub Khan, with the support of women's organizations like the All Pakistan Women's Association (APWA), was able to enact the Muslim Family Laws Ordinance of 1961, the scope of reform was less than that originally envisioned and the law remained a subject of controversy which would reemerge during the regime of General Zia ul-Haq." However Ayub firmly resisted pressures from the ulama to introduce state collection of *zakat* (a two and a half percent wealth tax), abolition of bank interest, flogging for certain Islamically proscribed crimes—issues which later would resurface and find sympathetic reception under Zia ul-Haq.

Zulfikar Ali Bhutto, who succeeded Ayub, allegedly pursued a policy of "socialist Islam": "Although ideologically and temperamentally Bhutto was a secular socialist, political realities within Pakistan and the Arab world led to an increasing appeal to religion in his domestic and foreign policy," John Esposito writes.[51] It would be more accurate, however, to characterize Bhutto as a feudal aristocrat in origins and style of life who was also politically inclined toward a directed welfare policy, if not socialism, in the interests of the people at large.[52] He sought and wanted power—Napoleon was his hero—and his politics followed from this a priori. His father, Shah Nawaz, was a Shiite Muslim, whose wife was a Hindu convert to Islam, but both parents and their son worshipped and asked for favors at the shrine of Lal Shahbaz, Sind's greatest Sufi saint.[53] Zulfikar Bhutto was by no means a pious Muslim, and his penchant for a luxurious social life, which included heavy drinking, extramarital flings (which certainly come under the ban of *hudud*), and hunting on his estates was a far cry from the precepts of the Islamicists. However, and this is the important aspect of his politics, from his youth he rhetorically yearned for a "great" and "sovereign" Muslim state of Pakistan that would be part of the larger conglomeration of Muslim peoples in India and the Middle East.[54] And, as Esposito indicates, the situational logic of his time required Bhutto to attend to certain Islamic issues.

The 1971 civil war that led to the secession of Bangladesh was blamed in Pakistan on the Ayub regime's failure to forge a national identity rooted in Islam. Moreover, Bhutto's pragmatic turning to Muslim oil countries, especially those located in the Gulf, for aid and as an outlet for Pakistani products, laborers, and military advisors was felicitously linked to the invocation of their common Islamic identity and heritage. "Improved relations with the oil sheikhdoms were accompanied by the Bhutto government's sponsorship of Islamic conferences, promotion of programs for the study of Arabic, introduction of Islamic regulations and laws restricting alcohol, creation of places for workers to perform their daily prayers of worship."[55] When the Jama'at-i-Islami and many religious leaders mounted a campaign against his socialist program, "Bhutto attempted to Islamize his socialism by identifying it with Islam and equating it with notions of Islamic egalitarianism and social justice. Bhutto's Pakistan People's Party (PPP) adopted Islamized socialist slogans like Islamic equality . . . and published materials which offered an Islamic justification for government socialist policies such as land reform and nationalization of banks, insurance companies, and many industries."[56]

But this attempt to Islamize socialism was roundly condemned by religious leaders such as Maulana Maududi of the Jama'at-i-Islami, who made the derisive comment that it was because his socialism had failed (and could not "dance naked") that Bhutto called it Islamic, in the hope of shoring it up. Bhutto was thus forced to make concessions such as omitting the words "Islamic socialism" from the constitution of 1973, and, perhaps more ignominiously, declaring the Ahmedi community to be a non-Muslim minority whose members were ineligible to hold the highest government positions. There was an escalation in the rhetoric concerning the proper and acceptable relation between Islam and politics, and "religion had so become a primary vehicle for mass politicization by both government and opposition . . . that in the general elections of March 1977 a broad coalition of secular and religious opposition parties, the Pakistan National Alliance (PNA), had placed itself under the umbrella of Islam, promising an Islamic system of government (nizam-i-Mustafa)."[57] Support was drawn from the traditional and modern middle class: urban intellectuals, merchants and businessmen, teachers, doctors, and clerical workers who opposed Bhutto's socialist measures. "The middle class nature of the PNA was reinforced by the presence and leadership of the religious parties . . . whose primary base was the urban and town based middle class."[58] But Bhutto and his PPP managed to hold on and win the elections, although the way they were conducted and the results were contested by his opponents. The dialectical interweaving of Islam and politics had by now taken such a feverish turn that in many ways the stage was set for General Zia ul-Haq's coup d'état in the name of Islam on July 5, 1977.

The attempt to Islamize state and society would reach its apogee under Zia. By the same token, that effort would also unleash all the complications and contradictions and animosities engendered by an attempt to employ the religion of Islam—which was by no means, as it turned out, a monolithic or generally agreed-upon system of beliefs, interpretations, and practices—as the encompassing framework for Pakistan's politics and policies.

The Pakistani Islamization drive, supported by Zia, who was president of the military regime for twelve years, from 1977 to 1988, sought an antidote in the shariʿah to the alleged oppression of Muslim countries by the West, especially the undermining of traditional practices and subversion of Muslim religious obligations by Western-style law and legal systems. A central Muslim perception is that Islamic law would restore traditional moral values and social order, which explains Muslims' fixation on shariʿah and the legal system as the focal point of reform, restoration, and change. As Anne Elizabeth Mayer puts it, contemporary Muslim fundamentalists tend to transform the shariʿah—an elaborate jurisprudence with extensive technical legal rules and interpretations elaborated by premodern jurists— "into an ideology, thereby treating it as a scheme for reorganizing society that, because of its divine origins, can serve as a panacea for political, economic and social ills."[59]

Thus a return to the shariʿah could mean "a pattern of hostile reactions to modernization measures, and a commitment to buttressing the patriarchal family, expanding religious instruction in public schools, imposing discriminatory measures on religious minorities, and Muslim dissidents, challenging the legality of land reform programs, or preventing women from working and serving in public office."[60]

It is in line with fundamentalist and reform tendencies that from the whole corpus of shariʿah rules, certain of them were selectively focused on and reinterpreted to suit contemporary preoccupations and challenges. Thus today's preoccupation with rules in criminal justice and the extension of the range of criminal conduct contrasts with the premodern jurisprudence's greater concern with civil matters. Aside from crimes listed earlier such as theft, apostasy, fornication, and use of alcohol, there have been modern extensions that seek to prohibit abortion, girls' and women's participation in sports, coeducational schooling, dancing and music, "immodest" and "un-Islamic" women's dress, women's participation in the professions and services, and "obscenity" in books, movies, and television programs.[61]

It is one thing for enthusiasts of Islamization policies, especially the members of the fundamentalist Jama'at-i-Islami, to advocate the reimposing of the shari'ah (and extending its interpretation to cover modern Western-inspired "immoralities"), but it is another for them to succeed in a country with a historical legacy of social and political developments under British rule, including secular education—a legacy of Anglo-Islamic and British law, the rise of a military, bureaucratic, and professional elite (including a legal profession) who had imbibed Western juridical, libertarian values, including the right of women to be educated and enter public life, which would resist and impede the fundamentalist "restoration."

Aside from this, Pakistan has a large minority of Shiite Muslims, who have a tradition of being liberal, and having little sympathy for the militant fundamentalist groups drawn from the Sunni majority. (In this respect Pakistan's Shiites present a strong contrast to the Iranian Shiite fundamentalists led by Ayatollah Ruholla Khomeini and his successors.) Moreover, the Islamic fundamentalists as such did not by themselves have the numbers and persuasiveness to win parliamentary elections.

In fact, the story of Pakistan's Islamization program is integrally tied to the alliance between a military dictatorship—under Zia for twelve years—and the fundamentalist movement, both of which, however, had their opponents within the country's military and bureaucratic elites. Zia, although personally a devout Sunni Muslim, found in the Islamization program a moral imperative and rationalization for perpetuating his military rule and postponing elections.

After staging his coup, Zia pledged himself to implement an Islamic system of government. "Zia employed Islam as a source of national identity, legitimacy, cultural interpretation and public morality to a degree which exceeded that of any previous government," John Esposito writes. He had Bhutto hanged for his un-Islamic behavior, appointed some members of the Pakistan National Alliance to key government positions, and appropriated the PNA slogan "Nizam-i-Islam" (Islamic government). He also appointed some prominent members of Jama'at-i-Islami, whose leader Maulana Maududi's writings strongly influenced him, especially his advocacy of Islam as a comprehensive way of life and assertions that the Qur'an and Sunnah must be accepted as the only source of law, and that all laws must conform to the tenets of Islam. In 1979, Zia announced reforms, crucial among which was the intention to establish shari'ah courts to determine whether specific laws were repugnant to Islam. Early in his administration (February 1979), Zia committed his government to enforcement of the shariʿah.

> Zia continued and expanded the scope of Islamic legal reforms introduced by Bhutto (such as the banning of alcohol and gambling, the closing of businesses and government offices for Friday congregational prayer, provision of space for workers to perform daily worship—salat or namaz). He introduced that part of the Islamic penal law known as the *hudud* (the limits of God), crimes expressly forbidden and appropriate punishment stipulated by Allah. Examples are flogging for consumption of intoxicants, false accusation of adultery, and banditry; amputation for theft; stoning to death for adultery. In actual fact, of these punishments, only flogging was administered, the others being considered controversial for various reasons such as that the *hudud* which presumed a socially just society was incommensurate with a society divided by poverty and need, or that the debilitating impact of colonialism required a period of education and preparation before ideal norms are imposed.[62]

Zia's mandate that the Islamic Ideology Council review Pakistan's laws to determine whether or not they were consonant with Islamic law, and to recommend appropriate legislation where required, went even further toward Islamizing Pakistan's legal system. At the same time, a shariʿah court was created to hear cases that challenged the Islamic character of existing laws or draft laws, and a shariʿah bench was created in the High Court in each of Pakistan's four provinces.

But in the judicial as well as other domains, Zia's Islamization policies were hobbled by contradictions and dissent, which indicate the difficulties of translating a religious charter into actual practice in contexts of cultural plurality, social differentiation, colonial experience, and the coexistence of modernity and tradition. A major contradiction and inconsistency stemmed from Zia's dictatorship, his military rule, and his virtual placing of himself above the law when it suited him. Thus the shariʿah court and its benches were barred by him from reviewing laws in three areas: the constitution and martial-law ordinances, Muslim family laws, and fiscal laws. "Second with the cancellation of elections and extension of martial law, the implementation of the courts' findings in the form of legislation meant in actuality the assent of Zia as CMLA. As Zia's critics posed the quandary: 'If the Sharia, God's law, was to reign supreme, then how could certain areas of law be exempted from review and why were the findings of the Sharia benches regarding God's law subject to review by the head of state?' "[63] In due course, the fact that martial-law ordinances and military courts were exempt from scrutiny undermined the implementation of many Islamization measures.

Other quasi-Islamic judicial reforms included the creation of *qazi* (*gadi*, judge) courts and the Department of Public Morality in the early 1980s. The primary beneficiaries of this move were the ulama, for the principal qualification for qazi status was knowledge of Islamic law (*fiqh*) and not a degree in modern law. "Aware that many of the ulama regarded Pakistan's legal system of law to be antithetical to Islam, the Pakistan Bar Council was quick to issue its own report which maintained that Islamic history confirmed that Pakistan's judicial system was in accord with Islam and that with some reforms the prevailing system of judges and lawyers were fully capable of meeting Pakistan's needs of Islamizing the law and providing swift and inexpensive justice."[64]

It was in economic matters that Islamic precepts collided critically with capitalist free-market principles and entrepreneurial interests. Islamic activists appealed to Islamic precedents for imposing property and wealth taxes and banning usury. Here again irony and ambivalence and lack of authoritative clarity came into play when alleged Islamic values were translated into practice. Although the shari'ah court upheld previous land reforms and nationalization measures introduced by the Ayub Khan and Bhutto governments, both Zia and the court "were responsive to the concerns of landowners, industrialists, and the majority of religious leaders, who had objected to Bhutto's socialism, and strongly supported the right to private property as the Islamic norm."[65]

Contentious and provocative and capable of generating divisive special pleading were, among others, two issues: the imposition of an alms (*zakat*) tax and the elimination of usury, especially in the form of interest charges by banks ("the curse of interest").

The government's compulsory collection of zakat found critics: some held that zakat is a tithe, a private obligation, not a tax; others, that zakat is a personal individual responsibility, which should not be bureaucratized. The most damaging result of imposing zakat was its exacerbation of sectarian tensions between Pakistan's Sunni majority and its Shiite minority (15 percent of the population). Shiites protested that impositions based on the Hanafi (Sunni) school of law did not necessarily accord with Jafari (Shiite) legal principles.[66] A case in point was zakat, which for Shiites is not compulsory on capital or trading money. Similar differences of interpretation occurred with respect to Islamic penal laws and the punishments attached to them. "In July 1980, Shiite leaders convened a conference in Islamabad which drew more than 100,000 Shii. This was followed by a protest demonstration on July 5 of some 25,000 Shii against compulsory zakat."[67] The government, faced with this dissent, revised the law, enabling

Muslims to obtain an exemption based on "faith and *fiqh*." On the whole, the large minority of Shiite Muslims have shown little sympathy for the militant fundamentalist groups drawn from the Sunni majority.

Similarly, a proposal made in a report prepared on behalf of the Council of Islamic Ideology to eliminate interest on all domestic transactions by stages over three years evoked opposition from within the government and its commissions. However, the government did proceed to introduce interest-free bank accounts on a voluntary basis in many branches of its nationalized commercial banks in 1981. Government institutions such as the House Building Finance [mortgage] Corporation, the National Investment Trust, and the Investment Corporation of Pakistan were also directed to run on an interest-free basis. By July 1985, bank interest was abolished on all bank accounts. Overall, in terms of practical consequences, Islamization, despite opposition, did result in extensive restructuring of the operations of financial institutions to eliminate interest; and in changes in the tax system after the enactment of the alms tax.[68]

The Zia regime had a restricting impact on women's rights, and women's movements and organizations arose and demonstrated vigorously. Fundamentalist forces and many ulama considered that Islamic norms of modesty required the separation of the sexes in public, the implementation of traditional Islamic laws, and the repeal of the modernizing reforms enacted in the Muslim Family Laws Act of 1961. They considered that veiling and seclusion of women should be enforced in education, the media, and business, and railed that modern changes allowing more freedom to women compromised their modesty. The following statement issued in early 1984 by the Central Committee of the Jama'at-i-Islami resonates with their vehemence:

> Open violation of Islamic ethics, rebellion from Islamic teachings has now reached an alarming point in our society. The public media organizations, with the connivance of certain corrupt officers, are bent upon converting our society into a mixed and shameless one. Vulgar songs, semi-nude and immoral advertising, programs of dance and music, encouragement of mixed gatherings on television, particularly unreserved [sic] dialogue delivered by boys and girls, the color editions of newspapers full of huge colored pictures of women and feminine beauty are only a few examples of this condemnable conspiracy. This dangerous wave of vulgarity has now gripped the country. Performances by foreign troupes attended by certain very important government officials, fancy dress shows, vulgar stage plays in the name of art, mixed gatherings, country-wide virus of VCR, dancing and musical programs, printing of girls' pictures in the newspapers in the name of sports, mixed education, employment of women in certain government departments to make them

more attractive and the day-by-day rising process of seating men and women under one roof in government and business offices and even in local councils are all "red" signs of dangers against the society and Islamic ethics.[69]

Such sentiments were voiced in Friday mosque sermons, pamphlets, newspapers, and Parliament.

It is interesting that unlike in Iran, the Pakistani fundamentalists were partially thwarted by women's movements and protests from imposing their restrictions and curbs on women's rights and freedoms. The Council of Islamic Ideology (CII), one of the organizations to which Zia entrusted the task of formulation of Islamization measures, was of the view that women should be confined to a domestic role, and that it was "westernized individuals" in Pakistan who want to bring women out of their homes and make them the center of attraction in society. Fundamentalists, given access to the media, broadcast claims that Westernized women were the source of decadence and immorality, and that sexual segregation was essential for the preservation of virtue.

A series of directives in the early 1980s were aimed at limiting women's public exposure and visibility, such as their appearance on television. Women broadcasters were required to cover their heads and wear the *dupatta* (a thin cloth worn over their dress). Women athletes were permitted to play only before all-female audiences and were banned from participating in international competitions. When finally admitted to the Islamic University, women were educated in separate facilities from men.

Women's groups organized opposition to the Zia regime when it threatened to infringe upon their rights. Restrictive measures such as those listed above "politicized women's organizations such as the All Pakistan Women's Association, which had been the oldest women's rights organization, the National Women Lawyers' Association, and the Women's Action Forum, which had sprung up as professional women in particular were increasingly mobilized" to counter the threat of Zia's program to women's status and interests.[70] Women engaged in public protests in Lahore in February 1983 to denounce a proposed law on evidence that would allow a woman's testimony to be devalued in relation to a man's. The original draft Evidence Bill asserted that the evidence of two women equaled that of one Muslim male, but this was later modified to apply only in specified cases.[71] "Although the evidence law was enacted in 1984, the regime was chastened by the feminists' response. Thus certain proposals for new laws, such as one that would have reinstated the Sharia rule that in cases of killings the value of a woman's life was to be calculated as being worth one-half that of a man's, were never actually enacted, despite strong support from fundamentalists."[72]

Zia's authoritarianism, which had banned political parties and had restricted political participation, inevitably engendered a cumulative thrust for the restoration of democracy. In February 1981, the banned political parties came together to form the Movement for the Restoration of Democracy (MRD). In due course, even religious leaders who favored Zia's Islamization program found common cause with other political parties in calling for elections. By the spring of 1984, the Jama'at-i-Islami, which had continued to support Zia, called for a joint front to oppose martial law and campaign for the restoration of democracy, and declared a nonconsultative military government to be un-Islamic.

In February 1985, national and provincial elections took place on a non-party basis, with Zia still maintaining that Islamic democracy did not permit political parties. However, by the end of 1985, martial law was terminated, civilian rule was restored, press censorship was lifted, and political parties were allowed to function with some restrictions. But even this transition to democracy was compromised by Zia's amendment of the constitution to assure the ultimate power of the president to appoint and dismiss the prime minister and to exempt from prosecution those associated with his martial-law regime.

Despite the inauguration of a civilian government under Prime Minister Muhammad Khan Junejo, there was a mounting political protest on the part of both the MRD and the Jama'at-i-Islami demanding free elections based on a political party system and the resignation of Zia as army chief of staff if he were to be a true civilian president. And then in 1986, Benazir Bhutto appeared on the scene to lead the protest and to revive and energize her father's party, the PPP.

After more than a decade of military rule and rule under martial law from 1977 to 1985, which while pushing for Islamization also permitted some dissent and had in some ways moved pragmatically in piecemeal fashion, Zia in June 1988 took the fateful step of issuing a presidential decree that asserted that all government policies would henceforth be guided by Islamic law, and that all laws contravening Islamic law would be nullified. "This *Islamic Law Enforcement Ordinance* was apparently designed to implement Islamic law across the board under clerical supervision and to make all laws, including the constitution, subordinate to the Sharia, as had been provided in article 4 of the Iranian constitution. To avoid problems with foreign aid donors and institutional creditors, one exception was made for international economic and investment agreements."[73] The Islamization decree, which may have been prompted by Zia's fears of the elections scheduled for the autumn, and his strategy of using Islamic criteria to disqualify Benazir Bhutto, on the grounds that a woman's serving in high political office contravened the shari'ah, was vigorously denounced from all parts of the political spectrum. "Zia's death on 17 August 1988 *before the decree had been formally ratified* left it a dead letter."[74]

Zia had saddled Pakistan with a constitutional arrangement that would plague the country's politics in the years after his death (1988–93, the terminal year for this account). When in 1983, the Movement for the Restoration of Democracy challenged the military regime, Zia agreed to restore democracy in the form of a Parliament elected on a nonparty basis, but "as a quid pro quo, he secured the Parliament's approval for the Eighth Amendment to the 1973 Constitution, which tilted the balance of power in the President's favour unlike the original version which granted Powers to the Prime Minister."[75] The president was to be elected for a term of five years by an electoral college consisting of two Houses of Parliament and the four provincial assemblies; he was empowered to appoint judges to the Supreme Court and the chiefs of armed services; he could appoint as prime minister a member of the National Assembly if, in his opinion, the person was likely to command the confidence of other members; and finally, the president could dissolve both the national assemblies if, in his opinion, a situation had arisen in which the government could not function in accordance with the provisions of the constitution. "To put it differently, the Prime Minister holds office at the pleasure of the President," Samina Yasmeen observed.[76]

If, from 1985 to 1988, the Eighth Amendment created an "unbalanced diarchy" in Pakistan (Zia was president as well as commander of the armed forces and had to deal with the elected national and provincial assemblies) after his death, the diarchy gave way to a troika, with a tug of war possible between the president, the army chief (and the army), and the prime minister.

Benazir Bhutto, who won the 1988 November elections and was asked to form a government, was the first prime minister to be trapped in this triangulation. Benazir and the PPP, which she led, despite invoking the memory of her father and benefiting from disillusionment with Zia's policies, managed to win only 92 of the 207 National Assembly seats. The acting president, Ghulam Ishaq Khan, and the military delayed handing over power until the PPP succeeded in establishing an alliance with the Muhajir Qaumi movement, giving it a majority in the Assembly, and until Benazir made certain compromises with the army.

The constraints under which Benazir operated were relevant to the subjects of ethnonational conflicts and the fate of Islamization. Given her uncertain hold on the country, and wary of alienating the ulama, she did not move to counter or diminish Zia's Islamic legacy, or to repeal the Islamic laws previously introduced. Deciding to present a public image consonant with Islamic practices, she went on a much-publicized pilgrimage to Mecca, contracted an arranged marriage with a businessman, and began to raise a family.

Even more problematic was the political problems of governance that assailed her against the backdrop of a hostile establishment that was prepared to move against her as opportunity arose.

> From the start, the federal government failed to establish a workable
> relationship with the provinces. Relations with the Baluchistan provincial
> government were tense throughout Bhutto's regime; growing political
> confrontation with Nawaz Sharif brought relations with Punjab to a low point;
> and the major cities in Bhutto's home province of Sindh suffered from the
> worst violence since independence. In addition, frequent allegations of
> corruption surrounded both the PPP and the Bhutto family. But most
> important, Benazir Bhutto frequently challenged the military, either directly
> or indirectly.[77]

In other words, she tried to interfere in army appointments.

With the reactivation of the Kashmir issue in 1990, and the army's alleged disapproval of her handling it, by August 1990, the rift between them had so widened that the army resolved to remove Benazir. The powers given the president by the Eighth Amendment provided the means. The military persuaded the president to dismiss Benazir's government on charges of maladministration and failure to work effectively with the provinces, nepotism, and corruption, and also to dissolve the assemblies.[78] General elections were thereupon held in October 1990, bringing Nawaz Sharif to power as leader of the Islami Jamhouri Itehad (IJI, or Islamic Democratic Alliance), an eight-party coalition. It seemed as if Sharif had better prospects of success than Benazir:

> From the outset, the Nawaz Sharif government operated under relatively
> different circumstances. In the 1990 elections, the IJI had gained a clear
> majority by winning 105 seats in the National Assembly. It also fared better
> than the PPP in elections for the provincial assemblies and was able to form
> governments in three of Pakistan's four provinces. Therefore, the everpresent
> tension between the federal and provincial administrations, which was a
> constant feature of the Bhutto regime, was not so apparent during the Sharif
> era, despite differences on various issues. In fact, the relative ease with which
> the Sharif government operated with the four provinces often enabled it to

settle long-standing disputes. In March 1991, for instance, the IJI government secured a long overdue accord among the provinces over apportionment of the Indus waters.[79]

Sharif's policies moved in two directions. He brought in his own bill, the Enforcement of Shariʿah Act, 1991, to make shariʿah law supreme in Pakistan, probably to ward off a more radical version from the religious parties; he also tried to attract Western investment by projecting pro-business and free-market orientations and downplaying Islamization. His drive for privatization and encouragement of foreign and local investment seemed to draw the support of small and large business interests, which saw the country's increased growth rate as proof of Sharif's business acumen.

But in due course Sharif, too, was entangled in the shifting politics of volatile interest groups, and, although he had initially come in with the support of the military, soon differences surfaced over Gulf War policy and the quicksand of army appointments. There were reports in 1992 that Sharif's efforts to steer Pakistan's economy toward "free markets and privatization" were being contested by fundamentalist groups.

In September 1992, journalists reported that Islamabad was rife with rumors of an impending crisis within the famed troika—the army, President Ghulam Ishaq Khan, and Prime Minister Sharif. The army had conducted an unprecedented crackdown (Operation Clean Up) in Sind against the MQM, with which the president was closely associated, and which was accused of being "neo-fascist" and letting its "armed thugs" plague the city of Karachi. (The composition and political activities of the MQM, which collided with the interests of the Sindhis in Sind Province, and which were most aggrandizing in the cities of Karachi and Hyderabad, are described in the first part of this chapter.) The MQM was in 1992 the major partner of the ruling coalition in Sind, and a key partner in the same coalition (IJI) at the center, whose dominant component was the Muslim League, led by Sharif. Both Ishaq Khan and Sharif were affected by the army's operation in Sind. Sharif's leadership of the Muslim League itself was shaken up when many of its parliamentary members, under the leadership of Ghulam Mustafa Jatoi (a former prime minister), formed a new group called the National Democratic Alliance (NDA). At this stage, Benazir Bhutto was said to be courting the army, despite her previous distaste for it, because this alliance might help to dissolve the elected government and make possible her return to power. A growing rift between the army and the prime minister was rumored as having been caused by the army's Sind cleanup and by an alleged working agreement between Benazir and the army chief.[80]

But what finally brought down both Prime Minister Sharif and President Ishaq Khan was the power struggle between them that began over the selection of the new chief of army staff (COAS) after the sudden death of General Asif Nawaz on January 8. The tug of war between them was a saga in itself, concluding in a double tragedy. Both antagonists were interested to have their candidate in this important position, which had a critical role to play in national politics. The president in particular wanted a dependable ally who would help maintain the powers invested in him by the Eighth Amendment and who would also aid his reelection, due in ten months. The president won this round by appointing General Abdul Waheed Kakar.

Nawaz Sharif soon countered by announcing on February 28 that he proposed to repeal the Eighth Amendment, so that power would return to the duly elected prime minister and Parliament. It is thought that this was an unrealistic move, seeing that Sharif did not have a two-thirds majority in the National Assembly to repeal the amendment. The presidential camp managed to engineer a split in the Pakistan Muslim League and was also negotiating with Benazir for PPP support in the coming presidential election, in exchange of the promise of fresh midterm elections to the National Assembly. Sensing his imminent dismissal, Sharif made a defiant televised speech on April 17 in which he blamed the president as the "root cause" of the crisis, and flung down the gauntlet, declaring, "I will not resign and I will not take dictation."[81] Calling the speech an act of subversion, and making the usual charges of corruption, and so forth,[82] President Ishaq Khan thereupon dismissed Prime Minister Sharif, dissolved the National Assembly, and announced fresh elections.

Then took place a dramatic reversal, which some commentators praised as the first demonstration in a long time of the independence of the Supreme Court. Sharif's petition against the dissolution of the National Assembly as unconstitutional was upheld by the Court. Undaunted, President Ishaq dissolved the provincial Punjab assembly, thus foiling Sharif's attempt to regain his base in his home province, and followed up by dissolving the NWFP assembly and getting a no-confidence motion directed against the chief minister of Sind. "By manipulating provincial politics, the president isolated the central government, making the prime minister realize the helplessness of the center vis-a-vis the provinces," Tamir Amin observes.[83]

When several mediatory efforts failed, the army chief, General Kakar, "brokered" a deal by which on July 18, 1993, both President Ishaq Khan and Prime Minister Nawaz Sharif stepped down. A new caretaker administration was formed, and it was announced that there would be a new midterm general election in October 1993.

In the midterm general election, held on October 6 for the National Assembly and October 9 for the provincial assemblies, and said to be remarkably free and fair, the Pakistan People's Party (PPP) led by Benazir Bhutto and the Pakistan Muslim League (led by Nawaz Sharif) emerged as the two leading parties, capturing 86 and 72 seats, respectively, in the National Assembly of 207 seats. "In the popular vote, the PML (Nawaz group) had an edge by securing 39.7 percent of the vote over the PPP, which got 38.1 percent."[84]

The National Assembly results showed that "the four Islamic Parties and other religious parties suffered a humiliating defeat, capturing even less seats (9) than the minorities in the National Assembly," Amin notes. One cannot, of course, project long-term trends on the basis of these results but one possibility is that the exit of Zia and the return to democratic party politics may have signaled the weakening of the fundamentalist Islamic thrust for total reinstitution of the shari'ah, and the bifurcation of support for two parties—one with majority support in Sind (the PPP) and the other in the Punjab (the Muslim League)—which, however, resembled each other in not carrying Islamization any further than where Zia left it, with the possibility that the extreme legislation already on the books would be left to gather dust.

The National Assembly elections also showed another important result. "Regional parties like the Awami National Party (ANP) in the NWFP [North-West Frontier Province], the Confederal Party in Sindh, and ethno-nationalist elements in Baluchistan also suffered stunning defeats in the national body; at the same time the PML (Nawaz group) and the PPP made significant inroads into the provinces."[85] This might signal an important trend toward the muting of radical secessionist regional ethnonationalist movements, although not, of course, the weakening of regional pressures for special policies on their behalf.

The MQM, which had been the strongest party in previous urban elections in Sind, boycotted the National Assembly elections, and the major beneficiaries of the boycott were the PPP and the PML (Nawaz). The MQM did participate in the Provincial Assembly elections in Sind, winning 27 seats, with the PPP gaining a majority of 56 seats, and the PML(N) getting 8 seats. Thus the MQM showed that it was a presence in that province. In the Punjab, the PML(N) with 106 seats was the single largest party, while the PPP won 94 and the splinter faction PML (Jatoi), its ally, won 18 seats.

The results of the elections in the North-West Frontier Province evinced a complex situation: the regional Awami National Party won virtually the same number of seats as the PPP (21 versus 22), while the PML(N) won 15, and others won 8. Here again, although the PPP and PML asserted their national importance, the locally rooted party, sponsoring its special interests, maintained a bargaining position. In Baluchistan, the PML(N) with 6 seats and the PPP with 3 got the better of an assorted group of smaller parties and independents. Amin writes:

> The 1993 elections saw the emergence of two genuinely national political parties led by two charismatic leaders with firm roots in the provinces. However, it was premature to predict whether a two-party democratic system would evolve. Although both the ruling party and the opposition were displaying mature behaviour toward each other, chances for stability remained precarious because of the absence of a democratic culture, fragile balance of civil-military relations, lack of cohesive political parties, and the interests of external powers in manipulating Pakistan's internal politics for their own objectives.[86]

The penetration of national parties into the provinces does not guarantee that the collisions between Pathans and Baluchis in Baluchistan, the tensions between Muhajirs and Sindhis in provincial politics, or the conflicts between Pathans (and Afghans) and Biharis (and Muhajirs) in Karachi over the issues of control of space, real estate, occupations, economic niches, and "criminalized" factions dealing in drugs and arms will cease.[87] The issues of the alleged domination of Punjabis in the army and bureaucracy and of Urdu as the sole national language will continue to simmer. Punjab is also the central base for fundamentalist pro-Islamization activist groups, who are likely to exert most pressure whenever the country is perceived to be fragmenting or "weak" in relation to India. Meanwhile, the issue of Kashmir will continue to unite army and civilians against India whenever an explosive issue erupts, as well as heightening the army's propensity to seek the power to wage that war, in which it has invested so much honor and valor, in the way it wants. It has to be conceded that the Islamization project pursued by Zia's regime with the support of the fundamentalists did not achieve a national unity and integration that superseded and transcended Pakistan's regional and ethnonationalist divisions. The circumstances that led to major violent conflicts in the 1980s between ethnic communities and regional ethnonationalist movements are still alive today, but there is also evidence in the years since Zia of an increasing commitment to democratic party politics, and there are signs of the national parties being more successful at working in alliance with regional ones.

PART TWO

RETHINKING THE NATURE
OF COLLECTIVE VIOLENCE

7   Some General Features of Ethnic Riots and Riot Crowds

The local histories of particular instances of ethnic riots no doubt differ as regards the group issues that are in contention and the circumstances in which they occur. The case studies presented in Part I, especially the Sinhala-Muslim riots of 1915, the Sinhala-Tamil riots in Colombo in 1983, the Sikh-Hindu eruptions in Delhi in 1984, the Pathan-Bihari clashes in Karachi in 1986, and the Sindhi-Muhajir encounters of 1988–90, to mention some major occurrences in South Asia, were by no means similar in regard to the concrete issues that fueled and triggered them.

I shall, however, group these occurrences together in this discussion, along with many others smaller in scale, such as the Hindu-Muslim clashes in Moradabad in the 1980s, the Sinhala-Tamil riots of 1958 in Colombo, the Bombay riots of 1984, and the flare-ups between 1989 and 1992 caused by the so-called Babri Masjid–Ramjanmabhumi controversy, which has intensified the militancy of both Hindus and Muslims, and also seriously affected the course and outcome of national and state elections in India. By indicating certain general features that all these incidents share, I hope to open a window onto the phenomenon of collective violence itself. The points being made here are elaborated in chapter 9, in which the mobilizational campaigns mounted by Hindu nationalists leading to the demolition of the Babri mosque in December 1992 and resulting in riots in Bombay and elsewhere are further discussed.

Typically, although not exclusively, the riots I have identified involved urban populations.[1] Among these populations, both those who actually engaged in physical acts of aggression and those who mobilized and directed the violence were primarily drawn from certain identifiable segments or categories of the population in question.

riots in larger context of viol.

The riots were not simply disconnected occurrences, but formed part of a larger incidence of violence, occurring in a wide range of social contexts and political circumstances, which can be ordered on a scale of increasing violence, premeditation, and participation. This larger universe ranged from abuse in family life to petty crime and robbery, to the use of henchmen and thugs to settle business disputes, and to organized thuggery during political elections. And when I refer to widespread violence in the society at large, I include terrorism and violence practiced by the state, principally by the police and security forces as routine practice in relation to the public. It is common knowledge that the police practice physical violence on those arrested, especially if they are of the lower orders, and use coercion to extract information and confessions. And in country after country, police, army, other security forces, paramilitary groups recruited by the state, and even some public officials participated in riots, either as onlookers slow to take preventive action or as vigorous participants favoring the cause of one side. Those entrusted with maintaining and enforcing law and order are rarely neutral in societies where ethnic conflict is rife.

! role of police

In many cities and towns, intermittent ethnic riots form a series, with antecedent riots influencing the unfolding of subsequent ones. Thus the 1983 riots in Sri Lanka, the most virulent so far, were preceded, to mention only the most destructive ones, by the riots of 1958, 1977, 1981. The city of Colombo was involved in all of them. In the city of Meerut in Uttar Pradesh, India, where the Muslims comprise about 45 percent of the population, tensions between them and the Hindus have led to communal rioting on eight occasions since independence, as in May 1987, when both civilian Hindus and the "provincial armed constabulary" committed atrocities.[2] Many other Indian and Pakistani cities have had similar experiences, implicating the same or different antagonists. A variant on the same issue that is not infrequent in large metropolitan cities containing a mosaic of differentiated communities is illustrated by the spate of clashes that have scarred Karachi, a city teeming with immigrants, where until 1985, annual Shia-Sunni sectarian clashes routinely took place at Muharram (the time of fasting and public mourning among Shiites commemorating the deaths of Hassan and Hussain in the seventh century). Karachi also saw anti-Ahmedi riots in the early 1950s and again in 1969–70. It has seen vicious Pathan-Bihari clashes in 1985, in 1986, at least twice in 1987 (in February and July), and in 1988 (May and October). Chronic Sindhi-Muhajir animosities exploded in Karachi in 1972–73 and repeatedly in the years 1988–90, and later.

crowds of mass movements focused on and orchestrated by charismatic

crowds *charisma* *leaders*

The crowds in ethnic riots in South Asia bear little resemblance to the crowds of mass movements focused on and orchestrated by charismatic leaders of the type associated with Gandhi's independence movement, Hitler's Nazi expansionism, and Khomeini's Islamic fundamentalism. Hence the plentiful literature about mass movements focused on charismatic leadership is not very relevant to my subject matter. The ethnic riots of their time were not induced by the leadership and intentional policies of the Gandhis and Nehrus of India, the Bhuttos of Pakistan, the Senanayakes and Bandaranaikes of Sri Lanka; but lesser politicians and local organizers have frequently been implicated as catalysts, ideologues, and mobilizers.

riots & everyday life

If the ethnic riots and incidents perpetrated by civilian crowds and factions are repetitive, they are also mercifully short-lived, not only because after an initial period of chaos and paralysis, the police and army can assert their dominance, but also because as human outbursts these riots have a short life cycle of orgasmic violence and spent energies. Moreover, these civilian destroyers seemingly return to the humdrum of everyday life and neighborly existence after their spasmodic bloodlettings. These features have also to be construed.

In order to comprehend these phenomena, it seems to me that ideally we should first travel on the highways and byways of ongoing social life and view the solidarities as well as the tensions of everyday existence in family and neighborhood, the cycles of festivals and ceremonies in public places, the routines and stratagems and factional battles deployed in mass politics, the risks and hopes of mass migration, the trials of urban coexistence, and so on, before we resort to what is usually labeled "crowd psychology" or "political psychology," which has its own distinctive contours and its own revelations.

rat. destruct.

South Asian rioters, like many riot crowds elsewhere, are "purposive" in their destruction of property. That is to say, property destruction and looting are not fickle, momentarily dictated "irrational" actions but are integral and repetitive feature of ethnic riots, linked to "leveling" objectives and tendencies. The riot crowds of ethnic conflict may also combine homicide and brutalities with property destruction and arson. The riots I have in mind typically involve urban populations, and they have occurred primarily in cities, towns, and in dense settlements (such as peasant colonization schemes) with bazaars and marketplaces.

It is tempting and comforting, especially for middle-class apologists and bureaucrats, to describe the riots that have periodically occurred in Delhi, Calcutta, Karachi, Colombo, Jakarta, and lesser urban places as the destructive and violent conduct solely or mainly of the lumpenproletariat, the unemployed, criminal elements, and slum or shantytown dwellers. But such scapegoating simply will not do, both because it is factually partial and because it blinds us to the important realization that ethnic riots emerge out of a larger context of social and political tensions and conflicts, and that the segments of the population involved in this larger context are more numerous and varied in status than those who are actually seen as the members of the marauding mobs.

The faces in the crowd reflect a part of the socioeconomic profile of cities like Bombay, Delhi, Calcutta, Karachi, Dhaka, Colombo, Kuala Lumpur, and Jakarta, a profile that combines modern architectural complexes, high-rise hotels, factories with shantytowns, squatter settlements, tenements, and urban villages. Many urban sites and spaces in these cities permit the dense contiguity of professionals, engineers, clerical workers, small shopkeepers, artisans, subcontractors, transport workers, factory workers, porters, unskilled laborers, the unemployed, and the underemployed. These cities are also the conspicuous locations of concentrations of schools and colleges, serving the needs not only of the urban masses but also of children from rural areas, who lodge with urban relatives in order to secure secondary and higher education. Schools and colleges, like factories, are places where large numbers habitually congregate, exchange news, provide mutual stimulation, and organize for concerted action in politics and public events. My case studies show that the faces in the ethnic crowds cannot simply be dismissed as vagrants, criminal elements, and the unemployed dregs, but include numbers of students, as well as most categories of the working class engaged in factory work, transport services, and artisan trades, and many gainfully employed in the running and servicing of bazaars and commercial zones. (When riots occur in peasant resettlement and land-development zones, as they did in Sri Lanka in 1958, labor gangs, peasant colonists, and small-town bazaar shopkeepers and their retinues become involved.) We must not, however, leave out of account national and municipal politicians, as well as their local bosses and agents, with their clients, retainers, and goondas capable of being mobilized as riot captains and thugs or who play an integral role in the organizing, triggering, and directing of the "purposive" violence of the mobs. Time and again, a large portion of the police force and paramilitary agents have been inactive or have acted in collusion with the rioters, a matter not so amazing if they are recruited from the local majority and have the same social prejudices and political interests as their kinsmen and ethnic friends, among whom they live. Finally, on the fringes of the crowds, we find the unemployed and criminal elements as well. In sum, we must not gloss over the fact that ethnic riots implicate a complex variety and several segments of the population, and for this reason, they cannot be dismissed or underplayed as marginal phenomena distanced from the main body of civilians.

I here advert to a point of comparative relevance. E. J. Hobsbawm, E. P. Thompson, George Rudé, Natalie Zemon Davis, Emmanuel Le Roy Ladurie, and other historians who have dealt with the crowd movements in Western Europe from the sixteenth to the eighteenth centuries agree that the participants in the popular protests and riots they have studied were mainly drawn, not from gin-swilling criminal elements, petty-thieving casual labor, or vagrants—they participated at the margins, parasitically— but from the more sober "lower orders" of the towns and countryside. The rioters were people of settled occupations and settled residence, if prone to temporary unemployment: domestic servants, small shopkeepers, journeymen, artisans, and craftsmen—carpenters, locksmiths, shoemakers, tailors, stonemasons, weavers, and woolcombers. Sometimes merchants and those in the professions were implicated. In other words, crowds in preindustrial Western Europe were fairly representative of the employment followed by the "lower" and "lower-middle" orders in rioting areas. And the main centers of popular outbreaks, strikes, and revolutionary agitation were central markets, the main centers of petty trades and crafts and shops, and stable residential areas. In short, the mobile *vulgus,* that hydra-headed monster fantasized about by the propertied classes and ruling authorities, had a more orderly shape than is commonly thought, and redirects our attention to society and the state at large.[3]

The cross-sectional composition of many South Asian and other third world riot crowds of our time distinctly and integrally links them to participatory democracy, population movements, and sprawling urbanization. The politicization of ethnicity, a hallmark of our time, tied to the politics of elections, has much to do with the winning of the benefits distributed by the modern state committed to welfare, development, and employment programs.[4] This political equation, combined with the capabilities of the mass media, radio, television, and print capitalism, so effectively deployed in our time, makes present-day ethnic riot crowds very different from the crowds of preindustrial Europe I have referred to. The contrast is striking when we take into account the "universalistic" slogans of popular democracy that have been transplanted to the political arenas of newly independent states.

Keeping European comparisons in mind, we may now ask what relation the South Asian phenomena bear to the political crowds of postindustrial Western Europe? It has been argued that a great deal of the democratic politics of modern Europe is transacted according to long-implanted traditions and interests of social class, as evidenced by trade unions, professional associations, political parties, and the like, which as organized solidarities to a significant degree transcend cleavages of language, ethnicity, race, and even religion. By comparison, the ethnic conflicts we are concerned with here are less relatable to manifest social class differences and more attributable to ethnic concerns and interests acting as a monolithic principle, vertically integrating a people differentiated by class. If class interest enters at all, it seems as if the diverse interests within a people united by the discourse of ethnicity coalesce and converge for a while in pursuit of their different goals.

The crowds of ethnic conflict thus on the one hand resemble the "industrial crowds" of modern Europe in engaging with participatory democracy, universal suffrage, and so on, but they on the other hand differ from them in action, finding their solidarity, not in divisive class interest, but in conceptions of collective ethnic identity whose continued salience and role, and adaptation and manipulation for winning collective entitlements and rewards, have to be given their proper weight. The interests of collective ethnic identity may link up with and be congruent to the converging interests of different "class fractions," but this signifies, not class war, but class collaboration and manipulation by dominant elites.[5]

One inevitably has to ask to what extent separatist movements in Eastern Europe today—the murderous animosities of Christian Armenians and Islamic Azerbaijanis, the conflicting claims of Croats, and Serbs, and Muslim Bosnians, and the fury of the Chechens—are activated by ethnic sentiments, solidarities, and techniques of mobilization similar to those operating in South Asian arenas. This question is further complicated in the case of Eastern Europe by the coincidence that ethnic crowds formed there at a time of aspirations to democratic politics, devolution and decentralization of power, and the loosening of authoritarian controls.

Like ethnic riots of South Asia and elsewhere, the explosions currently taking place in Eastern Europe and what used to be the southern USSR also raise the issue of how we are to understand the human brutalities and killings, the looting and destruction of property, perpetrated by mobs. There are plausibly common elements in these eruptions. The politicized ethnic consciousness of today draws its intellectual, and, more important, its emotional sustenance from appeals to religious, racial, linguistic, and territorial ties and mytho-historical claims. These are powerful forces for forming collectivities—they provide doctrine and legitimation, define and make self-conscious both personal and collective identity, and are effective boundary markers of collectivities in confrontation and conflict. The religious wars between Catholics and Protestants in Europe in earlier centuries fed on similar intensities: "Religious violence is intense because it connects intimately with the fundamental values and self-definition of a community," Natalie Zemon Davis writes.[6] Class wars have not resulted in massacres and destruction of the magnitude manifested by wars of an ethnic, communal, or religious nature. And as I have remarked before, class interests and class fractions, whatever reality they have in South Asia, seem either to interact with ethnicity or, more visibly, to be submerged in a more potent collective identity that cuts vertically through classes to rally people under the banner of race, religion, language, and homeland. This collective identity simultaneously fuses individual selves and at least for short periods of time grants them personal identity as members of a homogeneous "species." This "substantialized" or concretized identity acquires its forcefulness by activating, instigating, or projecting so-called primordial sentiments onto the political arenas of twentieth-century politics. Aggregating in terms of ethnic possessions and claims enables collectivities to compete, bargain, and collide in the pursuit of power, material rewards, and prestige at a time when parochial village and local forms and networks of sociation are giving way to larger regional or communal forms and networks. It is simultaneously a time when the hopes and possibilities of making unitary nations and nation-states out of societies internally divided by a variety of actual or potential ethnic claims have been seriously eroded, if not shattered. This has happened primarily because the objective of forming nation-states has provided opportunities for some groups and coteries to monopolize the state apparatus and to dominate, incorporate, or even reduce to inferior status other groups, who feel that their portions are being jeopardized. Interestingly, both majority groups and minorities, elites and masses, may find themselves feeling "victimized" and "beleaguered," depending on their share in the distribution of capital assets, educational advantages, occupational skills, and other forms of symbolic capital, on their patterns of urban-rural location, on their changing demographic proportions, and on the political arithmetic of majority rule and the formation of coalitions. But the haunting question remains: how does it come about that ethnonationalist collectivities intensify and transform their contests into wars of mutual elimination or of total displacement, into acts of murder and physical expulsions of people? One cannot forget that the genocide of the Jews attempted by the Nazis was fueled by similar demonic urges. To borrow some words from Marx, which he used in a different context: how does it happen that the opposition of ethnonationalist groups "should culminate in brutal contradiction, the shock of body against body, as its final dénouement?"[7]

8 The Routinization and Ritualization of Violence

There are three perspectives on collective violence in ethnic conflict that each in its own way and in its proper context provides illumination. They are not necessarily mutually exclusive and do in fact intersect. But each followed through to its ultimate does constitute a distinctive view.

One approach views collective violence in the form of riots as "eruptions" with two facets. On the one hand, they are caused by underlying tensions and conflicts in the society, such as competition for scarce resources, educational opportunities, employment prospects, political power, and so on among groups or categories in a social arena—whether they be ethnic groups, communities, classes or fractions of classes. On the other hand, these eruptions are seen as breaching the norms and arrangements and boundaries of everyday social order, and therefore as extraordinary and "excessive" in nature. The metaphor that may apply here is that of fault lines in the social fabric, through which volcanoes erupt under stress.

To some extent this perspective does fit some aspects of the accounts presented above. However, proponents of the breach-and-eruption perspective may actually differ as to whether the eruptions themselves are to be treated as irrational, destructive, and deserving of suppression or as purposive, directional, and positive in bringing about necessary social change (or as having both sets of implications).

A second perspective, which may intersect in places with the first stated above, but that pushes the exploration of riots in a different direction, which we might call "semiotic" and "performative," tries to see whether features of ethnic riots as collective behavior may be related to the wider context of political and moral norms, cultural practices and conventions, and traditions of public assemblies and public enactments, such as festivals, ceremonies, protests and rebellions. I have elsewhere elaborated three senses of what I understand to be the performative features of rituals and public events: the first is an extension of the Austinian sense of *performative*, wherein "saying" and naming something with words, voice modulations, gestures, and other kinesic movements is also doing and achieving effects as a legitimating conventional act with widely accepted public significance; the second is in the quite different sense of a staged sequential and recursive performance that uses multiple media and engages multiple sensory modalities by which the participants experience the event intensively and with heightened effect; and finally, there is the sense of "indexical" values (a concept derived from Charles Sanders Peirce) being existentially transferred to and inferred by the actors during the performance, thereby conferring on them prestige, legitimacy, authority, power, and other entitlements and forms of symbolic capital.[1] This semiotic and performative perspective thus illuminates the extent to which riots and associated contexts of collective violence are routinized, ritualized, and draw on the public culture's repertoire of presentational forms and practices; it also sensitizes us to the dynamic, elaborative, creative, constructive, and invented features of public events, by which participants relate to and address current issues and causes of contextual relevance and contingent and emergent circumstances, and also encounter unexpected open-ended outcomes.

My own anthropological interests in ritual and in cultural semiotics set me on this path of interpretation, encouraged and informed by the writings of Thompson, Hobsbawm, Rudé, Natalie Zemon Davis, Tilly, and others. Then, in the summer of 1990, after I had embarked on this road,[2] I began to read Sandria B. Freitag, whose work on urban riots in India under the British Raj in the nineteenth and twentieth centuries, influenced by the genre of writings cited above, had likewise taken a direction I found informative.

Riots, Freitag believes, should be linked "to the larger world of collective activities in public spaces, involving crowds and rites, music and swordplay, sacred space and sacred time"—that is, to a "world often labelled by scholars as 'popular culture.'" Referring specifically to Banaras, she remarks that "in many respects, collective activities in public spaces constitute the heart of shared urban experience." But Banaras is not unique: "Collective actions in the public spaces of an urban north Indian environment tended to be of three types: public space performances, collective ceremony, and popular protest.... Although distinct in ways, they developed out of shared cultural assumptions and, taken together, constitute a world that should be considered a coherent whole and analyzed on its own terms. This world may best be described as composed of 'public arenas,' or activities that represent public expressions of collective values and motivations."[3]

There is an important third perspective, which in a sense says something very different from the first perspective outlined above, and is closer in approach to the second. It applies in particular to situations of ethnic conflict that have become chronic. Conflict is not merely a situation of episodic and discontinuous riots with periods of peace and near-normal life in between; conflict has become an everyday and seemingly permanent state of affairs; it has turned into a state of civil war, in which the armed security forces of the state and armed rebels and opponents resort to violence as the primary vehicle of their dispute, so that it becomes a patterned mode of conducting politics by other means. I have suggested that the recent collective violence in the Punjab, the war between the Sri Lankan government forces and the Liberation Tigers of Tamil Eelam (LTTE), which is continuing (and with the Janatha Vimukthi Peramuna [JVP, or People's Liberation Front], which seems to have ended), the civil war in Kashmir, and the violent exchanges between Muhajirs, Sindhis, and the security forces in Karachi have virtually reached this state. Northern Ireland presents this condition of political warfare at its starkest. This third perspective, which has much to reveal, is impelled to focus on all the forms of collective violence being enacted, less as eruptions and results of underlying fissures and conflicts in the "infrastructure," "relations of production," or "institutional structure" of society, and more as a force and agency that has attained its own autonomy, has become "a self-legitimating sphere of social discourse and transaction" in its own right that actually structures and directs political action.[4] The antagonists in this political warfare develop their own semiotics of violence: each side develops its repertoire of strategies and counterstrategies, actions, conventions, codes, and countercodes and espionage. All sides thus engage in a discourse of violence whose logic, techniques, strategies, and objectives they increasingly understand, anticipate, and counteract.

The structuring role of this collective agonistic violence may reach a point at which it actually becomes efficacious in the construction, production, maintenance, and reproduction of ethnic identity and solidarity itself. What was previously seen as an effect now serves as a cause. Violence shapes the urban space of ethnic enclaves, barriers, shatter zones, liminal areas, barricades; it has become a mode of gaining or losing urban space, and of displacing, moving, and resettling populations. The organization, technology, and logistics of urban mass industrial production are adapted and applied to clandestine war. The military operations and arsenal of the state's security forces are reproduced among guerrillas and insurgents who have devised their own command structure and cells, their bomb factories and arms dumps, and their offensive and defensive strategies.

ELECTIONS AND VIOLENCE

In the course of this study of recent ethnic riots I increasingly realized that the manner in which political elections were staged, and violent events before, during, and after them, were germane to my subject of routinization and ritualization of collective violence. So as a prelude to this topic, let me recall three examples of recent election violence drawn from three different South Asian countries.

BANGLADESH

Local government elections were held in Bangladesh in 1988 to select more than 44,000 mayors and members of local councils. The keenness of participation in the elections can be gauged from the fact that

> more than 133,000 people sought posts on 4,376 village councils. Bangladesh has a population of about 105 million people. The councils in question serve for three years and are chiefly responsible for development activities at the local level.
>
> Supporters of rival candidates in local elections battled each other with rocks, guns, and homemade bombs today, and 80 people were reported killed and hundreds wounded across the country. The death toll was based on reports from the police, hospitals, and journalists in outlying villages. They also said the injury toll could exceed 2,000. The police said more than 200 people were arrested. Voting was suspended at dozens of polling places because of the violence. . . . Some sites were ransacked, and ballots were stolen in others.[5]

Less than a month later, national parliamentary elections were held in Bangladesh in similar circumstances:

> Rival party workers fighting with guns, knives, and bombs killed 13 people and wounded scores of others in Bangladesh during elections today, police officials said. Groups of up to several hundred men fought battles in several cities, and opponents of President H. M. Ershad [a former lieutenant general, who had seized power in a bloodless coup in 1982] tried to enforce a general strike to disrupt the parliamentary and municipal elections. The 12 party opposition alliance boycotting the election had called the polls a farce and urged the country's 46 million electorate not to vote.

Voting at 170 polling places had been suspended because of ballot rigging, violence, or lack of election officials. The voting was to be rescheduled there. The electoral commissioner said he could not detail the extent of fraud but added: "It was as if I was seeing an election in England. It was almost peaceful."

President Ershad, who had "been under increasing pressure to leave office since November, when the main opposition parties agreed to settle their differences and begin a campaign of strikes and protests," ordered the deployment of 9,000 troops to monitor the voting. The streets of Dhaka were nearly empty, and shops were shuttered because of the 36-hour general strike. Near Dhaka University, people demonstrating against the Ershad government burned vehicles and set a fire station ablaze "after police who had been besieged in the building fled." Ershad's Jatiya Party was leading in 41 of the 49 parliamentary seats for which partial results had been announced. The party was expected to win 245 of the 300 seats that were being contested. Ershad rejected the demands of the Awami League and the Bangladesh Nationalist Party for his resignation. Asked whether he expected the unrest to continue, he replied, "After this things certainly will improve."[6]

INDIA

The second example concerns the November 1989 Indian elections to the Lok Sabha, which Rajiv Gandhi lost, enabling V. P. Singh and his coalition government to assume power. There were widespread charges of violence and corrupt practices obstructing the holding of democratic elections.

Allegations were made that in Rajiv Gandhi's own constituency of Amethi, in Uttar Pradesh, policemen had been seen stuffing ballot boxes, and that the headquarters of the Janata Dal Party were ransacked. In the same constituency, the leader of a party of untouchables, Kanshi Ram, was shot in the arm during a scuffle with Congress Party (I) supporters; and Sanjay Singh, a nephew of the leader of the Janata Dal Party (V. P. Singh), was shot and wounded. It was reported that, on the first day of elections, "armed gangs roamed through the constituency of Prime Minister Rajiv Gandhi, terrorizing voters."[7]

It seems that the opponents of Congress (I) did not spurn similar intimidation and obstruction of polling. On the first day of voting, some twenty people died, and several dozen were wounded in election-related violence throughout the country. "In Srinagar, on India's northwestern border with Pakistan, antigovernment Muslim militants set fire to several polling stations and planted bombs near the homes of party members supporting the coalition between Prime Minister Gandhi's Congress Party and the locally based National Conference of Chief Minister Faroo Abdullah." In Andhra

Pradesh, another opposition-controlled state, "election officials threw out ballots from 125 polling stations and called for new voting on Friday. The officials said that unnamed politicians had snatched voting papers and ballot boxes."[8]

SRI LANKA

In Sri Lanka, violence before, during, and after elections has been a common occurrence since before independence, but has subsequently increased in intensity and frequency. It reached an unprecedented level at the time of the first referendum held in December 1982 by President J. R. Jayewardene to get the electorate's approval of an extension of the term of the sitting Parliament by six years. On October 22, Jayewardene had been reelected president, which apparently gave him the power and leverage to take this step. The referendum itself was a novel and highly controversial move, undertaken to prolong the tenure of the incumbent members of Parliament, especially those of the United National Party, which then held 84 percent of the seats. In the event, the government's victory was narrow (54.66 percent in favor; 45.34 percent against), and was secured by resort to blatant thuggery and electoral infractions more extreme and effective than the opposition parties could muster. Ironically enough, the referendum was justified by Jayewardene as a means of saving the nation from "a Naxalite type of people, bent on violence."[9]

The Conduct of the Campaign

A state of emergency had already been declared on October 20, ostensibly to check violence after the presidential election held earlier, which Jayewardene had won more or less fairly and squarely. "Under emergency regulation important opposition newspapers were banned, printing presses were sealed, opposition meetings were restricted and many opposition organizers and supporters and other critics of the government detained or arrested and interrogated. "The Referendum Act prohibited the display of flags, banners, and posters in public except on the premises when a meeting was being held and only on the day of that meeting. The government party's symbol (a lamp) and other propaganda devices were openly displayed, while the same privilege was virtually denied opposition groups by hostile police. "The increasing partisanship of the police . . . rendered opposition workers and 'pot' [the opposition's symbol] voters extremely vulnerable in the face of intimidation by government supporters," Priya Samarakone notes. [10] The government party seemed so omnipotent that neither the police nor the elections commissioner felt able to move against it.

The agents of the government successfully harassed the cadres of the chief opposition party, the Sri Lanka Freedom Party. One destabilizing tactic employed was the temporary arrest and detention of the SLFP's key organizers, including its general secretary. Other key party workers, such as the assistant secretary and his wife, were subjected to interrogation as the "main culprits" in an alleged "Naxalite plot," which was never proven to exist. Arrest and interrogation was an ordeal faced by opposition party workers at all levels.

"On many occasions, meetings were broken up by groups of government supporters, with the police watching but taking no action, or even protecting the disruptive elements." For example, in Kurunegala, an opposition meeting was disturbed by hooligans led by a UNP member of Parliament, and "the police intervened only to protect the MP when the crowd tried to eject the troublemakers," Samarakone observes. Several such disruptions were reported, and the active participation of MPs in such disruptions and the partiality of the police were not unusual. The banning of opposition newspapers and the sealing of their presses was another tactic adopted by the ruling UNP, while the state-owned newspapers and printing establishments flooded the country with government propaganda. This action against presses publishing on behalf of the opposition had already begun at the time of the presidential election and was carried further during the referendum. *Suthanthiran*, a Tamil-language opposition newspaper produced in Jaffna, was closed for preparing to print the Tamil-language text of a message to the Tamil people from Sirimavo Bandaranaike, the leader of the SLFP. *Aththa*, a Communist Party newspaper with wide circulation among the Sinhala-reading public, was closed for criticizing the referendum proposal itself. The state-controlled media—radio, television, and major newspapers—promoted the government's cause. The major dailies of Associated Newspapers of Ceylon Ltd., such as the *Daily News,* and of the Times Group, such as the *Daily Mirror,* both owned by the state, not only carried government views but engaged in character assassination of politicians and lay leaders who opposed the referendum. Similarly, broadcasting and television time, which was available for only a limited time at a high price to the opposition, was freely and amply available to the ruling party. In addition to existing propagandistic films and edited news broadcasts, several new programs were launched "to acquaint the masses with the performance of each minister in the interests of the common man."[11]

Television time was denied to independent organizations such as the Civil Rights Movement and theoretically available for a period of 45 minutes only to "recognized political parties." A state-produced film praising the government's effort began its screening on November 21, and on December 17, the National Film Exhibitors Guild presented President Jaye-wardene with a copy of *Towards the Dharmishta Society*, "which was screened that day in Sinhalese and English in cinemas in every district of the country."[12]

The Conduct of the Polling

Opposition campaigners had already faced threats and obstruction, and intimidation and thuggery increased as the election drew near, reaching a peak on the polling day itself. It appears, for example, that in the face of widespread intimidation, the SLFP Central Committee of Attanagalla electoral district decided to withdraw all its polling observers from the forty-seven stations in the electorate.

Many opposition polling observers were taken into custody on false complaints, and were usually released two or three days after the poll. For example, SLFP observers in Yatinuwara (Kandy District) suffered this fate. The left-wing parties were subjected to similar harassment. On election day, threats against and physical assaults on opposition polling observers apparently resulted in their totally vacating the polling stations in many places. There were several recorded instances of intimidation of public servants administering the polls. As usual, organized mass impersonation was practiced, the secrecy of the ballot was violated at some polling stations, and many opposition supporters were prevented from reaching or frightened away from the polling booths. In his official report, printed as a sessional paper, the commissioner of elections confirms many of these allegations in moderate and guarded language:

> The Commissioner of Elections and Inspector-General of Police received representation on the 16th December that some Agents/Polling observers expressed doubt about their safety and requested that those assigned to this Polling Division be withdrawn. This withdrawal was officially intimated to the Commissioner of Elections and the Inspector-General of Police one day before the poll. Alleged reason for such withdrawal was lack of security . . . and fear of intimidation and reprisals. Consequently they claim to have advised Agents not to attend the Polling Stations. . . .
>
> However divergent the interpretations could be, yet it becomes rather difficult in these circumstances, to deny the allegation that the failure to maintain the expected law and order in general and more specifically on the day of the poll, partly at least would have been the reason for the failure of some Polling Observers to assert their rights and be present at the Police Stations. . . .

The police assistance to the Elections Staff in the management of a Polling Station, therefore becomes indispensable. Allegations were made at the Referendum, that some impersonators had escaped while some were forcibly rescued, marked Ballot Papers were displayed by voters, Polling Observers had left the Polling Stations for lack of safety, and at times outside elements had disturbed the working of the Polling Stations. These allegations should not be dismissed as mere expression of disappointment and rancor.[13]

The Referendum of December 1982 reached a high-water mark in election violence and introduced some new excesses. The open display of marked ballot papers, removal of opposition polling observers, or their total withdrawal from polling stations, and unconcealed intimidation of public servants administering the referendum were probably new developments. And perhaps never before had the police shown active partiality to such a degree or demonstrated such unwillingness to enforce the law.

It seems not entirely accidental that the worst ethnic riots in the history of Sri Lanka took place in 1983, only six months or so after the referendum. "The fact that violence has been used to meet criticism and political dissent in the country as a whole, including the Sinhala areas, may well have encouraged the belief among certain sections of the population that the ethnic problem could be dealt with in a similar manner," a document put out by the Civil Rights Movement in Sri Lanka observed.[14]

A new set of developments characterized the presidential election of 1988. Two insurgent groups, the LTTE (Tigers) in the north and east, and the JVP in the south (and in certain other places, such as Matale and Anuradhapura), the latter group in particular, exercised widespread intimidation and violence to prevent citizens from voting. Furthermore, on the government side, the police and, more weightily, the army were deployed, ostensibly to protect voters and to ensure that the elections would be held and completed. But as usual the security forces also used violence, and both the UNP and the opposition parties resorted to the usual election stunts and violations.

In the event, the election was held and completed. The UNP's Ranasinghe Premadasa was elected president. But the pattern of voting and the variations in voter turnout indicated that the JVP and the LTTE were successful in keeping many people from voting in those constituencies in which they were concentrated.

All this underscores a point made before: that the Sinhala-Tamil ethnic riots since 1956 are part and parcel of the violence, political tensions, and economic inequities in the country as a whole. The JVP insurrection by Sinhala youth, in some ways a mirror image of the Tamil rebellion, was also generated by the defects of the island's political economy. Seen in this perspective, the brutalities of ethnic violence are an intensified and explosive version of the violence in other domains. This also applies to occurrences of ethnic violence in virtually all the instances outside of Sri Lanka alluded to above.

THE REPERTOIRE OF COLLECTIVE VIOLENCE

The concepts of *routinization* and, more important, *ritualization* of collective violence may help us to perceive some of the organized, anticipated, programmed, and recurring features and phases of seemingly spontaneous, chaotic, and orgiastic actions of the mob as aggressor and victimizer. These concepts should also go some way toward describing the syntactic features of ethnic riots, without claiming that they exhaust the contingent events of their pragmatic significance.

Some of the components of this repertoire may well be drawn from the everyday forms of ritualized life and from the ritual calendar of festivities. They may be imitated, inverted, or parodied, according to their dramatic and communicative possibilities. Since these features are recurrent, either the same actors, or actors who as contemporaries have social links or intergenerational ties with previous actors, participate in them and reproduce them time and again.

Focus on routinization and ritualization may also help us to comprehend why brutalities committed as a member of an inflamed mob pursuing what it considers to be a "righteous" political cause on behalf of the collectivity (whether it be an ethnic group or nationality) may not take a crippling psychic toll on the aggressor at the level of the individual/self. And why, after bouts of violence, the participants seemingly return to their normal daily lives and continue to live side by side with their erstwhile enemies.[15]

There is little evidence that as aggressors and victimizers—in Colombo, Karachi, Delhi, Calcutta, and elsewhere—rioters experience a collective malaise after the event or are in any overt sense burdened with concerns and reactions that impede their return to everyday life, although that return may be one of increasing unease. It is noteworthy that reports on riots, whether by official commissions, nongovernmental agencies, or the media, do not address this issue: they neither ask the question nor seek information about it.

 To mobilize crowd action, manage mobs, and manipulate the media, politicians, faction leaders, and the professional thugs who can be hired for the purpose deploy specific recipes, techniques, and stratagems. Elections are spectacles and contests of power; they are the performative enactment of power; they provide the pomp, terror, drama, and climaxes of crowd politics. Clifford Geertz's sketch of the traditional theater state,[16] which portrays state rituals as passively imaging the cosmic scheme, could be strengthened and energized by elucidation of the procedures and mechanisms used for domesticating and managing large crowds and persuading them to become adherents of the established order. Transposed and adapted to modern participatory democracy, the idea of the theater state will find in political elections an informative example of how participants are mobilized and deliberately urged to heightened action, which by an agonistic buildup eventuates in violent eruptions and spectacles—literal dances of death—before, during, and after elections. (Writing on religious riots in sixteenth-century France, Natalie Zemon Davis remarks: "We may see violence, however cruel, not as random and limitless, but as aimed at defined targets and selected from a repertory of traditional punishments and forms of destruction.")[17] The following examples of components that might form part of a manual of communal violence in South Asia (and many places elsewhere) are frequently combined in the production of public events imbued with violence:

1. Processions prominently displaying portraits of public figures and carrying emotive public symbols such as black flags, Buddhist flags, and placards with inflammatory slogans (which are also vociferously and rhythmically chanted).[18] Among public figures and charismatic persons today, some of the most effective crowd drawers and mobilizers are varieties of "holy men," be they Buddhist monks, Hindu sadhus (mendicant ascetics), Muslim ulama, or even Indian film stars who by virtue of having played the roles of gods in the cinema have become quasi-divine in the public's eye themselves (such as Rama Rao of Andhra Pradesh and the late M.G. Ramachandran of Tamil Nadu). Processions as public spectacle are surrounded and witnessed by "slow crowds" of spectators. Exhibitionism on the one side and admiring spectatorship on the other are the reciprocal components of spectacle.

2. Rallies that conclude with public speeches given in large open spaces (see figures 6 and 7). A core component of mass oratory is the vigorous declamation of stereotyped orations composed of stock formulae and peppered with mytho-historical allusions, inflated boasts, group defamation, and scurrilous insults to and insinuations against opponents. These orations are transmitted and amplified to earsplitting decibels with the aid

Figure 6.   Indira Gandhi at an election rally on her behalf around 1981. *India Today.*

of microphones, loudspeakers, and, nowadays, television and VCRs. This kind of noisy propaganda contributes effectively to the "demonization" of the enemy and feelings of omnipotence and righteousness among the participants as representatives of an ethnic group or race.

3.   Standardized forms of intimidation of the opponent, examples of which are obstructions by thugs at voting booths; throwing of bombs at public places and meetings; hate mail, including threats of assassination; and actual, selective cautionary murders. Some years ago, on a visit to Harvard University, Ambassador Karan Singh referred to the "criminalization of politics" in India, an apt phrase, so long as we remember that criminality too can become routinized.

4.   Distribution of bribes, usually monetary rewards, liquor, caps, shirts, flags, and so on, to "buy" votes and "inspire" workers and supporters. Although officially labeled "corruption," this is standard lubrication for the political process and facilitates the movement of crowds. It would seem that the exercise of democracy is an expensive business, and that it too generates its characteristic networks of patronage and forms of "alliance," protection, incorporation, and mobilization.

5.   An array of "triggering actions" that are publicly recognized as challenges, slights, insults, and desecrations inviting reprisal.

Figure 7.   A rally with posters staged on behalf of Rajiv Gandhi. Sharad
Saxena (*India Today*).

W. Norman Brown observed that the precipitating causes of Hindu-Muslim riots in nineteenth-century India "might be a quarrel over ownership of a parcel of land and the right to erect a religious building on it, or the playing of music by a Hindu wedding procession as it passed a mosque where such a noise constituted sacrilege, or exaction of exorbitant rent or interest by a landlord or money-lender of one religious persuasion from a tenant or debtor of the other, or sacrifice of a cow by Muslims, or the clash of crowds when a Hindu and a Muslim festival coincided."[19]

By one account, in the years 1900–1922, there were sixteen communal riots in India; from 1923 to 1926, there were seventy-two.[20] They were usually triggered by irritation caused to Hindus by the slaughter of cows and to Muslims by the playing of music in front of mosques. But such disputes have a history extending back at least to late medieval times. There is evidence that religious riots did occur widely in India between 1770 and 1860, although one must bear in mind that what is labeled a religious riot may in fact—in addition to whatever differences in religious practices and norms may become salient in that context—involve a number of other interests and differences, whose contention and resolution are also at the heart of the matter.[21] Diverse issues and the interests of multiple groups are involved in movements of collective violence that are retrospectively labeled and perceived as collisions between two monolithic population segments: Muslims versus Sinhalese, Hindus versus Muslims, and so on. That in retrospective summation the complex issues and diverse participants who participated in the events summarized as "riots" are reduced to a master principle of religious or ethnic allegiance is itself an important fact, whether that labeling is done by colonial rulers, independent governments, "ruling elites," or the "lower classes."

Apropos of the 1809 riots in Banaras (focused initially on the Lat Bhairava shrine) and the anti-tax agitation of 1810–11, Gyanendra Pandey devastatingly deconstructs "the communal riot narrative" adopted by the British colonial regime—stereotyped depiction of a permanent "religious" divide between Muslims and Hindus, construction of a diachrony into which the events of "riots" fitted, and "the description of violence as a means of describing native character"—by which diverse events and episodes in Indian politics were emptied of their "specific variations of time, place, class, issue" and reduced to the play of religious differences between the Hindus and Muslims.[22] Based on her "public culture" approach, Sandria Freitag says of the 1809 riots in Banaras between Hindus and

Muslims over the Bharat Milap shrine: "Beyond the overt level of symbolism that classifies this conflict as 'religious' lie further meanings. From this vantage point, the specific identification of the combatants, not as 'Hindus' and 'Muslims' but as Marathas, Rajputs, Gosains, and weavers, becomes significant. Thus while not denying the religious characterization, we can find much additional meaning by placing these acts in the larger context of the political economy of Banaras at the turn of the century."[23]

The so-called "Cow Protection Riots of 1893" offer another example of such labeling. These riots were preceded by movements to protect the sacred cow in the late 1880s and early 1890s in Uttar Pradesh. At a general level, the movements and the riots were focused on a religious issue and mobilized Hindus against "a common 'Other' of Muslims." They first manifested themselves in cities and towns such as Kanpur, Lucknow, Gazipur, Aligarh, Banaras, and, above all, Allahabad, where they engaged both reformist elites and neighborhood populations; in the next phase, they engaged the surrounding rural areas, where they intermeshed with the parochial rural interests of dispersed village populations, militating against the more unified impact made in the cities and towns.[24] Pandey argues that the clashes in Azamgarh, Ghazipur, and Ballia in 1893, and those in Shahabal twenty-five years later, reveal bitter antagonism between the dominant Hindu upper castes and Hindu lower castes seeking greater social mobility, and that there were simultaneously class issues that cut across the religious divide and united Hindus and Muslims on social and economic grounds. It is thus difficult to maintain that the anatagonism of Hindus and Muslims was the primary contradiction in the region.[25]

In the late 1980s, a television series called *Tamas* (Darkness), which portrayed and revived memories of the brutalities and violence of the early years of Partition (and by implication also addressed more recent clashes between Hindus, Muslims, and Sikhs), stirred disputes and violence in India, including demonstrations in several cities and an attack on a television station. The series began with scenes bound to agitate both Muslims and Hindus: "In the opening sequence . . . a low caste Hindu is hired by a sinister Hindu businessman to kill a pig, which is then placed in front of a mosque as a provocation to Moslems." In reply, a cow is slaughtered, "inflaming the Hindus and setting off a cycle of revenge in which the town is set ablaze and innocents are slain."[26]

In the recent past, violence and riots between the Sikhs and Hindus in the Punjab have been triggered by acts of ritual desecration. In the middle of political turmoil in 1982, with the talks between the Akali Dal politicians and the central government bogged down, radical young Sikhs, members of the Dal Khalsa, carrying guns adopted shock tactics to force people to take sides: "Just before dawn on the hot morning of 26 April, the bleeding heads of two cows were found in front of a Hindu temple in Amritsar. . . . The rioting in Amritsar following the discovery of the cows' heads resulted in one death and a 24-hour curfew. In retaliation, packets of cigarettes were tossed into Sikh *gurudwaras* [temples] to defile them [Sikhs spurn tobacco], and rioting spread to twenty Punjab towns."[27]

Speaking of a standard form of ritual desecration and its devastating effect, Uma Chakravarty and Nandita Haksar cite the anguish of a Sikh named Balwant Singh at the burning of his gurudwara before his eyes: "His deep hurt at finding that someone had urinated on the Guru Granth Sahib [the sacred scriptures] has perhaps not been captured in our translation," they observe.[28] Such symbolic challenges, which are calculated to inflame, and fiendishly embellished and distorted by rumors, can rapidly spawn a spiraling tornado of violence.

RUMORS AND DISTORTED NEWS

Among the components that figure in the mounting and the staging of ethnic riots (as in many other forms of crowd violence), mischievously and recklessly planted rumors attributing evil intentions and diabolical acts of outrage to the enemy have the dubious honor of inflaming the aggressor to orgasms of destructive violence. Rumors thus have a twofold character. On the one hand, they are a standard and expectable item in crowds formed for mass action against a nominated enemy. Most often the "stories" they relay cluster around themes and issues repeated again in history in diverse places and time. They relate to horrors such as the raping and disemboweling of pregnant women, the poisoning of public wells and water supply, and other standard kinds of desecrations and violations. At a time of charged emotions, such reports, repeated again and again, are seen as highly credible, although subsequently recognized, after the storm, to be improbable. They cause panic and paranoia, and they are also a product of fear and panic. They are believed at a time when distanced skepticism and critical evaluation are scarce, and when individuals are at the greatest risk of being provoked by one another into a state of collective frenzy. And to compound the matter, rumors planted by "riot captains" and agents provocateurs are circulated by the media and, in the telling and relaying, become elaborated and further distorted, in turn spawning other rumors. In time, it is virtually impossible to find out where and when and by whom a rumor was begun. In the end, the panic and fury rumors cause lead to the perpetration of horrendous acts of the very kind attributed to that enemy. Rumors can thus be self-fulfilling.

Just to keep in mind that we are not dealing with a peculiarly Asian diversion, recall a classic case. The cholera epidemic of Paris in 1832 coincided with the workers' armed insurrection of June of that year. "The cholera claimed 39,000 victims, many of them from the crowded streets and tenements adjoining the central markets and Hôtel de Ville. It was widely rumored that the government or the bourgeoisie had deliberately infected the wells and poisoned the inmates of the hospitals and prisons."[29]

One of the frightening aspects of our so-called revolution in mass media communications is that partisan newspapers and radio broadcasts by hasty commentators, or even calculating political leaders, can relay unconfirmed reports of incidents, many of them rumors or distortions of facts, and selective information about events, foregrounding the blame that accrues to the "enemy" and withholding blame that one's own side deserves. Such inflammatory news reaches thousands instantly and travels on with embellishments by word of mouth among gathering crowds. When television and radio are centralized government monopolies, and government controls the flow of news, both selective reporting and censorship contribute to the propagation of tendentious information.

Thus both official and unofficial inquiries into the anti-Sikh riots in Delhi in 1984 following the assassination of Indira Gandhi have highlighted a number of noteworthy features.[30] One is the mischievous, indeed diabolical, role of rumors. Rumors that the New Delhi water supply had been poisoned are said to have been broadcast from loudspeaker vans, and they were thereafter relayed around New Delhi by telephone. There were rumors, too, that Sikhs had large caches of weapons stored in their gurudwaras. Sikhs allegedly distributed sweets to celebrate Mrs. Gandhi's death and jubilantly danced the *bhangra*, a Punjabi dance associated with festivals. (In fact, this story seems to have begun when some college students, who had been preparing to stage a performance for a month, were noticed rehearsing on the day Mrs. Gandhi was killed.) A rumor, which reversed the actual truth, was that trains arriving in Delhi were filled with the corpses of assassinated Hindu passengers.

Television also provided some of the essential ingredients of the riots. Television as a natural medium has spread across India only since 1980. Indeed, at the end of 1984, the government claimed proudly that 70 percent of the population was at last within range of a television signal. That signal is highly controlled. Most of the programming still emanates from New Delhi, another mark of the centralization of the Indian state which Mrs. Gandhi fostered. In the wake of her assassination, the national television and radio networks repeatedly identified her killers as Sikhs. Television showed scenes of the crowds at the place where her body lay in state. Some people shouted slogans: "Blood for blood!"[31]

The ethnic riots in Sri Lanka provide another graphic example of the havoc caused by rumors and tendentious political statements. The rumors swirling around when some students and I were trapped in Gal Oya in 1956 during the first postindependence riots, such as the story of the raping of a young woman, followed by her exposure naked in the street, the imagined invasion of a mythical army, and the frenzied flight of the original aggressors, have already been described in chapter 4. Rumor also helped to raise the passions of the Sinhalese public in other cases, however. One of the incidents associated with the riots of 1958, the second outbreak of Sinhalese aggression against Tamils, and by far the most violent and destructive up to that date, involved the Tamil Federal Party's plans to hold its annual convention in Vavuniya in the north to rethink its strategy after the failure to implement the Bandaranaike-Chelvanayagam pact. The preparations of the Federalists to travel to Vavuniya to attend the convention were retailed to the Sinhalese public in grossly distorted form as a threatened invasion by Tamils from Trincomalee and from Batticoaloa to capture and occupy the historic Sinhalese capitals of Amuradhapura and Polonnaruwa! This spurred the Sinhalese to attack a train from Batticoaloa that was supposed to be carrying the Tamil invaders when it arrived at the railway station at Polonnaruwa. A spate of violence was subsequently unleashed in Polonnaruwa town.

As the violence spread from Polonnaruwa to the eastern provinces, the prime minister, Mr. Bandaranaike, made a broadcast to the nation. "By a strangely inexplicable perversion of logic . . . [he] tried to explain away a situation by substituting the effect for a cause," Tarzie Vittachi observes. In the course of the broadcast, Bandaranaike said: "Certain incidents in the Batticaloa District where some people lost their lives, including *Mr. D. A. Seneviratne*, a former [Sinhalese] Mayor of Nuwara Eliya, have resulted in various acts of violence and lawlessness in other areas—for example Polonnaruwa, Dambulla, Galawela, Kuliyapitiya and even Colombo" (emphasis in original). Vittachi comments: "The killing of Seneviratne on May 25 was thus officially declared to be the cause of the uprising, although the communal riots had begun on May 22 with the attack on the Polonnaruwa Station and the wrecking of the Batticaloa-Colombo train." Soon enough widespread arson occurred in the business sections of Colombo and in provincial towns of the southwest. "The cry everywhere in the Sinhalese districts was 'avenge the murder of Seneviratne'. Even the many Sinhalese who had been appalled by the *goonda* attacks on Tamils and Tamil owned kiosks, now began to feel that the Tamils had put themselves beyond the pale. . . . The Prime Minister's peace call to Nations had turned into a war cry."[32] Meanwhile, other fabrications were wreaking havoc:

> A female teacher from Panadura, the story went, who was teaching in a school in the Batticoaloa District, had been set upon by a gang of Tamil thugs. They had cut off her breasts and killed her. Her body was being brought home to Panadura for cremation. . . . In the bazaar [at Panadura] there was sudden pandemonium. The *goondas* [thugs] intensified their depredations. They ransacked Tamil-owned shops and beat up shopkeepers and passers-by. A gang of *goondas* rushed into the Hindu temple, and attempted to set fire to it. . . . They pulled an officiating priest out of the *Kovil* and burnt him into cinder.[33]

When the Ministry of Education examined its records, it found that there was no female teacher from Panadura on the staff of any school in the Batticoaloa District.

Examples from South Asia and all over the world of distorted communication adding fuel to the fires of internecine conflict can easily be multiplied to confirm the role of rumors in creating stereotypes, causing panic, and serving as justification for brutalities. Richard Lambert documents, for example, how a tendentious campaign conducted by the press in India and Pakistan fed into the gathering storm in Calcutta and the subsequent Hindu-Muslim riots of 1949–50. A spiral of alarm, beginning with stories of looting of merchants' houses in Dhaka, countered by allegations about the East Bengal government's forcible occupation of Indian homes, and followed by stories of mass requisition of houses and the forced participation of Hindu children in Muslim prayers in East Bengal schools, eventually climaxed with "stories of molested women."[34]

PROCESSIONS AND PARADES

Processions and parades, especially of a religious character or in celebration of national holidays, are usually fixed in a religious calendar. And especially in the case of the religious calendars of contiguous religious communities, it is not infrequent that different festivals calling for processions may fall at the same time. It is not unknown for the merrymaking of the Holi festival of the Hindus and the Shia Muslims' Muharram processions to be staged on the same days. In periods of benign coexistence, it is not unusual in India for Sunni Muslims to join in the Muharram celebrations of the Shias, as happened in Lucknow in the eighteenth and nineteenth centuries, and for Muslims to participate in the annual festivals of a Hindu guardian deity, and so on.[35] But in times of ethnic tension, processions predictably trigger violence between polarized communities, especially when they traverse the other's territory. Thus festival calendars can at sensitive times actually channel and direct the shape, expression, timing, and spatial location of ethnic violence. Sometimes the building of a new mosque or temple in an urban space where the community doing the building is gaining in strength and affluence has implications for the conversion of a neighborhood or locality that to start with was mixed, but is now on the way to becoming an exclusive enclave. Writing of Northern Ireland, Allen Feldman explains how it is that to march in and through an area is to lay claim to it:

> The typical spatial pattern of [Protestant and Catholic] parades is the movement from the center of the community (physical and/or symbolic), where the parade audience is ethnically homogeneous, to a march along the boundaries demarcating an adjacent community of the opposed ethnic grouping. Marching along the boundaries transforms the adjacent community into an involuntary audience and an object of defilement through the aggressive display of political symbols and music. . . . Ceremonial marches are important in the Catholic communities, but in the Loyalist (Protestant) community they are an axial rite. Among Loyalists marchers there is a tradition of "taking" a new street and incorporating it into the parade route. These new routes are either on the boundary or actually within the territory of adjacent Catholic communities. In the next year's marches, these new routes are vehemently defended from Loyalist incursions by outraged Catholics or the police. In the Loyalist community these parades synthesize historical symbolisms, the command of space, and boundary transgression.
>
> Violence symbolized or practiced, in this performative context is identified as the appropriate medium for colonizing the outer margins of community space, while kinship and residential structures are reserved as the central ordering apparatuses of the internal community proper.[36]

Processions and marches are not, of course, confined to the format of religious calendars and national holidays. Aside from processions at life-cycle rites such as marriages and funerals, they are standard when a public statement in a public arena is thought necessary, as in staging protests, strikes, and demonstrations; and in the course of electioneering and celebrating victories at the polls. Moreover, the actual enactment of politics is done in the form of competing and agonistic processions, public meetings, and oratorical rebuttals. The more the marchers, the louder their slogans, the more macho their getup, the more "powerful" the politician.

In May 1981, the All-India Sikh Students Federation, led by Jarnail Singh Bhindranwale's confidant, Amrik Singh, began a campaign to ban the sale of tobacco within the walled city of Amritsar. Hindu traders objected, and a Hindu-led pro-cigarette procession of 10,000, some carrying swords, marched through Amritsar on 19 May. On 31 May, 20,000 Sikhs, many brought in from the countryside by appeals from Bhindranwale, and almost all armed, paraded through the city. To understand this spiral of more and fiercer-looking processionists, one has to know that Sikhs spurn tobacco, while Hindus are not subject to this taboo. In the past, the question of smoking had not posed problems, but now it did. (As mentioned above, on another occasion, Hindus polluted Sikhs' sacred space by flinging to-bacco into their gurudwara.)

In the above example, processions were an integral medium, and indeed a *primary form*, in which an explosive religio-political issue was enacted. Any of these agonistic counterstatements could explode at one moment or another, both predictably and unpredictably, into a violent collision, a few killings, or even trigger a large riot.

Processions can be precursors of violence as well as actually develop into riots, and both politicians and religious leaders, who are often both, know their histrionic value as well as their instrumental efficacy in defining and inscribing the region or territory being claimed as an ethnic group's home-lands. In these days of motorized transport, loudspeakers, and mobile film and video shows, the spaces that are traversed and laid claim to can be vast. Bhindranwale's dramatic rise to political eminence in the Punjab was owing in part to his unflagging traveling in his bus along the network of newly constructed village roads and in part to his effective use of mass media and the expanding vernacular press at a time of dramatically rising literacy.

FESTIVALS, RALLIES AND VIOLENCE:
AN ILLUSTRATION FROM KASHMIR

Kashmir, a princely state during the British Raj, was divided between India and Pakistan after the two countries were separated in 1947. The city of Srinagar and the surrounding areas of the valley became part of the Indian state of Jammu and Kashmir.

The fact that the majority of the people of this state were Muslim (in 1980, Muslims constituted 64 percent of the state's population of 5 million) made for contention between Hindus and Muslims from the beginning. For some four decades, Muslim activists, especially the Jammu and Kash-mir Liberation Front, have been agitating for secession from India and union with Pakistan. More recently, many of the militants have demanded independence and the status of a neutral country.

It was also virtually inevitable that from the beginning Pakistan and India would be at loggerheads over border issues and Pakistan's alleged encouragement of the cause of the secessionists. India has already fought three wars with Pakistan. And India has accused Pakistan of arming and training and harboring Muslim militants from Jammu and Kashmir. The demands and protests leading to violence, after a period of relative quiet, intensified in the early months of 1990.

My reference to Kashmir at this point is not so much to give an informed account of its politics of secession but to illustrate some points made earlier about the repertoire of signs, devices, and strategies, such as processions, rallies, orations, and rumors, that is used to stage and enact mass politics. Furthermore, it is relevant that many of these components also constitute traditional festivals. It is, therefore, on the cards that festivals, rallies, demonstrations, and riots may spill over into one another as collective enactments, involving the participation of crowds experiencing heightened sensibilities.[37]

The turmoil in Kashmir in the early months of 1990 offers a good illustration of the overlaps, conjunctions, and processes of spillover between festivals and mass politics and collective violence. To make my point, I shall manipulate the chronology somewhat by describing a later set of events before preceding ones.

"Hundreds of thousands of demonstrators marched through the streets of Srinagar today to press demands for independence for the predominantly Muslim border region," the *New York Times* reported in February 1990. "It was the largest demonstration in decades." For the first time in seven weeks, "the state government lifted the curfew in the city today to allow the marches to take place. The demonstrations also coincided with a major Muslim festival and a Hindu festival. Large gatherings are expected at mosques and temples to mark the separate occasions later tonight." Many joined the processions after the noon prayers at the mosques scattered across the city. "Flags of the Kashmir Liberation Front fluttered from shops, roofs, and even a police-control point." Some demonstrators had traveled from the town of Anantnag, about thirty miles away. Wearing their traditional loose gowns (*phirin*), they sat on the tops of buses waving the green, white, and red flags of the Jammu and Kashmir Liberation Front and shouting slogans favoring independence. Thousands of protesters streamed into the heart of the city, largely on foot. According to a senior police official around 400,000 people—more than half the population of Srinagar city—were in the streets. The protesters eventually converged on the office of the United Nations military observers, where they delivered statements demanding a plebiscite in the Indian-controlled zone (and also in the adjoining area under Pakistani control, called Azad). Young men shouted slogans from the roof of a building opposite the UN office, while men and women waved flags as they walked about. Near the UN office, "young men served sweet watery milk to demonstrators from large drums." So far, the police, armed with bamboo staves and a few rifles, had watched quietly from a distance and had not intervened. Few paramilitary troops were visible.[38]

The festival atmosphere and the boisterous, but still peaceful, rallies and demonstrations were actually an interlude in a fraught political atmosphere, which had already seen violence and would within weeks deteriorate again into a violent ethnic conflict, with the youthful Muslim protesters many turned into "insurgents" and labeled "fundamentalists," combating the Indian police and armed forces, which did not refrain from shooting back.

Since January 20, in the month preceding the demonstrations described, "at least 82 people [had already] been killed . . . in frequent street clashes between militants and security forces in Srinagar and adjoining areas." Most of the victims were protesters defying the curfew imposed by the Indian government to stem the rising violence, incidents of which occurred daily. On February 10, for example, eight bombs exploded in Srinagar, the targets being two banks, a post office, shops, and businesses. A few hours earlier, a shopping complex in the city had been set on fire. Officials blamed the Jammu and Kashmir Liberation Front.[39] Kashmir's dissident militants may be expected to continue with their mass politics combining festivals, processions, demonstrations, and violence. Since 1990 there has been a continuing violent conflict between the Indian armed forces and the Muslim dissidents.

THE IDEOLOGY OF HINDU NATIONALISM

Especially since the mid 1980s, the limelight in Indian politics has fallen on the movement called "Hindu nationalism," whose clarion call is for the revitalized formation of the Hindu nation (Hindutva; Hindu Rashtra). Historically, the focal organization connected with the project of Hindu nationalism was the Rashtriya Swayamsevak Sangh (RSS), founded in Nagpur in 1925, whose mission was to regenerate the Hindu nation. Around it in succeeding years a family (*parivar*) of front organizations arose, namely, the Vishwa Hindu Parishad (VHP, or World Hindu Council), formed in 1965 as a quasi-militant body, and the Bharatiya Janata Party (BJP, or Indian People's Party), which was constituted as a political party around 1980, its predecessor being the Bharatiya Jana Sangh. Subsequently, around 1991–92, militantly nationalist offshoots such as the Bajrang Dal sprang up.

The first leader of the RSS was Dr. Keshav Baliram Hedgewar, whose successor in 1940 was Madhav Sadashiv Golwalkar, a Maharashtrian Brahman who had been a teacher at the Banaras Hindu University. The aims of the RSS were stated as follows: "To eradicate differences among Hindus; to make them realize the greatness of their past; to inculcate in them a spirit of self-sacrifice and selfless devotion to Hindu society as a whole; to build up an organized and well-disciplined corporate life; and to bring about the regeneration of Hindu society."[1]

The stress on the centrality of Hindu culture as the defining element of both religion and nation was given wide currency by Golwalkar in a little pamphlet, *We or Our Nation Defined,* first published in 1939. "The nation," he said, "is a compound of the famous five unities: geography, race, religion, culture and language."[2] This formulation obviously had significant implications for the identity and status of India's immense Muslim population of nearly 110 million, and other groups such as Sikhs, Buddhists, and Christians. (The RSS claims that Sikhs and Buddhists are Hindus, which is at odds with their own sense of commitment to their distinctive religions.)

Some RSS spokesmen do not choose to cite canonical authority from scripture or refer to any of the holy foundation texts of Hinduism or any defined dogma. Hinduism is not predicated on the historicity of an individual founder or on the authority of a book or canon. Hedgewar pointed to the overarching concept of *dharma* as forming the heart of Hinduism: on the one hand it relates to the proper "rehabilitation of the mind" and on the other to the "adjustment of individuals towards a harmonious corporate existence." Since "Hindu" coincided with *rashtriya*, "nationality," it was argued, Hindus were automatically true nationals of India. "Members of other religions, if they denied they were Hindus, were also denying that they were Indians."[3]

After the assassination of Mahatma Gandhi in January 1948, the RSS was declared an unlawful association, and Golwalkar and other leaders were arrested. The ban was later lifted.

RSS volunteers, or *swayamsevaks,* were encouraged to think of themselves as a brotherhood dedicated to the improvement of Hindu society and eventual creation of a Hindu *rashtra* (nation). The movement was especially active in the Punjab and in northern India during the period of high communal tension at Partition, to which the RSS leaders have never reconciled themselves, viewing it as a profound tragedy perpetrated by Muslims.

RSS ideology harps on the degradation and decline of Indian society by virtue of its disunity and the seduction of its elites by Western culture and values. There is a need, it argues, for a regeneration in order to recapture the glories of the past, and for a change in the life of contemporary Indians. After initiation in a public ceremony, youthful RSS neophytes, or *shakhas* (subordinate workers in local branches), experience an expanded identity as members of a collectivity devoted to the task of regeneration of Mother India—an identity larger than the parochial ones of caste and village.

In general, RSS literature berates sections of the "dehinduized intelligentsia" influenced by Western education and culture who think that the Indian nation is a modern construct, and that Hinduism was not a definable religion, only a conglomeration of superstitious practices. Golwalkar charged the Indian National Congress with the fabrication of a new sense of nationality on the basis of these British-hatched misconceptions. The commitment of the Indian National Congress, especially Jawaharlal Nehru, to a special definition of "secularism" as a solution to governing India and managing its religious diversity is rejected as concealing the reality of Indian life deeply grounded in Hindu culture. In terms of the RSS definition of the Hindu nation, four categories of people are enemies of India: Indian followers of foreign religions, such as Islam and Christianity; Communists and their sympathizers; westernized members of the Indian intelligentsia; and foreign powers.

The powerful and explosive charge the RSS leaders (followed by the VHP and the BJP) made against the Congress is that after independence, Nehru and the Congress Party failed to build a new society because of their allegiance to the false dogma of secularism, which was used to win the electoral support of minorities, especially the Muslims and Christians.

The success of the RSS and its allies is a reaction to a sense of personal failure or frustration experienced by many people, especially young men of the middle class, who feel that they have not shared in the benefits of the sweeping changes that have taken place in India since 1947 and that they have been marginalized by the urban elites in terms of opportunities for advancement and influence. The educated unemployed youth of India form a vast discontented and volatile constituency ready to be mobilized for populist politics of the kind promoted by the Hindu nationalists.

THE AYODHYA DISPUTE

"The Ayodhya dispute" is shorthand for the complicated, confused controversy surrounding the sometimes violent attempts by Hindu nationalists belonging to the aforementioned groups to destroy the mosque called the Babri Masjid in Ayodhya, if possible, and to build a Hindu temple devoted to the god Ram (Rama, one of the avatars of Vishnu) in its place. If this was not possible, it was felt, the next best move would be to build a temple to Ram at an adjoining site.

Ayodhya, near Faizabad in Uttar Pradesh, is a sacred city for Hindus, a pilgrimage center and place of many Hindu temples. The Babri Masjid is said to have been built in 1528 by one of the Mughal Emperor Bābur's generals on the site of an earlier Hindu temple dedicated to Ram, allegedly built by King Vikramaditiya in the fourth century A.D. It is popularly believed that this was the birthplace of Ram, the son of King Dasharatha of Kosala, whose capital Ayodhya was. (The use of some carved pillars in the construction of the mosque lends some credence to the claim of the preexistent temple, but the pillars might have been brought from elsewhere.) Hindus call the place Ramjanmabhumi. The affair is thus labeled the Babri Masjid–Ramjanmabhumi dispute.

While the fact that the mosque was built in Bābur's time is not disputed, everything about the antecedent state of affairs is.[4] In the nineteenth century, there had been some clashes between Hindus and Muslims in the Ayodhya locality. After the trauma of Partition, the Indian government closed the mosque and made it out of bounds to both Muslims and Hindus. In late December 1949, the image of the deity Ram (together with images of Lakshman, his brother, and Sita, his consort) "appeared" in the Babri Masjid. The Muslims considered this a defilement of their mosque, and riots ensued, which were quelled with great difficulty by police and army troops. However, in the following year, the Ramjanmabhumi Seva Committee managed to obtain permission to worship Ram's image once a year to commemorate its first appearance.

In 1984, the Vishwa Hindu Parishad began its campaign to have the mosque opened for regular worship by Hindus. The Ayodhya issue, which itself served as a condensed symbol of many criticisms and grievances on the part of the Hindu nationalists against the governments in power, in particular the Congress (I) regime, became the prime electoral issue for the political party of the Hindu nationalists, the BJP, whose leader, L. K. Advani, leapt into prominence as the political challenger of successive prime ministers, notably V. P. Singh, the leader of the Janata Dal Party in 1990, and later Narasimha Rao of the Congress (I).

Focusing on the Ayodhya issue enormously helped the BJP to achieve electoral success.[5] From a mere two seats in the Lok Sabha in 1984, the BJP's tally rose to 85 in 1989, and two years later it had expanded to become the main opposition, with 120 seats. In 1991, the building of the Ram temple was the main issue, which like an immense umbrella encompassed many others, such as alleged favoritism toward Muslims and the corresponding plight of the Hindu majority, as instanced by the Shah Bano case (1980) and the Rajiv Gandhi government's decision to allow Muslims to follow their own "personal laws";[6] the recommendation by the Mandal Commission of affirmative action in favor of the backward classes, which higher-caste Hindus found threatening; the violence in the Punjab and the threatened secession by the Sikhs; the violence likewise in Kashmir, exacerbating Hindu-Muslim animosities; the need for a uniform civil code for all Indian citizens; the "pseudo-secularism" of the nation-state fathered by Nehru and perpetuated by Congress (I); the rejuvenation of the nation by making Hindu culture a bulwark against Western secularism, consumerism, and sexual eroticism; the continued corruption of the Congress (I) regime and the train of scandals it has spawned. All these grievances were grist for the rhetoric, propaganda, and slogans purveyed on the road to Ayodhya. This combative rhetoric came to a climax in December 1992, when the Babri mosque was demolished.

THE DEMOLITION OF THE BABRI MASJID AND ITS CONSEQUENCES

On the one hand, the Bharatiya Janata Party tapped into and deployed traditional religious rituals, resources, and sentiments (avoiding narrow "sectarian" texts and doctrines) and also drew from the repertoire of "public culture"; on the other hand, it creatively used modern media for maximal propagandizing reach and modern modes of transportation for assembling its motorcades and *rath yatras* ("chariot processions") and for its "electioneering" in mass politics. The chariots themselves are an amalgam of the old and new: temple chariot superstructures mounted on modern trucks and vans, equipped with loudspeakers, electrical generators, and so on. They are, in fact, composite modern elaborations that also include decorative elements borrowed from Peter Brook's film of the *Mahabharata*, as in the case of the chariot in which Advani rode in 1990. The "religious" goals of "pilgrimage" and "holy war" were conflated with electoral calculations and pursuit of political power. Young recruits became voluntary "holy workers" (*karsevaks*); sadhus and *sants* mixed their ritual chantings with militant thuggery; and rituals of offerings called *pujas* and *yajnas* to deities were piously attended by politicians representing themselves as aspiring revivers of the Hindu nation and prospective ministers of state.

"Sacrifice for Unity" of Mother India (*Ekamata yajna*) rallies and processions were staged in 1983 to create national unity. Huge images of Mother India (Bharat Mata) were carried in chariots, and holy water from the Ganges was mixed in pots (*kalashas*) with water from other sacred rivers and sold to temples. This campaign is alleged to have mobilized some 60 million people, and processions traversing the sacred geography of the subcontinent, from Hardwar in the north to Kanyakumari in the south, and from Gangasar in the east to Somnath in the west, from Kathmandu in the northeast to Rameswaram in the deep south, are alleged to have covered 85,000 kilometers. India, as Bharatvarsha, has long been considered a "geographical unity" and a global sacred field (*kshetra*).

In 1984, the first procession to Ayodhya was staged. It was called "a sacrifice to liberate the spot where Rama was born" (Ram janmabhumi mukti yajna). The objective was to "open the lock" (*thala kholo*) to the mosque and thus "liberate Ram" and make the deity accessible to worship.

By 1989, with the temporizing of the courts, which were unwilling for good reason to adjudicate the rival Muslim and Hindu claims, passions over the Ayodhya mosque issue had mounted, and they escalated further in the face of the unstoppable violence by Sikh extremists in the Punjab and the resurgence of the Hindu-Muslim animosities in Kashmir. Sacred bricks (*Ramshilas*) were transported in convoys of trucks in 1989 for the *mahayajna* ("great sacrifice"), namely, the ceremony for the laying of the foundation of the temple of Ram (Ram Janmasthan Mandir). Sanctified bricks made of the "local earth" in multiple places were transported together with *sevaks* (workers) to the radial center of Ayodhya, and, in reverse, earth dug in Ayodhya was redistributed to different parts of India. This amounted to a periphery to center (centripetal) and center to periphery (centrifugal) double participatory process.

In 1990, there was a procession to build the platform (*Ram mandir*) of the temple. The most dramatic features of this campaign was BJP President Lal Advani's 10,000 kilometer rath yatra, planned to start at the Sonmath Temple in Gujarat and conclude at the disputed Babri Masjid site in Ayodhya, and his arrest on the way. Intruding upon this sequence and adding further spin to it were the riots and immolations by students (of upper- and middle-caste status) in many towns and cities triggered by Prime Minister V. P. Singh's decision to reactivate and implement the Mandal Commission's provisions for affirmative action in favor of the "Other Backward Classes" (OBC's).[7]

On December 6, 1992, as *mahants, pandits*, and sadhus were getting ready to start the puja on the newly built platforms for the temple to Ram, the Babri Masjid was demolished by karsevaks, who broke the security cordon, scrambled on top of the domes, and smashed them, some of them plunging down with the debris (see figure 8). There was evidence of preparations for the demolition among the rank and file, and it was preceded by an immense massing at Ayodhya of leaders, activists, and workers of the Sangh Parivar, the family of organizations of the Hindutva movement. All the leaders of the movement—Advani and Vajpayee of the BJP, Joshi of the VHP, and leaders of the RSS, the Bajrang Dal, and the Shiv Sena—were present. And, unsurprisingly, incidents of arson and injury accompanied the demolition.

By the end of December 8, two days after the demolition, virtually all the sevaks had left Ayodhya in buses and trains. But news of the destruction of the Babri Masjid—celebrated as the beginning of Ramraj and

Figure 8. Hindu nationalist militants storm and demolish the Babri mosque in Ayodhya on December 6, 1992. Prashant Panjiar (*India Today*).

Bharatvarsha by Hindu militants—plunged the country into a political crisis and set off murderous Hindu-Muslim riots, further compounded by police shooting in at least six Indian states, which was responsible for most of the deaths that resulted, and by the strike (*bandh*) called by the BJP to protest the arrest of its party leaders. It was the worst outbreak of sectarian violence in India since the assassination of Indira Gandhi in 1984.

After two days of fighting, more than 400 were reported killed in various parts of India, but the actual number was believed to be much higher. By this time, the arrest of the Hindu leaders, the banning of five Hindu and Muslim organizations, and the one-day general strike called by the BJP had added considerably to the intense tensions and violence. Among the Indian cities, the worst incidents of violence took place in Bombay, Delhi, Ahmedabad, Varanasi, and Jaipur. In Pakistan, Karachi and Lahore were much inflamed, as was Dhaka in Bangladesh. Incidents of arson involving Muslims and Hindus, Indians and Pakistanis, took place as far away as the United Kingdom.

By December 11, UPI News reported, "Authorities said Friday that violence was diminishing after five days of vicious communal clashes that killed 1,050 people and injured more." The BBC also reported a return to normalcy on the same day, with a death toll of "over 900 so far." The number of deaths throughout India frequently reported as the final count in numerous press reports was 1,200.

In virtually no case did the riots last longer than six or seven days (from the evening of December 6 to December 11 or 12), once again showing that civilian riots are generally short-lived and unstable, and that once past their peak, in about three days, they simmer down as the army and other security forces begin to exert their authority and take effective preventive action.

THE BOMBAY RIOTS

One notable departure from this pattern is the flow of events in the city of Bombay, where there were two spells of rioting, the first, as in other places, from December 6 to December 12, 1992, and then, after an interval of a month, with only minor incidents, a second outbreak of even greater intensity from January 7 to January 16, 1993.

On the face of it, Bombay was an unlikely site for the violence: it is a bustling center of finance and commerce and considered one of Asia's most cosmopolitan cities. It is also said to be India's most populous city. At the census of 1991, the population of greater Bombay was 9.9 million, and its density was an extraordinary 16,432 persons per square mile. The metropolitan agglomeration was estimated as 12.6 million in 1991, making Bombay the sixth most populated city in the world.[8]

But Bombay is also a city of startling economic disparities and mounting tensions. Between the 1960s and the 1980s, there was a large decline in the kinds of employment that fed and clothed numerous manual, semi-skilled, and skilled workers. Nearly 900,000 manufacturing jobs were lost, and textiles made way for chemicals as the city's major employer. Declining employment prospects were further compounded by deteriorating labor-management relations and large streams of migrants from other parts of India, adding to the variety of religious and linguistic communities living in close proximity. This could lead to explosive zero-sum contests between the local Maharashtrian "sons of the soil" (*bhumiputra*) and migrants, as exemplified by the attack of Shiv Sena militants on South Indian migrant labor in the late 1960s.

Bombay has its affluent residential enclaves and plush hotels and shopping centers, needless to say, but "more than half its population lives in slums in most miserable conditions. These slums have mixed populations of various religious and regional as well as caste communities. These are usually a maze of narrow lanes and bylanes, making it easy for the miscreants to hide themselves and difficult for the law-enforcing agencies to pursue them."[9]

"Taken together, the communal violence of December and January [1993] spread to every part of the metropolis. . . . In the first phase, south-central Bombay was the first and worst affected area. Rioting then spread to some suburbs. . . . In the second phase, the riots spread over almost all of greater Bombay, that is, downtown and central Bombay, as well as the western and eastern suburbs, to Dahisar in the west and Mulund and Deonar in the east."[10] In the first phase, in December, fifteen police station areas were under curfew; in the second, the number increased to twenty-four.

As noted earlier, exact casualty figures—the numbers of those killed, injured, displaced, or expelled—and details of damage to and looting of property, and so on, are notoriously difficult to compile in riot situations. In Bombay, widely diverging figures were cited by the police and army, by hospitals and morgues, by relief workers, by journalists and unofficial investigating teams, and by the local residents on both sides of the divide. Whatever the wide variations in figures—the government's official sources always depressing them and the victimized neighborhoods exaggerating them—it is clear that the Bombay toll was very large.

According to the figures compiled by the *Times of India*, 227 people died in the December riots, and 557 in the January riots; another 317 succumbed in March bombings related to the riots, allegedly the work of Muslim terrorists linked with the Gulf states (which unfortunately cannot be gone into here).[11] Somewhat higher estimates are given by Asghar Ali Engineer: "In the first phase, the Government admitted more than 200 deaths, but the number is more than 300." For the second phase, while the official figures put the toll at 650, Engineer surmises that "the figure may exceed 1000."[12]

The *Times of India* calculated that 10,000 houses, from 70 to 300 bakeries, over 70 percent of Bombay's timber warehouses, and about 500 trucks and 150 taxis were set on fire and damaged or destroyed. Some fifty thousand people were rendered homeless. Property damage was estimated at 40 billion rupees,[13] not counting damage to the public transport system (railways and buses) and electricity supply, or loss of manufacturing output, services, and trading and working days, which can only be very roughly quantified.

Although, especially in the second phase around January 10, middle- and upper-class residential areas such as parts of Malabar Hill, Warden Road, and Central Dalal Estate were attacked, by far the worst cases of arson, homicide, and displacement of people occurred in Bombay's sprawling working-class and poverty-stricken slums. In the first phase, the most frequently mentioned locality was Dharavi, others being Govandi, Mahim, Bhendi Bazar, and Null Bazar; in the second phase, localities such as Dongri, Nagpada, Pydhonie, and Tardeo figure in the reports. The terms *slum* and *shanty settlement* give the impression that these are merely dense concentrations of the very poor, but the areas mentioned include markets and bazaars, temples and mosques and saints' tombs, timber godowns, groceries, and artisans' shops. These so-called slums are where the majority of the urban population—shopkeepers, workers, artisans and craftsmen, transport workers, taxi drivers, "coolies," construction workers, and so on—live, but wedged inside them are also lower-middle-class and white-collar communities of brick-built *pakka* (proper) houses.

The areas in question were populated by different proportional mixes of Muslims and Hindus (themselves differentiated by region of origin, primary language, and sectarian affiliation). Some were predominantly Hindu or Muslim; others were characterized by co-residence and contiguity of the two groups. Although on various occasions, the Muslims (who made up 15 percent of Bombay's population) were the attackers or engaged in exchanges of violence, by far the largest number of victims were Muslims, most of them passive targets.

Perhaps to a degree unknown in the case studies previously outlined, the Bombay riots present us with the worst instances of active police participation in the shooting of victims. While in the rioting areas of Bombay, the police in some measure were taxed and had to act in self-defense, many reports charge the police with indiscriminate shooting, the larger number of their victims being Muslims. The vast majority of the police force in all ranks were non-Muslim, and, as I have argued before, a police force so constituted is bound to share the political values of the majority. When the rioting was over, the death count over the first week was reported as 259. Engineer estimates that in all over 400 Muslims were killed or injured.[14]

"What started off as a clash between Muslim youths and armed police trying to protect public property turned communal as the riots spread from the densely-populated Muslim areas of south and central Bombay to the huge slums of Dharavi, Deonar and Ghatkopar," *India Today* noted.[15] It was also accepted, and conceded by Police Commissioner Bapat, that the vast majority of deaths in Bombay were caused by police firing, and that Muslim crowds were the primary victims of this police action. Toward the end of the first phase of the upheaval, in the face of police complicity and mostly unilateral involvement, the home minister of Maharashtra State called for the deployment of thousands of Indian Army troops to head off further rioting.

The deliberate, calculated use of violence by the Shiv Sena movement as a mode of conducting politics, and to gain economic advantage and greater power for its leaders and their lieutenants, is a noteworthy aspect of the Bombay riots. The phrase "criminalization of politics," commonly used in India today, aptly applies to the activities of this organization. Virtually all reports on the Bombay riots unfailingly point to the Shiv Sena, led by Bal Thackeray, as taking the lead in organizing and planning violence against Muslims in what has been described as a pogrom. Thackeray's movement has been explicitly compared to Hitler's Nazis and its activities to present-day "ethnic cleansing" in Bosnia.

Founded in 1966 for the express purpose of conducting a campaign to reserve jobs for "sons of the soil," the Shiv Sena grew subsequently into a more organized and multifunctional mafia-style operation. At one stage in the mid 1980s, it captured power in, and virtually ran, the Bombay Municipal Corporation (BMC), and it still has its elected members in the BMC. Aside from Thackeray, the next most conspicuous figure is Madhukar Sarpotdar, a member of the Maharashtra State Legislative Assembly and an active figure in local politics and protection rackets. The Shiv Sena runs its own newspapers and has links with others, which support it; it controls certain labor unions, which function as right-wing enforcers against left-oriented unions; and it has ties to some of Maharashtra's barons of industry, who finance it.

By the early 1990s, the Shiv Sena's leaders found it advantageous to renew their political presence by supporting the cause of Hindu nationalism and became like the VHP, a militant body, participating in the rath yatras and espousing the BJP's political rhetoric. During the Bombay riots, especially in the days before and during the second phase in January 1993, it successfully staged *maha-aratis*, rituals of collective worship, at various Hindu temples in Bombay, in order to mobilize crowds for launching of violent actions. Devised to contest and rival the traditional Muslim Friday afternoon prayers (*namaaz*) at mosques, where large numbers of Muslims met and heard their preachers, the Shiv Sena used the maha-aratis to convene Hindu worshipers and urge them to put an end to the "appeasement" policies of the government toward Muslims by attacking and displacing the local Muslims. The nexus between Bombay's politicians, businessmen, police, and the Shiv Sena deserves deeper study, for it would also show how the city's politics is linked to the state's, and the state's to national politics. During the riots, one of the tangles that exacerbated the difficulties of slowing down the violence were the alleged rivalries and animosities between Naik, Bombay's chief minister, and Sharad Pawar, a fellow Maharashtrian, who had gone to Delhi as defence minister but later returned to Bombay, on the orders of Prime Minister Narasimha Rao, to replace Naik. These rival politicians were themselves patrons of, and associated with, allegedly criminal gangs.

The impact of the riots and the displacement of Muslims on the spatial and occupational distribution of population in metropolitan Bombay is also noteworthy. The spatial factor relates to the control of land as real estate in a city where land—including land occupied by slum dwellers—is expensive and has much more profitable alternate uses. The Shiv Sena's direction of attacks on Muslims, and their dispossession and displacement, and counteractions by Muslim gangs on a lesser scale were thus to a significant degree also concerned with the conquest of space. Concurrently, the displacement of Muslims in specialized crafts and artisanal work (weaving, leather working) affected the division of labor in the city and deprived it of essential services. The increased polarization of the Hindu and Muslim communities and the partial rearrangement by "ethnic cleansing" of Bombay's residential areas and business sites, and of its ethnic composition in employment, are serious consequences of the pogrom conducted against the Muslims of Bombay, both poor and rich, slum dwellers and occupants of middle-class or affluent apartments. The expulsion of occupants of shanties—even in the slums of Dharavi and Behrampada, their tiny spaces are valuable and salable—or pushing Muslims and Hindus into homogeneous enclaves, when previously they lived jumbled together at various sites and in interstitial areas, the invasion of the residences of upper-middle-class Muslims, and the looting of their property or complete takeover of their apartments—these actions, if not reversed, would lead to "a geographical reorganization of a complex and historic city along communal lines."[16]

The war against one another to capture real estate was engaged in by a number of interest groups—whether they be businessmen looking to redevelop, traders displacing rivals, the poor looking for tenement space, Shiv Sena youth gangs looting and burning, or other ad hoc gangs of both Hindus and Muslims on the rampage. Their acts had little to do, as the riots developed and continued, with the original "grand" cause of protecting the Babri mosque or of liberating Ram—that is, with the alleged great national communal divide between Hindus and Muslims. Such collective ethnonational charters become secondary to the pursuit of personal political and property concerns. At their worst moments, irrespective of whether they were Hindu or Muslim, the rioters may have been battening on and cannibalizing their own kind.

Equally significant, the "ethnic cleansing" furthermore had much to do in the context of high unemployment with displacing "outsiders" from the jobs they held and the occupations they followed. In 1966 and subsequently, the Shiv Sena was out to eject South Indian Tamils from jobs that Maharashtrians envied. The Bombay riots of 1992–93 resulted in the flight of many Muslim families, especially those of small business, craft, artisan, and other working-class status, and it is unclear how many of them will return, and, even if they return, whether they will be able or permitted to resume their former occupations.

Although the worst of the violence had passed by February 1993, the signs of hatred continued. It was reported that labor unions run by Shiv Sena were intimidating Muslim workers, preventing them from returning to their jobs in some of the city's largest industries, including Otis Elevator, the Mahindra jeep and tractor plants, and companies on the docks. There were also reports of warnings issued to Hindus not to patronize or work for establishments run by "antinational" Muslim employers.

THE PROCESSES OF NATIONALIZATION
AND PAROCHIALIZATION

Earlier chapters introduced and illustrated a pair of interrelated processes, namely, *focalization* and *transvaluation*, which were perceived in the unfolding and trajectory of the 1915 Sinhalese-Muslim riots in Sri Lanka and the Karachi riots between Pathans and Muhajirs in 1985. These two concepts were coined to label the manner in which microevents at the local level, through chainlike linkages, accelerate and cumulatively build up into an avalanche, whose episodes progressively lose their local contextual, circumstantial, and substantive associations, while the violence, lasting a few days, is retrospectively generalized and made into a macroevent or master narrative labeled an "ethnic conflict" between two antagonistic ethnic groups.

Now is the time to introduce another pair of concepts, *nationalization* and *parochialization*, to describe and sum up processes of unfolding that are the very opposite in sequence and significance to those pertaining to focalization and transvaluation.

The RSS, BJP, and VHP, which aspire to power at the union center and in state governments, claim to be movements sponsoring causes with national significance, exemplified by the very concept of Hindutva. The building of a new temple to Ram in Ayodhya was portrayed as an all-India Hindu nationalist cause. For these movements, Ayodhya was an *axis mundi* and a *locus classicus,* a condensed symbol signifying the whole. Processions carrying sacred bricks, unity campaigns, and rath yatras started from various dispersed peripheral points and radiated toward the center, the birthplace of Ram. Correspondingly, earth dug at the center and sacred water from the Ganges were distributed in centrifugal fashion to various parts of the subcontinent.

Radiating out from India's metropolitan centers to its peripheries, this phenomenon in due course affected hundred of towns and villages, engaging with local power structures, local complexes of castes, sects, and ethnic groups, and playing itself out in relation to these particular cleavages, which adapted and concretized the national cause to suit their local political contexts and contingencies. This reproduction of a national issue in diverse local places, where it explodes like a cluster bomb in multiple context-bound ways, I call *parochialization.* Nationalization and parochialization thus relate to each other as a top-down, center-to-periphery process, while focalization and transvaluation involve a bottom-up, periphery-to-center aggregating and generalizing process. The Bombay riots are a prime example of how a "national" cause and a "national" event worked themselves out in terms of local causes, networks, and interests, and thus became parochialized. The two contrasted sets of processes, focalization and transvaluation, and nationalization and parochialization, thus together provide us with a way of describing and interpreting current ethnonationalist conflicts and their paths of collective violence.

VIOLENCE IN DEMOCRATIC POLITICS

The rath yatras, juggernauts, and other processions associated with the Ayodhya dispute and enacted as a religiocultural cause dedicated to religious devotionalism and Hindu revival were also simultaneously political theater, carrying and employing a number of institutionalized and organized components, which constitute a repertoire of collective violence deployed in elections and the conduct of democratic politics. These components are part of that repertoire:

1. Motorized cavalcades, consisting of hundreds of cars and vans snaking through towns, stopping for roadside rallies and explosive speeches, sparking violent incidents, even riots.

2. The call for national strikes (*hartal*), usually lasting one day, that result in the stoppage of transport services and the closing of bazaars and shops.

3. Collisions between marchers and police, troops, and paramilitary forces, resulting in some deaths and injury to the people in the crowds, both protesters and onlookers, and to members of the security forces.

4. When collisions develop into "riots," standard actions are arson and destruction of vehicles (cars, jeeps, buses) and buildings, especially if these are "government property."

5. Timing rath yatras to take place at the time of festivals such as Dassehra, in October, when Ram and Ravana are alive and well in dramatic performance of the *Ramayana*,[17] and pilgrimage climaxes such as circumambulations which not only ensure the spectator-presence of hordes of pilgrims and celebrating civilians but also lend to the processions, which embody a large potential for violent acts, the atmosphere of permitted license, euphoria, and effervescence associated with "holi" days and carnivals. Moreover, politically motivated "self-immolations" and "homicides" are staged as "religious acts" and the slogans of past "holy wars" and "historical battles" serve as challenges and triggers to violence in the current holy war.

These acts and events form a repertoire of collective violence linking up with and drawing from the collective calendrical festivities and celebrations of public culture, and insofar as that repertoire is systematized through repeated performance over a period of time, it foregrounds violence itself as a mode of conducting politics and begins to shade into civil war, when violent conflict becomes an everyday state of affairs.

The Indian media have been effectively harnessed and deployed in various ways to propagandize causes such as the Ayodhya temple issue, notwithstanding that India is a country in which 65 percent of the population are illiterate (and only 2 percent know English). Lloyd Rudolph has recently perceptively commented that "the increasing prominence of the media has accelerated a trend away from locally based, bottom up politics, a trend that was already well launched before the 1989 elections." There is, Rudolph asserts, a

> shift in Indian politics from party based campaigns, relying on local workers who approximate ward organization, toward plebiscitary campaigning organized around simple slogans and whirlwind visits by great personalities. Since 1971, when the link between national parliamentary and state elections was broken, electoral waves (6 to 9 percent shifts in party vote shares) whipped up by nationally resonant slogans such as "abolish poverty," "restore democracy," or "preserve national unity" have come to settle parliamentary elections. Then came audio cassettes featuring candidates' and leaders' voice messages and party songs, followed by the spread of national television, radio and VCRs. The collaboration of television, radio and VCRs has clearly accelerated the shift from party-based campaigning to the plebiscitary mode."[18]

This observation catches much of the tenor and tempo of contemporary Indian electoral politics.

One may, however, wish to modify somewhat Rudolph's illuminating top-down globalizing plebiscitarian perspective by reminding ourselves that the "national" and "nationalizing" issues also have their distinctive "parochial" unfoldings and denouements, which are sensitive to local fault lines, local alignments and factions. Moreover, there are also bottom-up instances, where a chain of local events escalates and spreads, and, undergoing the processes of "focalization" and "transvaluation," cumulatively becomes more generalized and simplified, concluding as a binary global divide such as those between Muslims and Hindus, Sinhala Buddhists and Hindu Tamils, Pathans and Muhajirs, and so on. But here too local media have played their communicational roles.

All things considered, this observation seems valid: mass politics and mass religious fervor in many places—ranging from Iran to India to Armenia—now make efficacious and explosive use of communication media and high-tech devices. Aside from radio and films, followed by television, perhaps the most sensational recent development is the use of VCRs and audiocassettes, by means of which both villagers in remote rural areas and the unlettered in cramped urban slums can hear messages and see visual images propagated by leaders and ideologues from metropolitan centers. Moreover, the further import of these new cassette media, widely available and cheap to acquire and distribute, is that they can serve as a counterweight to, and a subverter of, governments, which have been hitherto monopolized television and radio broadcasting, censored newspapers, and been the primary sources and purveyors of information. The causes of ethnonationalities and minorities fighting the centralized powers of states and authoritarian regimes are advanced through this revolution in information transmission. Moreover, rumors, which are notorious for instigating and fueling violence by interweaving rage with panic and fear of the "enemy," circulate all the more speedily through the media.

THE WEINER PARADOX

"How does one explain why India's democratic institutional structure persists, and how does one explain the paradox of a democratic system continuing to function in the midst of sharp social cleavages and large scale violence?" Myron Weiner asks. India's democratic system continues to flourish, says Weiner, although "conflicts among religions, castes and tribal communities have shown no signs of abating," and although the record of democracy is not an unblemished one, as illustrated by the period of emergency from 1975-77.[19] The same question with some modification and greater skepticism can be asked about Sri Lanka.

Indian democracy is widely celebrated for good reasons. But my answer to the Indian puzzle is that participatory democracy, competitive elections, mass militancy, and crowd violence are not disconnected. They were not disconnected in Europe: in Britain, for instance, the latter part of the nineteenth century saw the parallel rise of democracy and industrial militancy, through the two suffrage acts and the emergence of the "new unionism." And before that the French Revolution had ushered in the crowd as an enduring political force, with the storming of the Bastille as the stereotypical image of crowd politics. Thereafter, the political doctrines of democracy had to speak directly of the people, for or against it, and governments had to shape techniques to control the militant crowd as a manifestation of people's power, just as intellectuals had to accommodate it as a central concern in their social and political theories.

It seems that theorists of South Asian politics should make room today for militant electoral politics and collective violence as an integral component of their theories of democracy at work. The ideal normative description of democracy is that of a rational system of representative government where citizens as individuals—with "one man, one vote"—make rational choices according, to their interests and values, about which parties to support and which candidates to elect. And this theory also holds that the governed hold their governors to account through periodic elections and by recourse to judicial process. But democracy in South Asia is also a manner of conducting mass politics. The mobilization of the crowds and the wooing of their support—through election speeches, rallies, mass media propaganda, and dispensation of favors through election machines—is the central process of persuasion and vote-getting. This reliance on crowds and mass mobilization opens the door to the invention and propagation of collective slogans and collective ideologies, to the appeal to collective entitlements for groups in terms of divisive "substance codes" of blood and soil (to borrow a term from McKim Marriott).[20] Today "ethnicity" is the most potent energizer, embodying and radiating religious, linguistic, territorial, and class and caste identities and interests; it is also the umbrella under which personal, familial, commercial, and other local scores are settled.

In the practice of democracy in India, Pakistan, Sri Lanka, and Bangladesh, the Weiner paradox is facilitated by presenting public policies through state-controlled media as though they were the outcome of rational debate, and by making public ritual and spectacles parade as the process of consultation of the masses and seeking their legitimacy and consent.

There are other processes in the practice of democracy that are also related to the generation of collective communal violence. An increasing number of commentators, both Indian and Western, are drawing our attention to the dangers of the Indian state becoming a relatively independent and dominant actor, with its own interests that dictate specific policies in relation to ethnic and cultural groups in the polity. Engaged in its unrealistic project of creating a homogenized nation-state, it frustrates the cultural and social pluralism of India.[21]

In addition, the nation-state project articulates two other, antithetical social aims. The alleged push toward equality and the goal of achieving the greatest good for the greatest number open the way to the proliferation of bureaucratic and hierarchical administrative structures, in which officials of various sorts make citizens subject themselves to obvious forms of obeisance, subordination, inequality, and extortion. To adapt and echo an argument made by Ralf Dahrendorf, the sensitive points of contest and conflict in modern societies, including third world countries, with their bureaucratic expansion, lies in the differential distribution of power among officials and citizens, and the dominance of the former over the latter in daily encounters. It should therefore come as no surprise when protesting crowds attack and destroy government buildings and public property and immobilize public services and utilities, the very social capital and the infrastructure allegedly instituted to serve them. It is a form of political Luddism.

CODA: ELECTIONS AND COLLECTIVE VIOLENCE

Ethnonationalist conflicts and collective violence are obviously nothing new. They have occurred at other times in many places. In third world countries, "democratic" political elections are, however, a major contributor to collective violence. Moreover, because the stakes in the election process and its outcome seem so high in these societies, and because elections permit and indeed encourage calculated expressions and enactments of polarizing hostility, such outbreaks may well overshadow earlier cases of routinized periodic violence.

The general theme of whether democracy as a political process and the democratic state as a system intensify the occurrence of violence is an old one in the history of political theory. From the Greeks onwards, even up to the nineteenth century, many theorists, perhaps most, associated democracy with civil strife, and it is only subsequently that this became a minority view. Gustave Le Bon's characterization of the crowd as violent and irrational was linked to his antipathy to the French Revolution and subsequent democratic development in France.

It is apposite here to mention the concerns and remedies voiced in *The Federalist,* composed by Alexander Hamilton, James Madison, and John Jay at the time of the drafting and ratification of the U.S. Constitution in 1787–88.[22] The authors used the term *republics,* by which they meant political systems that derived their legitimacy from the electoral process. A central argument against republics in the Federalist papers was that they have short lives, because they exhaust themselves in bouts of internal violence. This happens because the "principle of liberty" that they must endorse allows the open expression of hostility, and once such expressions are permitted, it becomes virtually impossible to check or defuse them.

Madison seems to have taken it as axiomatic that contentious motivations propelled human beings. In Number 10 of *The Federalist,* he asserted:

> The latent causes of factions are. . . sown in the nature of man. . . . A zeal for different opinions concerning religion, concerning government, and many other points, as well of speculation as of practice; an attachment to different leaders ambitiously contending for pre-eminence and power; or to persons of other description whose fortunes have been interesting to the human passions, have, in turn, divided mankind into parties, inflamed them with mutual animosity, and rendered them much more disposed to vex and oppress each other than to cooperate for the common good. So strong is this propensity of mankind to fall into mutual animosities. . . . the most common and durable source of factions has been the various and unequal distribution of property.[23]

My concern here is not to take a position on the essential contentiousness or goodness of human beings, but to take note that, concerned with "that intolerant spirit which has, at all times, characterized political parties," the framers of the Constitution fashioned "controls on government" that would check the "destructive passions" of democracy. In defending the separation of powers in the new government, Madison cited these words of Thomas Jefferson's: "An *elective despotism* was not the government we fought for; but one which should not only be founded on free principles, but in which the powers of government should be so divided and balanced among several bodies of magistracy, as that no one could transcend their legal limits, without being effectually checked and restrained by the others."[24]

South Asia exemplifies the widespread propensity to collective violence in the conduct of politics in the circumstances of our modern times. Majoritarian domination of minorities leads to elective despotism (the so-called "tyranny of majority rule"). Communal or ethnic collectivities, based on race, territory, religion, or language—or a combination of these— and committed to the cry of collective entitlements, result in exclusivist claims and in separatist remedies, thereby making negotiated settlements difficult. And overly centralized governments that are insensitive to the concerns of pluralities, balk at devolution of powers, and resist the idea of pluralism as the necessary coexistence and tolerance of diversity are in danger of being controlled by political and bureaucratic "elites" and sections of the army, or of being hijacked by a fundamentalist majority.

If competitive democratic politics, ethnic conflicts, and collective violence are linked in the postcolonial, postindependence politics of South Asia, it may be asked, are there defensible alternatives to democratic forms of government? Having become committed to democracy, it would now be ideologically impossible for these countries to entertain and justify any form of unelected authoritarianism, although in practice distortions toward it have occurred and will continue to occur.

If collective violence is an actual as well as potential destabilizing force in South Asia, we may be led to ask whether certain kinds of collective identity issues can be or may have to be regulated or taken out of the political arena. Ethnonationalist politics in its various forms continually escalates into disputes over community boundaries, exclusions and inclusions of persons, and separate but not equal group claims. These issues eventually deteriorate into riots, civil wars, pogroms of "ethnic cleansing," and secessions. (Some theorists would hold that social class politics are so different from ethnic contests because they are usually concerned with the distribution of power and resources within a society, without raising the question of community or collectivity boundaries and the explosive threat of secession.)

With regard to the issue of the top-heavy character of postcolonial governments and their failure to achieve political integration with and at all levels of society, James Manor has made observations about Sri Lanka that may have wider applicability. Among other things, Manor connects the regular swings and alternations of power between two parties and their coalition allies to weak political integration between the elite and the masses, the lack of intermediary organizations linking them, and the inability to settle ethnic conflict because politicians resist devolution of power to "local government" and regional constituencies. Elections, Manor points out, produce ecstatic hopes, soaring, unrealistic expectations, and postelection disappointments. The intoxication with politics and the air of unreality and unspecificity that swirls around it lead to heady elections and social turbulence.[25]

There are other matters diagnostic of an insufficiently grounded unitary nation-state. The crisis of the nation-state in South Asia (and many other places) is dialectically linked with the surge of ethnonationalism. In India, Pakistan, Sri Lanka, and Bangladesh, the attempt to realize the nation-state on a Western European model has virtually failed. The nation-state conception has not taken deep roots in South Asia or generated a widespread and robust participatory "public culture" that celebrates it in widely meaningful ceremonies, festivals, and rituals. The "independence day" parades and speeches, the opening of Parliament, the weak affirmations of the secular state in the face of sectarian claims to special treatment, and other markers of nation-state existence pale in public support and relevance when compared to the scale and intensity of calendrical religious and ethnic festivals. The rituals and affirmations surrounding the monarchy as embodying national unity in Britain and the celebrations of "civil religion" focused on nation-making events in the United States have no real parallels in the new nation-states of South Asia. The truly engaging foci of a public culture are to be found in the arenas and festivities linked to features of communal life, associated with literature, recitations, texts, sagas, mythologies, and popular theater, which celebrate and enact religiopolitical and social memories and concerns of collectivities in place for a long time. This is why, for instance, the divisive themes but effective presentations of Hindu nationalism, Sikh nationalism, Sinhala Buddhist nationalism, and Dravidian nationalism so greatly constitute and dominate mass politics and participation in elections.

10   Entering a Dark Continent
The Political Psychology of Crowds

So far we have investigated these sociological features of rioting crowds: the identity of the faces in the crowd (their social position, occupational status, sex); the extent to which the riots were organized (in the sense that there were leaders and agents provocateurs who mobilized crowds, fed them with information regarding the designated targets, armed them, provided vehicles); the sites and locations where the riots took place and the nature of the arson, looting, and killing; and, finally, the overall trajectories, phases, and duration of riots.

From the examination of these particularities, we then moved on to the interpretive tasks of locating certain patterns and processes. The concepts of *focalization* and *transvaluation* were introduced to describe the trajectory of riots, especially the way in which riots as particular incidents and local conflicts build up into a massive avalanche labeled "ethnic riots." The complementary concepts of *nationalization* and *parochialization* were coined to describe the processes in the opposite direction when nationally mounted issues at focal centers have their dispersed and fragmented manifestation in local places in terms of local cleavages. Patterns of *routinization* and *ritualization* of collective violence were established, and the stereotyped strategies and acts that syntactically and recursively constitute collective events such as riots, elections, festivals, and so on were identified. All this should be borne in mind as contributing to our understanding of crowd formation and crowd behavior as we move on to still another analytical and interpretive level, which concerns the processes by which individual participants merging into crowd formations experience and manifest certain heightened psychic states and convulsive behavioral impulsions. This exercise ideally calls for the matching and intertwining of communicational and interactional processes with psychic and experiential processes at both the personal and interpersonal levels when crowds form and move as collectivities. Unfortunately, the issue of dialectically linking these processes and their feedback at the individual and interpersonal levels has so far produced little systematic theorizing.

In fact, the territory of "crowd psychology," a label modern psychologists have eschewed in favor of "political psychology," despite well-known writing on the subject by Gustave Le Bon, Gabriel de Tarde, Sigmund Freud, Elias Canetti, George Rudé, and others, remains one of the least mapped in the social sciences. Some writers are attracted by the idea of archetypal fixations and expressions embedded in the collective unconscious that become manifest in crowds. Others are sympathetic to arguments in favor of processes of suggestibility, imitation, homogenization, weakened intellectual reasoning, and heightened emotional states that occur when people become massed as crowds. Still others have linked crowds to their central fixation on, and identification with, charismatic leadership, and seek in turn to link this propensity to relationships and experiences in the family between parents and children. And a few neanderthal theorists have even indulged in fanciful imaginings about the primordial human horde and its herd "instincts" and propensities, its bonding as a group, and its territorial and/or mating imperatives.

Given these interpretive possibilities, which in our present state of knowledge we obviously cannot accept as systematic truths, I have decided to present my thoughts and evidence in this chapter in the form of a "postmodern" discourse: episodic, even disconnected sometimes, suggestive, multivalent, and polyphonic.

It is generally regarded that, although he had predecessors in Thomas Carlyle, Hippolyte Taine, Jules Michelet, Gabriel de Tarde, and others, all retrospectively making judgments about the role of the crowds in the French Revolution, it was Gustave Le Bon's *Psychologie des foules,* published in 1895 and translated soon afterward as *The Crowd: A Study of the Popular Mind,* that initiated "crowd psychology" and the "crowd mind" as a subject of explicit formal study and intellectual theorizing. Le Bon's text, which I shall treat in detail later, had its special emphases and limitations. *Le Bon's* His "crowd," covering many phenomena, was discussed in the abstract as a *crowd* single entity. An admirer neither of the French Revolution nor of the trends toward popular democracy in the nineteenth century, the conservative Le Bon reduced the crowd to its lowest common denominator of intellectual weakening and irrational impulses, destructiveness, and imitative suggestibility. He finally attached the crowd to the phenomenon of the leader, a theme that Freud was to acknowledge and develop as his central theoretical issue in his *Massenpsychologie und Ich-Analyse,* translated as *Group Psychology and the Analysis of the Ego* (1926). Freud's discussions may be pertinent for the study of charismatic leaders spearheading revolutionary movements, such as Moses, Napoleon, Lenin, Hitler, Mussolini, Gandhi, and Khomeini.[1] Le Bon's and Freud's theses have been extended and magnified by Serge Moscovici, who apocalyptically identifies the twentieth century as the epoch of mass psychology. This dramatic claim stems from Moscovici's retrospective viewing of the mass characteristics of the Nazi and Fascist movements, whose leaders generated the euphoria that carried their publics enthusiastically into the imperial objectives of World War II, and imposed their genocidal policies on designated enemies, especially the Jews.[2]

But the ethnic riots and communal violence I am discussing are not sustained, large-scale movements led by charismatic leaders, whose dialectical relation to the crowd is seen by certain theorists as the central issue for explication. They are volatile formations that periodically erupt and are organized, if at all, by transitory and subnational leaders and by lower echelons of collaborators commanding parochial networks and acting according to political circumstance and context. They are not led by the Nehrus, the Bhuttos, or the Bandaranaikes, and their structure and dynamics are better approached in ways I have illustrated earlier.

LE BON'S HETEROGENEOUS CROWDS

Le Bon, who is of central relevance for us, even as a foil, and as an aid to clarification, phrased the problem of the "mental unity" of crowds in terms that are in some respects still valid for us today as setting one interpretive task:

> From the psychological point of view the expression "crowd" assumes . . . [this] signification. Under certain circumstances, and only under those circumstances, an agglomeration of men presents new characteristics very different from those of the individuals composing it. The sentiments and ideas of all persons in the gathering take one and the same direction, and their conscious personality vanishes. A collective mind is formed, doubtless transitory, but presenting very clearly defined characteristics.[3]

Le Bon classified crowds into two types, heterogeneous and homogeneous. Heterogeneous crowds are composed of "dissimilar" elements—that is, of individuals "of any description, of any profession, and any degree of intelligence."[4] They are "anonymous" crowds, best exemplified by street crowds. It is these heterogeneous, anonymous, and temporary crowds that form the primary subject matter of Le Bon's *Psychologie des foules.* Le Bon defined homogeneous crowds, which he excluded from his study, as formed of "elements more or less akin," exemplified by groups such as sects (political, religious sects), castes (military, priestly, or occupational), and classes (middle classes, peasant classes). Insofar as Le Bon applied this label to groups acting as special-interest associations and pursuing their objectives over a period of time, we can see the point of his dichotomy.

Thus the issue for elucidation posed by heterogeneous crowds is as follows: "Whoever be the individuals that compose it, however like or unlike be their mode of life, their occupations, their character, their intelligence, the fact that they have been transformed into a crowd puts them in possession of a sort of collective mind which makes them feel, think, and act in a manner quite different from that in which each individual of them would feel, think, and act were he in a state of isolation."[5] Although I myself would today avoid some of the words in this passage, Le Bon's problematic is not irrelevant, indeed, it must be faced, especially since the crowds he was concerned with are not unlike the civilian crowds I have described as taking part in the ethnonationalist conflicts of South Asia: crowds composed of cross sections of urban populations, especially of the middle and lower orders, and that as short-lived collectivities engage in volatile and violent actions that they would ordinarily avoid as individuals.

But with respect to South Asian riot mobs, there is a serious shortcoming to the way in which Le Bon set up his problem. In the organization and direction of the ethnic riots and communal violence I am dealing with, one quite frequently sees the hands of professional politicians and their parties or factions, of business or trading groups distinguished by caste or language, of agents provocateurs and their gangs, while the crowds so mobilized or called into action by them may well become the heterogeneous, anonymous, and temporary formations that Le Bon focused on.

This qualification is not unimportant. For where I shall deviate from, and, I hope, improve upon, Le Bon (and Canetti) is by insisting on the circumstances in which the politicization of ethnicity and communalism has occurred in contemporary plural societies, and on the claims to group entitlements that in current mass politics provide the initial basis for collective identity, mobilization, and action. There is, therefore, a certain politico-economic purposiveness and directedness in the actions of crowds to some degree backed and orchestrated by interest groups. What I label "leveling" tendencies are pegged to the larger historical contexts and considerations of political economy, and the distribution of power within the society in question, which must be aligned with and dialectically related to other manifestations of "leveling," the homogenization, suggestibility, and euphoria that Le Bon isolates as the key issues of crowd psychology. More-over, the two interwoven strands of leveling must also be keyed to inter-personal communicational processes, including especially the role of ru-mors, which operate throughout the period of violence. The role of the media in transmitting information and misinformation, and in the height-ening of aggressive sentiments, cannot be emphasized enough.

The comments of witnesses to the Delhi riots of 1984 clearly pose in graphic language the multiple, even paradoxical, facets of mob violence that Le Bon's simplified notion of "heterogeneous" crowds misses:

> See the mob is a mob. *Woh kuch nahin sunta.* [They don't listen to anything.] The mob is blind. It listens to no one. But all this could happen only if the mob had some backing or the promise of some reward. There was absolutely no sign of fear in the mob's actions. When we asked them, "Aren't you afraid of the army, aren't you afraid of the police?" they said they had nothing to fear.[6]

This comment by a middle-class housewife who witnessed the brutalities inflicted by crowds on the Sikhs in a train at the Tughlakabad railway sta-tion, on the line from Bombay to Delhi, contains many themes and many interpretive possibilities. The mob's intensified "blind" passions explain its conduct—but the mob is at the same time possibly backed by organized in-terests, both political and economic, and it has a stake in the rewards of looting and leveling, which imply that the mob's actions are to some de-gree purposive, directed, and legitimated in advance. Moreover, the mob is not afraid of the army or the police, either because it feels omnipotent as a mob, because it knows that the security forces are in sympathy with it and will not interfere (at least in the early phase of the riots), or because both these attitudes are co-present.

I find Elias Canetti a more congenial interpreter of crowds than Le Bon. In *Crowds and Power* (1978), Canetti speaks, not of the crowd in the ab-stract, but of different types of crowds, which are capable of enabling as well as destructive actions, and the bases and impulses of which can be dealt with apart from the apical leader as a necessary component. Canetti is not hobbled by a revolutionary and reactionary obsession about a crowd's perennial regression to irrational violence, and, although he himself does not situate his typologies in thick descriptions of politico-economic con-texts, he is open to the possibility that both archetypal and circumstantial features may be deciphered from their actions.[7]

Before engaging with Canetti's vivid sketches, let me provide an exam-ple of my own that resonates with his soundings.

A RIOTING MOB: AN ILLUSTRATION

These incidents occurred in a bout of rioting in Colombo on July 28, 1987. The proximate reason was the Indo–Sri Lankan Accord, which made it possible for an Indian Peace Keeping Force (IPKF) to occupy the Northern and Eastern provinces of Sri Lanka with the objective of implementing the accord. The rioting in Colombo was done by the Sinhalese majority, who opposed the Jayewardene government's alleged giving of too many concessions to the Tamils and allowing an Indian intervention and occupation. The riot lasted only one day, but enough damage was done: nineteen civilians were killed and more than a hundred were reported wounded when police fired into the crowds. The mobs set fire to eighty buses, scores of cars, and a number of buildings, including shops, hospitals, and the Ministry of Women's Affairs.[8]

The organizers had called upon the protesters to assemble at a junction in the Pettah shopping district in the center of Colombo, in close proximity to the central bus station and the Fort Railway Station, which facilitated travel to the site. Those who assembled at this well-chosen strategic spot were said to represent "The Movement for the Defense of the Motherland," a coalition of some twenty parties and associations, united in their opposition to the treaty. The ruling United National Party sent not only police to keep order but also its henchmen belonging to a government union called Jatika Sevaka Sangamaya to show muscle and to disrupt the gathering.

The SLFP was prominently represented by Mrs. Bandaranaike, her son Anura Bandaranaike, several members of Parliament, and party organizers. (Prins Gooneskera, a civil rights lawyer who had defended many people accused by the government of subversive activities, and Gamini Iriyagolle, a vocal nationalist, both anti-UNP, were also sighted.) The next most conspicuous presence was that of hundreds of Buddhist monks, the most prominent of whom were Reverend Muruttetwe Ananda, who held the unusual position of head of the Nurses Union (which had conducted a strike against the government), and Reverend Maduluwave Sobhita, who was known to be a left-wing sympathizer.[9] There were many young men and women present, and it was alleged that many members of the JVP were also there. The mood was generally antagonistic to President Jayewardene, who was seen as having betrayed the country.

The protest meeting was at first orderly. Reverend Sobhita said that there were only twenty-four hours left to stop the proposed Indo–Sri

Lankan Peace Accord from being signed. With emotions mounting, it seems that the police acted first by firing tear gas into the crowd—perhaps for "preventive" purposes, perhaps, at the same time, as a provocative serving of notice.

From Gas Station junction and the Fort Railway Station end, the packed crowd split and streamed out in different directions—toward the bus stand in Pettah; down Gas Works Street into Pettah; toward the Fort (where the president's house and the main department stores, banks, and posh shops were located); toward Maradana, Borella, Panchikawatte, and so on. The main thoroughfare of Colombo, Galle Road, was avoided.

The crowd in the vicinity of the Pettah bus stand burned some buses. The police appeared in vehicles and forced many monks into them. Seeing a massive crowd forming in the Fort with a view to besieging the president's house, the police fired tear gas again. And when a police van was immobilized, the police fired into the crowd and killed some sixteen to seventeen persons. An attempt by the crowd to block the road to Kotte where Parliament was to meet that day was foiled.

The physical damage done by the crowd on this occasion is instructive. Only a few shops were burned or looted. The fury was directed against government property—buses, buildings (including the Ministry of Women's Affairs, which was on the route taken by a crowd stream), and a couple of railway stations.

The protesters, many of whom were lay and monk students, who lived in the satellite suburbs ringing Colombo, such as Kelaniya, Nugegoda, and Moratuwa, where the new universities and cheap housing are located, planned to stage many processions into central Colombo the next day. But the government decided to block all the main arteries leading into the city—roadblocks were constructed at the Kelaniya Bridge and at main junctions in Ratmalana, Dehiwela, Nugegoda, and so on. This time, the crowds, blocked from entering the city's central parts, turned into destructive mobs, which went on a rampage, burning buildings mainly in suburbs such as Nugegoda and Ratmalana and farther afield in the satellite towns of Avissawella, Panadura, and beyond.

> The rioting and the Government's harsh response, a day before Mr. Gandhi is to fly in to sign the accord, increased doubts here about the chances for a peaceful resolution of the violent divisions in this nation of 16.6 million.
>
> Not far from the reviewing stand [being erected for the visiting prime minister], police retreated as windows were systematically smashed in the downtown shopping district, which also contains Government offices and international hotels.

In the back alleys of the central market area, rival mobs of young men armed with wooden staves, metal bars, and fluorescent light bulbs battled each other.

They broke down shuttered storefronts and made bonfires of their contents.

They tossed red and yellow grains into the air, smeared their faces with flour and hammered canned goods against the ground in a frenzy of destruction.

Store owners hid in back rooms or on rooftops as the sounds of breaking glass and shouting approached them. They spoke in whispers, as if afraid to be heard on the street outside.

Near the central railway station, amid black smoke from a burning police truck and several buses, the protesters taunted the police, hurling stones and bits of brick as well as rotting bones and hard fruits called wood apples from the marketplace.

Helmeted police officers, crouching behind wicker shields, dropped to their knees and fired at the protesters past the burning vehicles. With each volley, flocks of birds rose from the tin roofs of the market stalls.

Bodies lay in the hot sun as the melee swirled around them. A young woman in a blue dress, her head covered in blood, writhed slowly in the ground beside an overturned lottery booth.

The rioting began in the early morning when thousands of political supporters of a former Prime Minister, Sirima Bandaranaike, carrying small black plastic flags, joined 150 monks in orange robes who sat in the shade of a sacred Bo Tree near the market place.

The men with black flags stopped passing buses and forced their passengers to join them.

Speaking into a hand-held microphone, the monks urged the crowd to protect the nation from division and warned of an eventual takeover by India.

As the monks spoke, the police suddenly opened fire with small canisters of tear gas, and the day's running battle began.

Some members of the crowd held back angry monks as they tried to charge police.

As the police repeated volleys of tear gas, the crowd moved into the alleyways where Tamil, Sinhalese, and Moslem shop owners were already pulling shut their iron gratings.

As the crowds grew, racing from one part of the old city area to another, pockets of outnumbered police officers pulled back with promises not to fire tear gas if the protesters left them alone.

One chief inspector at the scene said the police were also having difficulty commanding their own mostly Sinhalese men.

"You cannot ask them to take strong action, you know," said the chief inspector, who asked that his name not be used. "When it is Sinhalese doing it, the police sort of soft-pedal."

The chief inspector, a Tamil, said: "I can't push my orders too hard. I have got to be careful."[10]

This description of crowd behavior in Colombo could be replicated from many other parts of our globe, especially at the present time, when explosive behavior on the part of crowds is being reported almost daily. Two examples will suffice. In December 1989, for example, in the context of civilian protest actions against the Noriega dictatorship, "Looters . . . swarmed through Panama City's downtown business district, leaving an ankle-deep carpet of glass shards that made many sidewalks all but impassable. In some areas, hardly a windowpane was intact. . . . Some store owners took up rifles and stood guard in front of their shops."[11] On the same day, in Bucharest, Romania, "Residents hurled portraits of [former president Nicolae Ceauşescu] onto bonfires that blazed around town. They fed the flames with signs ripped down from buildings that praised him and bore his statements on building communism."[12]

CANETTI'S SKETCHES

Elias Canetti's *Crowds and Power* is a storehouse of observations on the behavior of crowds, some of which illuminate the behavior of mobs involved in ethnic riots. Canetti lists four general attributes of the crowd: (1) it always wants to grow; (2) within it, there is equality; (3) it loves density; (4) it needs a direction—it is in movement and it moves toward a goal.

Ordinarily, human beings fear the touch of the unknown and avoid physical contact with anything strange, Canetti observes. "It is only in a crowd that man can become free of this fear of being touched. . . . The feeling of relief is most striking when the density of the crowd is greatest."[13] "Only together can men free themselves from their burdens of distance; and this, precisely is what happens in a crowd. . . . It is for the sake of this blessed moment when no one is greater or better than another, that people become a crowd."[14]

Bill Buford amplifies this point by Canetti. He gives a powerful sense of the "unusual intimacy" felt in a densely packed football crowd:

> Something, I felt, was being communicated there; just about every member of that crowd of nine thousand [watching a game between Cambridge United and Millwall] was pressed closely against someone else and was held, as we were held, tightly together, waiting for a goal . . . there is no sport in which the act of being a spectator is as *constantly* physical as watching a game of English football on the terraces. The physicalness is insistent; any observer not familiar with the game would say it is outright brutal. . . . The English football game expects the spectator to become *one* with the crowd.[15]

It seems that a physically dense crowd also produces a psychic density. Individuals surrender themselves to the crowd, they all become equal, and distinctions, even of sex, do not count. And this is why, says Canetti, a "crowd seeks to close in on itself." A rioting mob is an "open crowd":

"there are no limits whatever to its growth; it does not recognize houses, doors, or locks and those who shut themselves in are suspect." However, an open crowd's spontaneous growth is at the same time its danger, "for just as suddenly it originates, the crowd disintegrates."[16]

The destructiveness of riot crowds is their most conspicuous feature. "Of all the means of destruction the most impressive is *fire*. It can be seen from far off and it attracts even more people. It destroys irrevocably; nothing after a fire is as it was before. . . . After the destruction, crowd and fire die away."[17]

"The crowd particularly likes destroying houses and objects; breakable objects like window panes, mirrors, pictures, and crockery . . . the noise of destruction adds to its satisfaction; the banging of windows and the crashing of glass are the robust sounds of fresh life, the cries of something new born. . . . But it would be wrong to suppose that the ease with which things can be broken is the decisive factor. . . . Sculptures of solid stone have been mutilated beyond recognition"[18] or have been hauled down.

"The destruction of representational images is the destruction of a hierarchy which is no longer recognized. It is the violation of generally established and universally visible and valid distances. . . . The more usual kind of destruction . . . is simply an attack on all boundaries."[19] The destruction of windows and doors of houses is also the destruction of the individuality and separateness of houses and inmates.

AN UNDERLYING AXIS: DOUBLE EXCHANGE
BETWEEN ASSAILANTS AND VICTIMS

There is, I suggest, a double exchange between assailants and victims that functions as the underlying axis of their relationship. These exchanges are dialectically related and derive from the tensions between the "similarities" (shared features) and the "differences" that relate the two parties.

First, when a minority, or another community, is under attack by a crowd in the name of equalization of entitlements, *then the wanton destruction of the lives and property of the "enemy" is inseparably accompanied by the personal appropriation and incorporation of that enemy's status, genius, and wealth.* This orientation is what has already been labeled "leveling"—that is, eliminating the alleged advantages enjoyed by the opponent and redressing the inequality allegedly suffered by the aggressor, usually a majority.

The looting of the victim's possessions, the raping of his womenfolk, are simultaneously forceful acts of incorporating the enemy, while destroying him. Thus these actions, which seem to be at the negative pole of reciprocity between self and other, also imply an extreme cannibalistic form of the fusion of self and other, and the obliteration of that dyad. The obliteration of the body of the victim by fire, cremation, simultaneously removes all evidence of the killed and the killer. A double anonymity is sought.

The second exchange takes as its point of departure the fact that assailants and victims are frequently not strangers to one another. They have been "neighbors" in the loose sense of having lived in the same towns, or resided intermixed or side by side in contiguous districts and in neighboring towns, for long periods of time, and have had transactions of various kinds."The degeneration of a difference in convictions into hatred and fight occurs only when there were essential similarities between the parties," Georg Simmel notes. "The 'respect for the enemy' is usually absent where the hostility has arisen on the basis of previous solidarity. And where enough similarities continue to make confusions and blurred outlines possible, points of difference need an emphasis not justified by the issue but only by that danger of confusion."[20]

As Simmel has perceptively said, it is because of the sudden imposition of difference on the basis of previous solidarity and coexistence, and because of the "blurred" nature of the social landscape, that a perhaps overdetermined hatred and repudiation are unleashed in denial of "confusions" or lack of firm partitions between the antagonists. One might extend Simmel by saying that *the greater the blurrings of and ambiguities between the socially constructed categories of difference, the greater the venom of the imposed boundaries, when conflict erupts, between the self and the other, "us" and "them."* No international military code of humane treatment of "prisoners of war" deriving from "respect for the enemy" regulates the conduct of Serb and Bosnian Muslim, Armenian and Azerbaijani, Hindu and Muslim in Kashmir, Sinhalese soldier and Tamil insurgent in Sri Lanka.

Can we push this process of creating and repudiating the intolerable "other" in current ethnonationalist conflict any further? Can we say that it is because that component of "sameness" that the ethnic enemy shares with you, and because your enemy is already a part of you, that you must forcibly expel him or her from yourself, objectify him or her as the total other? Accordingly, that component of "difference" from you, whether it be allegedly "religious," "linguistic," or "racial," is so exaggerated and magnified that this stereotyped "other" must be degraded, dehumanized, and compulsively obliterated?

There is a third consideration which we should take into account as possibly central to the dynamics of ethnonationalist conflicts. The drive for the desired and imagined unity and homogeneity of an ethnic collective as "one nation" is frequently difficult to consummate and doomed to be contentious and fractious because of multiple internal contests and differences and cross-cutting interests. And this situation may also engender a process that René Girard has elaborated on in *Violence and the Sacred:* the internal divisiveness and conflicts within a group or collectivity may drive its members to seek out a scapegoat and "sacrificially" kill it to gain its own uncertain unity, making of this cleansing a sacred act of generative unanimity and duty.[21] This links up with the suggestion, made earlier, that the targeted and victimized enemy next door usually shares much content and texture with the aggressor, and that the expulsion or annihilation of that enemy may therefore be a substitute for expelling or annihilating the enemy one harbors within oneself, which may account for the overdetermined brutality against and guiltless obliteration of the "other."

INTERPRETIVE FORAYS

Canetti's allusive and intuitive reflections on the crowd's destructive and leveling tendencies are more soberly but perhaps even more powerfully recorded by Rudé, who appropriately cites Carlyle's aphorism: "A short argument, fire." The major devices of the preindustrial crowds of England and France for 150 years or more, the expression of their leveling instinct, "were direct action and the imposition of some form of elementary 'natural' justice." "Strikers tended to destroy machinery or 'pull down' their employers' houses; food rioters to invade markets and bakers' shops and enforce a popular price control or *taxation populaire;* rural rioters to destroy fences and turnpikes or threshing machines and work houses, or to set fire to the farmers' or landlords' stacks; and city rioters to 'pull down' dissenters' meeting houses and chapels, to destroy their victims' houses and property, and to burn their political enemies in effigy."[22] "In England, arson, particularly the burning of the farmers' stacks of hay and corn, was a well established weapon in agrarian disputes."[23]

Canetti's literary brushstrokes and Rudé's realism stir the memory of those of us who have seen riots, the smell of smoke and the sight of flames rising from rubber tires, serving as the necklaces of death, the burning cars and houses, the hauling down of statues of stately Queen Victoria, of proud British governors, of feared dictators like Stalin, and of once, and not so long ago, famous postindependence national leaders, the brazen crossing of boundaries by crowds, their invasion of the hitherto forbidden inner spaces of homes, and of the boardrooms and sanctums of government ministers and unapproachable bureaucrats, guarded by recalcitrant secretaries and officious "peons."

On the basis of many accounts of, and visual information on, ethnic riots, it seems that crowds in action, even when they have been organized and led, become in their density and anonymity aggregates of deindividualized equals, who engage in destructive attacks on property and possessions and unleash impulses aimed at leveling the society and its hierarchy, or to obliterate differences among its groups. This may include the desecration of sacred pantheons of gods, saints, and heroes who represent that hierarchy and differences of status. In these ways, a riot mob may be said to be temporarily crossing boundaries, dissolving category distinctions and classifications, and acting as the creator and embodiment of liminal time.

The rioting crowd is a "hunting pack" and a "baiting crowd"; it is out for killing and it knows whom it wants to kill and to expropriate. It strategically corners its enemy, and its feeling of omnipotence is a function of its immense superiority in numbers and weapons, and its knowledge that the victim can do nothing to retaliate. Also because the rioting is preceded by and can draw on the legitimation of populist politicians and populist tracts, the mob feels that the designated victim, if not actually sacralized for sacrifice in the Maussian sense, has nevertheless been made over to it for destruction, and that *it therefore need not fear the sanction attached to killing.* "A murder shared with many others, which is not only safe and permitted, but indeed recommended, is irresistible to the great majority of men," Canetti observes.[24] And a victorious crowd can hold together only as long as it scores successes in quick succession.

But a baiting and hunting crowd, so omnipotent and immunized against the guilt of killing, can also itself turn into a "flight crowd" the moment it feels that the enemy who survives, previously a helpless victim, but now feared as a threat, is on the warpath. Such is the black comedy and farce that surrounds crowds as fragile formations. During the Sri Lanka riots in 1983, after a few days when the Sinhalese mobs in Colombo had with some thoroughness destroyed Tamil houses and shops (but not actually taken many human lives), a rumor spread like wildfire that armed Tamil "tigers" had landed and were marching on the capital. The result was a headlong, undignified, panic-stricken stampede by masses of Sinhalese along Galle Road fleeing south—and when the fleers realized that the rumor was false the next day, they turned on the Tamils with added fury and committed brutalities from which they had previously refrained.

Such reversals and tendencies of mood in rioting crowds give us a glimpse of another insight: the baiting and hunting mob, in attempting to eliminate its enemy, is thereby also trying to exorcise the possibility of its own death. And the more it kills the enemy, the more it feels menaced by the enemy's imagined secret strength. And it is because fear sits side by side with the rage of destruction that a mob can by a sudden twist of events feel menaced by the enemy's revenge and its own death. At this point, it disintegrates and takes to flight. When in certain contexts of ethnic conflict, ethnic communities living side by side in their respective concentrations clash, chameleonlike reversals of hunters into fleers, and vice versa, are part of the sport of violence. And as long as this mood lasts, there is no dampening of passions, only periodic bloodletting, and a spiral of escalating violence. Eugène Ionesco describes this mutual entanglement and death embrace in war in terms that are perhaps equally applicable to ethnic violence:

> I must kill my visible enemy, the one who is determined to take my life, to prevent him from killing me. Killing gives me a feeling of relief, because I am dimly aware that in killing him, I have killed death. My enemy's death cannot be held against me, it is no longer a source of anguish, if I killed him with the approval of society: that is the purpose of war. Killing is a way of relieving one's feeling, of warding off one's death.[25]

To sum up, certain kinds of rioting crowds in pursuit of collective entitlements are essentially "levelers," destroying property and life in a public cause that absolves them of individual crime and guilt. The leveling down of an ethnic group as an overprivileged enemy, an acquisitive other, an obstacle to one's own group's prosperity, is an orgiastic, short-lived action. If the ethnic group that is victimized still has in its possession the specialized knowledge, the material and symbolic capital, the networks that provide access to resources, it can usually pretty quickly recoup and regain its former position, thus inviting another act of leveling and conspicuous, methodical destruction of its property, a reverse potlatching. It is when such periodic leveling is accompanied by systematic political acts of discrimination and denial that succeed in robbing the victimized group of its special skills, resources, and channels of attainment that ethnic conflict moves from periodic bloodlettings, destruction of property, and displacement of people from their homes to a different level of attempted permanent *subordination* of a minority by a majority, and the countermove of secession on the part of the minority.

JUBILANT DESTRUCTION

Canetti, Rudé, and others have missed out one conspicuous feature frequently noticed about riot crowds bent on arson, looting, and destruction. This is their ebullience and their near festive mood while engaging in destruction. The authors of two reports on the Delhi riots of 1984 wrote of this with some puzzlement. *Who Are the Guilty?* (1984)[26] authored by two eminent Indian political scientists, remarked:

> It is significant that wherever we went, we did not find any sign of mourning or grief on the faces of those who were participating in the looting and burning. Attempts to pacify them by the peace marchers were met with derisive laughter. Listening to their raucous exultation and looking at their gleeful faces, one would have thought it was a festival, but for the arson and looting that was going on.

The authors also report that when the peace procession in which they marched, organized to defuse the riots, pointed out that the innocent Sikhs who were being attacked were not responsible for Mrs. Gandhi's death, and raised the slogan "Hindu-Sikh bhai bhai," disrupters shouted the counter-slogan "Hindu-Hindu bhai bhai," proclaiming the brotherhood of Hindus and rejecting interethnic unity.

The official Misra Commission remarked in passing: "The mob was jubilating and dancing. There was no sign of sorrow and grief on their faces. They were no mourners of the Prime Minister."[27] This report, astounded that the mobs were not grief-stricken but actually jubilant, readily resorted to the comfortable explanation that the riots were perpetrated by "gangsters," "anti-social elements," who were driven by "mob frenzy" and a "lust for stolen articles." It was these elements who "monitored the activities of the mobs and played the principal role in killing, looting, and arson."[28] Little did the commission recognize the truth—which I have established earlier—that the rioters included a cross section of the ordinary citizens of the poorer urban settlement of Delhi and were quite often led by lower-level Congress (I) workers and activists, and by some higher-level politicians as well.

It is my thesis that the jubilant and festive moods of rioting crowds are of a piece with their collective identity, their temporary sense of homogeneity, equality, and physical intimacy, their sense of taking righteous action to level down the enemy's presumed advantage and claim their collective entitlements. The same configuration also explains the crowd's lack of a sense of grief or remorse at its acts of destruction: because what participants have done does not call for individual personal accountability, a sense emboldened by the collusion of the police; it has received a patriotic benediction and has merged in an impersonal anonymity. It also participates in routinized and ritualized sequences of violence that further remove conduct from personal choice. But as we have seen, these jubilant, righteous crowds are also stricken by lurking anxieties and fears, which may become collective panics. The invention and circulation of rumors also portrays the dual features of their energizing and stimulating the crowd as well as revealing the crowd's latent fears, which it projects onto its victims.

Before I discuss rumors, I would like at this point to reiterate two implications of the concept of leveling. One relates to the politically motivated, purposive character of crowd violence devoted to diminishing or erasing the margin of advantage allegedly enjoyed by the rival designated as the enemy. This is leveling conduct motivated by the ideology of group entitlements. The second implication of such leveling is its psychic manifestation: fused in a relationship of leveling identity, the participants seem to suspend their individual wills and everyday restraints as they are swept into a collective passion, which expends its energy in destruction. The two processes of leveling meet and fuse in crowd actions.

THE CIRCULATION OF RUMORS

I would like to suggest certain connections between rioting crowds and their suggestibility to rumors, in a state of intensified passions. Rumors, let us note, although they are frequently planted and disseminated by agents provocateurs, generally appear anonymous in origin, and they cannot be traced to definite culpable sources; they are eminently oral utterances, they circulate at high velocity by word of mouth, nowadays through telephones, the radio, and TV, and are the currency of mass movements—whether they be revolutions, insurrections, or riots.[29] In the case of ethnic riots, they take a vicious form.

All theorists of crowd psychology from Le Bon and Tarde to Freud are agreed that there is a leveling process in the second sense, by which individuals' reasoning powers are weakened or abrogated and reach a lowest common denominator. (The theorists diverge, however, on the precise relations between the individual and the crowd that engenders this state.)

It seems plausible to suggest that leveling crowds engaged in communal violence are simultaneously prone to two psychic tendencies. They are aggressive and aggrandizing in the service of an imagined collective cause, and their courage comes through mutual stimulation; what they will not do individually, they will together. At the same time, they exhibit a marked anxiety and a lurking fear that their fortunes might well be reversed if their victims retaliate. A hunting crowd quickly turns into a crowd in flight.

This double condition that makes aggressor crowds susceptible to rumors explains a curious twist. Frequently, the most inflammatory and gruesome rumors in riots are hatched and circulated by the aggressors about the victims (although at the later postmortem stage the victims in turn convey their own horror stories to the authorities). In riots that last only a few days, the rumors begin to circulate the first day and have done their worst in terms of impact by the second, and it is usually on the second and third days that the worst brutalities to life and limb are committed and justified as "reprisal."

Riots subside after a few days, not only because law and order are restored, after a fashion, and the police and army once again parade the streets, but also because the mob's heightened psychic state cannot last beyond that time. Two processes working at two levels thus bring about the subsidence. Most participants cannot long remain without the restoration or recovery of their sense of separateness and "individuality" and the need to break away from the collective euphoric oppressiveness that elated them and to return to their everyday lives. Once the violence is spent, as in an orgasm, there is a return to quiescence. Then there can be a slow buildup of tensions, quarrels, frustrations, and demands pertaining to the same or similar continuing political conflict, to erupt again in violence at another time.

THE SPIRALING OF RAGE AND PANIC: A WINDOW ONTO "EXCESSES" AND THE BREACHING OF BOUNDARIES

Right through these chapters on ethnic conflict and collective violence, I have tried to probe, among other things, one perplexing and absorbing issue: how do crowds engage in destructive aggression to the point of arson and homicide? Although murder is not unknown in daily life, mass homicide—that is, a number of killings by crowds in the brief period of a riot—is an excessive act that breaks through ordinary norms of restraint. Yet for the most part, this homicide in ethnic conflict is usually seen as legitimate and justified, and it is not accompanied by public remorse on the part of the aggressors. In any case, it is rarely followed by arrest and prosecution in courts of justice.

I have all along tried to provide some clues to this conduct: for example, the powerful stimulus and legitimation provided by a hegemonic mytho-historical ideology (compounded of race, religion, language, and territory) stating a collective entitlement to rule and dominate; the attribution of unfair differential advantages to the ethnic enemy, and purposive attempts at leveling by destruction of property, business, and manpower; from a certain point onwards, the direction of communal violence by "organized" leaders and riot captains and their henchmen; and the championing of ethnonationalist causes by political parties and movements that mobilize recruits and crowds for <u>militant action</u>. I have also suggested that the feeling that the community has endorsed the killing may free individuals from the burden of remorse and guilt.

Le Bon's elucidation of the puzzle as to "why crowds are not killers in their own eyes" is in accord with my preceding statements. "Certain acts of crowds are assuredly criminal, if considered merely in themselves," but the actors do not think so. "The usual motive of the crimes of crowds is a powerful suggestion, and the individuals who take part in such crimes are afterwards convinced that they have acted in obedience to duty, which is far from being the case with the ordinary criminal."[30] The marauding crowd participant acts in "obedience to a suggestion, which is all the stronger because of its collective origin, and the murderer's conviction that he has committed a very meritorious act, a conviction all the more natural seeing that he enjoys the unanimous approval of his fellow citizens.[31]

Now I want to push a little further into the mentality of killing crowds by advancing a more complex formulation than I have attempted so far. It takes as its point of departure the observation made a few pages earlier that a "hunting pack"—that is, a crowd bent on pursuing and killing its victims—can also quickly turn into a panic-stricken "flight crowd." (Incidentally, this phenomenon of mass flight is well illustrated in James Thurber's story "The Day the Dam Broke.")

Some well-known and oft-repeated incidents in Colombo in July 1983 nicely illustrate the co-presence and oscillations of anger and panic. On the fifth day after the riots began, a Thursday morning, a mob assembled at the Fort Railway Station (Colombo's largest station, located at its commercial core), met the train arriving from Kandy, beat a number of Tamil passengers, and burnt them to death. On the following day, Friday, July 29, in Gasworks Street in Pettah, shots were fired by soldiers (the exact circumstances are not known). This incident was converted into a panic story of an attack being launched by invading Tamil Tigers. Ambassador Dissanayaka reports that

> frightened city workers . . . who owned cars drove at breakneck speed on both sides of the road as well as on the pavements. Others clambered on any type of vehicles [*sic*], cars, buses, lorries, vans and trishaws. While office workers behaved in this pitiable manner the slums of Colombo erupted again. Slum dwellers came out armed with axes, crow bars, iron rods and kitchen knives. . . . That day there were six tigers in Colombo. They were all in Dehiwela zoo.[32]

There was a massive stampede of civilians, even policemen and soldiers, fleeing from the enemy, in a tidal wave down Galle Road, the main seafront artery to the south. When the same crowds in flight realized their mistake, they unleashed the worst brutalities thus far inflicted on the Tamils: cars were burned with passengers inside them, and any Tamil trapped by the crowd was branded a Tamil Tiger and lynched. Jonathan Spencer reports that after some stranded students got back to their provincial home in Sabaragamuva Province that weekend, carrying news of the alleged Tiger attack on Colombo, the dangerous presence of terrorists in that city had become an established fact for the residents in their remote village.[33]

The suggestion I am making is that two seemingly antithetical states of mind and sets of experienced emotions may be co-present in the aggressor community and interact with each other with regard to its perception of an ethnic "enemy." These are, simultaneously, rage and anger at the enemy's alleged attack on the integrity, values, or well-being of the community in question, on the one hand, and successively, or in oscillation, fear and mounting panic that the ethnic enemy is violent, dangerous by nature, and has the capacities and resources to launch an attack and do great harm, on the other. The rage and anger push the community to prepare to attack at the slightest "provocation." The panic and fear push it toward collective hysteria and may lead to a wild swing toward retreat and flight.

The two states of collective perception and emotion dialectically act on each other and produce a mounting tension and a heightened mood, which when it explodes may lead to terrible brutalities and acts of destruction, which may be labeled "excesses." In this spiral of rage and panic, rumors that attribute gross brutalities to the "enemy" play a vital energizing and instigating role. Thus we begin to see how the "demonization" of the enemy is produced. It entails the attribution to the "enemy" and victim of violent and inhuman intentions, as well as superhuman propensities. An increasing alienation and polarization between the self as a "son of the soil" and the other as alien develops, and much that was previously shared now gives way to a suspicion-ridden separation and dehumanization of the other, so that to treat him as nonhuman and deserving of degradation and destruction becomes imperative and justifiable. So the aggressor community in attacking its enemy finally comes to perceive its actions as defensive and protective. Even a majority community may feel beleaguered and imperiled in this way. The enemy, already converted to the status of "traitors" and "terrorists," must be punished, displaced, and destroyed.

Rioting crowds are heterogeneous in composition, short-lived, and unstable. On the one hand, the sheer massing of persons in a crowd gives them a feeling of great power, even of omnipotence. But at the same time, since the crowd's members have tenuous links, united by heightened affect

Crowds & conflict 2 reflect

but no long-lasting interactional bonds, they are liable, under certain circumstances, to disintegrate and lose their sense of mutuality. The reverse of their sense of power is their sense of vulnerability. The rumors that circulate from member to member like wildfire both energize them with anger and at the same time cause panic. One of the central features uncovered in this discussion is that neither the rumors nor the anger and panic that they create bear much realistic or "objective" relation to the danger that allegedly threatens the crowd. Panic frequently leads to the disintegration of the crowd and the evaporation of the emotional ties that hold it together temporarily. "The mutual ties have ceased to exist and a gigantic senseless fear is set free,"[34] which disperses the crowd in disarray. But the crowds reform again, spurred on by street leaders and riot captains and their use of rhetoric, rumor, and techniques of mobilization. They go on the attack again, feeling euphoric and omnipotent, but retreat is not far behind.

I would like to illustrate this thesis by reference to the outbreak of the 1983 riots in Sri Lanka. I shall use as my sources separate essays by two anthropologists, Elizabeth Nissan and Jonathan Spencer, who describe the mood of the Sinhalese before and during the violence they committed against Tamils, and the justification they gave for their actions.[35] It is noteworthy that Nissan's view of the riots is from the vantage point of Anuradhapura, a populous historic city in the "distant" North-Central Province, and Spencer's view is also from a relatively remote village on the southern edge of Sabaragamuwa Province in the central highlands. The 1983 riots began in Colombo and then spread outwards,[36] and our two commentators report first on the provincial moods at their field sites and then move from the periphery to the center and back as violence radiates out from the capital.

Nissan reports these views expressed by Sinhalese citizens of Anuradhapura just before and during the riots: "Those Tamils" had come to "our country"; "they come here and now they are trying to divide the country"; "we have given them a lot but they always want more." These judgments were grounded in the premise that Sri Lanka was inherently a Sinhalese state, and that Tamils challenged it, thus bringing the wrath of the Sinhalese down on their heads. They had only themselves to blame.

But at the same time, Nissan reports that although there were only a few Tamils now left in Anuradhapura after their extradition some six years previously, and no actual violence was unleashed there during the 1983 riots, yet "there was fear in Anuradhapura that the town would be attacked by Tamil Tigers, descending on this most northern Sinhalese town from the Jaffna peninsula." This fear was "not just local, but . . . had been generalized to the point where, in Colombo panic broke out on Friday 29 July when it was believed that Tigers were attacking the city."[37]

Spencer similarly reports many stories circulating in his village about Tamil Tigers being sighted in the vicinity and carrying out murders in the area. These are evidence of the "panic that swept through Sinhalese areas in the build up to the riots" and the expectation of imminent large-scale violence.[38] And the Sinhalese newspapers fed this mood by failure to report accurately or misreporting incidents as the work of Tamil terrorists.

In another essay, Spencer elaborates on the rumors feeding panic and the mounting demonization and fear of the Tamils:

> In the months before the rioting, fear of the Tigers, and the possibility of attacks in the south, had been built up in the Sinhala press. . . . With the imposition of curfew and censorship and the apparent breakdown of the civil administration, rumors about the Tigers grew and developed dramatically— how they were on their way to attack the Temple of Tooth in Kandy, how they were going to poison the water supply of major towns, how they had travelled south from Jaffna hanging on the underside of trains (for 300 miles in a week when the trains were not running) or dressed in military uniform under disguise as priests. . . . In other words, the actions of the Tigers in the north, filtered through a propagandist press and a mesh of cultural stereotypes about the violent Tamil provokes an air of panic in which ever more outlandish rumors spread and flourished. . . . The worst attacks in 1983 were, in the atmosphere, conceived as *defensive* responses to the threat of superhuman Tamil violence.[39]

Ever since the late 1970s, when Tamil youth in desperation became militant insurgents, and thereafter successfully withstood and even got the better of the Sinhala army of occupation, Sinhalese chauvinists had been frustrated and flustered over the puncturing of their virile right of domination, established by Dutthagamani.[40] Increasingly, then, "the actions of the Tigers began to be interpreted in terms of dominant representations of violence and otherness. They were believed to be superhumanly cruel and cunning and, like demons, ubiquitous."

"This is the background to the panic which gripped the country in July 1983. . . . The rumors . . . clearly express partly developed but usually unacknowledged collective fears, and in their rapid development they seem to represent a kind of instant mythologizing in which terrifying new experiences were reinterpreted in terms of more familiar cultural structures"[41]— especially, it would seem, a repertoire of demonic images, whose grip on the Sinhala imagination has been vividly described and interpreted to us by Bruce Kapferer.[42]

Yet another process of image transference, which both Nissan and Spencer document, ex post facto justified the killing of Tamil civilians to the rioters and their supporting public. This was an identification "between all Tamils and those involved in violent separatist activity,"[43] and, by extension, identifying all Tamils as both terrorists and enemies of the Sinhala state. The ultimate implication was that the Tamil is an inherently violent *primordial* and dangerous creature, made even more fearsome by his cunning. And "for many Sinhalese people, away from centers of trouble, the Tamils, far from being victims, were assumed to be at least equal partners if not the protagonists in the rioting."[44]

Spencer describes well how by converting every Tamil into a "terrorist" and reading any defensive act on the part of an ambushed Tamil to be evidence of terrorist inclinations, the rioters were able to justify and live with their violence. Although the greater part of the violence was directed at property and not at people, killings did take place. "Whenever any Tamil attempted to defend himself or his property he became, by definition, a 'terrorist', and the mood of the crowd (and, in some cases, of the security forces), changed dramatically." Firing into the air to disperse the crowd could actually provoke a massacre.[45] "In other words, a thread of insane logic links a number of these incidents—aggression against the crowd, even in some cases simply running away from the crowd, was, *ipso facto*, evidence of terrorism, of being a Tiger. Clearly and objectively, this was never the case; equally clearly and objectively, this was what the crowd *believed* to be the case." "Embarrassed and ashamed by the news of murder, many Sinhalese people were relieved to hear that those killed had been 'terrorists.'"[46]

FEAR AND PANIC DURING THE DELHI RIOTS

These examples from Sri Lanka can be matched with utterances and events pertaining to the Delhi riots of 1984. Although the growing antagonism between the Sikhs and Hindus has progressively involved large numbers on both sides in inter- and intra-community violence, especially in the Punjab and Uttar Pradesh, yet in the case of the riots of 1984 in Delhi, the aggressors were an enormous majority of Hindus and the victims a small minority of under 10 percent of that city's population. This radical situation suitably illustrates the double play of rage and panic on the side of the aggressors.

As the documentation of interviews with residents shows, it was the majority Hindu assailants who manufactured and propagated rumors of sinister unpatriotic and criminal behavior by the Sikhs and also attributed to their victims aggressive propensities and greater resources of wealth and knowledge. Speaking to the authors of *The Delhi Riots* about events in his colony, "which witnessed the murder of more than 300 Sikhs, large scale arson and looting," Mala Ram, a *pradhan* (local community leader) of Block 18 in Trilokpuri recalled that the day after Indira Gandhi's assassination, a factory in nearby Noida went up in flames:

> It was a very large fire and there was a lot of noise. . . . After the fire subsided a very large *kafila* [collection of people] . . . entered our colony and they were shouting "Sardars are coming, Sardars are coming. . . . They are armed with *kirpans* [dagger or sword, one of the five Sikh symbols]." Everyone got into a panic thinking that the Sardars would attack them and ran into their homes. That mob then did all the *gadar* [disturbance] in our colony.[47]

The interviewer then posed this question to Mala Ram (and his neighbors): "Tell us something about this panic you felt that the Sardars were coming. Everywhere in Delhi we have heard that people reacted in the same panic stricken way when they heard that the Sardars were coming. . . . Now suppose the word had gone around that the Harijans [depressed scheduled castes] were coming, no one would have run off." Mala Ram and his neighbors, who are themselves Harijans, had this to say: "We are weak so who would be scared of us?. . . . Harijans are weak economically as well as politically. Harijans are weak in every sense. . . . The Sardars are economically strong; they are also in good positions everywhere." No satisfactory reply came when the interviewers pointed out: "But the Sardars who were killed here were poor scheduled caste people."[48]

As we saw in chapter 5, a middle-class lady from Gujarat named Ratnabehn witnessed horrible attacks on Sikh passengers at Tughlakabad railway station by a crowd armed with iron rods, cycle chains, and kerosene. To the question, "What was the mob saying as they attacked?" Ratnabehn replied:

> They said that the trains were being fired upon by Sikhs at Nizamuddin with guns. They told us to hide in the upper berths to save ourselves, otherwise we might get killed. They said that the trains are coming from Punjab with dead bodies of Hindus. They said, "You don't know what the conditions of your brothers and sisters are, they are cutting off the hands of your Hindu sisters." [Hands wearing bangles and rings, which were looted?]

In fact, at no time during the Delhi riots, as such, did Sikhs attack trains or kill any passengers.

In the 1915 riots in Sri Lanka, A. P. Kannangara reports, rumors sped along the routes by which violence spread, "igniting riots in one place after another." These rumors, although "modified and embellished on their way, were everywhere of a religious character."

> In Kandy and its suburbs, and as far as Gampola, the rumour was that the Muslims had attacked or were about to attack the Dalada Maligawa [the Temple of the Tooth Relic]. Further afield the commonest rumour was that the Moors, some said armies of Moors, were advancing on the Sinhalese, intent on the destruction of Buddhist temples, and on murder and rape. These rumours were accompanied or followed by others which suggested that Sinhalese who joined in taking revenge against the Muslims would go unpunished. Since Great Britain was at war with Turkey, the government would, it was said, welcome attacks on the Moors, and had decided to allow six days during which Sinhalese would be free to carry out their attacks. Another rumour was that since the governor [Sir Robert Chalmers] was a Buddhist, he would pardon Buddhists who punished the Moors for their sacrilege.[49]
>
> The effect of these rumours on the bazaar-poor in Buddhist areas may be gauged from that which they had in some other quarters. In Kotte, a township outside Colombo, the rumours brought out several leading Sinhalese residents, including government officials. Near Kandy, Walgampaya, who . . . was the chief lay trustee of the Gadaladeniya Devale, collected a crowd on the premises and went out at their head, sword in hand, presumably to head off the advancing Moors. Some European officers engaged in trying to quell the riots felt impelled to check rumours that nearby temples and bazaars had been attacked by the Moors. There was also the police magistrate who was at Heneratgoda when rumours arrived that two thousand Moors were advancing towards that town, and crowds of Sinhalese gathered to defend it. He told the Police Inquiry Commission that he had believed these rumours, promised the Sinhalese to help them in repelling the invasion, and made preparations to do so. In Kotahena, Mutwal and other Catholic localities further north of Colombo, church bells were rung when rumours arrived that the Moors were coming to attack the churches, and large crowds came out in defence. In Mutwal it was the local policemen who first ran out to repel the Moors, shouting the alarm to local residents.
>
> To some places the rumours were brought from Colombo, Kandy and other towns and bazaars by people such as carters, pilgrims, traders, city-workers and visitors to weekly markets on their way home. But many set out in order to carry the fearful news or, like the gangs of people who moved from bazaar to bazaar attacking Muslim shops, the example of what ought to be done to punish the Muslims. At Nawagamuwa, and perhaps at some other temples too, Buddhist monks and others, convinced that a Muslim attack was imminent, sent men on bicycles to raise the alarm and summon help. In several bazaars

the rumours reached crowds which had already assembled for some special occasion or another. Kandy, as we have seen, was crowded with Wesak pilgrims. In Gampola the bazaar was crowded with people who had come to attend a religious procession which had been arranged for that day. In Wattegama and some other towns the rumours arrived while weekly fairs were in progress. But generally the crowds were assembled by the force of the rumours. Some of these crowds started at once to attack the local Muslims, to punish them for what their co-religionists had done elsewhere. Other groups moved from bazaar to bazaar attacking Muslim shops and mosques.

But in most places the first impulse was defensive. In Hanguranketa, Panadura and several other towns, the crowds collected in the local temple or marched towards it in order to defend it. Some crowds travelled several miles either to meet the advancing Moors or to make their stand at a point along the road leading to the township. Others made for places where their fellow caste members were said to be under attack. Yet the desire for revenge quickly supervened. Some crowds, having been turned back by force or by persuasion began, as for example at Malabe, to burn and loot the nearest Moorish shops, houses and mosques. Others turned to the attack when the Moors whom they were awaiting or marching to meet did not arrive. In many bazaars crowds often hesitated and hung back from attack, for several hours in one or two places. Then someone would throw a stone at a mosque or a Moor shop, and the rest would follow suit.[50]

Kannangara's account thus confirms a number of features noted in connection with other ethnic disorders: the aggressor group is the source of the initial rumors, which quickly spread; these rumors usually allege that the group to be attacked threatens the core values, institutions, and persons of the aggressor group; offensive actions are thus claimed to be defensive; the rumors themselves operate to collect crowds; while rumors are publicly, anonymously, and insidiously passed from mouth to mouth, there are usually a few key mobile circulating agents provocateurs and riot gangs who are key points of transmission, coining new rumors and embellishing old ones; and "panic and rage" feed each other in the spiraling of violence. This would seem to lend support to the supposition that we are touching here on phenomena typical of crowd actions.

PROJECTION AND AGGRESSION

Some aspects of the psychological theory of projection may be harnessed to add further depth to our exploration of the construction and transmission of rumors that in turn kindle physical violence. To begin with, when any group or community constructs its own myths of origin, stories of victories and conquests, and lives of exemplary culture heroes, it also directly and indirectly denigrates and blackens the traditions of the opponent neighbors and contestants against whom its accomplishments are measured.

There is a further dimension to projection. What is of greater significance is "the need to have others as containers for one's own disavowed aspects."[51] So in rumors during ethnic conflict, one can see that the aggressor's negative characterization of the other may in part at least consist of separating off negative propensities and tendencies one fears in oneself and then projecting and externalizing them and pinning them on the victim. The projection may substantively consist of excesses one fears in oneself as well as weaknesses one senses one harbors; they are the shapes of one's rage as well as one's panic. When, in the course of ethnic conflict, two groups are simultaneously or in turn aggressor and victim, the rumors and prejudices and distortions emanating from both sides may reveal the disavowed and feared aspects of one's own collectivity as much as the stereotyped misperception and mistranslation of the other's traditions and practices.

THE RELATIVE MOTIONS OF ETHNIC CROWDS

The illustrations given from the 1915 and 1983 Sri Lankan riots pertain to situations where a dominant majority community (the Sinhalese) launched riots against minority communities (the Muslims and the Tamils). (Unfortunately, we have no parallel account of the moods, anger, and fears of the Tamils and Muslims before and during the riots.) In the Delhi riots of 1984, it was again a majority that attacked a minority, and similar rumors were spawned by the aggressor majority against the demonized victims. In the 1958 riots in Sri Lanka, the same trends have been documented.

These trends suggest the following hypothesis. In ethnic conflict, when a majority periodically attacks a vulnerable minority, the physical violence directed by the former is also accompanied by distorted rumors detrimental to the victim. Thus while it may be that the prejudice and distorted perception may precede and lead to violence as cause and effect, the more important truth perhaps is that *the motion toward collision combines distorted perception and active violence as parallel and complementary processes,* and the faster the motion toward collision, the greater in intensity are the rumor-waves of prejudice and demonization produced. This process also implies the opposite motion: that when riots subside—and they do so quite rapidly—there is a cooling effect and a diminution of distorted rumors and prejudices, until the pressures toward collision mount again.

In grappling with conceptualizing processes manifested by collective violence in the course of widespread ethnonationalist conflict in the world today, processes that defy understanding in terms of traditional models of order, stability, and transformation and change, I was prompted to explore whether there were formulations in the physical sciences that I might, in a loose analogical sense, creatively try to "translate" into nonmechanistic theories of communicative processes and intersubjective understandings.

I request the indulgence of the reader with regard to the remaining part of this chapter while I try my experiment of translating certain notions pilfered from physics such as "the Doppler effect" and "catastrophe," "chaos," and "turbulence" theories to describe some of the processes of collective violence outlined earlier.

Thus let us go back to the hypothesis stated a few paragraphs back, the dynamics of which could be characterized as the two effects of the relative motions of ethnic collectivities described in terms of the Doppler effect.[52]

When two collectivities compete within the same arena and space for what are perceived to be limited resources and rewards, their misperceptions and animosity increase in tandem. The waves of prejudice, accusations, and rumors increase in frequency, and the preparedness for violence intensifies, as the waves cumulatively back into each other and create the "blue shift" effect—the high frequency of blue- and white-hot intensity. Again, as the sound waves of mutual reproach emitted on both sides approach each other, and their frequency of emission also increases, the louder and shriller the noise produced grows. The collision produces maximum noise and heat, generating a destructive explosion.

The opposite motion of two collectivities is conducive to the "red shift" effect. When two collectivities move away from each other, in the sense that they are not competitors within the same space, and each collectivity finds its niche in an environment of "division of labor," "pluralism," and therefore of tolerance, the waves of mutual antagonistic perception become weaker and are of lower frequency, and therefore of a warmer hue and lower pitch of sound. Ethnic groups in this context do develop their distinctive cultural stereotypes of one another, but they are not mutually annihilative and intolerant. There is in this phase a greater chance of a tolerance, accommodation, and even appreciation of diversity.

Attack and Flight: The Unstable Extreme

What is called catastrophic instability is also detectable in the volatile behavior of crowds.

Suppose that we can in some measure gauge the level of anger and rage in the members of a crowd (a state of affect produced dialogically and through interpersonal effects) and then postulate that when that anger reaches a certain threshold, it is expressed or transformed into the form of physical attack. Suppose that, as is plausible, the members of the crowd are simultaneously in a state of fear and panic, and that when panic reaches a certain threshold, it is expressed as or transformed into flight. If our two control variables anger/rage and fear/panic *increase together* among the members of a crowd, and if the two thresholds are approached simultaneously, the crowd's behavior becomes unpredictable and unstable, and can switch abruptly from attack to flight and vice versa. In this "catastrophe model," we have two incompatible control variables, which are continuous, but in interacting antagonistically produce discontinuous or unstable states. Such modeling, even if difficult to apply empirically to rioting crowds in terms of "measurement," at least helps us to understand dimly how in many of the descriptions of rioting crowds given earlier, there are many instances of crowds attacking and retreating, coalescing quickly and breaking up in flight equally quickly, the onslaughts coming in waves of attack and quiescence, especially at that phase of the riots when aggression, rumormongering, and fear have reached the climactic point of unpredictable oscillation, maximum brutality, and demonization.

Social Dissociation and Stereotyping

Continuing in the spirit of ludic speculation, let me now, taking a leaf from "psychology," propose that a process of "social dissociation" is increasingly at work in situations of collective violence as a result of the communicational processes discussed earlier (including rumors), thereby further sharpening and narrowing the stereotyped image of the ethnic or sectarian enemy in the eyes and minds of the aggressors, in terms of both perception and affect. An aspect of this social dissociation is the depersonalization of members of the opposed collectivity so that they are homogenized and leveled into an undifferentiated, simplified negative stereotype. Such intensified stereotyping allows for a narrowed and focused obsession directed at the vilified enemy, and under the sense of collective legitimation, permits people to engage with concentrated energy in transgressive acts of violence against which there are restraints in everyday life, but virtually none in the altered state.

Let me insert the reminder that these intensified collective communicational states and acts are temporary states, of relatively short duration, from which the actors make an exit when the riots are over. The temporary experience of merging the self in such narrowed, focused dissociation in a collective context may perhaps also give us a clue to why rioters, after a spate of orgasmic violence, retrospectively recollect and speak of their actions in a distanced and neutral tone, cordoning them off as separate and not imperative to remember and to bring into intimate relation to their everyday selves. (At the same time, we need to remember that riots can occur serially and intermittently, and that aggressors can therefore make *parallel* intermittent entries and exits.) By contrast, it is the victims who remember and tell and retell the story of the violence and their experience of victimization and suffering, and thus by repetition shape their narratives into a standardized or ritualized lament, which is then progressively shared by the community of sufferers as a collective memory, with its stereotyped narrations. On the victims' side, the individual, personal, familial, sudden, and inchoate experience of first strike, arson, displacement, and injury are progressively and retrospectively shaped into more coherent and ratified reports of collectively shared suffering, and crystallized into a collective memory. The collectivity of aggressors would in time prefer their individual remembrances to be eroded by amnesia. It is the victims who do the work of remembering and memorializing as a collective experience.

The Turbulence of Crowds

There are many features of the outbreak and trajectory of collective violence such as civilian riots that are difficult to predict or chart in terms of systematic process. When exactly—on what day and time—in the atmosphere of a charged political context does a riot break out? In which place and site among a number of possible sites does it begin? What phases does violence go through, and when and how does violence change into a frenzied state of arson and carnage? And how does it dissipate itself, and calm down? I have tried at several places to describe and chart the course and duration of the cases we have examined. It seems that while we are about it, we might with a sense of playful curiosity dip into some formulations in physics concerning "turbulence" and see what analogical transfers we can make. This is not an entirely outrageous move. Some anthropologists of the pre-postmodern era (especially the "structural-functionalists") did play with notions of "steady state equilibrium," "moving equilibrium," "oscillating equilibrium," and so on (I may add to this collection my own interest in the zoologist Stephen Jay Gould's concept of "punctuated equilibrium"), although none ventured into "chaos" theory.

Turbulence in fluid dynamics signifies "a mess of disorder at all scales, small eddies within larger ones," James Gleick writes. "It is highly unstable. It is highly dissipative, meaning that turbulence drains energy and creates drag."

When flow is smooth, or laminar, small disturbances die out. But past the onset of turbulence, disturbances grow catastrophically. . . .

Like much of chaos itself, phase transitions involve a kind of macroscopic behaviour that seems hard to predict by looking at microscopic details. . . .

At a certain temperature and pressure, the change becomes sudden and discontinuous. A rope has been stretching; now it breaks.[53]

The material has entered a new realm.

It is gratifying to find that physicists investigating various branches of "chaos theory" do not believe in unending and unaccountable disorder and are trying to discern the patterns and processes that lead to, maintain, and slow down turbulence. But the answers sought have to be in terms of a theory of nonlinear systems.

How does a social flow cross the boundary from smooth to turbulent? How might small-scale tensions and petty conflicts that are usually settled or mitigated by the usual norms of restraint and mechanisms of social control get out of hand and cumulatively produce social turbulence. Looking back to the allusion above to the "blue shift" and "red shift" effects of rumors created when two sources meet in collision or recede into distance—processes and effects that can be extended to all forms of agonistic communicative events—can we envisage a state of turbulence being generated by a piling up of competing and unstable new waves and motions, with their different frequencies, such that they not only simply additively accumulate but also create rhythms with overlapping speeds and sizes, quickly reaching a state of unstoppable turbulence? When more energy comes into a system a Russian expert on fluid dynamics has conjectured, "new frequencies begin one at a time each incompatible with the last, as if a violin string responds to higher bowing by vibrating with a second, dissonant tone, and then a third, and a fourth, until the sound becomes an incomprehensible cacophony."[54]

I have sought through the concepts of *focalization* and *transvaluation* to describe the piling up of different local conflicts to form a larger-scale turbulence, and the parallel crystallization of small-scale crowds in multiple locations, which at times merged in short-lived larger outbursts, to break up into fragments again once the orgasm of destruction had dissipated the frenzy of energy and passion. The concepts of *nationalization* and *parochialization* were employed to describe, as, for example, in the case of the demolition of the mosque in Ayodhya and the subsequent urban riots, the opposite, processes whereby causes and campaigns promoted as "national" in scope have an impact on multiple local sites and communities and work themselves out according to local fault lines and locally significant issues.

But these (and other processes) have to be fitted into the larger context of constraints, parameters, and capacities that obtain in a particular situation of ethnic conflict. The parameters and the degrees of freedom within which a particular instance of collective violence is staged have something to do with factors such as these: (1) the nature of the locality and the demographic distribution of the groups involved, and the presence of leaders who can organize and of personnel who can be mobilized for action; (2) the antecedent relations between these groups, both competitions, tensions, and collisions and cooperation, coalitions, and accommodation; (3) the logistics of the available transportation system and communication media; (4) the technology of violence currently available to the actors; (5) the disposition and commitments of the police and security forces, and of the larger apparatus of state power; and (6) the targets and sites chosen for attack and defense.

The repertoire and capacities that constitute the cultural capital and arsenal from which the component units and phases of collective violence are drawn include the following: the calendar of festivals; the stock of performances, processions, orations, and public protests; stereotyped labelings and rumors, formally recognized insults, triggering actions, and shamings; and the array of communications media (newspapers, posters, television, VCRs, tapes, etc.) available and deployed. All these help shape the swirls, cumulative rhythms, and phased transitions, in the rise and fall of collective violence in public arenas.

11 Reconfiguring Le Bon and Durkheim on Crowds as Collectives

Although he has been subject to many ambivalent evaluations—regarding the originality of his ideas (many of which had previously been articulated by the Italian Scipio Sighela and the Frenchman Gabriel de Tarde), regarding his political conservatism and deep antipathy to socialist and democratic ideals and practices (Robert Merton calls him "a dismayed if not hopelessly frightened conservative"),[1] and, finally, regarding his tendency to reduce the essentials of crowd psychology to a "racialist basis"—Gustave Le Bon's *Psychologie des foules* is nevertheless a classic, and even if it is flawed, it is worth treating as a foil.

Le Bon's characterization of his time, "the age we are about to enter will in truth be the era of the crowds," was prescient, in that it all too well described the epoch of Nazism and Fascism and World War II. Serge Moscovici has elaborated on this theme.[2] And now in the 1990s, with the competition among nationalities and subnationalities throughout Eastern Europe, and especially in the successor states to the defunct USSR and Yugoslavia, Le Bon's prophecy seems to have come alive again. It is alive not only in Europe but worldwide. Ethnic conflict, accompanied by civilian riots, army actions, and insurrectionary movements, is rife in many places.

I am not concerned here to restate and reexamine Le Bon's argument, but to recover from his work theses that seem relevant to my theme, which I shall adapt and reformulate to suit the style of our time.

I find these of Le Bon's ideas interesting and relevant to ponder: (1) that in crowds there is "an intensification of the emotions" and "the inhibition of the intellect"; (2) that in crowds "unconscious mental processes" dominate over conscious, rational, and critical processes; and (3) that because of

297

a "lack of emotional restraint" and "an incapacity for moderation and delay," there is thus a rush of "intolerance" toward the other. I am even tempted to leap over or bypass Le Bon's dichotomy between intellect and emotion—a lowered intellect and heightened emotion—by postulating that when large crowds form, there is a tendency for ideas with high emotional valence—like images of fatherland, motherland, one people, the brotherhood of man, and so on—to constitute collective sentiments with a strong impulsion toward their collective realization in action. Le Bon put the matter in this way: "We see then the disappearance of the conscious personality, the predominance of the unconscious personality, the turning by means of suggestion and contagion of feelings and ideas in an identical direction, the tendency immediately to transform the suggested ideas into acts."[3]

The processes of interaction between the persons who constitute a crowd that transform them into a fused collectivity are a related set of themes touched on by Le Bon, who speaks of the role of "emotional contagion" and "suggestibility" in the crowd and in organized groups, which create a homogeneity and conformity of sentiments and actions. (Tarde's notion of "imitation" focused on the same issue.)

It is in adumbrating these features of homogeneity and conformity of sentiments, and the impulsion to act upon them, that Le Bon uses the felicitous term *leveling*, which Elias Canetti seemingly coined independently or used without attribution. I have throughout this book referred to manifestations of leveling behavior on the part of rioting crowds in ethnic conflict. Let me now try to differentiate and formalize the various forms of leveling conduct: in the domain of collective ideology, mytho-history, and collective "entitlement claims," stemming from and rooted in conceptions of imagined communities of nation, people, language, and territory, we see leveling in terms of all members holding the same or similar images and visions of their legacy and their destiny. "Appeals to sentiments of glory, honour, and patriotism are particularly likely to influence the individual forming part of a crowd, and often to the extent of obtaining from him the sacrifice of his life."[4]

I have described rioting ethnic crowds, imbued with ideas of unfair and illegitimate advantages allegedly enjoyed by the enemy group, usually a minority, engaging in acts of destruction, arson, looting, and killing in order to reduce the enemy's margins of advantage in material resources, educational, professional, and commercial skills, manpower, and cultural capital. There is a double imagery here: the attempted leveling of social advantages is accomplished as a physical leveling to the ground of buildings and a mowing down of persons.

Another context and site of leveling is in the processes and techniques of indoctrination and transmission of collective dogmas by means of a tailored rhetoric of persuasion and incitement through oratory exercised in rallies, processions, electoral meetings, and legislative assemblies, printed propaganda, and the electronic media.

My earlier elucidation of the cultural repertoire of ritualized and stereotyped forms that are drawn upon in staging public events such as elections, protest movements and strikes, and civilian riots can be further enriched by grafting to it these insights. The oratorical rhetoric that influences crowds exploits these devices: themes and issues tend to be radically simplified and at the same time exaggerated, as often happens in advertisements. Furthermore, the simplified and exaggerated truth is simply affirmed as true, in the manner of axioms, and ex cathedra pronouncements, and not demonstrated by argument (crowds are impatient of reasoned lectures). Finally, "affirmation has no real influence unless it is constantly *repeated*, and so far as possible in the same terms."[5]

In my previous analysis, I have underscored and repeatedly returned to the matter of the invention and circulation of rumors that are simultaneously anonymous, secretive, and public, and that energize crowds with their distorted news. Le Bon's own treatment of this issue may well add something. How does one explain "the facility with which are created and propagated the most improbable legends and stories" noticed among crowds?[6]

There are two features to the answer Le Bon gives. The first, which we might expect once we grasp his perspective, is that crowds become "excessively credulous," because "hovering on the borderland of unconsciousness," they tend to lose their critical faculty and the influence of reasoning upon it. They uncritically fall prey to contagious suggestion.

The second feature represents a more interesting and also controversial interpretive move. The crowd's "imagination" in a throng is heightened and transformed because it thinks in, and is susceptible to, "images"; and an image, a distorted vision, once let loose by one individual, is the starting point for a "contagious suggestion." The crowd may thus actually see and confirm an illusion, such as St. George appearing on the walls of Jerusalem to all the Crusaders, or a candle signaling from an upper story to besiegers during the siege of Paris. "Such is always the mechanism of the collective hallucinations so frequent in history—hallucinations which seem to have all the recognized characteristics of authenticity, since they are phenomena observed by thousands of persons."[7] Le Bon raises, but does not actually explain "the mechanism of a collective hallucination." Nor to my knowledge have his successors. But we cannot deny the reports one repeatedly receives of collective illusory or hallucinatory visions that are "seen" by crowds and spur them to action. They are as potent as rumors similarly taken to be true.

The question of the role of leadership in the creation of the crowd mentality he described was up to a point taken up by Le Bon and not too well integrated into his general description. One important explanation of why crowds are so suggestible, credulous, and mobile, and show a decline in intellectual critical attitudes and an upsurge of unconscious emotional intensity, was that they fell under the influence of leaders. Le Bon dramatically referred to the "thirst for obedience" that marks the crowd conformist. "A crowd is a servile flock that is incapable of ever doing without a master"; the leader is "the first element in the organization of heterogeneous crowds, and paves the way for their organization in sects."[8]

Since Le Bon's "heterogeneous crowds," despite their simplified stereotyping, are similar in some ways to the kinds of crowds we have encountered in ethnic riots, it is of interest to see how he characterizes the role of crowd leaders. The leaders of these crowds "are more frequently men of action than thinkers. . . . their convictions are so strong that all reasoning is lost upon them."

> The leaders of crowds wield a very despotic authority, and this despotism indeed is a condition of their obtaining a following. It has often been remarked how easily they extort obedience, although without any means of backing up their authority, from the most turbulent section of the working classes.
> The ringleaders and agitators may be divided into two clearly defined classes. The one includes the men who are energetic and possess, but only intermittently, much strength of will, the other men, far rarer than the preceding, whose strength of will is enduring.[9]

The first-mentioned are violent and audacious, but their energy, although a force to be reckoned with, is transitory, and scarcely outlasts the exciting cause that has brought it into play. They themselves are led by, and follow as their beacon, a man or an idea. At the upper end of the hierarchy are the second category of leaders of enduring strength of will, the true founders of religious and great undertakings.[10]

We may well wonder how Le Bon's characterization of "ring leaders and agitators" in short-lived volatile heterogeneous crowds fits our information on civilian crowds engaged in ethnic conflict. In the cases I have examined, there are certainly no great charismatic leaders of enduring, stable mass movements and associations at work. What we have are vigorous, violence-prone, patronage-conscious lesser politicians, demagogues (such as Cyril Mathews in Sri Lanka and Dr. Ashok Kumar and H. K. L. Bhagat in the Delhi riots), riot captains, and leaders of gangs that employ force on behalf of their patrons, be they politicians, businessmen, or populist or fundamentalist leaders, who rise and fall quickly.

In one sense, however, our evidence and analysis goes beyond the framework of Le Bon's elucidation. Although he speaks of types of crowds and offers copious illustrations of crowd behavior from the French Revolution and nineteenth-century French politics (for example, the short-lived popular movement associated with General Boulanger in the later 1880s and mass politics in the Third Republic), Le Bon fails to describe and track in detail a single popular movement and its participants, the faces in the crowd, and the larger political and economic contexts in which these movements rose and fell. In failing to do this, Le Bon also fails to link the crowds he speaks of to the networks of power and politics of their time.

The trails I have mapped in my South Asian case studies do link ephemeral riot crowds and their agitators, agents provocateurs, and mobilizers to the less visible, but powerfully present, institutions of and participants in democratic party politics, state machinery, and bureaucratic stakes, and to competition between parties and by ethnic groups among themselves and vis-à-vis the centralizing state and the project of the nation-state. At certain points, the trails lead us to the shadowy depths of the party machineries of Congress (I) in India, the People's Party in Pakistan, and the UNP in Sri Lanka—to mention only some major actors—and their calculations and strategies.

Here the shortcomings of Le Bon's political prejudices emerge too. Because he abhorred and feared democracy and socialism, he argued that political institutions, structures, and personnel engaged in the practice of democracy were irrelevant to, and only superficially implicated in, the underlying, enduring, timeless, essentialized, unconscious, and basically racial propensities upon which were projected those processes that create crowds and make our epoch "the era of crowds." I have conversely sought to establish an altogether different thesis, that ethnic strife that generates civilian riots and other crowd phenomena is inseparably linked with the communicational processes and practices of mass politics in the societies I have examined, a thesis that is capable of extension to many other contemporary societies.

There is one other limitation to Le Bon's theorizing of the crowd as a general phenomenon in politics. As demonstrated in some of my case studies—especially the Sinhala-Muslim riots of 1915 in Sri Lanka, the Hindu-Sikh riots of Delhi in 1984, and the Karachi riots of the mid 1980s—what comes to be labeled a monolithic "ethnic riot" is not enacted by a single crowd, but by many crowds, and a number of "local" collisions fueled by "local" disputes may simultaneously or successively occur and build up by chain reaction and cumulative force into a regional or societywide explosion. The concepts of focalization and transvaluation were used to describe this snowballing process in which particular contextualized happenings progressively lose their local meanings and become assimilated to generalized ethnic and national slogans, claims, and rhetoric.

It is because of such internal structuring that we have to remind ourselves constantly that the subjective and interactional crystallizations of the large collectivities who call themselves Sinhalese, Tamils, Sikhs, Hindus, Maharashtrians, and so on are episodic and context-bound. These same collectivities are internally divided and crosscut by factional, sectarian, caste, class, regional, and economic interests, which provide the ground for cleavages and rivalries. This is one reason why ethnic riots that temporarily mobilize large numbers are short-lived. In this way, we should deconstruct the labels, causes, and identities grouped under the general term *ethnic conflict,* and save this concept from excessive reification.

Now if we apply this lesson to Le Bon's treatment of the crowd, we can say that the French Revolution and the political turbulence of the Third Republic should be viewed, not as unitary events enacted in each case by one monolithic, single crowd, but rather as the creations of many crowds, with many faces, fighting different causes and different local enemies, which must also be closely followed and monitored in their chainlike linkages, before we postulate a "revolution" as a generalized and unitary phenomenon. The French Revolution, aided by its very labeling, is all too often mistakenly seen as a single coherent movement that fought for the glorious ideals of liberty, equality, and fraternity under the charismatic leadership of Danton, Robespierre, and their ilk.

DURKHEIM ON THE EFFERVESCENCE
AND EUPHORIA OF CROWDS

Emile Durkheim published his epochal work *Les Formes élémentaires de la vie religieuse: Le Système totémique en Australie* in 1912. It was translated into English in 1915 with the title *The Elementary Forms of Religious Life: A Study in Religious Sociology.*[11] Le Bon's book, *The Crowd,* had been published in its original French version in 1895. Although Durkheim's work, published some seventeen years later, deals at important points with crowd behavior, he does not cite Le Bon as a relevant text.[12] But as Steven Lukes observes, in advancing the thesis that certain social situations characterized by collective effervescence generate and recreate religious beliefs and sentiments, Durkheim was

> doubtless affected by the crop of studies in crowd psychology that had appeared at the end of the nineteenth century, by Scipio Sighela, Gustave Le Bon and, indeed Gabriel Tarde among others, but there is no evidence that he was specifically influenced by any of them; and, unlike them, he did not see crowd behavior as pathological, undesirable and an argument against democracy. On the contrary, he argued that it was "out of this effervescence itself that the religious idea seems to be born," that "after a collective effervescence men believe themselves transported into an entirely different world from the one they have before their eyes," that sacred beings, the creations of collective thought, "attain their greatest intensity at the moment when the men are assembled together and are in immediate relations with one another, when they partake of the same idea and the same sentiment." Moreover, the "only way of renewing the collective *représentations* which relate to sacred beings is to retemper them in the very source of the religious life, that is to say, in the assembled groups."[13]

While Le Bon belongs to the tradition of viewing processes of crowd formation and the actions and sentiments stemming from them as destabilizing, destructive, and degenerative, Durkheim advances the opposite thesis of crowd contexts as positively enabling the generation of "sacred" sentiments and of collective representations and practices that produce and celebrate social solidarity and integration. Secondly, insofar as Durkheim sees heightened crowd contexts as generating the sense of the sacred and holy, we may ask to what degree this perspective enables us to appreciate how in the context of ethnic riots, participants accede to the call of violating and victimizing the enemy as a moral imperative, socially induced and legitimated. In other words, Durkheim may have something distinctive to contribute to the subject of how violence relates to the sacred and the religious as collectively experienced and legitimated sentiments.

There are many other observations and implications in Durkheim's work that in one way or other bear on the interactional and subjective processes generated when people assemble in crowds to celebrate their religious rites at sacred sites and in other public arenas.

Durkheim set out to analyze Australian totemism because he believed that through the analysis of "the simplest religion known," he could determine "the elementary forms of the religious life." He had chosen to study a "very archaic religion" "because it has seemed to us better adapted than any other to an understanding of the religious nature of man, that is to say, to show an essential and permanent aspect of humanity."[14] This stance is, I think, the very opposite of Freud's in both *Totem and Taboo* and *Group Psychology and the Analysis of Ego*. Freud, with his evolutionary paradigm and his aligning of the phylogeny of the "species" with the "ontogeny" of the individual, explained certain "obsessive" and "neurotic" features of modern man's conduct as a "regression" in his unconscious life to "primordial" infantile experience and desires. Durkheim's aim was to establish that the study of archaic religion reveals in a clear manner something universal and permanent in all humanity, including the modern man, that derives from the fact of his being a social being.

What is the origin of the "idea of totemic principle or mana"? The stimulating action of society is felt by us as some current of energy coming from outside us. Moral power, although immanent in us, represents within us something not ourselves, namely, moral conscience. In similar manner, "we are forced to localize [our cultural capital—our language, our treasury of knowledge and traditions] outside ourselves," since they exercise over us a pressure of which we are conscious.[15] (In modern jargon, Durkheim is discussing parallel processes of objectification.)

Collective sentiments themselves propel, constitute, and structure ritualized conduct. In this observation about the collective impulsion toward ritual, Durkheim has an insight that escapes Freud's theory of individual pathological rites being the basis of collective religious rites: "Since a collective sentiment cannot express itself collectively except on the condition of observing a certain order permitting co-operation and movements in unison, the gestures and cries naturally tend to become rhythmic and regular; hence come songs and dances."[16] One may add to this insight the suggestion that many situations of mass assembly—ranging from demonstrations, strikes, and public protests to audiences listening to an orator or watching a spectacle—quite easily allow for low-level leaders, cheerleaders, and the like to orchestrate a crowd and make it follow routines of sitting and standing, cheering and jeering, raising and lowering flags and placards, reciting slogans and singing rousing songs. The coupling of rhythmic conduct with social regimentation is a topic worthy of study.

Into this aspect of the discussion may also be fitted Durkheim's reference to "the demon of oratorical inspiration" as something dialectically generated by the interaction of public speaker and audience. The "exceptional increase of force" felt by the speaker "is something very real; it comes to him from the very group which he addresses. The sentiments provoked by his word come back to him, but enlarged and amplified, and to this degree they strengthen his own sentiment."[17]

In amplification of this, I may add that it is not only in public oratory that this intersubjective dialogical stimulation occurs between performer and a participatory audience. We constantly witness a phenomena in sports arenas whereby processes of interstimulation between athletes and cheering fans raise the performance level of the home-team athletes to an even higher level than that achieved in previous moments, which first lit up the fans. A crescendo of noise and a quick flurry of unstoppable plays by the home athletes go hand in hand. The visiting team, consisting of no lesser athletes, is for a while collectively deflated, dispirited, and out of rhythm and seems actually to have lost physical energy, while the home team seems to have acquired a higher energy level, a lift of the spirits, prowess, and skill that in retrospect amazes them. By virtue of the close surrounding presence of spectator fans, basketball produces this demon of athletic inspiration more visibly than other sports, and the so-called "home court advantage" applies supremely to that game.

I think it is possible to rephrase and extend Durkheim on another matter. One of his central theories in *Elementary Forms* was that "sacred things are simply collective ideals that have fixed themselves on material objects." He explains their sacredness thus: "They are collective forces hypostatized, that is to say, moral forces; they are made up of the ideas and sentiments awakened in us by the separate spectacle of society, and not from sensations coming from the physical world."[18] Aspects of this formulation may fruitfully be aligned with the concept of the "objectification of charisma" in statues, images, amulets, relics, and sacred spots that I first developed in *Buddhist Saints of the Forest*.[19] In that book, I discussed how the "charisma" of saintly persons is ritually transferred to objects, which are seen as embodying the virtues and energies of the saints and transmit and radiate them to their lay possessors or worshipers, who also in turn treasure them, care for them, and invest those objects with portions of their own biography and personal experiences. I employed the neo-Peircean terms *indexical symbols* and *indexical icons* to describe these object-person relations.

Durkheim can thus be seen as suggesting that the religious force and energy generated by collective assemblies are externalized and objectified in totems, sacred objects to which are attributed power in their own right. But then in turn, by their very display and presence in collective rites, these objects generate and constitute collective sentiments and cognitions in the human participants. We can see therefore why the embodiments of objectified charisma—national flags, banners, standards, holy books, images, and portraits—are deployed in the collective rites, ceremonies, protests, elections, and processions that I have identified as fundamental to ethnic conflict and collective violence, exemplifying the process of "participation" elaborated on in my book *Magic, Science, Religion and the Scope of Rationality.*[20]

It is possible to separate analytically at least two orientations to our cosmos, two orderings of reality that people everywhere are capable of experiencing, although the specific mix, weighting, and complementarity between the two may vary among individuals, among groups within a culture, and among cultures taken as collective entities.

These two orientations I label *participation* and *causality*. Causality is quintessentially represented by the categories, rules, and methodology of positive science and discursive mathematico-logical reason. In ideal terms, the scientific focus is perceived as involving affective neutrality to and abstraction from events in the world. Particularly in the so-called hard, natural sciences, cause and effect in space and time are conceived of in terms of measurable impacts of energy and force, and by the progressive atomization of information, by which entities are progressively broken down from molecules to atoms, and from atoms to subatomic particles, whose interactions then provide the image of causality.

Participation can be represented as occurring when persons, groups, animals, places, and natural phenomena are in a relation of contiguity and translate that relation into one of existential immediacy and contact and shared affinities. (In the language of semiotics, humans, on the one hand, and places, objects, and natural phenomena, on the other, are represented as mutually representing one another "iconically," and also as transferring energies and attributes "indexically.") Participation among people, places, nature, and objects is manifested when Trobriand Islanders relate their myths of origins in terms of emerging from holes in the ground or being associated with primordial rocks; when the name of a peasant in the Kandyan highlands of Sri Lanka is a lexical string that successively denotes his village of origin (*vasagama*), the ancestral house in that village (*gedera*) with which his family was associated, and finally his personal name, fusing location, territory, residence, caste, family status, and ancestry in a single composite identity; when in a present-day Calabrian village, grandparents speak of their ancient rootedness in farms and villages of origin; when Americans, young and old, terrified by nuclear devastation and industrial waste, turn out in droves to protect their environment and their ecology, their flora and their fauna; when the Romantic poets, Wordsworth, Coleridge, and Shelley, waxed eloquent in the presence of, and communion with, nature; when national monuments such as the Lincoln and

Jefferson memorials, graveyards such as the Arlington National Cemetery, and battlefields such as Gettysburg are believed to enshrine a people's history and radiate their national glories. And people participate in each other as well: the bonding and relation between parents and children, between kinsmen by the ties of blood and amity; the transmission of charisma, or *metta*, through amulets and talismans between a Buddhist saint and his followers, or between Thai royalty and their subjects; the Indian concept of the *darshan* of a deity, whose eyes fall upon the worshipers as much as the worshipers view their deity—all these are intimations of participation. The connectedness between persons and the sense of being a part of an ensemble of relationships are also bridges to the reality of participation.

Although "causation" and "participation" may seem different or contrastive orientations to the world, the analyst must maintain that both are projected on the experiential and symbolizing capacities of the *same* sensory modalities of man—the modalities of touch, taste, hearing, and seeing. While much of the discourse of causality and positive science is framed in terms of distancing, neutrality, experimentation, and the language of analytic reason, much of the discourse of participation can be framed in terms of sympathetic immediacy, performative speech acts, and ritual action. If participation emphasizes sensory and affective communication and the language of emotions, causality stresses the rationality of instrumental action and the language of cognition. But these are ideal type exaggerations, and neither can exclude the devices of the other.

Durkheim was well aware—and here perhaps he intersects with Le Bon—that the "effervescence" created and experienced in crowds could result in "excesses" of both a positive and a negative kind. Le Bon the conservative mainly saw the "negative" aspects of crowd conduct. Durkheim seems to have been more evenhanded about the creative and destructive aspects of crowd excitation: A "general effervescence . . . is characteristic of revolutionary or creative epochs," he observes.

> Men become different. The passions moving them are of such an intensity that they cannot be satisfied except by violent and unrestrained actions, actions of superhuman heroism or of bloody barbarism. This is what explains the Crusades, for example, or many of the scenes, either sublime or savage, of the French Revolution. Under the influence of the general exaltation, we see the most mediocre and inoffensive bourgeois become either a hero or a butcher.[21]

Indeed, the effervescence and agitation can lead to excesses: it "often reaches such a point that it causes unheard-of actions. The passions released are of such an impetuosity that they can be restrained by nothing."

Ordinary morals, such as rules governing sexual relations, are contravened. Australian tribal totemic rites, usually staged at night, "produce such a violent super-excitation of the whole physical and mental life that it cannot be supported very long: the actor taking the principal part finally falls exhausted on the ground."[22]

But he has experienced extraordinary powers, which excite him to the point of frenzy.

12 The Moral Economy of Collective Violence

George Rudé's judgment of the European preindustrial crowds he describes as methodically destroying property and indulging in arson is that they were moved by economic and political "injustices," and that their acts of destruction signified the "leveling instinct . . . common to all such occasions, which prompts the poor to seek a degree of elementary social justice at the expense of the rich, *les grands,* and those in authority regardless of whether they are government officials, feudal lords, capitalists, or middle class revolutionary leaders."[1] And, as we have seen, Le Bon and Canetti, too, refer to the leveling passions of the crowd. E. P. Thompson's thesis of the "moral economy" and Natalie Zemon Davis's perspective on "rites of violence" both address the issue of the purposive motivations of preindustrial crowd violence in Europe and the conventional moral parameters within which it was exercised. As Davis puts it, summarizing the cumulative work of historians such as Hobsbawm, Thompson, Rudé, Tilly, and Le Roy Ladurie:

> The sixteenth century itself had its own generalizations about crowd violence. . . . Most of the time . . . the image was of chaos. Learned writers talk of grain rioters in Lyon as "the dregs of populace, with no order, no rein, no leader . . . a beast of many heads . . . an insane rabble" and of the Paris mob as an "ignorant multitude, . . . governed by the appetite of those who stir them up [to] extreme rage, just looking for the chance to carry out any kind of cruelty."

Nowadays, this hydra-headed monster is perceived as having a more orderly shape:

> We may see these crowds as prompted by political and moral traditions which legitimize and even prescribe their violence. We may see urban rioters not as

miserable, uprooted, unstable masses, but as men and women who often have some stake in their community; who may be craftsmen or better; and who, even when poor and unskilled, may appear respectable to their everyday neighbors. Finally, we may see violence, however cruel, not as random and limitless, but as aimed at defined targets and selected from a repertory of traditional punishments and forms of destruction.[2]

Davis uses the phrase "rites of violence" to label the religious riots in sixteenth-century France. "Is there any way we can order the terrible, concrete details of filth, shame, and torture that are reported from both Protestant and Catholic riots?" she asks, and answers: "I would suggest that they can be reduced to a repertory of actions, derived from the Bible, from the liturgy, from the action of political authority, or from the traditions of popular folk practices intended to purify the religious community and humiliate the enemy and thus make him less harmful."[3]

The violence, however cruel, was not random or limitless, Davis suggests, but "aimed at defined targets and selected from a repertory of traditional punishments and forms of destruction."[4] Destruction by water and fire purified, exorcised, and removed pollution. Making victims wear crowns of thorns or ride backward on asses had their biblical precedents, now reproduced in mockery. Even the extreme ways of defiling corpses— dragging bodies through the streets and throwing them to the dogs, dismembering genitalia and selling them in mock commerce—and desecrating religious objects—roasting the crucifix, daubing human excrement on holy water basins, greasing one's boots with holy oil—had their perverse connection with concepts of pollution and purification, heresy and blasphemy.

From another angle of vision, the rites of violence merge with the realm of comedy and the ebullience of festivities, processions, and Mardi Gras games. Examples are mock trials imitating magistrates' proceedings and the killing of victims as enactments of "farce." Indeed, the occasion for most religious violence was during the time of religious processions and mass rituals. Collisions and confrontations were inevitable when different styles of worship collided in the same public space and during the same sacred time: "When festive Catholicism took over the streets with dancing, masks, banners, costumes and music, the sober Protestant procession was a parade of armed men and women in their dark clothes, going off to services at their temple or outside the city gates, singing Psalms and spiritual songs that to Catholic ears sounded like insults against the Church and her sacraments."[5]

South Asian riots also give ample evidence of such "rites of violence" drawn from the repertory of religious lore and ritual, folk sanctions and punishments, and rituals of purification and exorcism. Muslims and Buddhists clashing over processions; Hindus and Muslims fighting about cow killing; May Day rallies and Wesak festivities; inflammatory election speeches and the strident sermons of Buddhist monks at public rituals; collective vow-taking to eliminate the profane enemy in imitation of vows taken before the powerful god Kataragama in his manifestation in the Sinhalese Buddhist pantheon as a guardian of the island, granter of boons, and punisher of enemies—these all powerfully instigate and even legitimate acts of violence (in the eyes of the assailants) "for the sake of religion and country": the demonizing of victims and their expulsion or annihilation in the idiom of exorcism; ultimately, the forced immolation of defenseless and terrified victims in mock imitation of both the self-immolation of conscientious objectors and the terminal rite of cremation.

IS THERE A MORAL ECONOMY OF ETHNIC VIOLENCE?

One critical question we must confront is whether the demonstration that there is ritualized and patterned conduct in ethnic riots that finds its precedents in religious and other ideological lore and beliefs, cultural practices, and social customs automatically *legitimates* that violence in ethical and moral terms. There is no doubt that the majority of those involved in such violence, be they Hindu or Muslim, Sinhalese or Tamil, Sikh or Hindu, Bengali or Chakma, Pathan or Bihari, feel at some level that their cause is legitimate and justified—and this is why they can by and large live with their violence (although they cannot totally escape doubts and pangs of remorse).

But even if it manifests elements describable as "rites of violence," can collective action in ethnic conflict for that reason claim the *right* to commit violence—violence that violates human rights, equality before law, fair trial, and habeas corpus, and denies the premises of citizenship, rights to property, and freedom from fear and hunger and injury? Do these rights and criteria, which the United Nations and its agencies declare ought to apply to all humans in our time, supersede the interests, punitive traditions, and extralegal actions of a country's component groups, be they majorities or minorities? Must these groups not bow and bend to the general good of the country, constituted as a democracy, of which they are members? Moreover, how are we to understand "the right of self-determination" of peoples as a recognized "universal right," and when are the rights of self-determination of component "nationalities" or "ethnic communities" in a plural society held to be justified and to take priority over a centralizing authority in the name of nation-state making?

The concept of *moral economy* formulated by E. P. Thompson may help us to answer these questions. Thompson argues that eighteenth-century English "food riots" constituted "a pattern of social protest which derives from a consensus as to the moral economy of the commonwealth in times of dearth."[6] Rejecting "the spasmodic view of popular history" that denigrates the popular protests of that time as the actions of "mobs," a label that denies common people the status of historical agents in their own right, or vulgarizes their actions as merely attempts to stay the rebellions of the belly (a form of gross economic reductionism), Thompson advances this sympathetic portrayal of motive and normative expectations: "It is possible to detect in every eighteenth century crowd action some legitimating notion," the belief of the men and women of the crowd "that they were defending traditional rights or customs" and that they "were supported by the wider consensus of the community." "On occasion this popular consensus was endorsed by some measure of license afforded by the authorities." It is true that riots were triggered by soaring prices, by malpractice among dealers, or by hunger, but "these grievances operated within a popular consensus as to what were legitimate and what were illegitimate practices in marketing, milling, baking, etc." This in turn was "grounded upon a consistent traditional view of social norms and obligations, of the proper economic functions of several parties within the community," which can be said to constitute "the moral economy of the poor."[7] This moral economy impinged very generally upon eighteenth-century government and thought; it supported definite and passionately held notions of the commonweal, which found some support in the paternalist tradition of the authorities.

By a "paternalistic model of the marketing and manufacturing process," Thompson meant regulation by the authorities on behalf of the poorer segments of the populace: markets should be controlled and supervised to protect ordinary consumers: they should conduct sales at stated times and employ accurate weights and measures; the poor should have the opportunity to buy grain, flour, or meal in small parcels without hindrance; and dealers should be hedged around with restrictions against malpractice and profiteering. The authorities should also ideally provide consumer protection; millers and bakers should be considered servants of the community, working not for gross profit but for a fair allowance. The market practices of laissez-faire capitalism were resisted by the poor with decreasing success. The paternalist norms provided exasperated crowds with legitimation for their food riots, although direct action itself through rioting and confiscation or destruction of property in an effort to restore fair practices was not sanctioned by the paternalist authorities themselves.

THE MORAL ECONOMY PERSPECTIVE
AND THE SUBALTERN HISTORIANS

The moral economy perspective had its first interesting, and, in the eyes of many readers, persuasive Asian application in James Scott's *The Moral Economy of the Peasant* (1976),[8] in which he interpreted certain peasant rebellions in Burma and Indo-China in twentieth-century colonial times as motivated by peasant grievances against breaches of traditional understandings in landlord-tenant relations, especially with regard to the guarantee of subsistence security in times of poor harvests and uncertain prices. The erosion of these norms in an expanding market economy with monetized rents, which were not adjusted to cushion poor seasons, and inflationary prices fueled peasant insurrections such as the Saya San rebellion in Burma.

With regard to India, the moral economy interpretation has been invoked as a guiding principle in the reconstruction of Indian colonial history by some historians of the subaltern school. A case in point is Gyanendra Pandey's treatment of the peasant revolt and riots in Awadh, North India, in January 1921.[9] Pandey writes:

> The idea of a just, or moral, struggle appears to have been fundamental to the peasants' acceptance of the necessity of revolt. Exploitation as such was not unjust. It was inevitable that some ruled and some conducted prayers and some owned the land and some labored and all lived off the fruits of that labor. But it was important that everyone in the society made a living out of the resources that were available. . . . It was . . . when the landlord decided to levy new and oppressive imposts in a period of considerable hardship for substantial sections of the peasantry that resistance was taken up in Awadh as morally right and necessary.[10]

The peasant rebellion in Awadh studied by Pandey diverges from the pattern of most of the short-lived South Asian ethnic riots sketched in Part I of this book, in that it lasted some three years, from 1919 to 1922. Pandey's essay is thus more comparable with the discussion in chapter 9 above of Hindu nationalism and the Ayodhya dispute, a series of campaigns and contests that have occurred over a number of years and are still continuing.

Pandey's account is structured in terms of three phases. The first lasted until about the end of 1920, when the peasants were forming associations and in the main making protests against the excessive exactions of the landlords. The second was a militant phase from January 1921 onwards, when peasants rioted against and attacked landlords and merchants and their agents and properties, there were engagements between peasants and the police, and trials of the offenders were subsequently held by *panchayats* (village or local councils). The last phase erupted after a brief period of quiescence, toward the end of November 1921, in the form of the Eka (unity) campaign. This consisted of many Eka meetings, attracting hundreds of people and lasting a few days. The whole peasant movement, however, soon went under, being unable further to resist the police. A reason suggested for this outcome is that Indian National Congress politicians on the whole failed to support the movement, thereby preventing it from becoming more general and widespread. This in turn may also have contributed to the peasant movement's inability to sustain itself against the government's security forces.

Although he does not explicitly postulate a system of moral economy norms applicable to the society of Awadh at large, of which the rural population was a part, as Thompson does for England, or that orientated landlord-tenant relations, minimizing the risks of going under and of starvation for the peasants, as Scott does for Burma, Pandey convincingly demonstrates that the "inferior right holders" in land and tenant peasantry and laborers, already subject in the late nineteenth century to heavy taxations and exactions, suffered even more excessive, illegal, and "unjust" exactions and expulsions at the hands of their landlords in the years of depression and inflation following World War I. The peasants of Awadh, by this persuasive account, were justified in their revolt, for they had genuine grievances.

And when the peasants, organized as collectivities, were moved to militant action in 1920–21, they assembled in large numbers and "rioted" in unison in many parts of Awadh. For example, in the Rae Bareli, Faizabad, and Sultanpur districts, peasant violence took the forms of "the looting of bazaars, attacks on landlords, and battles with the police." There were several instances of attacks on landlords' property:

> In Rae Bareli large bands appeared in several estates, destroying the taluqdars' crops and looting and destroying storage places. "From 5 January for some days the district was in a state of anarchy.". . . In Faizabad the terminal weeks of 1920 and the early days of 1921 brought isolated attacks on the servants of taluqdars, and the looting and the burning of their straw. Then following a meeting on 12 January 1921 which led to an attack and the looting of Zamindars of Dankara, widespread rioting broke out in the district. Bands of

500–1000 men, women and children marched from place to place for the next two days, settling scores with their enemies.[11]

In the forefront of the riots, Pandey says, were "the lower castes and landless labourers" and members of " 'criminal' tribes," lower-caste Ahirs, Bhars, Lunias, and the untouchable Pasis and Chamars, "the castes that provided the majority of the small tenants and agricultural labourers."

It is noteworthy that after the initial attacks on the landlords, their agents and servants, and the houses and properties of "high-caste villagers," the actions of the rioters after December 1920 were "extended to the bazaars and other points where wealth was concentrated. The chief targets were the *banias* (merchants) who had exploited the difficult times to make large profits, but *sunars* (goldsmiths), weavers, and others who were thought to have profited from the situation were also attacked in some places. The houses of upper caste and prosperous villagers were attacked, and quantities of clothes, jewels and so on burnt and destroyed."[12]

Pandey is unequivocal about the purposiveness and motivation of the riots: the peasants organized for action in peasant associations; they were motivated by just grievances and inspired by consciousness of their condition; they mobilized effectively to hold meetings and protests; they pledged to resist oppression by landlords.

Although Pandey does interestingly, if all too briefly, refer to the energizing role of rumors (about the alleged multiple simultaneous appearances of the national charismatic Gandhi and the local charismatic Ramachandra in many places) and the mystical potency of slogans such as "Sita-Ram" for the mobilization of crowds, when the people were moved to riot, he does not entertain any possibility of crowds qua crowds under heightened circumstances engaging in collective violence—arson, looting, plunder—that may require probing beyond the normative limits of a moral economy paradigm. Indeed, at one point, he dismisses another contemporary historian's view thus: "[M. H.] Siddiqi seems to accept the contemporary officials' view that the peasants were 'indiscriminate' in their attacks, and describes the local Sabhas as becoming 'totally anarchic' at the level of action. Yet the weight of the evidence points to a quite different conclusion."[13]

In my view, Pandey's demonstration of the grievances behind the peasant revolt in Awadh, and of the peasants' capacity to organize politically in their own right (without the ambiguous and equivocal help of the national Congress politicians) and their transition to militant action, is illuminating and persuasive. It certainly reinforces Ranajit Guha's charge about "the myth, retailed so often by careless and impressionistic writing on the subject of peasant insurrections being purely spontaneous and unpremeditated affairs."[14] The jacqueries in the Allahabad and Ghazipur districts during the Sepoy Rebellion of 1857–58 and revolts such as those launched by the Kol (1832) and the Santal and the Munda (1899–1900), Guha says, "had all been inaugurated by planned and in some cases protracted consultation among the representatives of the local peasant masses. . . . They had far too much at stake and would not launch into it except as a deliberate, even if desperate, way out of an intolerable condition of existence. Insurgency, in other words, was a motivated and conscious undertaking on the part of the rural masses."[15] In much of the earlier historiography, he asserts, however, "insurgency is regarded as *external* to the peasants' consciousness."[16]

While accepting without demur a high content of purposiveness and planned action in the peasant revolt in Awadh, as demonstrated by Pandey, I think there is still some space left for asking how exhaustive that framework is (1) for dealing with the question of the representativeness of the peasant rebels with regard to the stratum they belonged to—that is, the issue of internal differentiation and conflict of interests among the varied peasantry itself, and (2) for fully accounting for the shape and intensity of the violent acts enacted by the peasant crowds themselves.

The first issue has been addressed by C. A. Bayly in his assessment of "the subaltern project." With regard to the relative propensity of peasants to violent protest, a theme that runs throughout the volumes of *Subaltern Studies,* Bayly remarks:

> Even at the height of these spectacular disturbances only a minority of villagers were involved in prolonged violent disturbance. . . . Again, at the height of the Depression and no-rent movements in 1931 a remarkably high proportion of peasants still paid up. It is not at all clear that resistance, let alone violence, is a defining characteristic of the poor or exploited. This may be an unfortunate fact, but it is not one that historians can ignore.
>
> What emerges from this is that a critical analysis of rural movements (and for that matter, working class movements) will be flawed if it fails to take into account the sectionalism of workers and peasants. The investment of the Congress in defence of the social status quo was paralleled by the concern of high and middle peasant groups for property, status and dominance, however poverty stricken they were in reality. . . . Down almost to the very bottom of society every subaltern was an elite to someone lower than him . . . , the rhetorical devices of "subaltern" and "peasant resistance" often impede [the subaltern historians] in this more subtle analysis.[17]

Bayly suggests that "the rural movement fell apart under the weight of its own internal conflicts and that propertied elements within the peasantry as much as the small landed class took a hand in suppressing the movement."[18]

The second issue arises out of the instances of ethnic riots represented in this book, all except one of which have occurred in postcolonial times. Two interrelated comments are in order. While there is considerable evidence for the purposiveness and directedness of the riots once they got under way, I have also tried to suggest that the communicational and interpersonal processes recursively and cumulatively at work in crowd situations may generate heightened violence that goes beyond premeditation and purposive political action. Moreover, the riots we have studied are not simply a monolithic contest between the "state" or "government" and the "people." There are many scenarios. Sometimes, as in Colombo in 1983 and Delhi in 1984, some government representatives and resources were clearly for a while involved in the production and direction of the riots. All too often it is a majority ethnonationalist community—as in the case of the aforementioned Colombo and Delhi riots, and in the case of the string of urban riots after the demolition of the Babri mosque in 1992, of which Bombay was the exemplary worst instance—that launches violence against a minority and is aided and given space to do so by the agents of law and order of the city or state, particularly the police. Sometimes as in the Pathan-Bihari riots in Karachi, a section of the civilian populace engages with another section, and the security forces of the state may have to intervene (it may be hoped as a neutral arm) to stop the violence. These are not necessarily separate scenarios—they could variably combine in ethnonationalist conflicts. Finally, we should not forget that sections of the civilian populace may collide, both with the aid of state agents whose loyalties are divided and against the representatives of the state taking part in the conflict. These are complexities that no contemporary witness of ethnic conflicts can forget or mute. There is no monolithic archenemy called "colonialism" available to be excoriated; and one cannot romanticize contemporary South Asian ethnic riots as pure "resistance" and the attendant acts of arson, homicide, and injury as commensurate with a "conscious undertaking" on the part of the rioters.

A SUBALTERN HISTORIAN LOOKS AT INDIA'S CONTEMPORARY SECTARIAN STRIFE

Gyanendra Pandey himself has recently written a study of Hindu-Muslim riots in India, showing how a subaltern historian constructs his own narrative about, and represents as well as evaluates, acts of collective violence enacted in India's contemporary sectarian and ethnic strife.[19]

Consonant with a postmodern stance, Pandey is critical of any attempt to write a grand and totalizing, even objective, history of sectarian strife. A discourse in "search for omniscience" is out of place. He also associates such attempts with a particular historiographic perspective, the view from the center, which is also the view of an elite sectional interest. This view accords "the rhetoric of nationalism a central place, and interprets nation state making as the mainstream historical process," and therefore treats all opposition to the nation-state as antinational, "whether this opposition has been located in the industrial working class, among the rural poor, or in other regional and local movements." This narrow nationalist perspective "is bolstered not only by reference to current world trends in the economic and political practice of states . . . but also by a 'modern' and avowedly secular nationalist historiography that has reinforced notions of natural Indian unity and an Indian national essence."[20]

Pandey, in riposte to this historiography elevating the nation-state, advocates his own reading "in defence of the fragments." The word *fragments* is rhetorically deployed in several ways. On the one hand, it refers to "the fragments of Indian society—the smaller religious and caste communities, tribal sections, industrialist workers, activist women's groups, all of which might be said to represent minority 'cultures and practices' that are expected to fall in line with the 'mainstream' national culture (Brahmanical Hindu, consumerist, and sectional)." *Fragments* "also designates the hazardous variety of the evidence a historian of modern strife has to deal with" and "the difficulties of evidence gathering and representation encountered," which point to "the folly of using accounts of, say fifty or a hundred years ago as if they were somehow 'transparent,' and capable by balanced setting off against one another, by appropriate additions and subtractions, to give an adequate reconstruction of history."

While nationalist Indian history finds its primary source in official archives (government records, court records), Pandey urges historians to use another kind of "fragment"—a weaver's diary, a collection of poems by an unknown poet, and those literatures that Macaulay condemned: creation myths and women's songs, family genealogies and local traditions of history. (One forgives him for failing to say that this is the stuff out of which social and cultural anthropologists of South Asia have constructed their monographs for decades.) These fragments might well, and do, challenge the state's construction of history and mark "those contested spaces through which particular unities are sought to be constituted and others broken up."[21]

Now, as a sympathetic reader of Pandey's essay, I see him positioning himself in this way to advance his own " 'fragmentary' point of view," which foregrounds the deeply contested nature of the territory of Indian nationalism and resists "the drive for a shallow homogenization and struggles for older, potentially richer definitions of the 'nation' and the future political community."[22]

Pandey decries the discourse that has represented sectarian strife in India, labeled "communalism," as a secondary story to the nationalist discourse, and has reduced Hindu-Muslim strife to a minor element in the main drama of India's struggle for independence from colonial rule. "Partition was, for the majority of people living in what are now the divided territories of northern India, Pakistan, and Bangladesh, *the* event of the twentieth century—equivalent in terms of trauma and consequence to the First World War (the "Great War") for Britain or the Second World War for France and Japan," Pandey asserts.[23] A few exceptions aside, most Indian intellectuals, Pandey complains, "have tended to celebrate the story of the Independence struggle rather than dwell on the agonies of Partition."[24] Differences and strife between Hindus and Muslims persist in India today, Pandey points out, and, while there are reasons for wanting to suppress or to evade representing this state of affairs, investigators and writers should deal with the Muslim-Hindu polarizing stereotypes that are generated by it, and also deal with the issue of violence itself, not push it aside as an aberration or an extraordinary phenomenon, or in the opposite direction as a "known" matter. (Having myself devoted much time recently to studying collective violence as a critical inquiry, I cannot but feel gratified by this view.)

Pandey's own characterization of Hindu-Muslim sectarian strife and violence is partly based on, and was triggered by, his visit, as a member of a ten-member team sent under the aegis of the People's Union of Democratic Rights (PUDR), Delhi, to investigate the Hindu-Muslim riots that took place in Bhagalpur in October–November 1989. Before sketching his impressions, Pandey signals the problems with collecting factual "evidence," dealing with informants' partial and tendentious reports, including their "preemptive narratives" and "ritualized accounts," and the willful destruction or erasure of both "official" and unofficial evidence—in short, the problem of using "fragments" of information in writing a history. Hence his defensive opening statement, "This is not a paper," and his play on the multiple meanings of *fragments*. But carefully read, Pandey's essay, despite its disavowals and equivocations, and agonizings over difficulties, does at crucial points make unqualified general observations and judgments on the shape and contours of contemporary sectarian strife:

It has become commonplace in India now to describe one instance of strife after another as "perhaps the worst since 1947"; such has been the magnitude and brutality of sectarian violence in the 1980s. In any event, Bhagalpur was indeed one of the most devastating examples of Hindu-Muslim strife in the country since Partition. This round of violence began in the last week of October 1989; arson, looting, and murder spread from the city to the surrounding countryside and raged practically unchecked for several days. The situation was then brought under some sort of control by military and paramilitary forces, but an atmosphere of fear and terror remained for months afterwards.

Given the scale of the "riots," and the infamous role of the local administration in encouraging the attacks and suppressing evidence, it is impossible to establish the "facts" of this occurrence—what traditional historians like to call the "nuts and bolts" of the story. Possibly as many as a thousand people were killed in the course of the violence, most of them Muslims, but estimates of the casualties still vary enormously. During the first days of the "riots," trains were stopped repeatedly at different places in Bhagalpur and its neighboring districts; from several of these, Muslim travelers were dragged out and lynched. No one can say for certain how many were killed in this way—not even disturbed Hindu travelers who happened to be caught on one of these trains and saw people being pulled from their particular carriage. In the major attacks, in the rural areas as well as in the city, neither old people nor infants, neither women nor children, were spared. There is widespread feeling that women were abducted and raped on a large scale, but none of the surviving victims will talk about rape; the five specific cases recorded by the PUDR team that conducted investigations in Bhagalpur in January 1990 were incidents that Muslim women informants had themselves heard about.

What is beyond question is that the extent and ferocity of the attacks were unprecedented, even for a district that has seen much sectarian strife before, including "riots" in 1946. At the worst stage of the violence in October–November 1989, some 40,000 people were forced to leave their homes and live in makeshift relief camps. Destruction and looting of property occurred on a massive scale for several weeks. The fears generated among the heavily outnumbered Muslims were such that a great many were unwilling to return to their homes even three months after the initial outbreak of violence; an estimated 10,000 were still in "relief camps" toward the end of January 1990, apart from those who had moved in with relatives or friends in "safer" places in or outside Bhagalpur district. At this time many Muslims were pressing for the permanent retention of military or paramilitary forces in the vicinity of their villages or wards (*mohallas*) as the only trustworthy means for their protection, and some were demanding that they be given arms by the government for the same purpose. The air was still thick with rumors, and isolated attacks and looting continued to occur; one such incident was reported as late as March 1990.[25]

These statements, strong reminders of many features I have already sketched and discussed in regard to my case studies in Part I, unequivocally convey one message: that contemporary ethnic conflicts can scarcely unproblematically be represented in terms of "subaltern resistance" and "justifiable premeditation." In fact, Pandey ventures the judgment that contemporary ethnic conflict and collective violence have intensified in scale and taken forms little known in the past:

> Sectarian violence in the 1980s appears to have taken on new and increasingly horrifying forms. Recent strife between people belonging to different religious denominations has not been restricted to pitched battles on the streets or cloak-and-dagger attacks and murders in side lanes, which were the chief markers of earlier riots. The worst instances of recent violence—Bhagalpur, 1989; Meerut, 1987; the anti-Sikh "riots" in Delhi in 1984; the anti-Tamil "riots" in Colombo in 1983; the Hindu-Muslim "riots" in Moradabad in 1980; and others—have amounted to pogroms, organized massacres in which large crowds of hundreds, thousands, and even, in places, tens of thousands have attacked the houses and property and lives of small, isolated, and previously identified members of the "other" community.[26]

The "excesses" of Hindu nationalism generated in the modern political context are set out with a fierce moral outrage and a sense of "evil" unleashed:

> Many observers have pointed to the new heights reached by Hindu militancy and propaganda over the last few years. This has been orchestrated most visibly by the VHP, and it plainly had much to do with the increased frequency and scale of Hindu-Muslim strife in the 1980s. The point that is perhaps not sufficiently stressed, however, is that the violent slogans and demands of organizations like the VHP, and the "riots" they have sparked, do not poison the minds of "the people" only for a moment. On the contrary—given our history, the resources available to "secular" and "communal" forces in the country, the opportunism of most of our major political parties, and the continued and repeated outbreak of sectarian violence—the most outrageous suggestions about the "evil," "dangerous," "threatening" character of the "other" community (or communities) come to be widely accepted and part of a popular dogma.
>
> Nothing but this acceptance can explain the kinds of atrocities perpetrated in recent instances of sectarian strife: the call to leave not a single Muslim man, woman, or child alive, which was acted upon in several places in Bhagalpur; the massacre of all eighteen Muslim passengers traveling in a tempo-taxi along with the Hindu taxi driver, when they were stopped on a major country road two-and-a-half weeks after the cessation of general

"rioting," and their burial in a field which was then planted over with garlic; the chopping off of the breasts of women; the spearing of infants and children, the spears with the victims impaled on them being then twirled around in the air to the accompaniment of laughter and shouts of triumph.[27]

THE MORAL ECONOMY ARGUMENT
AND MODERN SOUTH ASIAN ETHNIC VIOLENCE

Can the modern South Asian ethnic conflicts and riots that I have been describing be defended and legitimated as popular expressions of a moral economy grounded in a broad consensus spelled out by the authority of the nation-state and generally accepted by its citizens? Can the sort of argument E. P. Thompson provided for the eighteenth-century grain riots in England and that Pandey has advanced for the Awadh peasant revolt of the early 1920s also be sustained here?

The short answer is, no. Modern South Asian ethnic conflicts take place in an environment that lacks a crystallized and coherent nation-state ideology and a body of political norms and practices deriving from it that is acceptable to and shared by all (or the majority of) the components and members of the body politic. That there is a crisis of the nation-state in South Asia today is patently clear. True, the contending parties appeal to norms, traditions, and values that in their eyes grant legitimacy to their causes. But they are particularistic claims and divide the proponents into protagonists and antagonists in an arena that lacks a consensual unitary "moral political economy" that is an organic growth deriving from historical developments in late colonial and in postindependence times and claims the allegiance of all peoples in the country.

The concept of moral economy is only applicable to a situation where the contending parties refer and defer to a shared discourse of values and practices, although each party may try to interpret and apply those values to its advantage. It cannot apply to a situation where the rivals appeal to different norms and make mutually exclusive claims.

The English food riots, although not directly condoned by the state, derived their moral sense and justification from expectations of a fair division of labor in society and how its parts contributed and should contribute to the common wealth. The ethnic turmoils of our time derive from exclusive claims to resources and rewards by the component groups in plural societies; they revolve around "majoritarian democracy" and the rights of "minorities" and employ inflammatory and divisive labels and slogans such as "national identity," "mother tongue," "restoration of historical claims," "discrimination," "unfair domination," "affirmative action," "equality of citizenship," "the protection of civil rights," "traditional homelands," "majority rule," "minority rights," "self-determination", "ethnic cleansing," and "genocide." The violence that has occurred and the brutalities that have been practiced are intolerable by the standards of the International Bill of Human Rights, which all member states of the United Nations are urged to accept. Such violence is up to a point "purposive," "ritualized," and "repetitive," draws its shape from a repertory of practices widespread in the society at large, and can be recursively related to the sectional claims, identities, interests, and politics of the segments and communities and individuals that make up the society at large. It is therefore not merely an aberration, or an uncharacteristic phase of "irrationality," but has increasingly become a regularized mode of enacting mass politics and a central experience in the defining self-perception of collectivities and their expectations of social intercourse.

There might still be a case for hopefully asserting that pluralism and multiculturalism (and not a hegemonic national culture sponsored by the population segments that control the nation-state) are the true "moral economy" of countries such as India. It is possible to affirm that there are many precedents for coexistence, exchanges, reciprocities, and tolerance between religious, ethnic, and regional groups and collectivities in South Asia, although ethnonationalist movements such as the BJP, VHP, and RSS in India, Dravidian (and Tamil) ethnonationalism in South India, the Jama'at-i-Islami in Pakistan, and Sinhala Buddhist nationalism and the Tamil martial nationalism propagated by the LTTE in Sri Lanka are trenchantly nonaccommodative and urge exclusivist boundaries and loyalties and inferiorizing encompassment of minorities.

HUMAN RIGHTS AGAINST OPPRESSION

The concept of "human rights" may be understood as the set of rights articulated in the Universal Declaration of Human Rights, a statement of principles proclaimed by the United Nations in 1948, and in related international treaties. These treaties include the two international human rights covenants that the United Nations adopted in 1966 and that give legal form to the Universal Declaration. The Covenant of Civil and Political Rights guarantees rights such as freedom of thought and expression, freedom from arbitrary arrest and torture, and freedom of movement and peaceful assembly. The Covenant on Economic, Social and Cultural Rights provides for rights such as the right to work and receive fair wages, to protection of the family, to adequate standards of living, and to education and health care.

> Together, the Universal Declaration and the international Covenants with the Optional Protocols are known as "The International Bill of Rights." Numerous subsequent treaties elaborate aspects of this Bill of Rights, including covenants on: Prevention and Punishment of Genocide (adopted in 1948), Elimination of Racial Discrimination (1965), Elimination of Discrimination Against Women (1979), the Status of Refugees (1951) and Protocol on Refugees (1966), Rights of Children (1989), Elimination of Discrimination Based on Religion or Belief (1981), [and the] Draft Declaration on the Rights of Indigenous Peoples (1993) which awaits submission to the UN Commission on Human Rights.[28]

It is clear that the International Bill of Human Rights, taken to include all of the above, enumerates many principles and rights that have been violated, ignored, or compromised in current ethnonationalist conflicts all over the world, including those that have occurred and are taking place in South Asia.

It is only nations that have ratified the UN covenants and other human rights treaties that are legally bound to observe treaty provisions, and it is the responsibility of the international community to hold governments accountable for their treaty obligations. Not all the members of the United Nations have ratified the Bill of Rights, and the grounds on which they have refused to do so are instructive to consider.

Those nations that have ratified the covenants and treaties have conformed with their obligations to varying degrees. One criticism leveled at the Western nations who represent themselves as the primary sources and backers of the concept of universal human rights, including the United States, is that they have not observed or implemented the norms themselves, especially in relation to women, minorities and foreign migrants, "indigenous peoples," the poor, and the "underclass." The Western "gate keepers" are also criticized for applying the norms to other nations based on which are their allies and which their enemies, which favorable to their interests and which not. This accusation is irrefutable.

But it must be admitted that the most glaring failures in protecting basic rights by countries that have ratified the Bill of Human Rights are found outside Western Europe and North America. In this category must be included the countries of South Asia that are the focus of this book. Amnesty International, Human Rights Watch, and various other NGO's have published findings on state-inflicted abuses, including incarceration without trial, homicide, torture, and displacement of people in India, Pakistan, Sri

Lanka, Bangladesh, and Nepal. Reports by government-appointed commissions, private civilian commissions, NGO's, and a host of civilian sources attest to violence and human rights abuses by citizens against citizens (with or without the participation of the security forces and police) during and after elections, and during riots, rebellions, protests, and strikes.

Violations of the rights of women and children in South Asia are plentiful. India has been the scene of highly publicized "dowry burnings" of newly married women whose parents allegedly failed to provide adequate dowries to the bridegroom's side. Also much debated are the rights and wrongs of *sati* (immolation of widows); of allowing Muslims to continue to observe their "personal laws," which include the unilateral privilege of husbands to divorce their wives and avoid making adequate maintenance payments; and of the practices of female infanticide, child labor, child marriage, sale of children, and so on. A vexed question in India today is the question of devising a single uniform civil code for all of India's citizens despite their multicultural and plural religious affiliations.

In Pakistan, major human rights issues revolve around religious "orthodoxy" and tolerance of sectarian differences within Islam; implementing punishments allegedly authorized by the Qur'an and shari'ah that seem extreme by United Nations standards; and circumscribing the freedom of women with respect to public employment, forms of dress, movement outside the home, and so on.

Sri Lanka's infringements of human rights in regard to the conduct of democratic elections, the state's use of violence and armed force to suppress insurgencies mounted by elements of the Tamil minority and by the Sinhala youth (JVP), and the similar abuses and violations by both Tamil and Sinhalese insurgents, and by civilians who launch "riots" against minorities, have been quite well documented and are public knowledge.

Violence as a mode of conducting politics is a fact of life in South Asia. The legitimacy of the employment of violence by states and civilian groups and the right of civilian groups and citizens to be protected against that violence are two sides of the same coin. All the South Asian states named here are signatories of the International Bill of Rights. Their official recognition of these rights thus coexists with their infringement of them, official denial of deviations, and testy remarks about undue interference with their national sovereignty if the subject is mentioned.

Some nations have refrained from ratifying (in full or part) the International Bill of Rights—China is a major instance of refusal—because such an instrument contravenes "national sovereignty," or, after having signed on paper, continue to have reservations about the provenance and validity of the rights in question. It is asserted that the Universal Declaration of Human Rights (1948) and the subsequent elaborations, while claiming to be of universal significance and application, are really products of post-Enlightenment Western perspectives, value orientations, cultural preferences, and historical experiences, and that dressing them up and presenting them as of universal validity violates the experiences, insights, and valuations of non-Western cultural traditions and norms. It is also held that these Western human rights charters are imperialist and hegemonic. There is a widespread perception that the present normative notion of universal human rights is in tension with the moral and cultural diversity in the world. We are thus faced with the apparent incompatibility of the two conceptions: the *universality of human rights,* on the one hand, and the *relativity in human rights,* on the other.

Notwithstanding significant contributions by non-Western countries to the formulation of human rights covenants and treaties in the nearly fifty years since the Universal Declaration was adopted, and plausible claims by some interpreters of non-Western systems of thought that strands of their traditions independently parallel post-Enlightenment Western perspectives, it is undeniable that the package is primarily based on Western ideals.

However, pressures to allow culture-based deviations from international human rights norms have grown. "These pressures recently culminated, for example, in efforts by many Asian and Muslim states at the 1993 World Conference on Human Rights in Vienna to challenge the universality of human rights principles as they are currently set out in international law and to seek modification of these principles on the grounds that they are too ethnocentrically Western."[29] The final conference declaration appears to paper over the discussions voiced during the proceedings; it ambiguously proclaims that while human rights are universal in nature, regional differences, as well as historical, cultural, and religious backgrounds, should be taken into account. To quote two key resolutions in illustration:

> The World Conference on Human Rights reaffirms the solemn commitment of all States to fulfil their obligations to promote universal respect for, and observance and protection of, all human rights and fundamental freedoms for all in accordance with the Charter of the United Nations, other instruments relating to human rights, and international law. The universal nature of these rights and freedoms is beyond question.
>
> All human rights are universal, indivisible and interdependent and interrelated. The international community must treat humans globally in a fair and equal manner, on the same footing, and with the same emphasis. While the significance of national and regional particularities and various historical, cultural and religious backgrounds must be borne in mind, it is the

duty of States, regardless of their political, economic and cultural systems, to promote and protect all human rights and fundamental freedoms.[30]

It is not my intention to evaluate human rights from the perspective of universalism versus relativism. A social and cultural anthropologist of my sort will necessarily advocate that a collectivity's cultural practices are historically rooted, that they are interrelated and cannot easily be atomized or fragmented, that their meaningfulness is context-bound and instantiated in action, and that translation from one culture to another requires much care.

Some of the comparativists on both sides, universalists and relativists, have unduly totalized and essentialized cultures and civilizations as unified, monolithic entities. Many commentators, advocates, and activists respond to such "orientalism" by countering that their religious and cultural texts and normative traditions are many-stranded and rich, and are capable of, and invite, flexible interpretations. Of all contemporary civilizations, it is the Islamic ones that have been most subject to this stereotyping, both at the hands of Western orientalizers and at the hands of certain authoritarian state powers, who have tried to impose allegedly "orthodox" repressive regimes in the name of Islam as officially interpreted. But increasingly there have been critical voices from within Islamic societies that resist monolithic judgments of both kinds. Aside from a few clerics and scholars, the most powerful resistance to negative stereotyping and patriarchal authority comes from feminist groups and women's organizations in these societies. There is more actual diversity of opinions among Muslims on human rights issues than is generally supposed, and Muslims who reject the received orthodoxy are not to be dismissed as alienated from their traditions but are deeply embedded in them.

Two general observations hold in any case.

First, the positions of the universalists and the cultural relativists are not mutually exclusive and incompatible. There is some shared space between them, without which their discourses would be incommensurable. There are some human rights set forth in international law that remain uncontested by those who call for the recognition of cultural differences. "These rights include freedom from torture, slavery, genocide, and racial discrimination; the requirements of fair trial; and respect for the dignity of the human person" (that persons, groups, or states that cannot publicly contest these normative priorities may deviate from them in practice is another matter). However, between universalists and relativists, "certain other human rights norms, even if contested, must be presupposed for any legitimate dialogue to take place." The rights in question are the rights to freedom of expression, freedom of the press, freedom of religion, and freedom of association. "To allow the undermining of rights such as these would be to curb, if not eliminate precisely the freedoms that are needed to carry out meaningful dialogue on human rights and to seriously impede the project of more firmly establishing cultural foundations for a global human rights system. Affirming these human rights norms, even while distinguishing uncontested from contested norms, comprises a fundamental floor of moral agreement that permits constructive dialogue to take place."[31]

Second, there are many regimes allegedly committed to "democratic politics" that have nevertheless, in the name of "national sovereignty," the "rightful claims of majority" and "sons of the soil," "national emergency," "the requirements of economic development and growth," "the imperatives of religious orthodoxy," and so on, curbed freedom of the press and freedom of association; practiced religious intolerance (disallowing sectarian differences) and discrimination (preferential policies); imprisoned people, denied them fair trials, and resorted to torture, allegedly to prevent terrorism and "subversion of state"; restricted the dress of women and their rights to work and to travel freely.

But one lesson above all has been taught us moderns: where there is systematic oppression and violence by the state and by ruling groups, dissent, resistance, and counteraction by the victims usually arise in time. The official voices of the state or ruling groups try to deflect attention away from their abuses and to deny the legitimacy of the voices of the oppressed, be they women's groups, minorities, or inferiorized "indigenous peoples," but collective mobilization in the arenas of modern politics is possible, and counteraction is frequently violent.

COPING WITH COLLECTIVE VIOLENCE

It has been demonstrated that democratic politics and ethnonationalist conflicts are related in South Asia, and that violence as a mode of conducting politics has become established, even institutionalized. One might even go so far as to say that ethnonationalist conflicts combined with collective violence are not just isolated volcanic eruptions but are close to becoming systematized social formations. The evidence for the ritualized and routinized forms of conduct that comprise a repertoire of collective violence supports this assertion. In South Asia (and in many other places as well), violence is an integral part of the political process.

The traditional response of first world criminal justice systems to violent crime is not applicable to the kind of collective violence discussed in this book, and especially civilian ethnonationalist riots. In the United States, we are told, the criminal justice system takes the view that violent crimes (physical and mental injury inflicted on victims) "are morally wrong as well as simply harmful, and that those who commit such offenses should be held accountable for their misconduct. In this view, justice demands judgement and punishment for such acts, regardless of the practical effect of punishment on future criminal offending."[32]

It is clear, however, that in South Asian riots of the kind discussed above, violence (in part at least planned and directed) is committed by large "impersonal" crowds and frequently acquiesced in by significant segments of the police force (who collude in the violence or passively watch it). In these circumstances, it is virtually impossible, or made impossible, to arrest offenders or expect offenders to be arrested. If arrests are made, they are simply token acts, and the offenders are soon released. (Usually police and paramilitary punitive action against rioting is directed at the victimized minority rather than the aggressor majority.) The net result is that usually there is no prosecution of rioters in the criminal courts.

Even more significant, parts of the state system itself—in the form of prominent legislators, members of the security forces, and civil servants at both central and provincial/state levels—are directly or indirectly involved in the staging of such riots, in the belief that they are justified by a need to punish "dissenting," "disloyal" minorities and to eliminate imagined disparities between an "endangered" majority and a "privileged" minority. This is the logic of leveling crowds engaged in affirmative action on behalf of a majority that feels, or is made to feel, beleaguered.

In the criminal justice perspective, the institutions of justice, of law and order, and the officials employed by them are considered guardians and enforcers of rules and norms that are considered legitimate for the entire society. This can hardly be the definition of the situation when members of the legislature and administration are themselves involved in the enactment of collective violence for political purposes.

If a criminal justice perspective is inapplicable, the public health system is highly relevant with respect to the consequences of collective violence. The civil administration necessarily has to cope with the damage done during civil disorders. Hospitals and welfare agencies have to deal with the victims of violence who have suffered physical and mental injury, who have been rendered homeless, and have been reduced to the status of refugees and displaced persons. Refugee camps have to be established, relief administered, and compensation for injury provided to widows, care given to orphans, money distributed to enable people to resume their former occupations, and so on. The costs of collective violence—which are immense and sudden—are borne (1) by the official administration of the state and its agencies, which are already financially strained; (2) by citizens who have lost property, houses, businesses, shops, and industries to looting and arson (in most cases in South Asia, comprehensive insurance is not available or feasible); and (3) by nongovernmental organizations (NGOs), UN agencies, and foreign aid.

AN INTERNAL CONTRADICTION

Systematically organized ethnic riots of the kind described involve a massive internal contradiction at the level of the state and the government. On the one hand, one or more branches of government—politicians and political parties, and, more indirectly, some of the agents of law and order—are frequently involved in stirring up and managing such riots. On the other hand, other branches and agencies of government are involved in the work of repairing the damage done, however imperfectly, and in spending government resources on rehabilitation and relief.

A partial, but by no means insignificant, part of the answer to this contradiction is that it is in the nature of democratic politics as presently practiced in South Asia that political parties are oriented first and foremost to winning the votes of constituents by whatever means. Since ethnonationalism has many attractions as an ideology and political program, especially the claims of collective entitlements and privileges for one's own ethnic kind and collectivity, ethnonationalist conflict and violence are unleashed as part of the process of mobilizing support for electoral reasons. But once the damage is done, the civilian administration is faced with the obligation to cope with the rehabilitation of victims and restoration of services and has to spend much money and effort in doing so.

HIDDEN PAYOFFS FOR AGGRESSORS

Payoffs for the aggressors reinforce the purposive nature of collective violence. If the ethnic enemy that is attacked possesses assets or fills occupational and commercial niches that are envied by the aggressors, the displacement of the alleged enemy opens up economic and occupational and social opportunities for the aggressors, and thus space for the victors to occupy. There is one hitch, however. While it is easy enough to fill openings in unskilled and semiskilled work and lower levels of clerical work, it is much less so where skilled, professional, entrepreneurial, and business management qualifications and experience are required. This circumstance has sometimes aided variable numbers of the displaced minority to return and refill that space.

Moreover, a vital strategic calculation on the part of those who organize and direct violent actions is that by displacing existing populations from shantytowns and "slums" in urban areas, valuable real estate can be claimed for profitable schemes of urban redevelopment, middle-class housing estates, and manufacturing plants. This calculation has played an important part in the periodic riots in Karachi, in the Delhi riots of 1984, in the riots of December 1992–January 1993 in Bombay and other large Indian cities, and in the Colombo riots of 1983. Thus the euphoric and rousing identity claims of ethnonationalism and sons-of-the-soil populism are buttressed by pragmatic financial calculations.

There may also be another sinister calculation behind purposively staged pogroms and ethnic cleansing. In the abovementioned Delhi and Bombay riots, the majority of targeted victims were male adults and youths, whose deaths or injury most definitely resulted in the main income earners and heads of the households of the victimized community being eliminated, leaving the old, widows, and children to cope with their reduced circumstances. The demographic reduction of the most productive age cohorts of the ethnic enemy is an intentional strategy. Whereas in India and Sri Lanka, the rape of women and their impregnation—rape as a strategy of war—and the killing of women and children have not been major objectives (although they have occurred), such acts have been prominent in ethnonationalist conflict in the former Yugoslavia.

CAN WE PREDICT?

Is it possible to predict which individuals in an urban population are likely to participate in collective street violence? Is it possible to identify potential offenders so as to take preventive and protective action?

As noted earlier, a major limitation that an investigator of collective violence faces is that since individual rioters are rarely apprehended or easily available for questioning about their biographical particulars, it is virtually impossible to make predictions of future participation in riots on an individual basis. (It can be difficult to predict, in large numbers, who in a locality, individually identified, will participate, although intensive fieldwork in a locality may reveal to the investigator certain habitual "thugs" and "gang leaders" who are available for the work of violence and are known to have participated before.) However, a social scientist might reasonably predict on a probabilistic basis which segments of an urban population categorized by class, occupation, residential location, or political party affiliation might be expected to participate in violent politics at a particular time.

Although unable accurately to predict the date and time when a riot might occur months or even many days ahead, an investigator may certainly recognize the signs of a buildup that may eventuate in riots, such as the timing of and dates set for elections and competitive festivals; the inflammable issues that are being aired at public meetings and in street talk; and the increased rate of circulation of proliferating rumors in public places, markets, and places of worship. While one may concoct a causal account on the basis of ex post analysis, ex ante prediction on the basis of incomplete information, contingency of events, and uncertainty of developments has all the limitations of speculation. This problem is not new to the social sciences.

PREVENTATIVE ACTION: A RECOMMENDATION

Certain steps might be taken to deter and head off motivated collective violence in future. Wherever there is evidence that the central government or local government agencies are implicated, those agencies must be held responsible. The police should be multiethnic in composition and should be required to take a strong public stand against violence; prior knowledge on the part of the public that the police will not tolerate rioting is a strong deterrent. When it is suspected that violence might erupt because of certain well-known "triggering" events, the police must anticipate and make their purposive presence felt in the streets. A strong showing of police is necessary at the most frequent sites of violence: bazaars and business centers, bus depots, railway stations, and locations where a vulnerable minority is concentrated.

The importance of these suggestions is underscored by the fact that no subsequent riots have occurred in Colombo since the riots of 1983, despite a succession of assassinations and bombings. A primary deterrent has been the firm stance taken by the governments of presidents Jayewardene, Premadasa, and Chandrika Kumaratunga that there shall be no repetition in the capital of the events of 1983. The police and the army, it is thought, are firm in this resolve, although they are culpable of searches, detentions, and harassment of alleged enemies of the state. The absence of riots in Colombo since 1983 suggests that riots are neither inevitable nor can occur as spontaneous eruptions of anger when the government is vigilant and ready to restrain them. Commentators on the recent occurrences of ethnonationalist collective violence in Indian cities have similarly surmised that firm actions signaled and taken by the police and security forces on the lines indicated accounted for the nonoccurrence of riots in certain cities that might have otherwise broken out in violence.

My conclusions about the participation of police in race riots are in agreement with those reached in some previous studies. For example, Allen D. Grimshaw reminds us of a conclusion reached by Richard D. Lambert in his unpublished 1951 study of Hindu-Muslim riots in India, which he also affirms is applicable to his own study of race riots in the United States, such as the East St. Louis riots of 1918, the Chicago riots of 1919, and the Detroit riots of 1943. Lambert found that in the context of broad changes affecting the Indian polity in the period preceding Indian independence, there was a breakdown in the formal system of social controls:

> Policemen came to be regarded, not as neutral arbiters of social disputes operating within a system of legal redress for grievances, but rather as armed representatives of the communities from which they were originally recruited. This interpretation of their role was accepted by members of the rival community, by members of their own community, and increasingly by policemen themselves. When this occurred the usefulness of police in social control was sharply reduced and, in some cases, police activities contributed to further disruption of social organization.
>
> The role played by police forces in urban riots in the United States has not been uniform. In at least a few cases the situation, as defined both by the police and the conflicting racial groups, has been similar to that described above. . . . In other cases, prompt and non-partisan police action has been effective in either preventing the eruption of major interracial disturbances or in confining them and bringing them to a prompt close.[33]

Grimshaw aptly comments that formal police forces tend to retain the ideological orientations of the groups from which they themselves are recruited. One conclusion seems to stand the test of time and place: a highly visible display of force at the command of the police under the direction of a government that insists on uniform evenhanded application of protection and control by the police, and that is ready to call quickly on additional strength to back them when necessary, is usually an effective deterrent to the outbreak of civilian riots. The catch is that it is difficult to ensure these ideal conditions. The above proposal is not by any means a cure for the sporadic occurrence of collective violence closely linked to the competitive politics of organized groups pursuing articulated interests; it is also not an advocacy of authoritarian repression. As the Tillys put it in their account of "the rebellious century, 1830–1930," for the most part, as experienced by France, Germany, and Italy, "collective violence [has been] a by-product of collective action—a by-product, because the violence grows out of the in-

teraction of organized groups, which are carrying on sustained collective actions."[34]

With regard to South Asian ethnonationalist conflicts, it is also more accurate and illuminating to see contemporary violence as a conscious, even organized, mode of conducting mass politics on the part of significant political actors and their agents, rather than as a blind eruption caused by the breakdown of society and polity. The participants, of course, are not fully in control of the processes of collective violence, especially in the form of riots, or of its consequences, and if such violence is sustained and evokes organized counterviolence, it leads to civil war.

CODA: THE POLITICS OF ETHNONATIONALISM

In discussing the politicization of ethnicity in South Asia, I have tried to track the manner in which large numbers of people in the new polities have become, or been made to become, conscious of ethnic identity, and how in turn they have been energized as collectivities to engage in political action. The awareness that collective ethnic identity can be used and manipulated in political action is, of course, related to the increasing possibilities of contact through the improvement of transport, of the quick adoption and deployment of modern media, and of raised levels of education and literacy and the spread of what Benedict Anderson has called "print capitalism."[35] Another explanation lies in the proliferation and popularization of street theaters and public arenas, occasions for collective massing of people, ranging from political rallies and elections and referendums to strikes, demonstrations, sit-ins, and mass protests. These sites and stagings allow for distinctive interpersonal and communicational processes that intensify the propensities to negative stereotyping, distorted rumormongering, and collective violence. All these capabilities for, and features of, large-scale political action have occurred in tandem with population explosions in third world countries and the migration of vast numbers of rural people to metropolitan centers and places where industries or peasant resettlement schemes have been established. Another significant factor is the proliferation of schools, colleges, and universities, which have provided sites, just as factories had done in the history of industrial development, for the production, mobilization, and massing of activists for engaging in political action.

One setting for the politicization of ethnicity is the advent of "modern" states committed to welfare policies in the "developing" third world, which have become crucial and direct arbiters of economic well-being, as well as of political status and the benefits that flow from that. Within democratic governmental systems, there are many occasions, such as elections at municipal, regional, and central levels, for like-minded members to mobilize and make claims on behalf of ethnic groups and successfully win concessions for them.

This instrumental efficacy of ethnicity in making claims on the resources of the modern state inevitably in turn reinforces and maintains ethnic political machinery—patron/client networks, bossism, and patronage structures—through which affirmative action and pork-barrel distributions are dispensed. Of the monies earmarked for social services and welfare, as much or more may end up in the hands of those who dispense them as in those of the intended recipients.

While these considerations apply generally, there is a special chain of circumstances that has led third world democracies in particular to enact their politics on the basis of ethnicity. At the time of decolonization in the Caribbean, in many parts of Africa, and in South and Southeast Asia, the granting of independence and the transfer of power were packaged with constitutions framed in terms of Western concepts of "natural rights" and civil liberties and Western procedures and institutions of representative government. Framed in the secular political language of universal rights and government by representation, such charters conferred on the rural masses and migrants to fast-forming cities a massive dose of rights and the opportunity for involvement in the political process to a degree not previously experienced. Quickly transformed from a "passive" existence into political actors and banks of votes, with the power to elect politicians and parties to power, they discovered that they could even demand or extort rewards, reforms, and privileges from their elected representatives, who for a while constituted the central political authority.

But it became increasingly clear that the alleged secular constitution and institutions of representative government predicated on the individual rights of citizens and the willingness of citizens to form parties on the basis of competitive interests did not generate the expected outcomes. Instead, collectivities, which we may call ethnic groups, have become the political actors, seeking affirmative action for the achievement or restoration of privileges and life chances in the name of ethnic (or racial) equalization. Ethnic equalization, rather than freedom and equality of the individual, is the principal charter of participatory democracy in many of the plural and multiethnic societies of our time. It has been the experience in India, Pakistan, Sri Lanka, and Malaysia that once political demands are made on the basis of ethnic affiliation for the distribution of economic rewards, occupational positions, and educational privileges, the norm of "equality of opportunity" is progressively and irreversibly displaced by the norm of "equality of result."[36] It is commonly the case that affirmative action and quota allocations on the basis of depressed or backward status do not speedily produce results by way of the ladder of equality of opportunity and increased access to schools and educational institutions. Thus, in time, disadvantaged groups push toward equality of results, by fiat if necessary, and for direct redistributive policies in order to equalize income, living conditions, and so forth, on a group basis. But equality of result, or redistributive politics, frequently engenders zero-sum games, in which there are distinct losers and winners. And inevitably these invidious outcomes lead to more open political competition and conflict. Finally, as a result of the revolution in rising expectations, the more successful constituencies are in achieving their political rights to vote, to elect parliaments, and to wield the stick of accountability, the more assiduously they will advocate the provision of social rights—such as the right to a job, adequate health care, unemployment insurance, and so on—as entitlements from the state.

The equalization on a group basis of opportunities and rewards in the expanding universe of redistributive politics may equally be the slogan of majorities or minorities in a plural society. The language of claims is best described as that of ethnic group entitlements on the basis of relative comparison and relative deprivation. The entitlement claims of rewards equalization are contentiously sought through a privileged use of one language, or the additional use of a language so far excluded, or the imposition of special quotas providing privileged access to higher education, job opportunities, land grants, and business entrepreneurship. The "zero-sum" atmosphere of these quintessential entitlement claims reflects a restrictive worldview that has surfaced with vehemence precisely at a time when massive movements of people to urban places and to peasant resettlement schemes have taken and are taking place, and when mass educational and literacy programs are being implemented. Exhortations to a national effort of productive expansion that will increase the opportunities and rewards for all, thus obviating or mitigating the need for ethnic quotas, fall on deaf ears, partly because employment and income levels rise only slowly, and income distribution disparities continue to persist, and because distributive equality on ethnic lines is a politically rousing demand that promises rapid material results. A Weberian might be tempted to say that the postponement of present gratification for the sake of future prosperity and profit, the sterling ethic of capitalism, is less effective than immediate ethnic aggrandizement as the stimulant of the masses.

In countries engaged in postindependence participatory democracy, and in which the electoral process acts as a political marketplace, different scenarios for the cleavages and trajectories of ethnic conflict can be sketched, depending on the ethnic distributions and their relative standing. The relevant factors are how many groups are involved, their demographic proportions, their residential locations, their cultural, legal, and institutional distinctiveness, their levels of economic and educational achievements, and the degree of their participation in common institutional systems and of their common membership in corporate organizations.

For purposes of systematic discussion, the different scenarios and trajectories pertaining to ethnic conflict should be brought within the ambit of an interpretive framework that addresses questions of how ethnic groups in an arena see themselves as acquiring, maintaining, and protecting their claimed-to-be-legitimate group entitlements (1) to capacities and "symbolic capital" such as education and occupation, (2) to material rewards such as incomes and commodities, and sumptuary privileges that enable distinct styles of life, and (3) to "honors" such as titles and offices, markers of ethnic or national pride, and religious and linguistic precedence and esteem. These honors are accorded by the state and/or other authorities that are the principal arbiters of rank. In this version of invidious and comparative "group entitlements," power, prestige, occupations, material goods, aesthetic judgments, manners and morals, and religious convictions come together and naturally implicate one another.[37]

"Religion" is not purely a matter of belief and worship but also has social and political resonances and communitarian associations; "language" is not a mere communicative device but has implications for educational advantage, occupation, cultural identity, literary creation, and historical legitimation of social precedence. Similarly, "territory" has multiple implications that go beyond spatial locations to include charged claims about "homelands" and "sons of the soil." We have to comprehend an arena of politics where, as Donald Horowitz puts it: "Fundamental issues, such as citizenship, electoral systems, designation of official languages and religions, the rights of groups to 'special position' in the polity, rather than merely setting the framework for politics, become the recurrent subjects of politics."[38] The quests for group worth, group honor, group equivalence, and so on are central foci in the politics of ethnicity and critical ingredients in the spirals of intense sentiments and explosive violence that ensue.

I can envisage three overlapping scenarios that, although they are parts of a larger mural, can be presented as posing different issues and different outcomes. They cover a fair range of the major ethnic conflicts that have occurred in recent times.

The picture of a plural society that J. S. Furnivall, among others, sought to characterize is especially applicable to the political economies of countries under British or Dutch colonial rule in West Africa, East Africa, the Caribbean, Indonesia, and so on. In these societies, certain ethnic groups may occupy special economic and social niches as merchants and traders (Lebanese and Syrians in West Africa, Indians in Uganda, Chinese in Malaya and Indonesia, Indians in Fiji), as plantation labor (indentured Indian labor in Guyana and Sri Lanka), or as "bankers" and financiers (Natukottai Chettiars in Burma and Ceylon). Again, especially in colonial capitals, there might be more complex mosaics: certain trades, certain crafts, certain local "banking" and credit activities being the monopoly of both indigenous and foreign communities. The occupation of niches and specialization in certain activities tends to create a segmented labor market and militate against social class solidarities that cut across ethnic lines. Ethnic division of labor stunts working-class action and middle-class associational links.

Such a colonial heritage tends to crystallize expectations of "entitlements" as collective ethnic privileges. The colonial rulers helped to create these political maps when they distributed status honors, according to their calculations as to which groups should be rewarded, protected, or encouraged. But having persisted into the era of independence, these ethnic specializations and expectations have tended to generate ethnic conflicts when strains imperil the maintenance of boundaries. One such strain occurs when the importation of a category of manufactured goods from the industrial West threatens a local craft or makes a local service group redundant and dispensable. A fall in fortunes may threaten the group's access to the basic necessities of everyday life, and it may therefore face famine in a market of plenty and a depression in status in a political climate of expanding "development." But the most severe erosion of niche-equilibrium has come from those governments of new states that have tried to open up what they consider to be the privileged monopolies of ethnic enclaves, which are accused of restrictive practices as regards recruitment and provision of services. The dispossession of Natukottai Chettiars in Rangoon and the expulsions of Indian merchants from Uganda are examples of the new civilian authorities invading what they consider to be rich preserves to enrich themselves and their civilian supporters. Foreign specialized minorities are thus vulnerable to forcible ejection or dispossession by governments promoting the interests of "indigenous" minorities.

The second scenario relates not so much to the declining fortunes of well-placed communities as to the rising expectations and capacities of satellite minorities on the periphery who find themselves under the domination of majorities entrenched at the center and sometimes are in addition faced with the majority advancing into their frontier homelands. In Burma, Thailand, Laos, and northeast India, "hill people" or "hill tribes" are found opposed to "valley people." This bifurcation carries stereotyped other contrasts in agricultural styles (sedentary versus slash-and-burn), in written versus purely oral languages, espousal of Hinduism or Buddhism versus spirit cults (although in fact commonalities exist between segments on both sides). Sometimes these satellite communities have sought advance through the ministrations of Christian missionaries, and in any case, in the new postindependence polities, they have requested "affirmative action" proportionate to their demographic numbers, with regard to their participation in the task of nation-state making and in the education programs of the dominant centers. These satellite ethnic/tribal minorities tend to be potential secessionists, and as Horowitz puts it, "the largest number of secessionists can be characterized as backward groups in backward regions."[39] Examples are the Karens and Shans in northern Burma, Muslims (Moros) in the Philippines, the Nagas and Mizos in India, and the Kurds in Turkey, Iraq, and Iran.

The third scenario represents the kind of ethnic conflict and tensions with which I am especially concerned in this book. I have adapted some concepts coined by M. G. Smith in order to characterize them.[40]

In a situation in which there exist a fair amount of "cultural pluralism" (the diverse populations have distinctive markers of dress, marriage customs, and so on) and "social pluralism" (the ethnic populations have roughly equivalent standings in the polity as a whole, and for some purposes aggregate as corporations and collectivities, such as political parties or religious congregations), political moves may be made by a demographically dominant ethnic population to gain advantages over minority groups and to introduce elements of sociopolitical and even religious discrimination and asymmetry, thereby incorporating the minority groups into the polity on unequal terms. Smith has discussed how processes of "differential incorporation" lead to the outcome of "structural pluralism." Plural societies manifest differential incorporation within the larger polity when certain collectivities within it are subject to sectionally unequal distributions of legal, political, educational, and occupational rights, and are thus reduced to a subordinate status.

> The "second-class citizenship" of a social category identified by common disabilities and disqualifications, whether racial, religious, economic, or other grounds is merely one common mode of differential incorporation. Communal rolls, restrictive property franchises, and similar arrangements also express and maintain the differential incorporation of specific collectivities within a wider society. Such mechanisms are generally developed to enhance the power of the ruling section.[41]

Apartheid in South Africa and Guatemala are extreme and notorious cases of asymmetrical incorporation, but there are also somewhat more benign forms; current examples of majoritarian demands for "affirmative action" based on demographic strength and legitimated by mytho-historical sons-of-the-soil claims include those of the Malays, the Sinhalese in Sri Lanka, and Hindu nationalists in India. These claims lead inevitably to structural asymmetrical pluralism and are inevitably resisted by the minorities.[42]

Such attempts to subordinate previously unranked and equal groups who wield considerable capacities and skills, and to incorporate them unequally into the polity as inferior citizens, invite retaliation and counteractions. Alert to the threats of discrimination and subordination, and in the first instance fighting for inclusion within the polity on equal terms, they may as their situation worsens gradually gravitate toward the politics of devolution, and even secession, as has happened in Sri Lanka and India. Horowitz aptly phrases the options thus: "Unlike ranked groups, which form part of a single society, unranked groups constitute incipient whole societies."[43]

Let me conclude by returning to a general theme that applies to all three of the scenarios I have outlined. The present plethora of ethnic conflicts, whether viewed negatively as divisive and destructive of the state, or positively as a drive toward realistic devolutionary politics, coincides with an increasing sense of shrinking economic horizons and of political embattlement. Many things have gone awry with economic development: the declining terms of trade dictated by the industrialized West; internal bottlenecks; agricultural underemployment and migration to cities; increasing disparities of income distribution; rising unemployment among the expectant participants in the literacy explosion; the visible pauperization of the urban underclass; the feminization of poverty; the entrenchment of bureaucratic interests; the pork barrels of aggrandizing politicians. Thus the plausibility of "dependency theory" pertaining to the impingement of world-capitalist economic relations coincides with disenchantment with the nation-state and "bourgeois democracy" in internal politics, and with charges of "internal colonialism" exercised by dominant majorities over minorities. Such resentments in turn motivate politics compounded of new and powerful mixes, some of them seemingly contradictory and inconsistent. An example is that brand of politics that packages left radicalism or socialist goals, rightist majoritarian racism, and religious fundamentalism in one parcel. The resultant political activism—instanced by strikes, protests, and election rallies—and collective violence—instanced by riots, state terrorism, and guerrilla counteractions—undermines parliamentary democracy and the institutions of law and order on which the civil society of liberal thought rests.

It is obvious that, with regard to the ethnic conflicts under discussion, stark exclusionary dualities—such as stability and continuity versus change and revolution; tradition and its death versus modernity and its birth; primordial sacred realities versus secular modern associational interests—radiate little illumination. Between these options lie the contested middle ground and volatile co-presence of both modalities.

Ethnic conflicts manifest and constitute a dialectic. On the one hand, there is a universalizing and homogenizing trend that is making people in contemporary societies and countries more and more alike (whatever the actual fact of differential access to capacities, commodities, and honors) in wanting the same material and social benefits of modernization, be they income, material goods, housing, literacy and schooling, jobs, recreation, and social prestige. On the other hand, these same people also claim to be different, and not necessarily equal, on the basis of their ascriptive identity, linguistic difference, ethnic membership, and rights to the soil. In this latter incarnation, they claim that these differences, and not those of technical competence or achievement, should be the basis for the distribution of modern benefits and rewards. These compose the particularizing and separating trend among the populations of modern polities.

Moreover, in modern political arenas, the appeal to allegedly ancient origins, achievements, and affiliations, recast and re-presented in "revivalist" or "fundamentalist" dress, enables a mobilization of people on a scale never known or possible before, partly by the use of modern media of communication and propaganda, by the transmission through printed textbooks of tendentious ideas in proliferating schools, and by the promise of benefits and concurrent release of energies, both creative and destructive, at levels never before achieved, for deployment in elections and in mass activities.

These developments are not merely old wine in new bottles, or new wine in old bottles, for there are more potent transformative processes at work by which old categories and definitions of ethnic identity and interests are revalued and given new dimensions and contours. For example, for all their appeals to old labels and historical claims, in their present manifestations, the Sinhalese, the Malays, and the Fijians are collectivities formed in the late colonial and postcolonial epochs. Their ethnic boundaries are porous and flexible. At the same time, we witness the new values of modernization and progress—industrial employment, professional skills, and the practice of Western medicine—being recategorized as entitlements and sumptuary privileges indexed as quotas assignable to preexisting ethnic or racial or indigenous groupings. The time of becoming the same is also the time of claiming to be different. The time of modernizing is also the time of inventing tradition, as well as traditionalizing innovations; of revaluing old categories and recategorizing new values; of bureaucratic benevolence and bureaucratic resort to force; of participatory democracy and dissident civil war. The time is not simply one of order, or disorder, or antiorder: it is compounded of all three. Ubiquitous and violent ethnic conflict is one of the marks of these intense times through which we are living, and which we can see only darkly in the looking glass.

In the late twentieth century, a surprising number of militant and seemingly "irrational" eruptions have occurred. They challenge the confident post-Enlightenment prophecies that the decline of religion was inevitable, or that at best, it could only survive in a demythologized form; that primordial loyalties and sentiments would fade into oblivion as national integration took effect, or be carried away as flotsam by the currents of world historical process. These violent and ubiquitous explosions also challenge and strain our conventional social science explanations of order, disorder, and conflict. However inadequately, we must cope somehow with the phenomenon of destructive violence that accompanies ethnonationalist conflict today.

Notes

1. Nathan Glazer and Daniel P. Moynihan, eds., *Ethnicity: Theory and Experience* (Cambridge, Mass.: Harvard University Press, 1975), p. 5.

2. See, e.g., Walker Connor, "Nation Building or Nation Destroying," *World Politics* 24, no. 3 (1972): 329–55, and "The Politics of Ethnonationalism," *Journal of International Affairs* 27, no. 1 (1973); and Milton J. Esman, ed., *Ethnic Conflict in the Western World* (Ithaca, N.Y.: Cornell University Press, 1977).

3. Some scholars would include the struggles of blacks against discrimination in the United States and in South Africa as falling within the ambit of ethnic conflict.

4. Although 75 percent of the population of the mountainous Nagorno-Karabakh region are ethnic Armenians, it was included in the Soviet Republic of Azerbaijan in 1923. The former USSR is said to have had more than 100 distinct nationalities and ethnic groups, living in 15 republics.

5. The ethnologist Galina Komarova reported at a conference I attended in 1991 that at that time, "there were more than ninety points of ethnic tension" in the former USSR, three times more than in the conflicts prevailing in 1990. Between 725,000 and 1,500,000 persons had been displaced and forced to migrate.

6. The list must now include the genocidal violence in 1994–95 between the Tutsi and Hutu in Rwanda, and the Russian offensive against secessionist Chechnya.

7. There are many listings of ethnic conflict and displacement of people as a worldwide phenomenon—see, e.g., Sven Tägil, *Regions in Upheaval: Ethnic Conflict and Political Mobilization* (Solna, Sweden: Esselte Studium, 1984), and Donald L. Horowitz, *Ethnic Groups in Conflict* (Berkeley: University of California Press, 1985).

8. Under the caption, "Pakistan Arms-Dealers Hail God and the AK-47," the *New York Times*, March 8, 1988, reported that the following wares were on show in an arms store in Darra Adam Khel, an hour's drive south of Peshawar: "In addition to various versions of the Soviet AK-47 rifle, the arms dealer said he supplies [Afghan guerrillas] with ammunition, at nine cents a round, and such weapons as

Chinese and Soviet rocket launchers, pistols from various countries, Soviet, Chinese and American land mines, and machine guns, largely of Soviet manufacture." The smuggling route is a saga in itself: some goods are sent by ship from Europe to Singapore, and from there to the Soviet Union, from whence they are sent by truck to Kabul!

9. *Time*, March 14, 1988.

10. *New York Times*, March 15, 1988.

11. Edward B. Tylor, *Primitive Culture: Researches into the Development of Mythology, Philosophy, Religion, Language, Art and Custom*, vol. 1 (London: John Murray, 1873), p. 26.

12. Benedict R. O'G. Anderson, *Imagined Communities: Reflections on the Origins and Spread of Nationalism* (London: Verso and NLB, 1983), pp. 104–5.

13. Partha Chatterjee, *Nationalist Thought and the Colonial World: A Derivative Discourse* (London: Zed Books for the United Nations University, 1986).

14. Frantz Fanon, *The Wretched of the Earth* (1961; New York: Grove Press, 1963), p. 233.

15. See Jawaharlal Nehru, *An Autobiography* (London: Bodley Head, 1936); *Toward Freedom: The Autobiography of Jawaharlal Nehru* (New York: John Day, 1941); and *The Discovery of India* (New York: John Day, 1946). See, too, Chatterjee, *Nationalist Thought and the Colonial World*, ch. 5, where it is observed that Nehru situated Indian nationalism "within the domain of state ideology" (p. 132).

16. Myron Weiner, *Sons of the Soil: Migration and Ethnic Conflict in India* (Princeton, N.J.: Princeton University Press, 1978), p. 31.

CHAPTER 2. ORIENTATION AND OBJECTIVES

1. Benedict R. O'G. Anderson, *Imagined Communities: Reflections on the Origins and Spread of Nationalism* (London: Verso and NLB, 1983).

2. Donald L. Horowitz, *Ethnic Groups in Conflict* (Berkeley: University of California Press, 1985), p. 187.

3. Gyanendra Pandey, *The Construction of Communalism in Colonial North India* (Delhi: Oxford University Press, 1990).

4. This is illustrated in Gyanendra Pandey, "Rallying round the Cow: Sectarian Strife in the Bhojpuri Region, c. 1888–1917," in *Subaltern Studies II: Writings on South Asian History and Society*, ed. Ranajit Guha, pp. 60–129 (Delhi: Oxford University Press, 1993).

5. Jawaharlal Nehru, *An Autobiography* (London: Bodley Head, 1936), p. 138.

6. Will Kymlicka, *Liberalism, Community and Culture* (Oxford: Oxford University Press, Clarendon Press, 1989; paperback reprint, 1991), p. 1.

7. Pandey, "Rallying."

CHAPTER 3. THE 1915 SINHALA BUDDHIST–MUSLIM RIOTS IN CEYLON

1. It has been suggested that the name "Hambankaraya" derives from *sampankaraya* (boat people).

2. Charles Blackton, "The Action Phase of the 1915 Riots," *Journal of Asian Studies* 29, no. 2 (1970): 236.

3. Ibid., 238

4. For illuminating accounts of Anagarika Dharmapala, see Sarath Amun-ugama, "Anagarika Dharmapala (1864–1933) and the Transformation of Sinhala Buddhist Organization in a Colonial Setting," *Social Science Information* 24, 4 (1985): 697–730; Gananath Obeyesekere, "Personal Identity and Cultural Crisis: The Case of Anagarika Dharmapala of Sri Lanka," in *The Biographical Process,* ed. Frank Reynolds and Donald Capps, pp. 221–52 (The Hague: Mouton, 1979); and Heinz Bechert, *Buddhismus, Staat und Gesellschaft in den Ländern des Theravada Buddhismus,* vol. 1 (Frankfurt and Berlin: Metzner, 1966).

5. Amunugama, "Anagarika Dharmapala," gives this breakdown of the rules for the laity:

1. The manner of eating food. (25 rules)
2. Chewing betel. (6 rules)
3. Wearing clean clothes. (5 rules)
4. How to use the lavatory. (4 rules)
5. How to behave while walking on the road. (10 rules)
6. How to behave in public gatherings. (19 rules)
7. How females should conduct themselves. (30 rules)
8. How children should conduct themselves. (18 rules)
9. How the laity should conduct themselves before the Sangha. (5 rules)
10. How to behave in buses and trains. (8 rules)
11. What village protection societies should do. (8 rules)
12. On going to see sick persons. (2 rules)
13. Funerals. (3 rules)
14. The carter's code. (6 rules)
15. Sinhalese clothes. (6 rules)
16. Sinhalese names. (2 rules)
17. What teachers should do. (2 rules)
18. How servants should behave. (9 rules)
19. How festivals should be conducted. (5 rules)
20. How lay devotees should conduct themselves at temple.

6. Anagarika Dharmapala, "A Message to the Young Men of Ceylon," 1922 Calcutta pamphlet reprinted in *Return to Righteousness: A Collection of Speeches, Essays and Letters of the Late Anagarika Dharmapala,* ed. Ananda Guruge, pp. 501–18 (Colombo: Government Press, 1965).

7. See Richard Gombrich and Gananath Obeyesekere, *Buddhism Transformed: Religious Change in Sri Lanka* (Princeton: Princeton University Press, 1988).

8. Some of the problematic issues have already been raised in H. L. Seneviratne's review of *Buddhism Transformed,* by Gombrich and Obeyesekere, *Journal of Ritual Studies* 4, 2 (Summer 1990), and John Holt's review of the same: "Protestant Buddhism?" *Religious Studies Review* 17, 4 (Oct. 1991): 306–12.

9. On this point, see also Donald K. Swearer, "Fundamentalist Movements in Theravada Buddhism," in *The Fundamentalist Project,* vol. 1: *Fundamentalisms Observed,* ed. Martin E. Marty and Scott Appleby (Chicago: University of Chicago Press, 1991).

10. E. B. Denham, *The Census of Ceylon* (Colombo: Government Press, 1912), p. 232, citing an essay by P. Ramanathan.

11. Ibid., p. 230.

12. Throughout the nineteenth century, the majority of the Sinhalese representatives appointed to the Legislative Council were Protestant Christians of the Goyigama caste elite, such as James Alwis and J. P. Obeyesekere (James Pieris later became the first Karava Christian to be appointed). No Buddhist was elected to the Legislative Council of 1921, in which all the elected Sinhalese members were Protestant or Catholic. Buddhist activists managed to change the pattern for the first time in the elections of 1924, when the majority of Sinhalese elected were Buddhist. At the General Election of 1931, of the 38 Sinhalese returned, 28 were declared Buddhists. See Kingsley M. de Silva, *Managing Ethnic Tensions in Multi-Ethnic Societies: Sri Lanka, 1880–1985* (Lanham, Md.: University Press of America, 1986), pp. 63–68.

13. Kumari Jayawardena, *Ethnic and Class Conflicts in Sri Lanka* (Colombo: Naragama Printers, 1986), pp. 16–17.

14. See *Report of a Commission Appointed by the Governor to Inquire into the Causes Which Led to the Riots at Kotahena*, Sessional Paper No. 4 of 1883 (Colombo: Ceylon Legislative Council, 1883) [hereafter cited as *Report*]; G. P. V. Somaratna, *Kotahena Riot, 1883: Religious Riot in Sri Lanka* (Colombo: Deepanee, 1991), which reprints a comprehensive set of source materials, including the report of the commission; K. H. M. Sumathipala, "The Kotahena Riots and Their Repercussions," *Ceylon Historical Journal* 19 (1969–70): 65–81; and John D. Rogers, *Crime, Justice and Society in Colonial Sri Lanka* (London: Curzon Press, 1987), ch. 5, pp. 167–83.

15. The Roman Catholic cathedral of St. Lucia in Colombo received its cathedral status in 1838 but dates back at least to the eighteenth century. Work on rebuilding and enlarging it started in 1852 and was completed in 1887. At the time of the 1883 riot, the nave had been completed.

16. Gunananda had been an ordained monk earlier in his life, then disrobed to become a layman, and subsequently rejoined the Sangha in the capacity of *samanera* (novice). He was not reordained.

17. Somaratna, *Kotahena Riot*, p. 396. See also Rogers, *Crime, Justice and Society*, pp. 176–79.

18. *Report;* Somaratna, *Kotahena Riot*, p. 8.

19. Somaratna, *Kotahena Riot*, pp. 8–9.

20. The Riot Commission report records that the Buddhists, elated by securing their license, are alleged to have sent taunting anonymous letters to Catholics, saying, "You fools! You tried to stop our wedding on the funeral day of that God of yours! You couldn't do it! We will come in with the procession on Friday—stop it if you can!" (ibid., p. 12).

21. *Report;* Somaratna, *Kotahena Riot*, p. 14.

22. Somaratna, *Kotahena Riot*, pp. 409, 415, notes that some Buddhist monks connected with Gunananda's Dipaduttama Vihara held processions and caused trouble in Ratnapura and Balangola on the same Easter Sunday. A procession in Galle was planned to take place on the same Sunday in order to clash with the procession staged by Roman Catholics. Subsequent Buddhist peraheras similarly

processed past the localities and villages of Catholics. Somaratna plausibly infers that these events could not be considered "spontaneous, isolated and unconnected."

23. Rogers, *Crime, Justice and Society*, p. 178.

24. *Report;* Somaratna, *Kotahena Riot*, pp. 23–24.

25. Rogers, *Crime, Justice and Society*, p. 179; *Report*. Rogers also suggests that although the ferocity of Catholic feelings took the priests of St. Lucia by surprise, "the desire of Pagnani and his colleagues to use their authority to defuse the situation may be questioned."

26. Somaratna, *Kotahena Riot*, p. 402, reports that Gunananda apparently maintained good relations with Governor Longden, and constantly proclaimed his loyalty to the British government. A tantalizing tit-bit is that "the Royal Arms of England were emblazoned above the recumbent figure of the Buddha at the Kotahena temple," the same image that was the focus of the March festivities. The story among the people at this time was that the British sovereign gave official sanction to Buddhism and for holding the processions without interference.

27. Memorandum from Olcott to the earl of Derby, May 17, 1884, reproduced in Somaratna, *Kotahena Riot*, pp. 76–77. Eventually, the British restored the right to hold processions with tom-toms under certain conditions, and Vesak became a holiday. (Rogers, *Crime, Justice and Society*, p. 180, reports that after the clash at Kotahena, a prominent "Buddhist response was to increase the number of processions through Catholic neighborhoods and by churches," and that "these processions became a permanent source of contention" in the ensuing years.) But the "temporalities" question remained unsolved, because the Sangha resisted surrendering its property rights to lay control. The request for "Buddhist registrars" was denied by the Colonial Office at this time.

28. See Kingsley M. de Silva, *A History of Sri Lanka* (Berkeley: University of California Press, 1981), pp. 343–46, for additional information on the Kotahena episode and its aftermath.

29. Rogers, *Crime, Justice and Society*, p. 186.

30. P. T. M. Fernando, "The British Raj and the 1915 Communal Riots in Ceylon," *Modern Asian Studies* 3, 3 (1969): 245. See also Michael Roberts, "Plotters or Local Elite Chauvinists? Directions and Patterns in the 1915 Communal Riots," *A Symposium on the 1915 Communal Riots* (Peradeniya: Ceylon Studies Seminar, 1970). The documentation for the 1915 riots, in the form of British administrative reports, correspondence with the Colonial Office, and detailed contemporary accounts by Sri Lankans, is quite extensive. In 1970, the *Journal of Asian Studies* 29, 2, published a symposium on the subject: "Introduction," by Robert Kearney; "Economic and Political Factors in the 1915 Riots," by Kumari Jayawardena; "The Action Phase of the 1915 Riots," by Charles Blackton; and "The Post Riots Campaign for Justice," by P. T. M. Fernando. Other sources that I have consulted include Ameer Ali, "The 1915 Racial Riots in Ceylon (Sri Lanka): A Reappraisal of Its Causes," *South Asia*, n.s., 4, 2 (1981): 1–20; A. P. Kannangara, "The Riots of 1915 in Sri Lanka: A Study in the Roots of Communal Violence," *Past and Present* 102 (1983): 130–65; James T. Rutnam, "The Rev. A. G. Fraser and the Riots of 1915," *Ceylon Journal of Historical and Social Studies*, n.s., 2 (1971): 151–96; and Michael Roberts, "Hobgoblins, Low-Country Sinhalese Plotters or Local Elite Chauvinists? Directions and Patterns in the 1915 Communal Riots," *Sri Lanka Journal of Social Sciences* 4 (1970): 157–98.

31. Fernando, "British Raj," p. 245.

32. Blackton, "Action Phase," p. 235.

33. The colonial secretary of Ceylon, Reginald Stubbs, who together with the officer commanding the troops, Brigadier General H.H.L. Malcolm, was the architect of British military action, believed that the rioting had been organized by Western-educated Ceylonese who were determined to undermine the imperial power. Stubbs informed the Colonial Office in London that the disturbances were initiated by "a set of skunks—mostly I regret to say men educated in Europe—one or two Cambridge men among them if stories are true" (C.O. 54/782, 29924, letter of R.E. Stubbs to A.E. Collins, July 16, 1916).

34. Blackton, "Action Phase," p. 236. Parliamentary Under-Secretary of State Sir Arthur Steel-Maitland told the House of Commons that "German intrigues were at the bottom of the rising in Ceylon." See also Blackton, "Action Phase," pp. 251–52; Jayawardena, "Economic and Political Factors," p. 223.

35. On March 2, when the centenary occurred, the Sinhalese newspaper *Dinamina* printed a copy of the treaty in Sinhalese, articles of a nationalist tone on Ceylon's history by E.W. Perera and D.B. Jayatilaka, and a reproduction of the Lion flag of the Sinhalese. There was such a demand by crowds for this memorable issue that it was reprinted on March 6. See Blackton, "Action Phase," p. 236.

36. Ibid.

37. Jayawardena, "Economic and Political Factors," p. 224.

38. Ceylon, Government Archives, Report 14502: Report of the Riots of 1915 by the Inspector General of Police; *Mahabodi Journal*, October 1909; *Sinhala Bauddhaya*, 1912, *Lakmina*, 1915, and *Dinamina*, quoted in Jayawardena, *Ethnic and Class Conflicts*, pp. 24–25.

39. Blackton, "Action Phase," p. 238.

40. Kannangara, "Riots of 1915," p. 135.

41. The Tooth relic preserved at Kandy, the palladium of the Kandyan kingdom, is said to have belonged to the Buddha, although according to one account, the Portuguese captured and destroyed the original relic in the sixteenth century.

42. Blackton, "Action Phase," 239.

43. Rutnam, "Rev. A.G. Fraser and the Riots," pp. 189–90. Fraser included an account of the events in Kandy, and of the valorous conduct of his students and teachers, in a report circulated to the school's well-wishers in England, some four of whom were apparently members of parliament. Speaking on behalf of the secretary of state for the colonies, Sir Arthur Steel-Maitland unjustifiably cited Fraser as supporting his "conspiracy" theory of the riots. This subsequently led to a prolonged and unpleasant controversy between E.W. Perera, a prominent Sinhalese politician, and a reluctant Fraser as to what Fraser had written in his report. This controversy itself is not germane to my account of the riots, but what Fraser had to say about the origins of the riots, that they were "organized in advance," without being "designed against British rule" is of relevance to us.

44. Ibid., p. 191.

45. Fraser reports this but does not give the observer's name.

46. Rutnam, "Rev. A. G. Fraser and the Riots," p. 155.

47. Ibid., p. 156.

48. Blackton, "Action Phase," p. 241.

49. Ibid.

50. George Rudé, *The Crowd in the French Revolution* (Oxford: Clarendon Press, 1959), p. 2.

51. E.g., D.C. Vijayavardhana, *The Revolt in the Temple* (Colombo: Sinha Publications, 1953), p. 121.

52. Jayawardena, "Economic and Political Factors," p. 228.

53. Ibid., p. 228.

54. Ibid., p. 230, 231. In quoting Jayawardena, I omit her own citation of sources for her quotations.

55. Rutnam, "Rev. A.G. Fraser and the Riots," p. 186.

56. This letter is reproduced in *Return to Righteousness*. Dharmapala was interned in Calcutta in 1915.

57. Ibid., p. 540.

58. De Silva, *Managing Ethnic Tensions*, p. 63.

59. The Buddhist temperance movement appears to have brought under the same umbrella a wide spectrum of leaders of nationalist aspirations, ranging from Dharmapala, John Silva, and C. Batuwantudave through F.R. Senanayake to D.S. Senanayake. The last-named was the least involved in traditionalist Buddhist revivalism.

60. Jayawardena, "Economic and Political Factors," p. 226.

61. Sarath Amunugama, "John de Silva and the Sinhalese Nationalist Theatre," *Ceylon Historical Journal* 25, 1–4 (1978): 285.

62. Ibid., p. 294.

63. Vijay Samaraweera, "Arabi Pasha in Ceylon, 1883–1901," *Islamic Culture* 50, 3 (1976); id., "The Muslim Revivalist Movement," in *Collective Identities, Nationalism and Protest in Modern Ceylon*, ed. Michael Roberts (Colombo: Marga Institute, 1979); Ameer Ali, "The 1915 Racial Riots in Ceylon (Sri Lanka): A Reappraisal of their Causes," *South Asia* 4, 2 (1981).

64. Ali, "1915 Racial Riots," p. 2; Kannangara, "Riots of 1915," p. 159; Blackton, "Action Phase," pp. 249–50.

65. Samaraweera, "Arabi Pasha in Ceylon." In exile in Ceylon, Arabi became a law-abiding citizen. His nationalist role in Egypt gave him prestige, however, and his very presence in Ceylon gave him a charismatic status. He played a role in the Muslim revivalist movement, in particular emphasizing the necessity for the backward Muslims of Ceylon to become educated.

66. Ali, "1915 Racial Riots," p. 7.

67. Ibid., pp. 9–10. See also M.M.M. Mahroof, "Muslim Education in Ceylon, 1881–1901," *Islamic Culture* 47, 4 (1973). Samaraweera (1976, 1979) is somewhat less enthusiastic than Ali (1981) in assessing the actual progress made in education, in forming associations, and in literary activities by the Muslim community, as for instance compared with the achievements of the Sinhalese and Tamil revivalist movements.

68. Ali, "1915 Racial Riots," p. 11.

69. Ibid., p. 15.

70. Kannangara, "Riots of 1915," p. 155.

71. Ibid., p. 158; Ali, "1915 Racial Riots"; Blackton, "Action Phase," pp. 249–50.

72. Kannangara, "Riots of 1915," p. 158.

73. Ibid.

74. Blackton, "Action Phase," pp. 242–43.

75. Jayawardena, "Economic and Political Factors," p. 231, quoting J.G. Fraser (C.O. 54/784).

76. Kannangara, "Riots of 1915," p. 152.

77. Ibid., pp. 152–53.

78. Ibid., pp. 153–54.

79. Ibid., p. 148.

80. Ibid., p. 141.

81. It is also curious that while Kannangara asserts that Vahumpura rioters crossed into Colombo allegedly to defend merchants of their caste in the Pettah, he fails to link this action to the Buddhist-revivalist-nationalist movement.

82. Roberts, "Hobgoblins," p. 104. Typical representatives of the national elite Roberts identifies are the Panabokkes; descendants of Francisco de Mel of Moratuwa and of Harmanis Dias of Panadura, and of Ponnambalam Mudaliyar of Colombo; the Pedrises of Galle and Colombo; the Senanayakes of Botale; the Diases and Dias Bandaranaikes of Veyangoda; and the six advocate Jayewardenes. The *pelantiyas* of local elite status are many, and the leading individuals Roberts identifies for urban areas include C. Don Bastian, Piyadasa Sirisena, Thomas Karunaratne, and P. H. Abraham Silva.

CHAPTER 4. TWO POSTINDEPENDENCE ETHNIC RIOTS IN SRI LANKA

1. Accounts of the 1958 riots are found in Tarzie Vittachi, *Emergency '58: The Story of the Ceylon Race Riots* (London: André Deutsch, 1958); James Manor, *The Expedient Utopian: Bandaranaike and Ceylon* (Cambridge: Cambridge University Press, 1989); and Stanley J. Tambiah, *Buddhism Betrayed? Religion, Politics and Violence in Sri Lanka* (Chicago: Chicago University Press, 1992).

2. It was mistakenly stated in my book *Sri Lanka: Ethnic Fratricide and the Dismantling of Democracy* (Chicago: University of Chicago Press, 1986) that I and the students were caught up in Gal Oya in the 1958 riots.

3. For fuller information on the events leading up to the 1956 riots, see W. Howard Wriggins, *Ceylon: Dilemmas of a New Nation* (Princeton, N.J.: Princeton University Press, 1960); R. N. Kearney, *Communalism and Language in the Politics of Ceylon* (Durham, N.C.: Duke University Press, 1967); B. H. Farmer, *Ceylon: A Divided Nation* (London: Oxford University Press, 1963); A. Jayaratnam Wilson, *Politics in Sri Lanka, 1947–1979* (London: Macmillan, 1979); and Manor, *Expedient Utopian*.

4. Manor, *Expedient Utopian*, p. 234.

5. The MEP and UNP members of Parliament voted for the bill, while LSSP and Communist MPs and the representatives of Tamil areas opposed it.

6. Cited in Mithran Tiruchelvam, "Gandhian Civil Disobedience in Sri Lanka," *Pravada* 2, no. 7 (Aug.–Sept. 1993): 19.

7. Tiruchelvam (ibid., p. 20), cites an account written by A. Amirthalingam, a Tamil member of Parliament, in which the latter alleged that "a large number of unruly elements were mobilized and brought to Galle Face Green . . . volunteers

who went around distributing leaflets were beaten up by the mob. Notwithstanding this assault . . . they proceeded towards the Parliament. Before they could move very far a mob waving the lion flag attacked them, beat them with fists and sticks and kicked them" (A. Amirthalingam, in *The Memorial Volume of the Federal Party* [1972]).

8. Wriggins, *Ceylon: Dilemmas*, p. 261.

9. Manor, *Expedient Utopian*, p. 262.

10. See A. Jeyaratnam Wilson, *The Break-Up of Sri Lanka: The Sinhalese—Tamil Conflict* (Honolulu: University of Hawaii Press) 1988, p. 108.

11. Unfortunately, the student reports are no longer available to me, although my memorandum refers to them.

12. Stanley J. Tambiah, *Sri Lanka: Ethnic Fratricide and the Dismantling of Democracy* (Chicago: University of Chicago Press, 1986). For other relevant accounts and analyses, see Committee for Rational Development, *Sri Lanka: The Ethnic Conflict—Myths, Realities and Perspectives* (New Delhi: Navrang, 1984); *Sri Lanka: Racism and the Authoritarian State*, vol. 26, no. 1 of *Race and Class* (1984); Social Scientists' Association, *Ethnicity and Social Change in Sri Lanka* (Colombo: Navamaga Printers, 1985); Jonathan Spencer, ed., *Sri Lanka: History and Roots of Conflict* (London: Routledge, 1990); and James Manor, ed., *Sri Lanka in Change and Crisis* (London: Croom Helm, 1984); Neelan Tiruchelvam, "July '83 and Collective Violence in Sri Lanka," *Lanka Guardian* 16, no. 7 (Aug. 1, 1993): 6–7.

13. Neelan Tiruchelvam, "July '83 and Collective Violence," p. 6.

14. T. D. S. A. Dissanayaka, *The Agony of Sri Lanka* (Colombo: Swastika, 1983), p. 80.

15. Ibid., pp. 80–81.

16. It has been estimated that almost a hundred industrial plants, including twenty garment factories, were severely damaged or destroyed. The cost of industrial reconstruction was estimated at 2 billion rupees. This figure excludes the damage done to hundreds of shops and small trading establishments (see Neelan Tiruchelvam, "July '83 and Collective Violence," p. 6). Ambassador Dissanayaka (*Agony in Sri Lanka*, p. 81) has this to say about the targeting of Tamil business interests: "The Tamil owned Maharaja Organization is the largest commercial establishment in Sri Lanka next to the Upali group. They lost six factories in Ramalana, including Ponds, S-lon, and Berec. By evening their Head Office in Bankshall Street and their new subsidiary Hettiaratchi Brothers, which still bore its Sinhala name, were set on fire. Barring the Maharaja Organization, the largest Tamil commercial establishments in Sri Lanka were St. Anthony's Hardware Stores, K. G. Industries and Easwaran Brothers. They were also situated in Grandpass. They were all consigned to the flames."

17. On these developments, viewed as contributing to the direction and scale of the anti-Tamil violence in 1983, see Newton Gunasinghe, "The Open Economy and Its Impact on Ethnic Relations in Sri Lanka," ch. 6 of Committee for Rational Development, *Sri Lanka: The Ethnic Conflict—Myths, Realities and Perspectives* (New Delhi: Navrang, 1984); and Sunil Bastian, "The Political Economy of Ethnic Violence in Sri Lanka: The July 1983 Riots," ch. 11 of *Mirrors of Violence: Communities, Riots and Survivors in South Asia* ed. Veena Das (Delhi: Oxford University Press, 1990).

CHAPTER 5. SIKH IDENTITY, SEPARATION, AND ETHNIC CONFLICT

1. In sketching this background, I draw from these sources: Robin Jeffrey, *What's Happening to India? Punjab, Ethnic Conflict, Mrs. Gandhi's Death and the Test of Federalism* (London: Macmillan, 1986); Rajiv Kapur, *Sikh Separatism: The Politics of Faith* (London: Allen & Unwin, 1986); W. H. McLeod, *Evolution of the Sikh Community* (Oxford: Oxford University Press, 1976); Kushwant Singh, *A History of the Sikhs* (Princeton, N.J.: Princeton University Press, 1963, 1966); and Joseph T. O'Connell, Milton Israel, and William G. Oxtoby, eds., *Sikh History and Religion in the Twentieth Century* (Toronto: University of Toronto, South Asian Studies Papers, no. 3 [1990]). Other relevant sources are: Gopal Singh, *The Religion of the Sikhs* (New Delhi: Allied, 1987); Joyce Pettigrew, "The Growth of Sikh Community Consciousness, 1947–1966," *South Asia*, n.s., 3, no. 2 (1980): 43–62, and "In Search of a New Kingdom of Lahore," *Pacific Affairs* 60 (1987): 1–25; Murray Leaf, "The Punjab Crisis," *Asian Survey* 25, no. 5 (1985): 475–98; Harjot Oberoi, "From Punjab to 'Khalistan': Territoriality and Metacommentary," *Pacific Affairs* 60, no. 1: 26–41, and *The Construction of Religious Boundaries: Culture, Identity and Diversity in Sikh Tradition* (Delhi: Oxford University Press, 1994); and Richard G. Fox, *Lions of the Punjab: Culture in the Making* (Berkeley: University of California Press, 1985).

2. Jeffrey, *What's Happening to India?*

3. The Sikh sacred book, the Granth Sahib, is written in Sant Bhasa Punjabi using the Gurmukhi script.

4. Paul Brass, *Language, Religion and Politics in North India* (Cambridge: Cambridge University Press, 1974), pp. 277–366.

5. In 1955 the Congress Government of Punjab directed the police to enter the Golden Temple to arrest Tara Singh and his followers, a move that led to the fall of the Hindu chief minister.

6. Jeffrey, *What's Happening to India?*

7. Apparently, large numbers of Jats were converted to Sikhism in the seventeenth and eighteenth centuries. "The religion of the Sikhs and the culture of the Jats have blended closely since the eighteenth century" (Jeffrey, *What's Happening to India?* p. 49).

8. On factionalism in Punjabi politics, see Joyce Pettigrew, *Robber Noblemen: A Study of the Political System of the Sikh Jats* (Boston: Routledge & Kegan Paul, 1975; reprint, New Delhi: Ambika, 1978).

9. Jeffrey, *What's Happening to India?* p. 126.

10. Guru Gobind, who founded the Khalsa as an organized, militant body, also ended the line of personal gurus. Not all Sikhs belong to the Khalsa, and those who do not belong are called Sahajdhari. Bhindranwale was unclear and equivocal as to whether he wanted a Khalistan within or outside the Indian Union.

11. Harjot Oberoi, "Sikh Fundamentalism: Translating History into Theory," in *Fundamentalisms and the State*, ed. Martin E. Marty and R. Scott Appleby (Chicago: University of Chicago Press, 1993), p. 372, says that "Nirankari associations with the Sikh tradition go back to the mid-nineteenth century when their founder Baba Dayal tried to introduce reforms in Sikh practices and doctrines. He made little headway and the Nirankaris emerged as a sort of sect within the larger Sikh tradition."

12. Ibid., p. 273.

13. Zail Singh stepped down as chief minister of Punjab in May 1977 when Congress lost the state elections. Between 1977 and 1980, he was out of office. In 1980, he became union home minister, and in June 1982, he was made president of India.

14. Jeffrey, *What's Happening to India?* p. 146.

15. Ibid.

16. Darshan Singh Maini in *Voices from a Scarred City: The Delhi Carnage in Perspective,* ed. Smitu Kothari and Harsh Sethi (New Delhi: Lokayan, 1985), p. 4.

17. Rajni Kothari, "The How and Why of It All," in *Voices from a Scarred City,* pp. 15–16.

18. The main sources for this study are *Report of the Citizens' Commission: New Delhi, 31 October–4 November 1984* (New Delhi: Tata Press, 1985) [hereafter cited as *RCC*]; People's Union for Democratic Rights and People's Union for Civil Liberties, *Who Are the Guilty? Report of a Joint Inquiry into the Causes and Impact of the Riots in Delhi from 31 October–10 November* (New Delhi: Gobinda Mukhoty and Rajni Kothari, 1984) [hereafter cited as *WTG*]; Uma Chakravarty and Nandita Haksar, *The Delhi Riots: Three Days in the life of a Nation* (New Delhi: Lancer International, 1987); *Report of Justice Ranganath Misra Commission of Inquiry,* vols. 1 and 2 (New Delhi: S.N., 1986) [hereafter cited as *MCR*]; *Voices from a Scarred City,* ed. Kothari and Sethi.

19. *MCR,* p. 28.

20. *WTG,* p. 1.

21. *RCC,* p. 29.

22. *MCR,* p. 1.

23. *RCC,* pp. 12–13.

24. *MCR,* p. 29.

25. *RCC,* p. 13.

26. *WTG,* p. 2.

27. Ibid., pp. 1–2. Regarding the first rumor of Sikh celebration of Mrs. Gandhi's death, the authors of *Who Are the Guilty?* say that after careful inquiry, they are of the view that while some instances of "demonstrative gestures" may have been enacted by some Sikhs and non-Sikhs, "such cases were few and isolated." The *Report of the Citizens' Commission* also refers to the mischievous role of rumors, and regarding the allegation that Sikh students had danced the *bhangra* (a Punjabi festive dance) on hearing of Mrs. Gandhi's death: "A University Professor investigated the allegation . . . her findings, which were published in a newspaper, revealed that some Sikh students had been rehearsing for a college cultural show and that bhangra was one of the featured items. As soon as they heard the news of the assassination, they stopped their rehearsal" (pp. 36–37).

28. *RCC,* pp. 14–15.

29. Chakravarty and Haksar, *Delhi Riots,* p. 108.

30. Ibid., pp. 449–50.

31. *MCR,* p. 25.

32. *RCC,* p. 35.

33. The next of kin were entitled to a compensation of Rs 20,000.

34. Ibid., p. 23.

35. The Delhi administration also claimed that by 1986, it had helped to repair 131 of these gurudwaras and all 11 of the schools.

36. *MCR*, p. 32.

37. *RCC*, pp. 20–21.

38. Ibid., p. 17.

39. "The element of greed and envy against the relatively more prosperous life-styles of Sikh neighbors added a further motive particularly in poor and congested areas. The arson indulged in widely both in poorer and more affluent areas was generally due to mass frenzy" (ibid., p. 37).

40. Ibid., p. 37.

41. *WTG*, p. 11.

42. Ibid., p. 11.

43. Chakravarty and Haksar, *Delhi Riots*, p. 33.

44. Ibid., p. 35.

45. *WTG*, p. 2.

46. Ibid., p. 21.

47. Ibid., p. 22.

48. Ibid.

49. Ibid., p. 4.

50. Ibid., p. 32. While pointedly accusing the ruling party, the Commission did not exonerate other parties: "We have been equally disturbed by the apathy and ambivalence of other political parties. We have received no information that any of them played any significant role in providing either protection or shelter, relief or succor, in any of the affected localities."

51. In a column by M. Mitta titled "Riot and Retribution," *India Today* (February 15, 1996, p. 14) reports that "former Union minister H. K. L. Bhagat," whose "name repeatedly figured in the string of inquiries into the 1984 anti-Sikh riots in Delhi . . . was arraigned for the first time last fortnight. . . . Sessions judge, S. N. Dhingra, issued a non-bailable arrest warrant against Bhagat after a riot victim, Satnami Bhai, deposed on January 15 this year that he had personally instigated the mob that killed her husband." The trial that began ten years ago against 150 persons, including Bhagat, has until now made little headway. It pertained to the killings that took place in Trilokpuri, "the worst-affected locality in Delhi . . . and part of Bhagat's then East Delhi constituency."

It is further reported that the Misra Commission set up in 1985 "had received 16 affidavits alleging that Bhagat had addressed meetings in his constituency inciting [Congress] party workers to violence. Also, the Jain-Aggarwal Committee, which was a follow-up to the Misra Commission, recommended the registration of a murder case against Bhagat in 1991 for the killing of a Sikh head constable during the riots."

This information thus at least implicates a high-ranking member of the Congress (I) Party and a union minister in the staging and direction of the 1984 riots. Another leader whom the Delhi police are seeking permission to prosecute is Delhi MP Sajjan Kumar, who is accused of "leading a mob that killed one Navin Singh at Sultanpuri in west Delhi." Thus plausible evidence of the role of some prominent members of the Congress government in the riots is slowly surfacing.

52. *WTG*, p. 11.

53. *MCR*, p. 30.

54. Ibid., p. 28.

55. Ibid., p. 29.

56. Ibid., p. 32.

57. Ibid., p. 33.

58. Ibid., p. 25.

59. One hears this view frequently, wherever ethnic riots take place: "If only the army had been called out in time, the riots could have been scotched." The fact is that politicians and civil authorities usually are loath to call in the army at the beginning, when the dam bursts, and the authorities usually say they are "surprised" by the sudden disorder. The politicians are reluctant to suppress by force a political outburst by a public whom they electorally represent, and whose support they need for reelection. Frequently, members of the police force find it difficult to enforce law and order when they themselves share the interests and views of the civilians they serve and consort with them.

60. *MCR*, p. 34.

61. Ibid., p. 36.

62. Ibid., p. 38.

63. *MCR*, p. 42. The "Investigating Agency" referred to is the Misra Commission's own investigating unit, which it set up to collect information and evidence.

64. *Voices from a Scarred City*, ed. Kothari and Sethi, p. 14.

65. Ibid., p. 16.

66. *WTG*, p. 12.

67. *RCC*, p. 31.

68. For this discussion of Bhindranwale's movement, I am particularly indebted to Mark Juergensmeyer, "The Logic of Religious Violence: The Case of the Punjab," *Contributions to Indian Sociology*, n.s., 22 (1988): 66–88; and T. N. Madan, "The Double-edged Sword: Fundamentalism and the Sikh Religious Tradition," in *Fundamentalisms Observed*, ed. Martin E. Marty and R. Scott Appleby (Chicago: University of Chicago Press, 1991), pp. 594–627; and Harjot Oberoi, "Sikh Fundamentalism: Translating History into Theory," in *Fundamentalisms and the State*, ed. Martin E. Marty and R. Scott Appleby (Chicago: University of Chicago Press, 1993), pp. 256–85.

69. Oberoi, "Sikh Fundamentalism," p. 257.

70. Juergensmeyer, "Logic of Religious Violence," pp. 76–86.

71. Madan, "Double-edged Sword."

72. Oberoi, "Sikh Fundamentalism," p. 278.

73. Joyce Pettigrew, "In Search of a New Kingdom of Lahore," *Pacific Affairs* 60 (1987): 4–5.

74. Juergensmeyer, "Logic of Religious Violence," 74.

75. Ibid., 78.

76. See Oberoi, "Sikh Fundamentalism," p. 269. The Panthic Committee, a leading organization within the Sikh resistance movement, was set up in January 1986. Its most prominent leader was Gurbachan Singh Manochal. The Bhindranwale Tiger Force was the armed wing of the older Panthic Committee.

77. Ibid., p. 267.

78. The Golden Temple complex was rebuilt and restored in the time of Ranjit Singh.

79. Madan, "Double-edged Sword," citing Kushwant Singh's *A History of the Sikhs,* 1: 63.

80. Oberoi, "Sikh Fundamentalism," p. 259.

81. A particular irritant to Sikh nationalists is Article 25, section 2b, of the Indian Constitution, which in giving all Hindus the right of access to public Hindu shrines, includes within the category of "Hindu" all "persons professing the Sikh, Jain or Buddhist religion." In the case of civil marriage, Sikhs are still governed by the Hindu Code (1955–56), and inheritance among Sikhs is governed by the Hindu Succession Act.

82. I am here referring to the battle between the Sinhala government and the JVP, whose members were Sinhalese youth. The civil war between the militant Tamils, especially the Tigers (LTTE), was also taking place at that time.

83. *Political Killings in Southern Sri Lanka: On the Brink of Civil War,* a compilation and report by Eduardo Marino, an International Alert Publication, 1989, p. 2.

84. V. S. Naipaul, "The Shadow of the Guru," *New York Review of Books,* Dec. 20, 1990, p. 72.

85. Barbara Crossette, *New York Times,* Dec. 19, 1990.

86. *New York Times,* Nov. 27, 1990.

87. James Clad, "India—Crisis in the System," *Lanka Guardian* 14, no. 1 (May 1, 1991). Clad's comments reinforce the thesis proposed in my AAS presidential address in 1990: that contentious mass politics staged in the form of elections generates violence that is of a piece with the violence of ethnic riots. See Stanley J. Tambiah, "Some Reflections on Communal Violence in South Asia" (AAS presidential address), *Journal of Asian Studies* 49, no. 4 (Nov. 1990): 741–60.

88. Oberoi, *Construction of Religious Boundaries,* p. 49.

89. Ibid., p. 51.

90. Ibid., pp. 58, 59.

91. Ibid., p. 74.

92. Ibid., pp. 75–76.

93. Ibid., p. 76.

94. Ibid., p. 86.

95. Ibid., p. 90.

96. For example, Guru Nānak was a Bedi, and the Bedis, together with the Sodhis, enjoyed eminence and a wide religious patronage in Central Punjab. Sahib Singh Bedi was greatly respected by Ranjit Singh, accompanied him on several military expeditions, and officiated at the coronation ceremonies when Ranjit Singh proclaimed himself maharaja of the Punjab. Sahib Singh was endowed with extensive land rents, and the Bedi families were an important segment of the ruling elite of Lahore state.

97. Ibid., p. 124.

98. Ibid., pp. 306, 316.

99. Ibid., p. 421.

100. Ibid., p. 344.

101. Ibid., p. 344.

102. Ibid., pp. 330–31.

103. Ibid., p. 332.

104. Ibid., pp. 336, 338, 339. Harjot Oberoi's historical and ethnographic study stops at around 1920.

105. Rahit-namas dealt with life-cycle rites, behavioral taboos, transgression of Khalsa boundary rules, the specification and constitution of sacred space, and so on. For example, they laid down the procedure for the famous initiation rite of *khande ki pakul* (drinking of sweetened water stirred with a double-edged sword), specified that mortuary rites should not be followed by public lamentation, and recommended that during the mourning period, the complete Adi Granth should be read (together with the singing of *kirtan* (hymns) and the distribution of alms). But they did not interfere with marriage rituals, which followed the caste and lineage customs of the wider Punjabi society.

106. The Nānakshahi Calendar commencing in 1469, the year of Guru Nānak's birth, replaced the Bikrami Calendar (starting in 57 C.E.), the Sikh New Year was to start on the first day of the month of Baisakh (April–May) instead of the month of Chet (March–April), and Guru Nānak's birth was changed to coincide with the New Year's day. A campaign was also launched to dissuade Sikhs from taking part in Hindu festivals such as Holi and Diwali.

107. Gurmukhi is one of the several scripts in which Punjabi can be written, and the Granth itself is composed in a "melange of various languages coalesced under the generic title of Sant Bhasa" (Oberoi, *Construction of Religious Boundaries*, p. 348).

108. Oberoi, *Construction of Religious Boundaries*, p. 372.

109. Ibid., p. 357.

110. Ibid., p. 361.

111. Ibid. The perceptions and predilections of the Indian Army authorities regarding Sikhism were not necessarily shared by other British official and administrative circles in India, and there were conflicts among them about the regulation of Sikh shrines.

112. Fox, *Lions of the Punjab*, p. 10. Fox reiterates this thesis throughout the book, saying, e.g.: "The British military selectively recruited the cultural meanings defining Sikh identity from the past, then validated, spread, and, most important, constituted them in the very organization of their colonial army" (p. 178).

113. See, e.g., Ian J. Kerr, "Fox and the Lions: The Akali Movement Revisited," in *Sikh History and Religion in the Twentieth Century*, ed. Joseph T. O'Connell, Milton Israel, and Willard G. Oxtoby (University of Toronto, South Asian Studies Papers, no. 3 [1990]). Kerr says that Fox's emphasis on the recruiting and organizational policies of the British Indian Army is "strained, overdone" (p. 218).

114. Fox, *Lions of the Punjab*, p. 11.

115. Ibid., p. 87.

116. Ibid., p. 178.

117. Both the Arya Samaj and the Singh Sabha as conflicting reformist religions arose among the lower middle class in urban Punjab. "The Arya Samaj successfully converted only the low caste menials in the rural areas, but this success of urban reformers alienated the major cultivating castes" (ibid., p. 162). The Arya Samaj also lacked the kind of strong separatist identity that helped mobilize both urban and rural Sikhs under one banner.

118. Ibid., p. 171.
119. Ibid., p. 172.
120. Kerr, "Fox and the Lions," p. 216.
121. Ibid., p. 177.
122. Ibid., p. 219.
123. Attar Singh, "The Shiromani Gurudwara Prabandhak Committee and the Politicization of the Sikhs," in *Sikh History and Religion in the Twentieth Century,* ed. Joseph T. O'Connell, Milton Israel, and Willard G. Oxtoby (University of Toronto, South Asian Studies Papers, no. 3 [1990]), p. 227.

CHAPTER 6. ETHNIC CONFLICT IN PAKISTAN

1. Ayesha Jalal, *The State of Martial Rule: The Origins of Pakistan's Political Economy of Defence* (Cambridge: Cambridge University Press, 1990), p. 1.
2. Ali Amineh Azam and Farida Shaheed, "Karachi Riots, April 1985: A Report on the Pathan-Bihari Clashes in Orangi" (paper read at the Kathmandu Conference of the International Centre for Ethnic Studies, February 15–17, 1987).
3. Farida Shaheed, "The Pathan-Muhajir Conflicts, 1985–6: A National Perspective," *Mirrors of Violence: Communities, Riots and Survivors in South Asia,* ed. Veena Das (Delhi: Oxford University Press, 1990), pp. 194–214.
4. The riots that exploded in 1953, resulting in the murder of many Ahmedis in the Punjab province, are one example. This precipitated a crisis, leading to the first martial-law government. During the constitutional debates, religious leaders had argued for an amendment declaring the Ahmediyya a non-Muslim minority, on the grounds that their leader Ghulam Ahmad (1835–1908) proclaimed himself a prophet and thus defied the essential Islamic tenet that Muhammad was the last of the prophets. They also pressed for Ahmedi officials, including Pakistan's foreign minister, Zafrullah Khan, to be dismissed from office, since non-Muslims cannot be entrusted with high positions in light of their want of commitment to the state's Islamic tenets.
5. Shaheed, "Pathan-Muhajir Conflicts," p. 197. In 1974 the National Assembly under Bhatti amended the Constitution to declare the Ahmedis to be a non-Muslim minority.
6. The Ahmedi issue surfaced in 1983–84 in a potentially explosive manner. Reacting to a worldwide conference of Ahmedis at Rabwah in 1983, a large number of Sunni and Shiite *ulama* (Muslim clerics) met and called for government action to prohibit Ahmedis from using Islamic terms, remove them from civil and military posts, and confiscate their newspapers and literature. They also wanted the death penalty to be imposed for apostasy. The government inserted an ordinance in the Penal Code stipulating punishment for any Ahmedi who called himself a Muslim, used Islamic terms, preached or propagated his faith, and so on.
7. Anwar H. Syed, "Political Parties and the Nationality Question in Pakistan," *Journal of South Asian and Middle Eastern Studies* 12, no. 1 (1988): 42–75.
8. Theodore P. Wright, Jr., "Center-Periphery Relations and Ethnic Conflict in Pakistan: Sindhis, Muhajirs and Punjabis," *Comparative Politics* 23, no. 3 (Apr. 1991): 300.
9. Ibid. p. 301.
10. Ibid. p. 308.

11. Shaheed, "Pathan-Muhajir Conflicts," 198–99.

12. Ibid., p. 199.

13. Syed, "Political Parties and the Nationality Question," p. 55.

14. Ibid., p. 58.

15. Ibid., p. 60.

16. Ibid., p. 52. Emphasis in original.

17. Wright, "Center-Periphery Relations and Ethnic Conflict," pp. 300–301, 305.

18. Syed, "Political Parties and the Nationality Question," p. 61.

19. Ibid., p. 62.

20. See ibid., pp. 60–62, and Wright, "Center-Periphery Relations and Ethnic Conflict," p. 305.

21. *Herald* (Karachi), Nov. 1988.

22. *New York Times*, Oct. 2, 1988.

23. *Herald* (Karachi), June 1990.

24. A similar incident of police firing on a women's procession in Latifabad Unit 8 was reported.

25. *Herald* (Karachi), June 1990.

26. Ibid.

27. Ibid.

28. Akmal Hussain, "The Karachi Riots of December 1986: Crisis of State and Civil Society in Pakistan," in *Mirrors of Violence: Communities, Riots and Survivors in South Asia*, ed. Veena Das (Delhi: Oxford University Press, 1990) p. 190.

29. Jalal, *State of Martial Rule*, p. 4. Emphasis added.

30. Ibid., pp. 1–2.

31. Shaheed, "Pathan-Muhajir Conflicts," p. 210.

32. Ibid., p. 211.

33. See Stanley J. Tambiah, "Some Reflections on Communal Violence in South Asia," *Journal of Asian Studies* 49, no. 4 (1990): 741–60.

34. Jalal, *State of Martial Rule*, p. 1.

35. Ibid., p. 142.

36. Another religious group that also sought a political presence was the Jamiat-ul-Ulema-i-Islam, which aspired to link up with other Islamic parties in the Muslim world.

37. Sandria B. Freitag, *Collective Action and Community: Public Arenas and the Emergence of Communalism in North India* (Berkeley: University of California Press, 1989), pp. 296–97. Freitag cites Philip Oldenburg's " 'A Place Insufficiently Imagined': Language, Belief, and the Pakistan Crisis of 1971," *Journal of Asian Studies* 44, no. 4 (1985) as her source for the two notions of Pakistan before 1971.

38. Edward A. Gargan, "Divided Pakistan Torn by Lawlessness and Scandal," *New York Times*, Nov. 19, 1991.

39. Azam and Shaheed, "Karachi Riots."

40. Shaheed, "Pathan-Muhajir Conflicts," pp. 204–5.

41. Quoted by Shaheed from Arif Hassan, "Karachi's Godfathers," *Herald* (Karachi), Dec. 1986.

42. My chief source is Azam and Shaheed, "Karachi Riots," much of the contents of which is restated in Shaheed, "Pathan-Muhajir Conflicts." A subsidiary source is Hussain, "Karachi Riots."

43. Azam and Shaheed, "Karachi Riots." The otherwise unattributed quotations that follow in this section are from ibid. Emphasis has been added.

44. Allen Feldman, *Formations of Violence: The Narrative of the Body and Political Terror in Ireland* (University of Chicago Press, 1991), pp. 26, 30.

45. In *The Sole Spokesman: Jinnah, the Muslim League and the Demand for Pakistan* (Cambridge: Cambridge University Press, 1985; paperback edition, 1994), Ayesha Jalal gives a penetrating analysis of Jinnah's deliberations before Partition. "What Jinnah was clamouring for was a way of achieving equal say for Muslims in any all-India arrangements at the centre. By denying that Indian Muslims were a minority and asserting that they were a nation, Jinnah advanced the... argument that since India contained at least two nations, a transfer of power necessarily involved the dissolution of British India's unitary structure of central authority, and any reconstitution of the centre would have to take account of the League's demand that Muslim provinces, the territorial expression of this claim to nationhood, should be grouped to constitute a separate state" (p. 241). But the realization of this Muslim state as part of a larger Indian union was not possible in the case of Punjab and Bengal, which could not become part of a Muslim state within their existing boundaries because they had large non-Muslim minorities. This was the "fatal contradiction" in the demand that eventually led to Partition. Lacking the assurance that Punjab and Bengal would be territorially included in the proposed state of Pakistan, which would have given him a position of strength from which to negotiate broader all-India arrangements, including division of the armed forces, Jinnah finally had to settle for the "mutilated and moth-eaten Pakistan" he had previously rejected, stripped of the eastern Punjab and western Bengal and Calcutta (ibid., p. 246).

46. Included among such groups were the Jamiyyat i-Ulama Islam (the Organization of Islamic Ulama), the Jamiyyat i-Ulama-i-Pakistan (the Organization of Pakistan Ulama), the Jama'at-i-Islami (the Islamic Society).

47. Cited by T. N. Madan, "Secularism in Its Place," *Journal of Asian Studies* 46, no. 4 (1987): 747–59. Madan's source is Sir Muhammad Iqbal, *The Reconstitution of Religious Thought in Islam* (Delhi, 1980), p. 155.

48. Quoted by Anne Elizabeth Mayer, "The Fundamentalist Impact on Law, Politics, and Constitution in Iran, Pakistan and the Sudan," in *Fundamentalisms and the State*, ed. Martin E. Marty and R. Scott Appleby (Chicago: University of Chicago Press, 1993), pp. 113–14. Mayer's source is Abdul Ala Maududi, *The Islamic Law and Constitution* (Lahore: Islamic Publications, 1980), p. 263.

49. John L. Esposito, "Islam in State and Society: Pakistan" (paper presented at conference on "Democracy and Development in South Asia," Tufts University, Apr. 1990), p. 4.

50. Ibid., p. 7.

51. Ibid., p. 9.

52. When Bhutto's Pakistan People's Party was inaugurated on December 1, 1967, in Lahore, the party's motto was repeated "with passionate approval" by the delegates: "Islam is our Faith, Democracy (*Jumhuriet*) is our Polity, Socialism (*Musawat*) is our Economy, All Power to the People" (Stanley Wolpert, *Zulfi Bhutto of Pakistan: His Life and Times* [New York: Oxford University Press, 1993], pp. 115–16).

53. As prime minister of Pakistan, "Zulfi prayed at the same shrine, and ordered a pair of solid gold doors to be installed there" (ibid., p. 19).

54. See ibid., chs. 3 and 4.

55. Esposito, "Islam in State and Society" p. 10. See, too, by this author, "Islam: Ideology and Politics in Pakistan" in *The State, Religion and Ethnic Politics: Afghanistan, Iran, and Pakistan,* ed. Ali Banuazizi and Myron Weiner (Syracuse, N.Y.: Syracuse University Press, 1986).

56. Esposito, "Islam in State and Society," p. 11.

57. Ibid., p. 12.

58. Ibid.

59. Mayer, "Fundamentalist Impact," p. 110.

60. Ibid., p. 111.

61. Ibid., p. 113.

62. Esposito, "Islam in State and Society," p. 13.

63. Ibid., p. 23.

64. Ibid., p. 24.

65. Ibid., p. 26. With regard to the *ushr,* an agricultural tax, critics likewise exposed the contradiction—declaring the tax to be compulsory, but allowing voluntary payment—as a concession favoring wealthy large landowners.

66. Ibid., p. 27.

67. Ibid., p. 28.

68. See Mayer, "Fundamentalist Impact," p. 128.

69. Quoted by Kemal A. Faruki, "Pakistan: Islamic Government and Society," in *Islam in Asia: Religion, Politics and Society,* ed. John L. Esposito (New York: Oxford University Press, 1987), p. 60.

70. Esposito, "Islam in State and Society," p. 38.

71. "In classical Islamic law, the evidence of one woman was regarded as equal to half that of one man, with the exception of midwives attesting to the maternity of a child and wives denying adultery on oath, which prevailed over the oath of accusing husbands. Reformist Islamic legal thinking and the increasingly strong women's lobby are insisting on the value of the testimony of a man and a woman as equal" (Faruki, "Pakistan: Islamic Government and Society," p. 68).

72. Mayer, "Fundamentalist Impact," p. 128.

73. Ibid., p. 126.

74. Ibid., p. 126. Emphasis in original.

75. Samina Yasmeen, "Democracy in Pakistan: The Third Dismissal," *Asian Survey* 34, no. 6 (June 1994): 575–76.

76. Ibid., p. 576.

77. Ibid., p. 573.

78. Esposito, "Islam in State and Society: Pakistan," p. 46, sums up Benazir Bhutto's trials and tribulations, which focused her energies on political survival, as follows: "Lacking the required parliamentary majority for bold leadership, in need of broadening the base of her support in the face of significant political opposition in the Punjab from the Islamic Democratic Alliance as well as in Baluchistan, faced with ethnic violence in Sind and charges of incompetence and corruption in her government and family, Benazir Bhutto [had] not been able to demonstrate effec-

tive leadership. Afghanistan and [later] Kashmir further complicated the political situation."

79. Yasmeen, "Democracy in Pakistan," p. 574.

80. See, for details, "Pakistan: Changing Power Equations," *India Today*, Sept. 30, 1992, pp. 14–20.

81. Tamir Amin, "Pakistan," *Asian Survey* 24, no. 2 (Feb. 1994): 193.

82. There was also an implied accusation that some of the politicians close to Sharif had been responsible for the "political assassination" of the former army commander, General Asif Nawaz.

83. Amin, "Pakistan," p. 194.

84. Ibid., 195.

85. Ibid.

86. Ibid., p. 196.

87. The July 15, 1995, issue of *India Today* devoted its cover story, entitled "City of Death," to a gruesome account of riots that erupted in Karachi from Muhajir strongholds and the standoff between Benazir Bhutto (whose army and police virtually abandoned the city) and Altaf Hussain, the exiled leader of the MQM and its terrorists. The death toll since January 1, 1995, was reported as being 850. Pakistan's commercial capital is now hobbled by the MQM's battles with the security forces as well as with its own divisive factions and Sindhi militant groups.

CHAPTER 7. SOME GENERAL FEATURES OF ETHNIC RIOTS
AND RIOT CROWDS

1. Mention has already been made of writings by Gyanendra Pandey and Sandria Freitag on the so-called Hindu-Muslim riots that occurred at rural and urban sites in Uttar Pradesh in the late nineteenth and early twentieth centuries. Ethnic riots also occur in border regions whose local inhabitants and "tribes" feel that their homelands are being appropriated by immigrants and "aliens," and that they themselves are being demographically swamped by the new colonists. Similar attitudes are generated in interior provinces where new peasant resettlement schemes are instituted and populated by peasants transplanted from other over-crowded and poverty-stricken areas. In Sri Lanka, this is a major issue in the ongoing ethnic conflict among Sinhalese, Tamils, and Muslims. For treatment of this issue in India, see Myron Weiner, *Sons of the Soil: Migration and Ethnic Conflict in India* (Princeton, N.J.: Princeton University Press, 1978).

2. See Amnesty International, *India: Allegations of Extrajudicial Killings by the Provincial Armed Constabulary in and around Meerut, 22–23 May, 1987* (London: Amnesty International, 1987). It is likely that there have been other occurrences since this report was written.

3. See E. J. Hobsbawm, *Primitive Rebels: Studies in Archaic Forms of Social Movements in the Nineteenth and Twentieth Centuries* (New York: Norton, 1959); George Rudé, *The Crowd in History: A Study of Popular Disturbances in France and England, 1730–1848* (New York: John Wiley & Sons, 1966); id., *The Crowd in the French Revolution* (Oxford: Oxford University Press, Clarendon Press, 1959); E. P. Thompson, "The Moral Economy of the English Crowd in the Eighteenth

Century," *Past and Present,* no. 50 (Feb. 1971); Natalie Zemon Davis, "The Rites of Violence: Religious Riots in Sixteenth-Century France" *Past and Present,* no. 59 (May 1973); Emmanuel Le Roy Ladurie, *Carnival: A People's Uprising at Romans, 1579–1580* (London: Scholar Press, 1980).

4. See Stanley J. Tambiah, "Ethnic Conflict in the World Today," *American Ethnologist* 16, no. 2 (May 1989): 335–49, for elucidation of this issue.

5. The "racially" motivated attacks in Germany and France in recent years by fascist groups and youths on guest workers and immigrants of Turkish and Algerian origin may, however, require some qualification of this statement.

6. Davis, "Rites of Violence," p. 90.

7. Karl Marx, *The Poverty of Philosophy* (New York: International Books, 1963), p. 175.

CHAPTER 8. THE ROUTINIZATION AND RITUALIZATION OF VIOLENCE

1. See Stanley J. Tambiah, *Culture, Thought and Social Action: An Anthropological Perspective* (Cambridge, Mass.: Harvard University Press, 1985), ch. 4, "A Performative Approach to Ritual."

2. Thus, for example, my essay entitled "Some Reflections on Communal Violence in South Asia," *Journal of Asian Studies* 49, no. 4 (November 1990): 741–60, was innocent of Freitag's work.

3. Sandria B. Freitag, *Collective Action and Community: Public Arenas and the Emergence of Communalism in North India* (Berkeley: University of California Press, 1989), pp. xi–xii; id., ed., *Culture and Power in Banaras: Community Performance and Environment, 1800–1980* (Berkeley: University of California Press, 1989), pp. 25, 205.

4. See Allen Feldman, *Formations of Violence: The Narrative of the Body and Political Terror in Northern Ireland* (Chicago: University of Chicago Press, 1991), p. 5.

5. "80 Die in Bangladesh Election Violence," *New York Times,* Feb. 11, 1988

6. "Election Violence Is Said to Kill 13 in Bangladesh," *New York Times,* Mar. 4, 1988.

7. See Barbara Crossette, "Wounded India Candidate Is Reported Near Death," *New York Times,* Nov. 24, 1989.

8. See Barbara Crossette, "Gandhi Foes Cite Disruptions in First Day of India Voting," *New York Times,* Nov. 23, 1989.

9. *Daily News,* October 29, 1982. President Jayewardene said these words to the government parliamentary group. A chilling discussion of these occurrences is to found in Priya Samarakone, "The Conduct of the Referendum," in *Sri Lanka in Change and Crisis,* ed. James Manor (London: Croom Helm, 1984), pp. 84–117. See also *Report on the First Referendum in Sri Lanka,* Second Paper No. 11 (Colombo: Department of Government Printing, 1987). "Naxalite" is an Indian name for radical, militant, anarchistic insurgent groups, which have been especially prominent in Bengal and South India.

10. Samarakone, "Conduct of the Referendum," p. 88.

11. Ibid., pp. 95, 98.

12. Ibid., p. 99.

13. *Report on the First Referendum*, pp. 58, 59, 63.

14. *Communal Violence—July 1983* (Colombo: Civil Rights Movement, 1983).

15. To the concept of "ritualization of collective violence," I would contrast the reverse concept "disruption of a routinized life marked by life cycle and calendrical rituals" to highlight the trauma of dislocation and disorder experienced by the victims of collective violence who feel the consequences of mob violence at the most individual and personal levels: as the loss of one's own father, mother, daughter, or son; loss of one's home and belongings, imprinted with a particular personal and domestic history; and the inability to cope with the work of mourning when the deaths have been sudden and meaningless, and the bodies summarily burnt, spirited away, or shoveled into collective graves, thereby denying the survivors even the consolation of mortuary rites to formulate coping and offer comforting sentiments. This topic of the disruption of the routinized life of victims will not, however, be dealt with in this book.

16. Clifford Geertz, *Negara: The Theater State in Nineteenth-Century Bali* (Princeton, N.J.: Princeton University Press, 1980).

17. Natalie Zemon Davis, "The Rites of Violence: Religious Riots in Sixteenth-Century France," *Past and Present* 59 (May 1973): 53.

18. Key words recorded in the case of Sri Lanka are *apey anduwa* (our government), *dharmayuddaya* (holy war), *Sinhala namaduwa* (Sinhalese army), *Sinhala virriya* (Sinhala heroes). "Sita-Ram" was used as a rallying cry in a peasant revolt in India in the early 1920s (see Gyanendra Pandey, "Peasant Revolt and Indian Nationalism: The Peasant Movement in Awadh, 1919–22," in *Selected Subaltern Studies*, ed. R. Guha and G. C. Spivak [Oxford: Oxford University Press, 1988]). Political slogans of a stereotyped kind are likely to circulate throughout a country. "Some of the slogans Hindus shouted in Bijnor on 30 October [1990] were exactly the same as the slogans that were shouted during riots in Indore, Jaipur, and New Delhi between October and December 1990," Amrita Basu notes ("Why Local Riots Are Not Simply Local: Collective Violence and the State of Bijnor, India," *Theory and Society* 24 [1995]: 57).

19. W. Norman Brown, *The United States and India and Pakistan* (Cambridge, Mass.: Harvard University Press, 1963), p. 142.

20. S. Gopal, *The Viceroyalty of Lord Irwin, 1926–31* (Oxford: Oxford University Press, 1957), p. 8.

21. C. A. Bayly, "The Pre-history of 'Communalism'? Religions in Conflict in India, 1700–1860," *Modern Asian Studies* 19, no. 2 (1985): 177–203.

22. Gyanendra Pandey, "The Colonial Construction of 'Communalism': British Writings on Banaras in the Nineteenth Century," in *Mirrors of Violence: Communities, Riots and Survivors in South Asia*, ed. Veena Das (Delhi: Oxford University Press, 1990), pp. 94–134.

23. Freitag, *Culture and Power in Banaras*, p. 212.

24. Freitag, *Collective Action and Community*, ch. 5, "The Cow Protection Riots of 1893."

25. Gyanendra Pandey, "Rallying round the Cow: Sectarian Strife in the Bhojpuri Region, c. 1888–1917," in *Subaltern Studies II: Writings on South Asian History and Society*, ed. Ranajit Guha (Delhi: Oxford University Press, 1993), pp. 60–129.

26. "India Confronts Horrors of the Past in TV Series," *New York Times*, Feb. 15, 1988.

27. Robin Jeffrey, *What's Happening in India? Punjab, Ethnic Conflict, Mrs. Gandhi's Death and the Test of Federalism* (London: Macmillan, 1986), pp. 161–62. For another treatment of the continuing relevance of the sacred cow in ethnic conflict, see Anand A. Yang, "Sacred Symbol and Sacred Space in Rural India: Community Mobilization in the Anti-Cow Killing," *Comparative Studies in Society and History* 22, no. 4 (1980): 576–96.

28. Uma Chakravarty and Nandita Haksar, *The Delhi Riots: Three Days in the Life of a Nation* (New Delhi: Lancer International), 1987, p. 34.

29. George Rudé, *The Crowd in History: A Study of Popular Disturbances in France and England, 1730–1848* (New York: John Wiley & Sons, 1966), p. 245.

30. See People's Union for Democratic Rights and People's Union for Civil Liberties, *Who Are the Guilty? Report of a Joint Inquiry into the Causes and Impact of the Riots in Delhi from 31 October–10 November* (New Delhi: Gobinda Mukhoty and Rajni Kothari, 1984; *Report of the Citizens' Commission: New Delhi, 31 October–4 November 1984* (New Delhi: Tata Press, 1985); and Madhu Kishwar's report in *Manushi*, no. 25 (Nov.–Dec. 1984).

31. Jeffrey, *What's Happening in India?* p. 12. In the national elections of December 1984, which returned the Congress (I) Party with the largest majority in postindependence times, garish posters of Mrs. Gandhi, blood spurting from her body, told voters of " 'Indira's final wish—save the country with every drop of blood.' . . . Congress (I) campaigners in Calcutta placed a garlanded portrait of Mrs. Gandhi by the roadside, played tape-recordings of her speeches behind it and then placed a microphone in front of her picture. . . . Passers-by, however, seemed to accept the scene as unremarkable" (ibid., p. 17).

32. Tarzie Vittachi, *Emergency '58: The Story of the Ceylon Race Riots* (London: André Deutsch, 1958), pp. 44–45, 47. It appears that Seneviratne, who was given special prominence as a wealthy person, may have been the victim of a private feud, as suggested by S. J. V. Chelvanayagam (ibid., p. 45).

33. Ibid., p. 47.

34. Richard D. Lambert, "Religion, Economics and Violence in Bengal," *Middle East Journal* 4, no. 3 (July 1950): 206–328.

35. See, e.g., Freitag, *Collective Action and Community*, ch. 8, and id., ed., *Culture and Power in Banaras*, esp. chs. 4 and 7.

36. Feldman, *Formations of Violence*, pp. 29–30.

37. For a celebrated discussion of a similar phenomenon in France see Emmanuel Le Roy Ladurie, *Carnival: A People's Uprising at Romans, 1579–1580* (London: Scholar Press, 1980).

38. Sanjoy Hazarika, *New York Times*, Feb. 24, 1990.

39. *New York Times*, Feb. 11, 1990.

CHAPTER 9. HINDU NATIONALISM, THE AYODHYA CAMPAIGN, AND THE BABRI MASJID

1. M. S. Golwalkar, *We or Our Nation Defined* (Nagpur: M. N. Kale). See Ainslie T. Embree, "The Function of the Rashtriya Swayamsevak Sangh: To Define

the Hindu Nation," in *Accounting for Fundamentalisms: The Dynamic Character of Movements,* ed. Martin E. Marty and R. Scott Appleby (Chicago: University of Chicago Press, 1994) p. 619.

2. Ibid., p. 631.

3. Ibid., p. 623.

4. The mythic claims and pseudo-historical inventions are critically examined in *Anatomy of a Confrontation: The Babri Masjid–Ramjanmabhumi Issue,* ed. Sarvepalli Gopal (New Delhi: Penguin Books India; New York: Viking, 1991).

5. The story of the Hindutva movement since 1925—its ideology and political and social activities; the social composition of its component units (the Sangh Parivar); its increasing focus on the Ayodhya issue; and its increasingly successful electoral performance, combined with spectacular techniques and campaigns for mobilization of crowds, especially since 1984—and the alleged crisis of secular politics it has precipitated cannot be fully told here and is the subject of another book, now in preparation.

6. Shah Bano, a Muslim woman divorced by her Muslim husband, sued for maintenance in 1980. The court decision was in her favor, but some Muslim *ulama* protested, saying that the decision was against traditional shari'ah practice. Rajiv Gandhi, then prime minister, had the decision overturned by means of a parliamentary regulation permitting Muslims to observe their traditional "personal laws." The BJP objection is that whereas the government had already subjected all Hindus to the Hindu Code (1955–56), which effected a drastic reform of Hindu law, it was now giving a special exemption to Muslims, thereby negating the goal of instituting a unified civil code for all Indian citizens.

7. The Mandal Commission report, written in 1980 and shelved for a time, calculated the OBC's to amount to around 52 percent of India's population and recommended reservation of 27 percent of certain levels of central government employment for them. Since the Scheduled Castes and Scheduled Tribes already had 22.5 percent of central government (services and public sector) jobs reserved for them, the implementation of the Mandal recommendations would give *all* "backward classes" a total of 49.5 percent of the jobs. Upper- and middle-caste youth objected to this allocation.

8. *Frontline,* Feb. 12, 1993, p. 5.

9. Asghar Ali Engineer, "When Bombay Erupted," *Frontline,* Feb. 26, 1993, p. 128.

10. V. K. Ramachandran, "Reign of Terror: Shiv Sena Pogrom in Bombay," *Frontline,* Feb. 12, 1993, p. 12.

11. See Dileep Padgaonkar, ed., *When Bombay Burned* (New Delhi: UBS Publishers' Distributors, 1993), pp. xi–xiv. It is reported that 175 deaths were caused by (mainly police and army) gunfire, 309 died in the course of violent mob incidents, and 37 died through arson of homes and buildings.

12. "Secular Forces Must Unite: Interview with Asghar Ali Engineer," *Frontline,* Feb. 12, 1993, p. 16.

13. Padgaonkar, *When Bombay Burned,* pp. xi–xiv.

14. Asghar Ali Engineer, "When Bombay Erupted," *Frontline,* Feb. 26, 1993, p. 128.

15. "Bloody Aftermath," *India Today,* Dec. 31, 1992, p. 41.

16. M. Rahman with Lekha Rattanani, "Savagery in Bombay," *India Today*, Jan. 31, 1993, p. 26.

17. In many parts of India, including Banaras, the *Ramayana* is staged as part of the Dassehra festivities. The Durga Puja is a central feature, of course, and the slaying by the goddess Durga of the demon is melded with Ram defeating the demon king, Ravana.

18. Lloyd I. Rudolph, "The Media and Cultural Politics," in *India Votes: Alliance Politics and Minority Governments in the Ninth and Tenth General Elections*, ed. Harold Gould and Sumit Ganguly (Boulder, Colo.: Westview Press, 1993), p. 165.

19. Myron Weiner, *The Indian Paradox: Essays in Indian Politics* (London: Sage, 1989), p. 9.

20. McKim Marriott, "Hindu Transactions: Diversity without Dualism," in *Transactions and Meaning: Directions in the Anthropology of Exchange and Symbolic Behavior*, ed. Bruce Kapferer (Philadelphia: Institute for Human Issues, 1977), pp. 109–42.

21. See Paul Brass, *Ethnic Groups and the State* (London: Croom Helm, 1985), pp. 1–58. And see, too, Ashis Nandy, "The Political Culture of the Indian State," *Dædalus* 118, no. 4 (Fall 1989): 1–26; and Rajni Kothari, "The Indian Enterprise Today," ibid.: 51–67.

22. See *The Enduring Federalist*, ed. Charles Beard (New York: Frederick Ungar, 1959), esp. nos. 9 and 10. I am particularly indebted to David C. Rapoport for bringing this example to my attention and for indicating its relevance to my discussion of the linkage between elections, mass politics, and violence.

23. Ibid., p. 14.

24. Ibid., p. 15.

25. James Manor, "The Failure of Political Integration in Sri Lanka (Ceylon)," *Journal of Commonwealth and Comparative Politics* 17, no. 1 (1989): 21–46.

CHAPTER 10. ENTERING A DARK CONTINENT

1. We should also note that in *Massenpsychologie und Ich-Analyse*, Freud explicitly states that he is not concerned with Le Bon's "heterogeneous" and volatile crowds, but with Le Bon's "homogeneous" groups, examples of which for Freud were organized and enduring institutions such as churches, armies, and political parties. For this reason, we can leave aside Freud's text as largely peripheral to our subject.

2. See Serge Moscovici *L'Age des foules* (1981), trans. by J. C. Whitehouse as *The Age of the Crowd: A Historical Treatise on Mass Psychology* (Cambridge: Cambridge University Press), 1985.

3. Gustave Le Bon, *La Psychologie des foules* (1895), trans. as *The Crowd: A Study of the Popular Mind* (New York: Viking Press, 1960), pp. 23–24.

4. Ibid. p. 156.

5. Ibid. p. 27.

6. Uma Chakravarty and Nandita Haksar, *The Delhi Riots: Three Days in the Life of a Nation* (New Delhi: Lancer International, 1987), p. 453.

7. Elias Canetti, *Crowds and Power* (New York: Farrar, Straus and Giroux, 1984).

8. This last bit of arson was not aimed at women; the point is that the building in question was government property.

9. Information regarding these two prominent politically active monks can be found in Stanley J. Tambiah, *Buddhism Betrayed? Religion, Politics and Violence in Sri Lanka* (Chicago: University of Chicago Press, 1992), ch. 10.

10. Seth Mydans, *New York Times*, July 29, 1987.

11. Lyndsey Gruson, "Cities Are Looters' Jungles as Chaos Consumes Panama," *New York Times*, Dec. 23, 1989.

12. David Binder, *New York Times*, Dec. 23, 1989.

13. Canetti, *Crowds and Power* pp. 15–16.

14. Ibid., p. 18.

15. Bill Buford, *Among the Thugs: The Experience and the Seduction of Crowd Violence* (New York: Norton, 1992), pp. 102–65.

16. Canetti, *Crowds and Power* p. 16.

17. Ibid., p. 20.

18. Ibid., p. 19.

19. Ibid., p. 19.

20. Georg Simmel, *Conflict* (Glencoe, Ill.: Free Press, 1955), ch. 1.

21. René Girard, *Violence and the Sacred* (1977; Baltimore: Johns Hopkins Paperbacks, 1979).

22. George F. E. Rudé, *The Crowd in History: A Study of Popular Disturbances in France and England, 1730–1848* (New York: John Wiley & Sons, 1966), p. 238.

23. Ibid., p. 241.

24. Canetti, *Crowds and Power*, p. 49.

25. Quoted by Robert J. Lifton, *The Broken Connection: On Death and the Continuity of Life* (New York: Simon & Schuster, 1979), p. 332. The source is Eugène Ionesco's "Diaries," *Encounter*, May 1966.

26. People's Union for Democratic Rights and People's Union for Civil Liberties [Gobinda Mukhoty and Rajni Kothari], *Who Are the Guilty? Report of a Joint Inquiry into the Causes and Impact of the Riots in Delhi from 31 October–10 November* (New Delhi: Excellent Printing Services, 1984), p. 4.

27. *Report of Justice Ranganath Misra Commission of Inquiry,* vol. 1 (New Delhi: S.N., 1986), p. 29.

28. Ibid, p. 32.

29. Rumors also of course circulate via newspapers, pamphlets, and fly sheets—but even there, they are passed on by readers to nonreaders by word of mouth. Especially in situations where literacy is low, oral transmission is critical.

30. Le Bon, *The Crowd*, p. 160.

31. Le Bon's description, based on Taine's account, of the mood and the acts of the crowds that enacted the massacres of September 1792 during the French Revolution is worth reading in full. See ibid., pp. 162–64.

32. T. D. S. A. Dissanayaka, *The Agony of Sri Lanka* (Colombo: Swastika, 1983), p. 80.

33. Jonathan Spencer, "Popular Perceptions of the Violence: A Provincial View," in *Sri Lanka in Change and Crisis,* ed. James Manor (London: Croom Helm, 1984).

34. Sigmund Freud, *Group Psychology and the Analysis of the Ego* (New York: Norton, 1959), p. 28.

35. See Elizabeth Nissan, "Some Thoughts on Sinhalese Justifications for the Violence," and Spencer, "Popular Perceptions," in *Sri Lanka in Change and Crisis,* ed. James Manor (London: Croom Helm, 1984). See also Jonathan Spencer, "Collective Violence and Everyday Practice in Sri Lanka," *Modern Asian Studies* 24, no. 3 (July 1990): 602–23.

36. See Stanley J. Tambiah, *Sri Lanka: Ethnic Fratricide and the Dismantling of Democracy* (Chicago: University of Chicago Press, 1986).

37. Nissan, "Some Thoughts," pp. 175–76.

38. Spencer, "Popular Perceptions," p. 190.

39. Spencer, "Collective Violence," pp. 618–19.

40. In a mytho-historical chronicle composed by Buddhist monks in the fifth century A.D., the Sinhalese hero and king Dutthagamani is celebrated for mounting a war against the Tamil king Elara, recapturing the ancient capital Anuradhapura, and uniting the island on the basis of Buddhism. To modern-day Sinhalese Buddhist nationalists, he represents the glorious past that has to be regained.

41. Spencer, "Collective Violence," p. 620.

42. Bruce Kapferer, *A Celebration of Demons: Exorcism and the Aesthetics of Healing in Sri Lanka* (Bloomington: Indiana University Press, 1983); id., *Legends of People, Myths of State: Violence, Intolerance, and Political Culture in Sri Lanka and Australia* (Washington: Smithsonian Institution Press, 1988).

43. Nissan, "Some Thoughts," p. 176.

44. Spencer, "Popular Perceptions," p. 191.

45. Here is a chilling example reported by D. Beresford in the *Guardian* (Aug. 13, 1983), independently verified by Spencer, and cited by the latter. On July 27, a crowd collected to attack Tamil homes in a street in Badulla, a town in Uva Province. When the police failed to respond to the desperate summons of the Tamil residents, a well-known Tamil merchant who lived on the street fired a shotgun in the air to scare the crowd away. At this point, soldiers from the Sri Lankan army arrived and fired on the house. "The men in the Tamil homes in the street who were not beaten and hacked to death, were shot by the soldiers." The merchant's wife was then told by the soldiers to go into her house and bring "the other Tigers and guns" (Spencer, "Collective Violence," p. 618).

46. Spencer, "Popular Perceptions," p. 193.

47. Chakravarty and Haksar, *Delhi Riots.*

48. Ibid., pp. 402, 410–11.

49. Governor Sir Robert Chalmers was a highly regarded Pali scholar who admired Buddhism and sympathized with Buddhist interests. When the riots broke out, however, he lost his nerve, and, after declaring martial law, gave the army virtual carte blanche to enforce it and to hold courts-martial. He vacated his position as governor soon afterwards.

50. A. P. Kannangara, "The Riots of 1915 in Sri Lanka: A Study in the Roots of Communal Violence." *Past and Present* 102 (1983): 155–58.

51. Sudhir Kakar, "Some Unconscious Aspects of Ethnic Violence in India," in *Mirrors of Violence: Communities, Riots and Survivors in South Asia,* ed. Veena Das (New Delhi: Oxford University Press, 1990), p. 137.

52. In physical theory, the frequency of blue light is about twice as high as the frequency of red light. "As a swift luminous object approaches you the frequency

of its light appears enhanced—it becomes 'blue' or at least shifts in the direction of the high-frequency, blue end of the spectrum. Physicists and astronomers call it a blue shift. Conversely, an object going away appears 'red'—its light is red shifted . . . Blue, the high-frequency light, corresponds with high energy and high temperatures, while red, the low-frequency, represents lesser energy and cooler conditions" (Nigel Calder, *Einstein's Universe* [New York: Greenwich House, 1979], p. 9). Christian Doppler was a Viennese physicist, working in the early nineteenth century, who described the effect carefully, extending it from sound to light.

The Doppler effect translated into sound effect is perhaps even more apposite for conceptualizing some aspects of ethnic riots and crowd violence. As the eminent physicist Stephen W. Hawking explains: "This relationship between frequency and speed, which is called the Doppler effect, is an everyday experience. Listen to a car passing on the road: as the car is approaching, its engine sounds a higher pitch (corresponding to a higher frequency of sound waves), and when it passes and goes away, it sounds at lower pitch. The behavior of light or radio waves is similar. Indeed, the police make use of the Doppler effect to measure the speed of cars by measuring the frequency of pulses of radio waves reflected off them" (*A Brief History of Time: From the Big Bang to Black Holes* [New York: Bantam Books, 1988], pp. 38–39).

53. James Gleick, *Chaos: Making a New Science* (New York: Penguin Books, 1988), pp. 122, 127, 124.

54. Quoted in ibid., p. 124.

CHAPTER 11. RECONFIGURING LE BON AND DURKHEIM
ON CROWDS AS COLLECTIVES

1. "He is an apprehensive conservative, worried by the growth of the proletariat with its socialist orientation," Robert Merton says in his introduction to Gustave Le Bon, *The Crowd: A Study of the Popular Mind* (New York: Viking Press, 1960), p. xxxvii.

2. Serge Moscovici, *The Age of the Crowd: A Historical Treatise on Mass Psychology,* trans. J. C. Whitehouse (Cambridge: Cambridge University Press, 1985).

3. Le Bon, *The Crowd,* p. 32.

4. Ibid., p. 57.

5. Ibid., p. 125. Emphasis added.

6. Ibid., p. 40.

7. Ibid., p. 42.

8. Ibid., p. 118.

9. Ibid., p. 120.

10. On leadership of the second kind, functioning in stable groups and associations such as the army and the church, see Sigmund Freud, *Group Psychology and the Analysis of Ego* (New York: Norton, 1959). Something will be said later about the relevance of Freud's discussion of this.

11. Emile Durkheim, *Les Formes élémentaires de la vie religieuse: Le Système totémique en Australie* (1912), trans. as *The Elementary Forms of Religious Life: A Study in Religious Sociology* by Joseph Ward Swain (London: Allen & Unwin, 1915).

12. It is interesting to note that the original German edition of Freud's *Group Psychology and the Analysis of Ego* was published in 1921. Freud's major point of reference was Le Bon. He does not engage with Durkheim.

13. Steven Lukes, *Emile Durkheim: His Life and Work. A Historical and Critical Study* (London: Allen Lane, Penguin Press, 1973), pp. 462–63.

14. Emile Durkheim, *The Elementary Forms of the Religious Life* (New York: Collier Books, 1961), p. 13.

15. Ibid., pp. 242–43.

16. Ibid., p. 240.

17. Ibid., p. 241.

18. Ibid.

19. Stanley J. Tambiah, *The Buddhist Saints of the Forest and the Cult of Amulets: A Study of Charisma, Hagiography, Sectarianism, and Millennial Buddhism* (Cambridge: Cambridge University Press, 1985).

20. Stanley J. Tambiah, *Magic, Science, Religion and the Scope of Rationality* (Cambridge: Cambridge University Press, 1990).

21. Durkheim, *Elementary Forms*, pp. 241–42.

22. Ibid., pp. 247, 248.

CHAPTER 12. THE MORAL ECONOMY OF COLLECTIVE VIOLENCE

1. George F. E. Rudé, *The Crowd in History: A Study of Popular Disturbances in France and England, 1730–1848* (New York: John Wiley & Sons, 1966), p. 224.

2. Natalie Zemon Davis, "The Rites of Violence: Religious Riots in Sixteenth-Century France," *Past and Present* 59 (May 1973): 52–53. George Rudé's *The Crowd in the French Revolution* (Oxford: Oxford University Press, Clarendon Press, 1959), makes similar remarks in the final chapter, "The Revolutionary Crowd in History."

3. Davis, "Rites of Violence," pp. 81–82.

4. Ibid., p. 53.

5. Ibid., p. 74.

6. E. P. Thompson, "The Moral Economy of the English Crowd in the Eighteenth Century," *Past and Present* 50 (Feb. 1971): 76–126.

7. Ibid., pp. 78–79.

8. James C. Scott, *The Moral Economy of the Peasant: Subsistence and Rebellion in Southeast Asia* (New Haven, Conn.: Yale University Press, 1976). An interesting debate was initiated when Samuel Popkin, in his *The Rational Peasant: The Political Economy of Rural Society in Vietnam* (Berkeley: University of California Press, 1979), contested the validity of Scott's thesis and paradigm.

9. Gyanendra Pandey, "Peasant Revolt and Indian Nationalism: The Peasant Movement in Awadh, 1919–22," in *Selected Subaltern Studies*, ed. Ranajit Guha and Gayatri Chakravorty Spivak (New York: Oxford University Press, 1988), pp. 233–87.

10. Ibid., p. 261.

11. Ibid., pp. 267–68.

12. Ibid., p. 269.

13. Ibid. Pandey is referring to M. H. Siddiqi, *Agrarian Unrest in North India: The United Provinces, 1918–22* (New Delhi, 1978), ch. 2.

14. Ranajit Guha, "The Prose of Counter-Insurgency," in *Subaltern Studies II: Writings on South Asian History and Society,* ed. id. (New Delhi: Oxford University Press, 1993), p. 1.

15. Ibid., p. 2.

16. Ibid., p. 3. Guha obviously cannot be referring to the writings on Europe of Hobsbawm, Thompson, Rudé, Davis, and Tilly, or to those of James Scott on Southeast Asia. Can he be saying that *all* earlier writing on rebellions in India represented them as totally spontaneous and unpremeditated?

17. See C. A. Bayly, "Rallying around the Subaltern," *Journal of Peasant Studies* 16, no. 1 (Oct. 1988): 119–20.

18. Ibid., p. 118.

19. Gyanendra Pandey, "In Defence of the Fragment: Writing about Hindu-Muslim Riots in India Today," *Representations* 27 (Winter 1992): 27–55.

20. Ibid., pp. 28, 29.

21. Ibid., p. 50. M. S. Sathyu's film *Garam hawa,* Pandey says, is an exceptional and "remarkable statement of the early 1970s that sensitively portrayed the collective insanity, the uprooting, the meaninglessness of existence and the fear-laden searches for new meaning 'elsewhere' that were the lot of so many people in the aftermath of Partition."

22. Ibid., pp. 28–29.

23. Ibid., p. 31.

24. Ibid., p. 33.

25. Ibid., pp. 33–34.

26. Ibid., p. 46.

27. Ibid., p. 42.

28. *Religion and Human Rights,* ed. John Helsay and Sumner B. Twiss (New York: Project on Religion and Human Rights, 1994), pp. iii and iv.

29. Ibid., ch. 3, "Universality vs. Relativism in Human Rights," p. 34.

30. *World Conference on Human Rights : The Vienna Declaration and Programme of Action, June 1993* (New York: United Nations, 1993), pp. 28, 30.

31. *Religion and Human Rights,* ch. 3, "Universality vs. Relativism in Human Rights," p. 43.

32. Mark H. Moore, Deborah Prothrow-Stith, Bernard Guyer, and Howard Spivak, "Violence and Intentional Injuries: Criminal Justice and Public Health Perspectives on an Urgent National Problem," in *Understanding and Preventing Violence,* vol 4: *Consequences and Control,* ed. Albert J. Reiss, Jr., and Jeffrey A. Roth (Washington, D.C.: National Research Council, National Academy Press, 1994), p. 167.

33. Allen D. Grimshaw, "Actions of Police and the Military in American Race Riots," in *Racial Violence in the United States,* ed. id. (Chicago: Aldine, 1969), pp. 269–70. Grimshaw refers to Richard D. Lambert, "Hindu-Muslim Riots" (diss., University of Pennsylvania, 1951).

34. Charles Tilly, Louise Tilly, and Richard Tilly. *The Rebellious Century, 1830–1930* (Cambridge, Mass.: Harvard University Press, 1975), p. 243.

35. See Benedict R. O'G. Anderson, *Imagined Communities: Reflections on the Origins and Spread of Nationalism* (London: Verso and NLB, 1983).

36. I have taken these expressions from Daniel Bell, "Ethnicity and Social Change," *Ethnicity: Theory and Experience,* ed. Nathan Glazer and Daniel P. Moynihan (Cambridge, Mass.: Harvard University Press, 1975), pp. 146–47.

37. This proposal combines concepts taken from the writings of Amartya Sen, Pierre Bourdieu, and Donald L. Horowitz.

38. Donald L. Horowitz, *Ethnic Groups in Conflict* (Berkeley: University of California Press, 1985), p. 187.

39. Ibid., p. 36.

40. See M. G. Smith, "Some Developments in the Analytical Framework of Pluralism" and "Institutional and Political Conditions of Pluralism," in *Pluralism in Africa,* ed. Leo Kuper and M. G. Smith (Berkeley: University of California Press, 1969).

41. Ibid., p. 430.

42. An instructive example of this special pleading on behalf of a majority in place is Prime Minister Mohamad bin Mahathir's political tract *The Malay Dilemma* (Singapore: Time Books International, 1970).

43. Horowitz, *Ethnic Groups in Conflict,* p. 31.

Bibliography

Ali, Ameer. "The 1915 Racial Riots in Ceylon (Sri Lanka): A Reappraisal of Their Causes." *South Asia*, n.s., 4, no. 2 (1981): 1–20.

Alinsky, Saul. "The Professional Radical: Conversations with Saul Alinsky." *Harper's*, June 1965.

Amin, Tamir. "Pakistan." *Asian Survey* 24, no. 2 (Feb. 1994): 195–97.

Amnesty International. *India: Allegations of Extrajudicial Killings by the Provincial Armed Constabulary in and around Meerut, 22–23 May, 1987*. London: Amnesty International, 1987.

Amunugama, Sarath. "Anagarika Dharmapala (1864–1933) and the Transformation of Sinhala Buddhist Organization in a Colonial Setting." *Social Science Information* 24, no. 4 (1985): 697–730.

———. "John de Silva and the Sinhalese Nationalist Theatre." *Ceylon Historical Journal* 25, nos. 1–4 (Oct. 1978): 285–304.

Anderson, Benedict R. O'G. *Imagined Communities: Reflections on the Origins and Spread of Nationalism*. London: Verso and NLB, 1983. Reprint, 1985.

Azam, Ali Amineh, and Farida Shaheed. "Karachi Riots, April 1985: A Report on the Pathan-Bihari Clashes in Orangi." Paper read at the Kathmandu Conference of the International Centre for Ethnic Studies, February 15–17, 1987.

Bastian, Sunil. "Political Economy of Ethnic Violence in Sri Lanka: The July 1983 Riots." In *Mirrors of Violence: Communities, Riots and Survivors in South Asia*, ed. Veena Das. Delhi: Oxford University Press, 1990.

Basu, Amrita. "Why Local Riots Are Not Simply Local: Collective Violence and the State of Bijnor, India." *Theory and Society* 24 (1995): 35–78.

Bayly, C. A. "The Pre-History of 'Communalism'? Religions in Conflict in India, 1700–1860." *Modern Asian Studies* 19, no. 2 (1985): 177–203.

———. "Rallying around the Subaltern." Review of the writings of the subaltern school. *Journal of Peasant Studies* 16, no. 1 (Oct. 1988): 110–20.

Beard, Charles, ed. *The Enduring Federalist*. New York: Frederick Ungar, 1959.

Bechert, Heinz. *Buddhismus, Staat und Gesellschaft in den Ländern des Theravada-Buddhismus*. Vol. 1. Frankfurt and Berlin: Metzner, 1966.

Bell, Daniel. "Ethnicity and Social Change." In *Ethnicity: Theory and Experience*, ed. Nathan Glazer and Daniel P. Moynihan. Cambridge, Mass.: Harvard University Press, 1975.

Blackton, Charles. "The Action Phase of the 1915 Riots." *Journal of Asian Studies* 29, no. 2 (1970): 235–54.

Bond, George D. *The Buddhist Revival in Sri Lanka: Religious Tradition, Reinterpretation, and Response.* Columbia: University of South Carolina Press, 1988. Reprint, Delhi: Motilal Banarsidass, 1992.

Brass, Paul R. *Language, Religion and Politics in North India.* Cambridge: Cambridge University Press, 1974.

———. *Ethnic Groups and the State.* London: Croom Helm, 1985.

Brown, W. Norman. *The United States and India and Pakistan.* 1953. Cambridge, Mass.: Harvard University Press, 1963.

Buford, Bill. *Among the Thugs: The Experience and the Seduction of Crowd Violence.* New York: Norton, 1992.

Calder, Nigel. *Einstein's Universe.* New York: Greenwich House, 1979.

Canetti, Elias. *Crowds and Power.* New York: Farrar, Straus and Giroux, 1984.

Ceylon. Government Archives. Report 14502: Report of the Riots of 1915 by the Inspector General of Police.

Chakravarty, Uma, and Nandita Haksar. *The Delhi Riots: Three Days in the Life of a Nation.* New Delhi: Lancer International, 1987.

Chatterjee, Partha. *Nationalist Thought and the Colonial World: A Derivative Discourse.* London: Zed Books for the United Nations University, 1986.

Committee for Rational Development. *Sri Lanka: The Ethnic Conflict—Myths, Realities and Perspectives.* New Delhi: Navrang, 1984.

Communal Violence—July 1983. Colombo: Civil Rights Movement, 1983.

Connor, Walker. "Nation Building or Nation Destroying." *World Politics* 24, no. 3 (1972): 319–55.

———. "The Politics of Ethnonationalism." *Journal of International Affairs* 27, no. 1 (1973).

Das, Veena, ed. *Mirrors of Violence: Communities, Riots and Survivors in South Asia.* Delhi: Oxford University Press, 1990.

Davis, Natalie Zemon. "The Rites of Violence: Religious Riots in Sixteenth-Century France." *Past and Present* 59 (May 1973): 51–91.

Denham, E. B. *The Census of Ceylon, 1911.* Colombo: Government Printer, 1912.

de Silva, Kingsley M. *A History of Sri Lanka.* Berkeley: University of California Press, 1981.

———. *Managing Ethnic Tensions in Multi-Ethnic Societies: Sri Lanka, 1880–1985.* Lanham, Md.: University Press of America, 1986.

Dharmapala, Anagarika. *Return to Righteousness: A Collection of Speeches, Essays and Letters of the Late Anagarika Dharmapala.* Edited by Ananda Guruge. Colombo: Government Press, 1965.

Dissanayaka, T. D. S. A. *The Agony of Sri Lanka.* Colombo: Swastika, 1983.

Durkheim, Emile. *Les Formes élémentaires de la vie religieuse: Le Système totémique en Australie.* 1912. Trans. as *The Elementary Forms of Religious Life: A Study in Religious Sociology* by Joseph Ward Swain. 1915. New York: Collier Books, 1961.

Embree, Ainslie. "The Function of the Rashtriya Swayamsevak Sangh: To Define the Hindu Nation." In *Accounting for Fundamentalisms: The Dynamic Character of Movements,* ed. Martin E. Marty and R. Scott Appleby. Chicago: University of Chicago Press, 1994.

Engineer, Asghar Ali. Interview. "Secular Forces Must Unite." *Frontline.* Feb. 12, 1993.

———. "When Bombay Erupted." *Frontline.* Feb. 26, 1993.

Esman, Milton J., ed. *Ethnic Conflict in the Western World.* Ithaca, N.Y.: Cornell University Press, 1977.

Esposito, John L. "Islam in State and Society: Pakistan." Paper presented at conference on "Democracy and Development in South Asia," Tufts University, Apr. 1990.

Fanon, Frantz. *The Wretched of the Earth.* 1961. New York: Grove Press, 1963.

Farmer, B. H. *Ceylon: A Divided Nation.* London: Oxford University Press, 1963.

Faruki, Kemal A. "Pakistan: Islamic Government and Society." In *Islam in Asia: Religion, Politics and Society,* ed. John L. Esposito. New York: Oxford University Press, 1987.

Feldman, Allen. *Formations of Violence: The Narrative of the Body and Political Terror in Ireland.* Chicago: University of Chicago Press, 1991.

Fernando, P. T. M. "The British Raj and the 1915 Communal Riots in Ceylon." *Modern Asian Studies* 3, no. 3 (1969): 245–55.

———. "The Post-Riots Campaign for Justice." *Journal of Asian Studies* 29, no. 2 (1970).

Fox, Richard G. *Lions of the Punjab: Culture in the Making.* Berkeley: University of California Press, 1985.

Freitag, Sandria B. *Collective Action and Community: Public Arenas and the Emergence of Communalism in North India.* Berkeley: University of California Press, 1989.

———, ed. *Culture and Power in Banaras: Community Performance and Environment, 1800–1980.* Berkeley: University of California Press, 1989.

Freud, Sigmund. *Massenpsychologie und Ich-Analyse.* 1921. Translated by James Strachey as *Group Psychology and the Analysis of the Ego.* 1926 New York: Norton, 1959.

Furnivall, J. S. *Colonial Policy and Practice.* 2d ed. New York: New York University Press, 1956.

Gargan, Edward A. "Divided Pakistan Torn by Lawlessness and Scandal." *New York Times,* November 19, 1991.

Geertz, Clifford. *Negara: The Theater State in Nineteenth-Century Bali.* Princeton, N.J.: Princeton University Press, 1980.

Girard, René. *Violence and the Sacred.* Translated by Patrick Gregory. 1977. Baltimore: Johns Hopkins Paperbacks, 1979.

Glazer, Nathan, and Daniel P. Moynihan, eds. *Ethnicity: Theory and Experience.* Cambridge, Mass.: Harvard University Press, 1975.

Gleick, James. *Chaos: Making a New Science.* New York: Penguin Books, 1988.

Golwalkar, M. S. *We or Our Nation Defined.* Nagpur: M. N. Kale.

Gombrich, Richard, and Gananath Obeyesekere. *Buddhism Transformed: Religious Change in Sri Lanka.* Princeton, N.J.: Princeton University Press, 1988.

Gopal, Sarvepalli. *The Viceroyalty of Lord Irwin, 1926–31.* Oxford: Oxford University Press, 1957.

———. *Anatomy of a Confrontation: The Babri Masjid–Ramjanmabhumi Issue.* New Delhi: Penguin Books India; New York: Viking, 1991.

Grimshaw, Allen D. "Actions of Police and the Military in American Race Riots." In *Racial Violence in the United States,* ed. id., pp. 269–70. Chicago: Aldine, 1969.

Guha, Ranajit. "The Prose of Counter-Insurgency." In *Subaltern Studies II: Writings on South Asian History and Society,* ed. id., pp. 1–42. New Delhi: Oxford University Press, 1993.

Gunasinghe, Newton. "The Open Economy and Its Impact on Ethnic Relations in Sri Lanka." In Committee for Rational Development, *Sri Lanka: The Ethnic Conflict—Myths, Realities and Perspectives.* New Delhi: Navrang, 1984.

Hassan, Arif. "Karachi's Godfathers." *Herald* (Karachi), Dec. 1986.

Hawking, Stephen W. *A Brief History of Time: From the Big Bang to Black Holes.* New York: Bantam Books, 1988.

Helsay, John, and Twiss, Sumner B. *Religion and Human Rights.* New York: Project on Religion and Human Rights, 1994.

Hensman, Rohini. "Refugees: Their Potential as a Force for Reconciliation and Peace." *Pravada* 1, no. 3 (1993).

Hobsbawm, E. J. *Primitive Rebels: Studies in Archaic forms of Social Movements in the Nineteenth and Twentieth Centuries.* New York: Norton, 1959.

Holt, John. "Protestant Buddhism?" *Religious Studies Review* 17, no. 4 (Oct. 1991): 306–12.

Horowitz, Donald L. *Ethnic Groups in Conflict.* Berkeley: University of California Press, 1985.

Hussain, Akmal. "The Karachi Riots of December 1986: Crisis of State and Civil Society in Pakistan." In *Mirrors of Violence: Communities, Riots and Survivors in South Asia,* ed. Veena Das, pp. 185–93. New Delhi: Oxford University Press, 1990.

Jalal, Ayesha. *The Sole Spokesman: Jinnah, the Muslim League and the Demand for Pakistan.* Cambridge: Cambridge University Press, 1985. Paperback edition, 1994

———. *The State of Martial Rule: The Origins of Pakistan's Political Economy of Defence.* Cambridge: Cambridge University Press, 1990.

Jayawardena, Kumari. "Economic and Political Factors in the 1915 Riots." *Journal of Asian Studies* 29, no. 2 (1970): 223–33.

———. *Ethnic and Class Conflicts in Sri Lanka.* Colombo: Navagama Printers, 1986.

Jeffrey, Robin. *What's Happening to India? Punjab, Ethnic Conflict, Mrs. Gandhi's Death and the Test of Federalism.* London: Macmillan, 1986.

Juergensmeyer, Mark. "The Logic of Religious Violence: The Case of the Punjab." *Contributions to Indian Sociology,* n.s., 22 (1988): 66–88.

Kakar, Sudhir. "Some Unconscious Aspects of Ethnic Violence in India." In *Mirrors of Violence: Communities, Riots and Survivors in South Asia,* ed. Veena Das. New Delhi: Oxford University Press, 1990.

Kanapathipillai, Valli. "July 1983: The Survivors' Experience." In *Mirrors of Violence: Communities, Riots and Survivors in South Asia,* ed. Veena Das. New Delhi: Oxford University Press, 1990.

Kannangara, A. P. "The Riots of 1915 in Sri Lanka: A Study in the Roots of Communal Violence." *Past and Present* 102 (1983): 130–65.

Kapferer, Bruce. *A Celebration of Demons: Exorcism and the Aesthetics of Healing in Sri Lanka.* Bloomington: Indiana University Press, 1983.

———. *Legends of People, Myths of State: Violence, Intolerance, and Political Culture in Sri Lanka and Australia.* Washington, D.C.: Smithsonian Institution Press, 1988.

Kapur, Rajiv. *Sikh Separatism: The Politics of Faith.* London: Allen & Unwin, 1986.

Kearney, Robert N. *Communalism and Language in the Politics of Ceylon.* Durham, N.C.: Duke University Press, 1967.

———. "Introduction." The 1915 Riots in Ceylon: A Symposium. *Journal of Asian Studies* 29, no. 2 (1970).

Kerr, Ian J. "Fox and the Lions: The Akali Movement Revisited." In *Sikh History and Religion in the Twentieth Century,* ed. Joseph T. O'Connell, Milton Israel, and Willard G. Oxtoby. South Asian Studies Papers, no. 3. Toronto: University of Toronto, 1990.

Kishwar, Madhu. Editorial. *Manushi,* no. 25 (Nov.–Dec. 1984).

Kothari, Smitu, and Harsh Sethi, eds. *Voices from a Scarred City: The Delhi Carnage in Perspective.* No. 4 (Feb. 1985) of *Lokayan* (New Delhi).

Kothari, Rajni. "The How and Why of It All." In *Voices from a Scarred City: The Delhi Carnage in Perspective,* ed. Smitu Kothari and Harsh Sethi. *Lokayan* (New Delhi), no. 4 (Feb. 1985).

Kothari, Rajni. "The Indian Enterprise Today." *Dædalus* 118, no. 4 (Fall 1989): 50–67.

Kymlicka, Will. *Liberalism, Community and Culture.* Oxford: Oxford University Press, Clarendon Press, 1989. Paperback reprint, 1991.

Lambert, Richard D. "Hindu-Muslim Riots." Diss., University of Pennsylvania, 1951.

———. "Religion, Economics and Violence in Bengal." *Middle East Journal* 4, no. 3 (July 1950): 206–328.

Leaf, Murray. "The Punjab Crisis." *Asian Survey* 25, no. 5 (May 1985): 475–98.

Le Bon, Gustave. *La Psychologie des foules.* 1895. Translated as *The Crowd: A Study of the Popular Mind.* 1897. New York: Viking Press, 1960.

Le Roy Ladurie, Emmanuel. *Le Carnaval de Romans, de la Chandeleur au mercredi des Cendres, 1579–1580.* Paris: NRF/Gallimard, 1979. Translated as *Carnival: A People's Uprising at Romans, 1579–1580.* London: Scholar Press, 1980.

Lifton, Robert J. *The Broken Connection: On Death and the Continuity of Life.* New York: Simon & Schuster, 1979.

Lukes, Steven. *Emile Durkheim: His Life and Work. A Historical and Critical Study.* London: Allen Lane, Penguin Press, 1973.

Madan, T. N. "Secularism in Its Place." *Journal of Asian Studies* 46, no. 4 (1987): 747–59.

———. "The Double-edged Sword: Fundamentalism and the Sikh Religious Tradition." In *Fundamentalisms Observed,* ed. Martin E. Marty and R. Scott Appleby. Chicago: University of Chicago Press, 1991.

Mahathir, Mohamad bin. *The Malay Dilemma.* Singapore: Time Books International, 1970.

Mahroof, M. M. M. "Muslim Education in Ceylon, 1881–1901." *Islamic Culture* 47, no. 4 (1973).

Manor, James. *The Expedient Utopian: Bandaranaike and Ceylon*. Cambridge: Cambridge University Press, 1989.

———. "The Failure of Political Integration in Sri Lanka (Ceylon)." *Journal of Commonwealth and Comparative Politics* 17, no. 1 (1989): 21–46.

———, ed. *Sri Lanka in Change and Crisis*. London: Croom Helm, 1984.

Marino, Eduardo. *Political Killings in Southern Sri Lanka: On the Brink of Civil War*. Los Angeles: International Alert Publication, 1989.

Marriott, McKim. "Hindu Transactions: Diversity without Dualism." In *Transactions and Meaning: Directions in the Anthropology of Exchange and Symbolic Behavior*, ed. Bruce Kapferer, pp. 109–42. Philadelphia: Institute for Human Issues, 1977.

Marty, Martin E., and Scott Appleby, eds. *The Fundamentalist Project*. Vol. 1: *Fundamentalisms Observed*. Vol. 3: Fundamentalisms and the State. Chicago: University of Chicago Press, 1991. Vol. 1, 1993 Vol. 3.

Marx, Karl. *The Poverty of Philosophy*. New York: International Books, 1963.

Mayer, Anne Elizabeth. "The Fundamentalist Impact on Law, Politics, and Constitution in Iran, Pakistan and the Sudan." In *Fundamentalisms and the States*, ed. Martin E. Marty and R. Scott Appleby, vol 3. Chicago: University of Chicago Press, 1993.

McLeod, W. H. *Evolution of the Sikh Community: Five Essays*. Oxford: Oxford University Press, Clarendon Press, 1976.

Moore, Mark H., Deborah Prothrow-Stith, Bernard Guyer, and Howard Spivak. "Violence and Intentional Injuries: Criminal Justice and Public Health Perspectives on an Urgent National Problem." In *Understanding and Preventing Violence*, vol 4: *Consequences and Control*, ed. Albert J. Reiss, Jr., and Jeffrey A. Roth, pp. 167–216. Washington, D.C.: National Research Council, National Academy Press, 1994.

Moscovici, Serge. *L'Age des foules*. 1981. Translated by J. C. Whitehouse as *The Age of the Crowd: A Historical Treatise on Mass Psychology*. Cambridge: Cambridge University Press, 1985.

Naipaul, V. S. "The Shadow of the Guru." *New York Review of Books*, Dec. 20, 1990.

Nandy, Ashis. "The Political Culture of the Indian State." *Dædalus* 118, no. 4 (Fall 1989): 1–26.

Nehru, Jawaharlal. *An Autobiography*. London: Bodley Head, 1936.

———. *Toward Freedom: The Autobiography of Jawaharlal Nehru*. New York: John Day, 1941.

———. *The Discovery of India*. New York: John Day, 1946.

Nissan, Elizabeth. "Some Thoughts on Sinhalese Justifications for the Violence." In *Sri Lanka in Change and Crisis*, ed. James Manor. London: Croom Helm, 1984.

Oberoi, Harjot. "From Punjab to 'Khalistan': Territoriality and Metacommentary." *Pacific Affairs* 60, no. 1 (Spring 1987): 26–41.

———. "Sikh Fundamentalism: Translating History into Theory." In *Fundamentalisms and the State*, ed. Martin E. Marty and R. Scott Appleby. Chicago: University of Chicago Press, 1993.

———. *The Construction of Religious Boundaries: Culture, Identity, and Diversity in Sikh Tradition*. New Delhi: Oxford University Press, 1994.

Obeyesekere, Gananath. "Personal Identity and Cultural Crisis: The Case of Anagarika Dharmapala of Sri Lanka." In *The Biographical Process*, ed. Frank Reynolds and Donald Capps. The Hague: Mouton, 1979.

O'Connell, Joseph T., Milton Israel, and Willard G. Oxtoby, eds. *Sikh History and Religion in the Twentieth Century*. Toronto: University of Toronto Press, 1988.

Padgaonkar, Dileep. *When Bombay Burned*. New Delhi: UBS Publishers' Distributors, 1993.

Pandey, Gyanendra. "Peasant Revolt and Indian Nationalism: The Peasant Movement in Awadh, 1919-22." In *Selected Subaltern Studies*, ed. Ranajit Guha and Gayatri Chakravorty Spivak, pp. 223-87. Oxford: Oxford University Press, 1988.

———. "The Colonial Construction of 'Communalism': British Writings on Banaras in the Nineteenth Century." In *Mirrors of Violence: Communities, Riots and Survivors in South Asia*, ed. Veena Das, pp. 94-134. Delhi: Oxford University Press, 1990.

———. *The Construction of Communalism in Colonial North India*. New Delhi: Oxford University Press, 1990.

———. "In Defence of the Fragment: Writing about Hindu-Muslim Riots in India Today." *Representations* 27 (Winter 1992): 27-55.

———. "Rallying round the Cow: Sectarian Strife in the Bhojpuri Region, c. 1888-1917." In *Subaltern Studies II: Writings on South Asian History and Society*, ed. Ranajit Guha, pp. 60-129. New Delhi: Oxford University Press, 1993.

People's Union for Democratic Rights and People's Union for Civil Liberties [Gobinda Mukhoty and Rajni Kothari]. *Who Are the Guilty? Report of a Joint Inquiry into the Causes and Impact of the Riots in Delhi from 31 October-10 November*. New Delhi: Excellent Printing Services, 1984.

Pettigrew, Joyce. *Robber Noblemen: A Study of the Political System of the Sikh Jats*. Boston: Routledge & Kegan Paul, 1975. Reprint, New Delhi: Ambika, 1978.

———. "The Growth of Sikh Community Consciousness, 1947-1966." *South Asia*, n.s., 3, no. 2 (1980): 43-62.

———. "In Search of a New Kingdom of Lahore." *Pacific Affairs* 60, no. 1 (1987): 1-25.

Popkin, Samuel L. *The Rational Peasant: The Political Economy of Rural Society in Vietnam*. Berkeley: University of California Press, 1979.

Rahman, M., and Lekha Rattanani. "Savagery in Bombay." *India Today*, Jan. 31, 1993.

Ramachandran, V. K. "Reign of Terror: Shiv Sena Pogrom in Bombay." *Frontline*, Feb. 12, 1993.

Report of a Commission Appointed by the Governor to Inquire into the Causes Which Led to the Riots at Kotahena. Sessional Paper No. 4 of 1883. Colombo: Ceylon Legislative Council, 1883.

Report of the Citizens' Commission: New Delhi, 31 October-4 November 1984. New Delhi: Tata Press, 1985.

Report of Justice Ranganath Misra Commission of Inquiry. Vols. 1 and 2. New Delhi: S.N., 1986.

Report on the Census of 1911. Colombo: Government Press, 1912.

Report on the First Referendum in Sri Lanka. Second Paper 11. Colombo: Department of Government Printing, 1987.

Roberts, Michael. "Hobgoblins, Low-Country Sinhalese Plotters or Local Elite Chauvinists? Directions and Patterns in the 1915 Communal Riots." *Sri Lanka Journal of Social Sciences* 4 (1970): 157–98.

Rogers, John D. *Crime, Justice and Society in Colonial Sri Lanka.* London: Curzon Press, 1987.

Rudé, George F. E. *The Crowd in the French Revolution.* Oxford: Oxford University Press, Clarendon Press, 1959.

———. *The Crowd in History: A Study of Popular Disturbances in France and England, 1730–1848.* New York: John Wiley & Sons, 1966.

Rudolph, Lloyd I. "The Media and Cultural Politics." In *India Votes: Alliance Politics and Minority Governments in the Ninth and Tenth General Elections,* ed. Harold A. Gould and Samit Ganguly, pp. 159–79. Boulder, Colo.: Westview Press, 1993.

Rutnam, James T. "The Rev. A. G. Fraser and the Riots of 1915." *Ceylon Journal of Historical and Social Studies,* n.s., 2 (1971): 151–96.

Samarakone, Priya. "The Conduct of the Referendum." In *Sri Lanka in Change and Crisis,* ed. James Manor. London: Croom Helm, 1984.

Samaraweera, Vijay. "Arabi Pasha in Ceylon, 1883–1901." *Islamic Culture* 50, no. 4 (1976): 219–27.

———. "The Muslim Revivalist Movement." In *Collective Identities, Nationalisms and Protest in Modern Sri Lanka,* ed. Michael Roberts, pp. 243–76. Colombo: Marga Institute, 1979.

Scott, James C. *The Moral Economy of the Peasant: Subsistence and Rebellion in Southeast Asia.* New Haven, Conn.: Yale University Press, 1976.

Seneviratne, H. L. Review of *Buddhism Transformed,* by Richard Gombrich and Gananath Obeyesekere, *Journal of Ritual Studies* 4, no. 2 (Summer 1990).

Shaheed, Farida. "The Pathan-Muhajir Conflicts, 1985–86: A National Perspective." *Mirrors of Violence: Communities, Riots and Survivors in South Asia,* ed. Veena Das, pp. 199–24. New Delhi: Oxford University Press, 1990.

Simmel, Georg. *Conflict.* Glencoe, Ill.: Free Press, 1955.

Singh, Attar. "The Shiromani Gurudwara Parbandhak Committee and the Politicization of the Sikhs." In *Sikh History and Religion in the Twentieth Century,* ed. Joseph T. O'Connell, Milton Israel, and Willard G. Oxtoby. South Asian Studies Papers, no. 3. Toronto: University of Toronto, 1990.

Singh, Gopal. *The Religion of the Sikhs.* 1971. New Delhi: Allied, 1987.

Singh, Kushwant. *A History of the Sikhs,* vols. 1 and 2. Princeton, N.J.: Princeton University Press, 1963, 1966.

Smith, M. G. "Some Developments in the Analytical Framework of Pluralism." In *Pluralism in Africa,* ed. Leo Kuper and M. G. Smith. Berkeley: University of California Press, 1969.

———. "Institutional and Political Conditions of Pluralism." In *Pluralism in Africa,* ed. Leo Kuper and M. G. Smith. Berkeley: University of California Press, 1969.

Social Scientists' Association. *Ethnicity and Social Change in Sri Lanka.* Colombo: Navamga Printers, 1985.

Somaratna, G. P. V. *Religious Riot in Sri Lanka: Kotahena Riot, 1883.* Colombo: Deepanee, 1991.

Spencer, Jonathan. "Popular Perceptions of the Violence: A Provincial View." In *Sri Lanka in Change and Crisis*, ed. James Manor. London: Croom Helm, 1984.

———. "Collective Violence and Everyday Practice in Sri Lanka." *Modern Asian Studies* 24, no. 3 (July 1990): 603–23.

———, ed. *Sri Lanka: History and Roots of Conflict*. London: Routledge, 1990.

Sri Lanka: Racism and the Authoritarian State. Vol. 26, no. 1 of *Race and Class* (1984).

Stirrat, R. L. *Power and Religiosity in a Post-Colonial Setting: Sinhala Catholics in Contemporary Sri Lanka*. Cambridge: Cambridge University Press, 1992.

Sumathipala, K. H. M. "The Kotahena Riots and Their Repercussions." *Ceylon Historical Journal* 19 (1969–70): 65–81.

Swearer, Donald K. "Fundamentalist Movements in Theravada Buddhism." In *Fundamentalisms Observed*, ed. Martin E. Marty and Scott Appleby. Chicago: University of Chicago Press, 1991.

Syed, Anwar H. "Political Parties and the Nationality Question in Pakistan." *Journal of South Asian and Middle Eastern Studies* 12, no. 1 (1988): 42–75.

Tägil, Sven. *Regions in Upheaval: Ethnic Conflict and Political Mobilization*. Solna, Sweden: Esselte Studium, 1984.

Tambiah, Stanley J. *World Conqueror and World Renouncer: A Study of Buddhism and Polity in Thailand against a Historical Background*. Cambridge: Cambridge University Press, 1976.

———. *The Buddhist Saints of the Forest and the Cult of Amulets: A Study of Charisma, Hagiography, Sectarianism, and Millennial Buddhism*. Cambridge: Cambridge University Press, 1984.

———. "A Performative Approach to Ritual." In *Culture, Thought and Social Action: An Anthropological Perspective*. Cambridge, Mass.: Harvard University Press, 1985.

———. *Sri Lanka: Ethnic Fratricide and the Dismantling of Democracy*. Chicago: University of Chicago Press, 1986.

———. "Ethnic Conflict in the World Today." *American Ethnologist* 16, no. 2 (May 1989): 335–49.

———. *Magic, Science, Religion and the Scope of Rationality*. Cambridge: Cambridge University Press, 1990.

———. "Some Reflections on Communal Violence in South Asia." AAS presidential address. *Journal of Asian Studies* 49, no. 4 (Nov. 1990): 741–60.

———. *Buddhism Betrayed? Religion, Politics and Violence in Sri Lanka*. Chicago: University of Chicago Press, 1992.

Thomas, Keith. *Religion and the Decline of Magic*. New York: Charles Scribner's Sons, 1971.

Thompson, E. P. "The Moral Economy of the English Crowd in the Eighteenth Century." *Past and Present* 50 (Feb. 1971): 76–126.

Tilly, Charles, Louise Tilly, and Richard Tilly. *The Rebellious Century, 1830–1930*. Cambridge, Mass.: Harvard University Press, 1975.

Tiruchelvam, Mithran. "Gandhian Civil Disobedience in Sri Lanka." *Pravada* 2, no. 7 (Aug.–Sept. 1993): 19.

Tiruchelvam, Neelan. "July '83 and Collective Violence in Sri Lanka." *Lanka Guardian* 16, no. 7 (Aug. 1993): 6–7.

Tylor, Edward B. *Primitive Culture: Researches into the Development of Mythology, Philosophy, Religion, Language, Art and Custom*, vol. 1. London: John Murray, 1873.

Vijayavardhana, D. C. *The Revolt in the Temple*. Colombo: Sinha Publications, 1953.

Vittachi, Tarzie. *Emergency '58: The Story of the Ceylon Race Riots*. London: André Deutsch, 1958.

Weiner, Myron. *Sons of the Soil: Migration and Ethnic Conflict in India*. Princeton, N.J.: Princeton University Press, 1978.

———. *The Indian Paradox: Essays in Indian Politics*. London: Sage, 1989.

Wilson, A. Jeyaratnam. *Politics in Sri Lanka, 1947–1979*. London: Macmillan, 1979.

———. *The Break-up of Sri Lanka: The Sinhalese-Tamil conflict*. Honolulu: University of Hawaii Press, 1988.

Wolpert, Stanley. *Zulfi Bhutto of Pakistan: His Life and Times*. New York: Oxford University Press, 1993.

World Conference on Human Rights: The Vienna Declaration and Programme of Action, June 1993. New York: United Nations Department of Public Information, 1993.

Wriggins, W. Howard. *Ceylon: Dilemmas of a New Nation*. Princeton, N.J.: Princeton University Press, 1960.

Wright, Theodore P. Jr. "Center-Periphery Relations and Ethnic Conflict in Pakistan: Sindhis, Muhajirs and Punjabis." *Comparative Politics* 23, no. 3 (Apr. 1991): 299–312.

Yang, Anand A. "Sacred Symbol and Sacred Space in Rural India: Community Mobilization in the Anti-Cow Killing." *Comparative Studies in Society and History* 22, no. 4 (1980): 576–96.

Yasmeen, Samina. "Democracy in Pakistan: The Third Dismissal." *Asian Survey* 34, no. 6 (June 1994): 191–99.

Index

Compositor:	Impressions Book and Journal Services, Inc.
Text:	10/13 Aldus
Display:	Aldus
Printer and Binder:	Edwards Brothers, Inc.